Dynamic Risk Factors

Dynamic risk factors are the children of risk prediction. They were identified to help practitioners assess risk of recidivism and to set treatment targets likely to reduce reoffending. This resulted in the development of intervention programs designed to modify the characteristics of individuals and their environments associated with crime. The predictive nature of their legacy lies in their ability to provide reliable information about the likelihood of future reoffending. In this respect, dynamic risk factors are useful complements to static risk factors such as age, gender and history of offending, and add incremental validity to recidivism prediction. Their treatment utility resides in the fact that practitioners increasingly rely on the identification of dynamic risk factors to direct correctional assessment and interventions. Thus, dynamic risk factors have a dual status. They are both useful predictors of reoffending and measures of risk status, and potential causes of reoffending, capable of serving an explanatory role as well as a predictive one. It is a simple and powerful conceptualization that has streamlined forensic and correctional research, program development and the delivery of treatment. Despite its conceptual elegance, we believe that the dual conceptualization of dynamic risk factors is problematic and these difficulties spill over into their role in assessment, treatment and desistance contexts. In this book, the nature and function of dynamic risk factors are investigated and their strengths and limitations identified. This book was originally published as a special issue of *Psychology, Crime & Law*.

Tony Ward, PhD, DipClinPsych, received his PhD and trained as a Clinical Psychologist at Canterbury University, Christchurch, New Zealand. He was the former Director of the Kia Marama Sexual Offenders' Unit at Rolleston Prison in New Zealand and has taught clinical and forensic psychology at Victoria, Deakin, Canterbury and Melbourne Universities. He is currently a Professor of Clinical Training at Victoria University of Wellington, New Zealand. Tony has published 400 chapters, articles, books and other scholarly works in the areas of male sexual offending and general rehabilitation and practice. He is particularly interested in the critique and generation of theory within forensic psychology as well as the examination of ethical constructs in psychological practice.

Clare-Ann Fortune, PhD, PGDipClinPsyc, is a Lecturer in Clinical Forensic Psychology in the School of Psychology, Victoria University of Wellington, New Zealand. She teaches on the forensic and clinical psychology postgraduate programs. Her research interests include the development of and desistance from antisocial behavior amongst youth offenders, risk assessment and offender rehabilitation. She has published numerous articles in theses areas.

Dynamic Risk Factors

What role should they play in the explanation, assessment and rehabilitation of offenders?

Edited by
Tony Ward and Clare-Ann Fortune

Routledge
Taylor & Francis Group
LONDON AND NEW YORK

First published 2017by Routledge

2 Park Square, Milton Park, Abingdon, Oxfordshire OX14 4RN
52 Vanderbilt Avenue, New York, NY 10017

Routledge is an imprint of the Taylor & Francis Group, an informa business

First issued in paperback 2018

British Library Cataloguing in Publication Data
A catalogue record for this book is available from the British Library

ISBN 13: 978-1-138-29073-0 (hbk)
ISBN 13: 978-0-367-10956-1 (pbk)

Typeset in MyriadPro
by diacriTech, Chennai

Publisher's Note
The publisher accepts responsibility for any inconsistencies that may have arisen during the conversion of this book from journal articles to book chapters, namely the possible inclusion of journal terminology.

Disclaimer
Every effort has been made to contact copyright holders for their permission to reprint material in this book. The publishers would be grateful to hear from any copyright holder who is not here acknowledged and will undertake to rectify any errors or omissions in future editions of this book.

Contents

Citation Information

The chapters in this book were originally published in *Psychology, Crime & Law*, volume 22, issues 1–2 (January–February 2016). When citing this material, please use the original page numbering for each article, as follows:

Chapter 1
Dynamic risk factors: scientific kinds or predictive constructs
Tony Ward
Psychology, Crime & Law, volume 22, issues 1–2 (January–February 2016) pp. 2–16

Chapter 2
Putting risk factors in their place: an evolutionary-developmental approach to understanding risk
Russil Durrant
Psychology, Crime & Law, volume 22, issues 1–2 (January–February 2016) pp. 17–32

Chapter 3
A conceptual kaleidoscope: contemplating 'dynamic structural risk' and an uncoupling of risk from need
Kelly Hannah-Moffat
Psychology, Crime & Law, volume 22, issues 1–2 (January–February 2016) pp. 33–46

Chapter 4
Dysfunctional expertise and its relationship with dynamic risk factors in offenders
Zarah Vernham and Claire Nee
Psychology, Crime & Law, volume 22, issues 1–2 (January–February 2016) pp. 47–67

Chapter 5
Problems in the measurement of dynamic risk factors in sexual offenders
Anthony R. Beech, Helen C. Wakeling, Filip Szumski and Nick Freemantle
Psychology, Crime & Law, volume 22, issues 1–2 (January–February 2016) pp. 68–83

Chapter 6
Challenges for the theory and application of dynamic risk factors
Jacinta R. Cording, Sarah M. Beggs Christofferson and Randolph C. Grace
Psychology, Crime & Law, volume 22, issues 1–2 (January–February 2016) pp. 84–103

Chapter 7

Dynamic risk and sexual offending: the conundrum of assessment
Sharon Casey
Psychology, Crime & Law, volume 22, issues 1–2 (January–February 2016) pp. 104–123

Chapter 8

Understanding dynamic risk factors for violence
Gabrielle Klepfisz, Michael Daffern and Andrew Day
Psychology, Crime & Law, volume 22, issues 1–2 (January–February 2016) pp. 124–137

Chapter 9

Developing a theory of dynamic risk
David Thornton
Psychology, Crime & Law, volume 22, issues 1–2 (January–February 2016) pp. 138–150

Chapter 10

Dynamic risk and protective factors
Ralph C. Serin, Nick Chadwick and Caleb D. Lloyd
Psychology, Crime & Law, volume 22, issues 1–2 (January–February 2016) pp. 151–170

Chapter 11

Desistance and dynamic risk factors belong together
Devon L. L. Polaschek
Psychology, Crime & Law, volume 22, issues 1–2 (January–February 2016) pp. 171–189

Chapter 12

From dynamic risk factors to causal processes: a methodological framework
Tony Ward and Clare-Ann Fortune
Psychology, Crime & Law, volume 22, issues 1–2 (January–February 2016) pp. 190–202

Notes on Contributors

Anthony R. Beech is a Professor in Criminological Psychology and Head of the Centre for Forensic and Criminological Psychology, University of Birmingham, Birmingham, UK.

Sharon Casey is a Senior Lecturer at the School of Psychology, Faculty of Health, Deakin University, Melbourne, VIC, Australia.

Nick Chadwick is based at the Department of Psychology, Carleton University, Ottawa, ON, Canada.

Sarah M. Beggs Christofferson is a Lecturer in Clinical Psychology at the Department of Psychology, University of Canterbury, Christchurch, New Zealand.

Jacinta R. Cording is a PhD Candidate at the Department of Psychology, University of Canterbury, Christchurch, New Zealand.

Michael Daffern is a Professor in Clinical Forensic Psychology at Swinburne University of Technology, Victorian Institute of Forensic Mental Health, Australia.

Andrew Day is a Professor at the School of Psychology, Deakin University, and an Associate Director for the Centre of Mental Health and Wellbeing at Deakin University, Australia.

Russil Durrant is based at the School of Social and Cultural Studies, Institute of Criminology, Victoria University of Wellington, New Zealand.

Clare-Ann Fortune, PhD, PGDipClinPsyc, is a Lecturer in Clinical Forensic Psychology in the School of Psychology, Victoria University of Wellington, New Zealand. She teaches on the forensic and clinical psychology postgraduate programs. Her research interests include the development of and desistance from antisocial behavior amongst youth offenders, risk assessment and offender rehabilitation. She has published numerous articles in theses areas.

Nick Freemantle is a Professor of Surgery at the Department of Primary Care and Population Health, University College London, London, UK.

Randolph C. Grace is a Professor at the Department of Psychology, University of Canterbury, Christchurch, New Zealand.

Kelly Hannah-Moffat is a Vice Dean Undergraduate at the Centre for Criminology and Sociolegal Studies, University of Toronto, Canada.

Gabrielle Klepfisz is based at the Centre for Forensic Behavioural Science, Swinburne University of Technology, Melbourne, Australia.

Caleb D. Lloyd is a Professor in the Department of Psychology, University of Texas at El Paso, USA.

Claire Nee is a Reader in Forensic Psychology at the Psychology Department, University of Portsmouth, Portsmouth, UK.

Devon L. L. Polaschek is a Professor at the School of Psychology, Victoria University of Wellington, Wellington, New Zealand.

Ralph C. Serin is a Sabbatical Professor at the Department of Psychology, Carleton University, Ottawa, ON, Canada.

Filip Szumski is based in the Institute of Psychology, Adam Mickiewicz University, Poznań, Poland.

David Thornton was trained as a Psychologist in the United Kingdom where he developed treatment programs for Her Majesty's Prison Service. In 2001, he moved to the United States where he developed treatment services for high-risk mentally disordered sex offenders in Wisconsin. Together with colleagues like Karl Hanson and Ruth Mann, he has been involved in developing widely used instruments for evaluating the risk presented by sexual offenders. He is currently a Professor in the Department of Clinical Psychology at the University of Bergen in Norway and in private practice in the United States and the United Kingdom.

Zarah Vernham is a Lecturer at the Psychology Department, University of Portsmouth, Portsmouth, UK.

Helen C. Wakeling is based in the Commissioning Strategies Group, National Offender Management Service, London, UK.

Tony Ward, PhD, DipClinPsych, received his PhD and trained as a Clinical Psychologist at Canterbury University, Christchurch, New Zealand. He was the former Director of the Kia Marama Sexual Offenders' Unit at Rolleston Prison in New Zealand and has taught clinical and forensic psychology at Victoria, Deakin, Canterbury and Melbourne Universities. He is currently a Professor of Clinical Training at Victoria University of Wellington, New Zealand. Tony has published 400 chapters, articles, books and other scholarly works in the areas of male sexual offending and general rehabilitation and practice. He is particularly interested in the critique and generation of theory within forensic psychology as well as the examination of ethical constructs in psychological practice.

Dynamic risk factors: scientific kinds or predictive constructs

Tony Ward

School of Psychology, Victoria University of Wellington, Wellington, New Zealand

ABSTRACT
There are a number of theoretical problems evident in the concept of dynamic risk factors that arise from their (increasing) importation into the explanatory and treatment domains of forensic and correctional practice. More specifically: (a) the concept of dynamic risk factors has not been well defined; (b) relatedly, there is a lack of clarity whether dynamic risk factors refer to causal processes or are predictive constructs; and finally (c) because of the above problems no one is sure how best to integrate them into clinical assessment and treatment. I will examine each of these three conceptual problems in this paper and make some suggestions about how to utilise dynamic risk factors in explanations of offending.

Practitioners in the fields of correctional and forensic psychology have a duty of care to the individuals they work with to assist them to live more fulfilling lives. In addition, they have a responsibility to the community to identify, reduce, and manage the risk posed by offenders. The contrasting values of harm reduction and well-being enhancement create challenging ethical problems and may even result in a type of professional paralysis where practitioners do not know what course of action they should undertake in certain circumstances (Ward, 2013). There can be a conflict of roles caused by varying professional values and their associated practices. One of the attractions of the contemporary focus on risk management is that at first glance it seems to provide a solution to this dual role problem. On the one hand, empirically supported interventions are employed to lower individuals' level of risk to other people. On the other hand, offenders are offered the opportunity to live more productive and fulfilling lives.

Irrespective of the scientific and ethical merits of risk management approaches such as the Risk-Need-Responsivity model (Andrews & Bonta, 2010), there are a number of conceptual problems that arguably undermine the attempt to translate risk management principles into effective practice, and weaken the explanatory power of dynamic risk factors (see Heffernan & Ward, 2015; Thornton, 2015; Ward & Beech, 2015; Ward & Maruna, 2007). The conceptual problems relate to the concept of dynamic risk factors and their (increasing) use in the explanation and treatment of offending and its related problems (Ward, 2014). The understandable eagerness to predict crime and reduce reoffending has resulted in neglect of the need for good theoretical analysis to direct the development of sound programmes and assessment practices. More specifically, I argue that (a) the concept of dynamic risk factors has not been well defined and as a consequence of the resulting vagueness it is unclear whether it is a scientific (explanatory or classificatory) or normative concept; (b) relatedly, there is a lack of clarity whether dynamic risk factors refer to causal processes or are best viewed as predictive constructs; and finally (c) because of the above problems, no one is sure how best to integrate them into case formulation and treatment.

I will examine each of these conceptual problems in the remainder of this paper. My aim is to stimulate constructive discussion among researchers and to alert practitioners that some of the assumptions underpinning forensic and correctional programmes are problematic. I suspect that it is widely accepted that the concept of dynamic risk factors is under-theorised. While there have been recent attempts to explain how dynamic risk factors cause offending (Beech & Ward, 2004; Heffernan & Ward, 2015; Thornton, 2015; Ward & Beech, 2015), there has been virtually no sustained analysis of what they actually are (but see Hannah-Moffat, 2016). It seems to me that it is timely to undertake such a task.

Scientific or normative concepts?

It is fair to say that the definitions of dynamic risk factors offered in the literature are conceptually thin and amount to little more than a few general suggestions and associated comments. The classic account is that given by Andrews and Bonta (2010) who state that, 'Dynamic risk predictors (dynamic risk factors) are ones in which assessed change is associated with subsequent criminal behaviour' (p. 27). In other parts of their book, *The psychology of criminal conduct*, criminogenic needs are viewed as those dynamic risk factors that 'when changed, are associated with changes in the probability of recidivism' (p. 49). In other words, they are viewed as potential causal factors that if effectively targeted by cognitive behavioural techniques will reduce reoffending rates.

It is apparent that the definition of dynamic risk factors and their inclusion in risk management principles is normative in at least two senses. First, the link with recidivism reveals that they are partly defined with respect to legal norms; that is, individuals acting contrary to the law. Second, there are also ethical norms at stake as well. The assumption is that when criminal laws are broken individuals and members of the community are significantly harmed. The types of dynamic risk factors, for example, intimacy deficits or offence-supportive attitudes and beliefs, specify particular types of harm and their sources. For example, relational style problems indicate the infliction of suffering or abuse on adults and children who are close to the offender, while self-regulation deficits suggest a tendency to behave impulsively, possibly resulting in damage to other people.

The inclusion of legal and ethical norms in the definition means that dynamic risk factors are not causal factors in any straightforward sense. They are conceptualised with reference to social, political, and legal institutions, and while they may be underpinned by psychological mechanisms, are not themselves causal processes. Why does this matter? It simply reminds us that if you adopt the Andrews and Bonta (2010) definition of dynamic risk factors, they are not scientific concepts but are rather, at least in part, normative ones.

A second major weakness of the Andrews and Bonta (2010) definition is that they assume that psychometric instruments that assess dynamic risk factors are valid. By 'valid' I mean that the attributes they refer to actually exist and variations in that attribute cause the different responses on the measures concerned (Borsboom, 2005). Another way of stating this is that dynamic risk factors are assumed to refer to specific processes within individuals and their interactions with the world. This is a problematic assumption, as I will discuss later.

A final problem with the Andrews and Bonta (2010) definition of dynamic risk factors is that it is a definition of risk predictors, not causal factors. A close inspection of what they call the 'central eight' risk factors indicates that they are composite or multifaceted risk factors and are not conceptually integrated. For example, the dynamic risk factor of antisocial cognition incorporates a wide range of variables including attitudes, values, beliefs, rationalisations, and an antisocial personal identity (Andrews & Bonta, 2010, p. 59). The inclusion of multiple and minimally moderately correlated variables within a general domain makes sense if the aim is to predict offending but the downside is that the dynamic risk factor concerned will lack theoretical coherency and therefore have little explanatory value in accounting for crime. Speaking about test validity Borsboom (2005) makes a similar point, arguing that predictive tests lack validity but have utility:

> focusing on predictive properties will destroy, rather than enhance, measurement properties such as validity. The reason for this is simply that items that measure the same attribute will be correlated. Correlated items, however, are relatively useless in prediction, because they generate multicollinearity (they do not explain unique variance in the criterion). ... What one selects when optimizing predictive utility are items that are mutually uncorrelated, but highly correlated with the criterion. (163)

The extension of the risk management models, and more specifically the concept of dynamic risk factors, to the aetiological research and practice domains mistakenly presupposes that they do have explanatory value, whereas they are essentially aspects of predictive measures (see Ward & Beech, 2015). In their analysis of dynamic risk factors, researchers such as Mann, Hanson, and Thornton (2010) rely on data reduction techniques such as meta-analysis to identify the factors that are highly correlated across studies with offending. The origin of these dynamic risk factors is almost always in predictive scales of some type, and therefore, the above points stand.

In an attempt to deepen our understanding of risk factors, Beech and Ward (2004) proposed that historical and static risk factors, such as number of victims, function as markers of underlying psychological vulnerabilities to commit offences. They argued that the reason why risk assessment instruments for sex offenders, such as the Static-99 (Hanson & Thornton, 2000), are good predictors of future offending is because the static (i.e. fixed or unchangeable) factors mark offence-related proclivities in certain individuals (Beech & Ward, 2004). In Beech and Ward' s (2004) risk-aetiology model, stable dynamic risk factors are viewed as psychological traits or properties that create vulnerabilities for sexual offending (e.g. intimacy deficits). Acute dynamic factors are conceptualised as acute mental states that are caused by stable dynamic factors and are activated in specific contexts such as social rejection. Beech and Ward argue that the major explanatory work is accounted for by stable dynamic risk factors.

A problem with the Beech and Ward model is that the dynamic risk factors are simply listed as vulnerabilities and there is no mention of how they collectively cause offending, or are translated into psychological and social processes. A second weakness is that they also assume that each dynamic risk factor as formulated in the general offending, and sexual offending fields, refer to *psychological* processes. As argued above, they are partly normative concepts, and because of this fact, are not psychological constructs. Third, they share the problematic assumption apparent in Andrews and Bonta's (2010) classic definition that dynamic risk factors can serve as explanatory constructs, when due to their multifaceted nature, they cannot.

In a recent paper, Mann et al. (2010) identify a number of what they call psychologically meaningful risk factors which they believe to be prima facie causes of sexual offending and validated predictors of recidivism. They propose that to qualify as psychological meaningful risk factors: (1) there should be plausible reasons for regarding the factor in question as a cause of sexual offending and (2) strong evidence should exist that it actually predicts sexual offending. Mann et al. state that another way to understand risk factors, instead of classifying them as static or dynamic, is by adopting the concept of *psychologically meaningful risk factors*. Such risk factors can be conceptualised as individual propensities, which may or may not manifest during any particular time period (p. 194). The list of empirically supported meaningful risk factors for child sexual abuse in their paper includes: sexual preferences for children, emotional congruence with children, offence-supportive attitudes, and lack of adult intimate relationships. Mann et al. conclude that:

> the causal factors for sexual recidivism will ultimately be drawn from variables similar to those included in our list. We believe that it is these variables that should be emphasized in treatment. (p. 210)

Mann et al. (2010) make a similar mistake to the researchers discussed above, by assuming that it is theoretically defensible to transfer the concept of dynamic risk factors from the prediction domain to the explanatory and practice domains without significantly reworking them (see below). Second, relabelling dynamic risk factors as psychologically meaningful risk factors does not avoid the objection that they are, in part, normative concepts. This is because the criterion variable is offending behaviour and as such is value laden. Third, the relationship between indicators of the various risk factors (e.g. score on scales, ratings by clinicians, etc.) and the latent construct (i.e. attributes, such as intimacy deficits), the dynamic risk factor, is unclear. How does the attribute cause the different values in score; how is it translated into response tendencies?

What can we conclude from the above analysis of the way dynamic risk factors are defined? The most obvious difficulty is that they are poorly specified and are essentially risk predictors rather than referents of causal processes. While Beech and Ward (2004), and Mann et al. (2010), attempt to provide a deeper conceptual unpacking of dynamic risk factors they are saddled with the theoretical problems attending the original Andrews and Bonta (2010) definition. Part of the difficulty is that there is confusion about what is being addressed: prediction or explanation. As we will see below, it makes little sense to develop theories of dynamic risk factors until there is at least a rough understanding of what they are. Once the task shifts to an explanatory one then researchers owe us an account of how dynamic risk factors track causal processes and how they culminate in offending.

Explanatory or predictive constructs?

Are dynamic risk factors predictor variables or psychological constructs that refer to causal processes? This is an important question as it helps to justify whether they can legitimately be used in research and clinical contexts. The only thing you can reasonably expect from a measure that is designed to predict recidivism is that it does this as well as possible. However, once you conceptualise dynamic risk factors as possible causes then you are licenced to use them to explain why individuals commit offences and what particular causes ought to be targeted in treatment. The whole point of clinical assessment is to detect the relevant phenomena associated with offending, infer the mechanisms that generate them, and to then construct an intervention plan that seeks to modify or remove the causes.

In my view, there are four major questions that emerge from reading the literature on dynamic risk concerning their theoretical status. First, are they composite constructs rather than coherent theoretical terms, arising from their origin in risk prediction? Second, if they are genuine psychological constructs do they refer to aetiological factors, causal processes, or offence-related phenomena? Third, accepting that they may play an explanatory role, to what level of causes do they refer? Finally, are dynamic risk factors scientific kinds or simply summaries of disparate processes, properties, and states of affairs? These questions are conceptually linked and overlap with the definitional issues discussed earlier.

Composite or coherent concepts?

The general concept of dynamic risk factors and the various types such as deviant sexual interests, distorted attitudes, or self-management problems have their origin in measures of risk variables such as the Structured Risk Assessment Need framework (Thornton, 2013) or the Level of Service Inventory–Revised (LSI-R) (Andrews & Bonta, 2010). The major aim of measures such as these is to identify factors that predict reoffending, especially dynamic, variables that can be used to direct treatment and/or function as indicators of change in recidivism risk. As stated earlier, ideally a measure of risk would include a wide range of variables that each adds predictive value, and in this respect they should not be too highly correlated. If they are, then some of the correlated items are redundant and will be discarded. Thus, what test designers strive for are measures that cover the relevant domain as widely as possible so that their ability to detect risk-related variables is high. Over time, the focus of reviews of dynamic risk factors has been less on specific risk assessment tests and more on the individual dynamic risk factors, and their associated constituent variables (Beech & Craig, 2012; Mann et al., 2010). However, it is important not to lose sight of the fact that dynamic risk factors are essentially psychometric constructs, introduced to assess and monitor risk of recidivism. They were not originally developed as components of theories of offending and its associated psychological problems. Subsequent researchers such as Mann et al. (2010) and Beech and Ward (2004) did not question their fundamental nature as risk predictors and thus their analyses failed to demonstrate systematic conceptual relationships between the individual risk factors and the psychological and social processes thought to generate offending.

In a recent paper, Ward and Beech (2015) suggested that dynamic risk factors are composite constructs composed of multiple variables, arising from their initial status as risk predictors. Ward and Beech argue that in an overview of risk assessment the composite nature of dynamic risk factors is made perfectly clear. More specially, they point out that:

> Russell and Darjee (2013) identified social influences, intimacy deficits, general self-regulation problems, sexual self-regulation difficulties, pro-offending attitudes and lack of cooperation with supervision as stable dynamic factors. Each of these stable factors is subdivided into more specific factors; for example, intimacy deficits incorporate emotional identification with children, lack of concern for others and general social rejection. (p. 104)

What follows from the argument that dynamic risk factors are composite constructs rather than coherent theoretical concepts developed within the context of an explanation of offending? The first implication is that they do not pick out psychological processes at all but rather are labels or summaries of multiple factors (Borsboom, 2005; Ward & Beech, 2015). In a strict sense, they do not really refer to anything real; they do not exist. Second, the various types of dynamic risk factors (e.g. antisocial personality, relationship problems, intimacy deficits, self-management problems, emotional dysregulation, and distorted attitudes – see Thornton, 2013) are *markers* for psychological and social causal processes, aetiological factors and symptoms or clinical phenomena (see below). On their own they only function as predictors of reoffending; but as such they arguably track casual processes and to that extent provide a valuable function. In the field of medical epidemiology, Giroux (2015, p. 183) observes, '... the predictive value of a factor is not always symmetrical to its etiological part'. He further comments, '... the identification of risk factors for disease quickly lead to the question of their causal status' (p. 184). To be useful in an explanatory context, risk factors need to be analysed further, interpreted, specified, and linked to offence-related problems and actions. Only then can they be used to formulate cases and guide the construction of treatment plans. It is not surprising that the conclusion is that dynamic risk factors are not coherent theoretical concepts. The story is in their origins. The real difficulty is that the failure to grasp that the contexts of prediction and explanation are conceptually distinct has mislead researchers and clinicians into viewing them as putative causes.

What do dynamic risk factors refer to?

One of the difficulties in making judgements about the theoretical status of dynamic risk factors is that there are so many of them, in different offending contexts, that generalisations are problematic. What you end up with depends on which particular variables are chosen and incorporated into risk measures. However, research in the areas of sex offending and general offending risk prediction has consistently found two things (a) similar types of general dynamic and static risk features are apparent in the work of different research groups, and (b) there is a plethora of specific attributes within each risk factor domain.

The major eight risk factors featured in Andrews and Bonta's (2010) theory of criminal conduct are a mixture of static and dynamic factors, although for most of the risk factors, a set of dynamic needs or targets have been identified. One or two of them, for example, antisocial personality pattern, are broken down into different traits, attitudes, and behaviours. However, what is clear is that they are a ragbag of personality traits, capacities, emotional properties, attitudes, beliefs, and behaviours. Similarly, dynamic risk factors identified in the sexual offending field tend to fall under general domain descriptions such as those listed in Mann et al. (2010), Russell and Darjee (2013), and Thornton (2013). For example, Thornton (2013, p. 63) lists the following subdomains of dynamic risk factors within his general domain of sexual interests: intense impersonal sexual interests, sexual coping, diverse sexual outlets, sexualised violence, and sexual interest in prepubescent and pubescent children. While Mann et al. (2010, p. 199) include impulsivity, recklessness, and employment instability within the general domain of general self-regulation problems. Each attribute within the general dynamic risk factor domain can be further broken down into more specific variables (see below for a discussion of the problem of levels of analysis). Once it is appreciated that the major purpose of collections of dynamic risk factors is to predict reoffending, this should come as no surprise. After all, accurate prediction of a relatively vague criterion such as offending requires the recruitment of multiple variables. Thus, dynamic risk factor domains comprised heterogeneous factors, many of which, if cashed out in causal terms, could not occur at the same time; they are mutually exclusive (Ward & Beech, 2015).

At this point I will not press home the claim that, because they are composite constructs, dynamic risk factors do not genuinely refer to causal processes, and accept for the sake of argument that some might do so, even if in a tangential way. The issue I would like to concentrate on here picks up on the heterogeneous nature of dynamic risk factors and I make three claims arising from this fact: (a) they refer to a wide range of psychological factors, such as causal processes, aetiological factors, and symptom or clinical phenomena; (b) because of this vagueness of reference it is hard to know exactly what is being referred to in explanatory, assessment, and treatment contexts; and (c) it is necessary to refer to theories of offending to narrow the focus and, furthermore, to model the relationships between dynamic risk factors, and also the interactions within each category.

If you take a general dynamic risk factor such as *relational style*, and consider what Thornton (2013, p. 63) calls the subdomains within each, it is immediately obvious that they are a mixture of events, mental states, psychological processes, and social states of affairs. For example, emotional congruence with children refers to an emotional need and problematic attitudes to adult relationships; lack of emotionally intimate relationships is a social state of affairs and a contextual factor; grievance thinking points to the existence of ruminative mental states; and callousness is a personality feature. Furthermore, an attribute such as emotional congruence with children could be further analysed to mean a number of distinct and/or related things: feels safe with children, believes children understand him or her, can communicate effectively with children, can only experience true intimacy with children, and so on.

How do you resolve the vagueness of reference evident here and ascertain what is being referred to by dynamic risk factors and their constituent factors in a particular context? The only way to sharpen the focus is by utilising *theories* that explain how mental states, contextual factors, psychological structures and processes, and aetiological factors (e.g. in the case of relationship problems, childhood neglect or abuse) combine to cause relationships problems (there might be a number of possible types of problems) and, therefore, heighten reoffending risk. If space permitted I would be able to provide examples of this kind of heterogeneity problem for the majority of dynamic risk factors in the sexual offending domain, and general offending field. In short, unless theories of offending and offending-related problems are put to work, it would be logically and practically impossible to operationalise dynamic risk factors for explanatory and intervention purposes.

Level of abstraction

The earlier discussion of dynamic risk factors indicates that they vary in their level of abstraction. At their most abstract they consist of general domain names such as *relational style* or *self-management* difficulties and at a more concrete level these are unpacked into factors such as emotional congruence with children and employment difficulties. There are two issues that I think are important to consider if you accept that dynamic risk factors can be construed as causes of offending. The first matter concerns how to determine the most appropriate grain of analysis: How do researchers or clinicians decide what level of abstraction is reasonable for the tasks in which they are engaged? Second, from a theoretical perspective, the critical question is what are the dangers of constructing causal explanations based on dynamic risk factors at the wrong level? The reason the level of abstraction question is theoretically and practically important is that it highlights the degree to which explanation, assessment, and treatment of offending can rely solely on dynamic risk factors. It also suggests what additional conceptual and methodological resources should be recruited when importing dynamic risk factors from the prediction arena into aetiological and practice domains.

The issue of levels of abstraction is conceptually linked with that of levels of explanation. The key issue becomes: What is the most appropriate level of explanation (analysis) for the offending behaviour I wish to understand and to intervene in? If my interest is in risk prediction – and I assume that risk factors track causal processes in some way – then I could simply use the aggregate score from risk measures or look at the relationship between general domain factors and reoffending. However, if I wish to track the relationship between types of relationship difficulties and the onset of further offending, I would need to concentrate on a specific causal pathway. Or again, if the goal is to grasp how dynamic risk factors work together to increase the chances of individuals committing crimes, it would be necessary to construct a dynamic casual model. The danger of overlooking the issue of levels of abstraction when employing dynamic risk factors in research and practice is that you might unwittingly adopt the wrong level of analysis for the problem in hand. Haynes (1992) has expressed this worry well in the context of psychopathology:

> The difficulty with a high-level causal variable is that it includes many lower-level variables. Therefore, higher-level variables and models do not permit distinction among the multiple possible causal variables and paths they represent. For example, the active elements in 'marital distress' can include hostile verbal exchanges, physical abuse, sarcastic comments, defensiveness, withdrawal, infrequent presence in the home, feeling unloved, anxiety and emotional arousal, or lack of positive statements to the spouse. (p. 63)

The level at which you should formulate dynamic risk factors depends crucially on your particular interests and explanatory target, and ought to be informed by theoretical understanding of the pertinent causal mechanism and aetiological processes. Thus, there is no uniformly 'right' way to employ dynamic risk factors in explaining offending or when predicting recidivism. What is apparent is that once researchers and clinicians have decided what matters they are interested in, then dynamic risk factors should be formulated in ways that enable them to achieve their goals. However, it is hard to conceive of any situation in which additional theory will not be required, whatever the task. Appealing to dynamic risk factors on their own, without some idea of how the relevant causal process and aetiological factors are operating, is unlikely to be successful. They are simply too conceptually thin.

Are dynamic risk factors scientific kinds?

I have suggested that dynamic risk factors are vaguely defined and normatively laden, that they do not refer in any straightforward sense to psychological processes, are composite constructs, and are often formulated at the wrong level of abstraction. However, I have also accepted that it is possible that suitably reworked, they may be able to be used in causal explanations of offending and its associated problems. I am somewhat sceptical of this possibility but am prepared to accept it. In part it is an empirical question, although there are significant conceptual problems to be overcome. The most glaring is the conflation between the contexts of prediction and explanation.

An implicit question in the above discussion and in the literature on dynamic risk factors is whether they are scientific or natural kinds, or social kinds. According to Cooper (2005, p. 46) 'natural kind':

> … Is a technical term used by philosophers to refer to the kinds of things or stuff studied by the natural science. Sodium, fleas, dandelions, and electrons are all examples of natural kinds. Members of natural kinds are naturally similar to each other, and there is some explanation for this. Fleas for example, are all similar in that they jump, drink blood, and are poisoned by flea-spray, and fleas are alike in these respects because they are similar in some fundamental way, plausibly because they are all genetically similar.

There has been a considerable body of theoretical writing on the topic of natural kinds and its implications for classification and scientific explanation in natural science and in areas such as psychopathology (see Kincaid & Sullivan, 2014; Murphy, 2006). Some authors prefer the term *scientific* kind because it does not require that all members of a category possess every property. Rather, the argument is that there are prototypical examples of members of a category and although individual members may depart from the ideal in some respects, they generally share most properties. Thus while there are no necessary and sufficient conditions for scientific kinds, they are constituted by properties that tend to cluster together. The identification of scientific kinds is important as they licence us to make causal inferences and to predict outcome based on our understanding of the central properties in question. Social kinds, by way of contrast, are not classification independent and depend for their existence on social practices. That is, there are no objective or classification-independent properties, or clusters of properties to be discovered.

There has been some very interesting work on scientific and natural kinds in the area of psychopathology, probably the most relevant area for correctional and forensic researchers. To cut to the chase, it is now commonly accepted that mental disorders are conditions that involve some type of psychological or biological dysfunction *and* that cause harm to the person involved or other people (Cooper, 2005; Graham, 2013; Kincaid & Sullivan, 2014; Murphy, 2006). Rachel Cooper rather colourfully employs the metaphor of plants and weeds to capture the combination of objective impairment and normative judgements required to make a diagnosis of a mental disorder. She proposes that while plants share a cluster of physical properties that make them members of the genus *plants*, whether or not they are thought of as weeds depends on an additional, normative judgement that they are *unwanted* in certain contexts. A plant may be desired (so to speak!) in some countries, or at some times, while judged to be a weed in another place or time. Thus, a psychological dysfunction may be objectively acknowledged (e.g. extreme social anxiety) but only considered to be a mental disorder in some contexts (e.g. societies that highly value public interaction).

Are dynamic risk factors scientific kinds or social kinds? Their reliance on normative judgement is not in itself a problem, as we have seen in the case of mental disorders and plants. The crux of the matter is do they refer to conditions (capacities, personality features, sexual interests, etc.) that can be objectively identified as dysfunctional rather than simply morally wrong?

A first objection is that they do not appear to refer to any specific condition at all, such as a dysfunctional threat detection system (anxiety mechanism) or dysfunction in positive valance system (addiction). They refer to a ragbag collection of different things, including capacities, states of affairs, mental states, emotions, behaviours, and social contexts. Because they are not conditions they cannot be candidates for scientific kinds.

The best way to respond to this objection is to acknowledge that some components or variables incorporated within specific categories of dynamic risk factors will not be scientific kinds, but others may qualify. I suggest that impulsivity could be an example of a possible scientific kind. I think there are reasonable grounds to think that it is caused by impairment in the psychological capacities constituting agency. However, this move is a stretch because kinds are typically kinds of stuff or things, such as plants or fleas that share a number of properties. Alternatively, it could be argued that psychopathy is a scientific kind; although the degree to which it is considered a coherent category is disputed.

The issue is that dynamic risk factors cannot really be scientific kinds unless they can be viewed as things characterised by common properties. The only other alternative is that dynamic risk factors could be utilised to group offenders into categories such as high risk, moderate risk, and low risk; creating (scientific) kinds of offenders. The problem with this strategy is that it is theoretically empty as the only common features offenders possess in these groups are associated with their likelihood of reoffending. Theories of offending based on risk bands are likely to be fairly general and collapse into features such as impulsivity, antisocial attitudes, and behaviour.

So, what is the verdict? In my view dynamic risk factors are not scientific kinds and it is doubtful whether in their current, under-theorised form, they could be the basis of scientific kinds. Certainly offenders who have mental disorders of some type may be categorised in such terms. However, in these instances, risk factors do not play a role in the classification process. It seems to me that while some dynamic risk factors are markers for some types of psychological impairment, given their terminal vagueness and poor specificity, it is unclear what this dysfunction actually involves at the present time.

How to clinically utilise dynamic risk factors

The above analysis has come to a rather disappointing conclusion: in their typical formulation, dynamic risk factors are conceptually unable to play an explanatory role in the forensic and correctional domains. Furthermore, because treatment aims to modify the causes of offending and its associated problems, they should not be used to formulate cases and guide treatment. At least, not in their current form because they are not causes. They should only be used in the way they were originally intended to be: to complement static risk assessment measures and to monitor changes in risk over treatment, and when individuals are on probation. I agree with Mann et al. (2010) and Beech and Ward (2004) that at least some dynamic risk factors are *markers* of causal processes and in this respect have an important function in highlighting areas for research and clinical case formulation. They can tell us where to focus research attention, and how to engage with theory and methodology to search for the mechanisms generating offending. This will put case formulation and subsequent treatment on a much stronger foundation than a reliance on dynamic risk factors.

Research and clinical applications

In a recent paper, Heffernan and Ward (2015) argue that the current understanding of dynamic risk factors is deeply flawed, pretty much for the reasons outlined above. They propose that one way of thinking about how dynamic risk factors may influence sex offending (but their idea generalises to all types of offenders) is by conceptualising them in terms of the components of agency (goal-directed action). They draw from biological research and dynamic systems theory in concluding that the capacity for agency is inherent in all living things. They note that human beings possess the ability to intentionally structure learning and physical environments (i.e. niche construction) and are extremely sensitive to contextual variables. According to Heffernan and Ward, the major components of agency are (1) goals, plans, and strategies; (2) implementation of plans and their evaluation; and (3) the subsequent revision of goals and plans in light of outcomes. Furthermore, in their agency model of risk (AMR), there are three levels of agency each associated with its own distinct set of goals, plans, and strategies, and each capable of influencing the other types of agency. The levels of agency in the AMR are the *system* level (goals related to physical integrity and functioning such as sexual interest and emotion), *social* role (goals concerned with specific social roles such as being a teacher), and *personal* (concerns individuals' overall sense of identity and core normative commitments). The type of goals offenders possess and the plans they construct to achieve their goals and to evaluate their effectiveness are partly a function of *the contexts* in which they live and the resources available to them. Goals are activated or selected in response to external contexts and their cues such as the presence of threats, and by internal cues such as hunger, fear, sexual desire, or anger. Dynamic risk factors can be viewed as flaws in individual functional capacities, social supports, and opportunities. Thus, dynamic risk factors, once broken down into their causal elements, are seen as psychological and social processes (i.e. those associated with goals, plans, strategies, and action implementation) that impair normal functioning and hence disrupt persons' internal and external relationships to their social, cultural, and physical environments.

The research and clinical implications of this depiction of dynamic risk factors are significant and help address the problems of vagueness and lack of reference discussed earlier. For example, the dynamic risk factor of intimacy deficits in sex offenders can be understood as (1) maladaptive beliefs and norms concerning relationships (e.g. adults are untrustworthy); (2) interpersonal and emotional regulation strategies that damage relationships with adults (e.g. do not talk about feelings and avoid social contact with adults) and that isolate individuals from social support; and (3) the active search for, and construction of, social environments in which such individuals feel comfortable and where their needs seem to be met (e.g. paedophilic networks and spending a lot of time with vulnerable children).

The Heffernan and Ward (2015) AMR provides *one* way of marshalling supporting theories and research to facilitate the translation of dynamic risk factors into a form that is potentially explanatory and clinically useful. There are other ways of doing this, as is evident from a number of papers in this special issue (see Thornton, 2015, and Hannah-Moffat, 2016), each with its own strengths and weaknesses. But irrespective of their individual merits, the important point is that we need to enlist the help of aetiological theories and descriptive models to capitalise on what is of value in the concept of dynamic risk factors. On their own they are incapable of contributing theoretical power to aetiological, assessment, and treatments practices and their associated tasks.

Where do we go from here?

It was my intention in writing this paper to think more deeply than we have done previously about the theoretical status of dynamic risk factors and to identify any areas of concern. It is fair to say that whether dynamic risk factors suffer from substantial theoretical deficits depends partly on your viewpoint. From a psychometric perspective, the primary function of dynamic risk factors is to predict recidivism and to monitor risk. The priority is to develop reliable and valid measures of risk that can contribute to risk management. The degree to which such measures actually do this is contestable, and there are some doubts whether they are valid in the sense that dynamic risk factors are real attributes that cause variations in risk scores (see Borsboom, 2005). Despite these theoretical concerns, measures of risk incorporating dynamic risk factors such as the LSI-R (Andrews & Bonta, 2010) and the Stable-Acute (Hanson & Harris, 2000) are widely employed and endorsed by researchers and practitioners. From an explanatory perspective, although they are used to inform research, assessment, and treatment, and at least some researchers believe that they may be causes of crime, there is no consensus on this matter. My view is that dynamic risk factors are poor candidates for the status of scientific kinds and, additionally, because they lack theoretical coherency should not be included in explanations of offending. Their epistemic value is more that of boundary riders: they can alert researchers of possible areas of interest and then should retreat in the background while causal theories are developed and evaluated. In this respect, they are similar to static risk factors and are best construed as proxies or markers for the causes of offending.

The field of medical epidemiology provides a good illustration of how to take into account statistical relationships between risk variables and sets of mechanisms in the process of identifying the causes of diseases (Giroux, 2015; Illari & Russo, 2014). The use of case-control and cohort study methodologies enabled researchers to establish that there was a significant statistical relationship between smoking and lung cancer, raising the possibility that it was one of the causes of this disease. The subsequent discovery of the P53 gene, and an understanding of the mechanisms creating harmful mutations, led to the conclusion that the relationship is indeed a causal one.

According to this model of causal reasoning, in order to justify causal claims you need to first establish statistical associations between risk factors and offending, and then discover (infer) causal mechanisms that are capable of generating crime. The problem is that with dynamic risk factors there are reservations about whether or not they are conceptually coherent and therefore plausible causes, and also, they have not often been formulated in mechanistic terms. While there are theoretical accounts of offence-related problems such as intimacy deficits and emotional dysregulation problems in sexual offenders, they are rarely conceptually integrated with research on dynamic risk factors (Ward & Beech, 2015).

Where do we go from here? The guidelines for causal inference in epidemiology developed by Bradford Hill (1965) provide a helpful stating point. He suggested that it is reasonable to infer that a risk factor is a cause of a disease if it is consistent with the following guidelines: (1) a strong association with an specific outcome, (2) consistency (e.g. place, circumstances, time, and observers), (3) specificity (e.g. to particular groups, body systems and sites, and diseases), (4) temporality (a putative cause precedes outcome), (5) biological gradient (e.g. expect decrease in effect with decrease in cause), (6) plausibility (i.e. is the cause reasonable within the context of current knowledge?), (7) coherence (i.e. does it cohere with knowledge about the domain?), (8) experimental (evidence), and (9) analogy (i.e. the existence of other similar causal relationships). If you accept the argument of this paper, and adjusting for the fact that offending is not a disease, dynamic risk factors do not meet guidelines (3), (6), (7), (8), or (9). They do not meet (9) because there is rarely any theoretical modelling undertaken by researchers based on analogies, which require coherent constructs and specified relationships. Mann et al. (2010) propose that in order to establish whether risk factors are causes of sexual offending you first need to establish that there is a reasonably strong statistical association between them and offending and, in addition, present plausible accounts of their causal impact. While their proposals mirror Bradford Hill's guidelines (1) and (6), they do not address the other ones. Based on the argument of this paper, I consider all the guidelines to be important, especially those relating to the coherency of theoretical constructs and their evidential support (guidelines 6–9). Explicitly analysing dynamic risk factors in light of these guidelines, and employing them as evaluative standards, may advance research and treatment in the forensic and correctional domains. Bradford Hill (1965) argues that it is not possible to construct a set of strict criteria that, if met, guarantee there is a causal relationship between sets of factors; the best we can hope for are reasonable grounds for drawing causal inferences. More specifically, he proposes that:

> None of my nine viewpoints can bring indisputable evidence for or against the cause – and – effect hypothesis and none can be required as a sine qua non. What they can do, with greater or less strength, is to help us make up our minds on the fundamental question – is there any other way of explaining the set of facts before us, is there any other answer equally, or more, likely than cause and effect? (p. 299)

Bradford Hill's (1965) point is that it makes sense to adapt a pragmatic, somewhat humble, perspective and not to be overly rule-directed when attempting to identify, and subsequently justify, causal relationships between factors. Furthermore, the appropriate epistemic stance to adopt is a pluralistic one, where phenomena are detected (data patterns) and multiple methods are utilised to generate models and to develop and evaluate theories arising from such models (Haig, 2014). Thus, appeal to theory and the employment of systematic and careful reasoning is imperative if comprehensive explanations of offending are to be achieved.

Conclusions

The take-home message from this paper is simple, and the various strands of the argument all converge on one point: dynamic risk factors are not explanatory concepts but are rather, predictive constructs. The implications of this conclusion are far reaching and challenging. First, researchers and practitioners need to stop using this construct as the foundation for the explanation of offending and for the assessment and treatment of individuals who commit crimes. Second, practitioners should be trained how to formulate cases in psychological terms drawing from the relevant aetiological and treatment theories. Listing dynamic risk factors and allocating individuals to programmes that target them is unlikely to be effective. It is ineffective because it ignores the unique features of each person's situation and runs the risk of substituting behavioural control strategies for psychological interventions based on a sound understanding of the relevant causal mechanisms. Finally, it is myopic for policy-makers to assume that there is little more to correctional interventions than the employment of behavioural technology, and that this task can be undertaken by anyone who has undertaken only a basic level of training. Effective rehabilitation planning and programme delivery relies on an advanced knowledge of psychological principles of change, and cannot be translated into a few 'tricks' and guidelines. At the centre of this issue is the realisation that dynamic risk factors are best understood as general problem indicators rather than as providing detailed blueprints for change. Turning to another metaphor, they are more like scaffolds than completed buildings, and are at their best in explanatory and practice contexts when viewed primarily as instigators of inquiry.

Disclosure statement

No potential conflict of interest was reported by the author.

References

Andrews, D. A., & Bonta, J. (2010). *The psychology of criminal conduct*. New Providence, NJ: Anderson.

Beech, A. R., & Craig, L. (2012). The current status of static and dynamic factors in sexual offending risk assessment. *Journal of Aggression and Peace Research*, *4*, 169–185. doi:10.1108/17596591211270671

Beech, A. R., & Ward, T. (2004). The integration of etiology and risk in sexual offenders: A theoretical framework. *Aggression and Violent Behavior*, *10*, 31–63. doi:10.1016/j.avb.2003.08.002

Borsboom, D. 2005. *Measuring the mind: Conceptual issues in contemporary psychometrics*. Cambridge: Cambridge University Press.

Bradford Hill, A. (1965). The environment of disease: Association or causation? *Proceedings of the Royal Society of Medicine, 58*, 295–300.

Cooper, R. (2005). Classifying madness: A philosophical examination of the diagnostic and statistical manual of mental disorders. New York, NY: Springer.

Giroux, E. (2015). Risk factor and causality in epidemiology. In P. Huneman, G. Lambert, & M. Silberstein. (Eds.), *Classification, disease and evidence: New essays in the philosophy of medicine* (pp.179–192). New York, NY: Springer.

Graham, G. (2013). *The disordered mind: An introduction to philosophy of mind and mental illness* (2nd ed.). Oxford: Routledge.

Haig, B. D. (2014). *Investigating the psychological world: Scientific method in the behavioural sciences*. Cambridge, MA: MIT Press.

Hannah-Moffat, K. (2016). A Conceptual Kaleidoscope: Contemplating 'dynamic structural risk' and an uncoupling of risk from need. *Psychology, Crime, & Law*, 22(01–02), 33–46.

Hanson, R. K., & Harris, A. J. R. (2000). Where should we intervene? Dynamic predictors of sexual offense recidivism. *Criminal Justice and Behavior, 27*, 2–35. doi:10.1177/0093854800027001002

Hanson, R. K., & Thornton, D. (2000). Improving risk assessments for sexual offenders: A comparison of three actuarial scales. *Law and Human Behavior, 24*, 119–136. doi:10.1023/A:1005482921333

Haynes, S. N. (1992). *Models of causality in psychopathology: Toward dynamic, synthetic and nonlinear models of behavior disorders*. New York, NY: Macmillan.

Heffernan, R., & Ward, T. (2015). The conceptualization of dynamic risk factors in child sex offenders: An agency model. *Aggression and Violent Behavior, 24*, 250–260. doi:10.1016/j.avb.2015.07.001

Illari, P., & Russo. F. (2014). *Causality: Philosophical theory meets scientific practice*. New York, NY: Oxford University Press.

Kincaid, H., & Sullivan, J. A. (2014). *Classifying psychopathology: Mental kinds and natural kinds*. Cambridge, MA: MIT Press.

Mann, R. E., Hanson, R. K., & Thornton, D. (2010). Assessing risk for sexual recidivism: Some proposals on the nature of psychologically meaningful risk factors. *Sexual Abuse: A Journal of Research and Treatment, 22*, 191–217. doi:10.1177/1079063210366039

Murphy, D. (2006). *Psychiatry in the scientific image*. Cambridge, MA: MIT Press.

Russell, K., & Darjee, R. (2013). Managing the risk posed by personality-disordered sexual offenders in the community. In C. Logan & L. Johnstone (Eds.), *Managing clinical risk: A guide to effective practice* (pp. 88–114). Abingdon: Routledge.

Thornton, D. (2015). Developing a theory of dynamic risk. *Psychology, Crime, & Law.*, 22(01–02), 138–150.

Thornton, D. (2013). Implications of our developing understanding of risk and protective factors in the treatment of adult male sexual offenders. *International Journal of Behavioral Consultation and Therapy, 8*, 62–65. Retrieved from http://dx.doi.org/10.1037/h0100985

Ward, T. (2013). Addressing the dual relationship problem in forensic and correctional practice. *Aggression and Violent Behavior, 18*, 92–100. doi:10.1016/j.avb.2012.10.006

Ward, T. (2014). The explanation of sexual offending: From single factor theories to integrative pluralism. *Journal of Sexual Aggression, 20*, 130–141. doi:0.1080/13552600.2013.870242

Ward, T., & Beech, A. R. (2015). Dynamic risk factors: A theoretical dead-end? *Psychology, Crime & Law, 21*, 100–113.

Ward, T., & Maruna, S. (2007). *Rehabilitation: Beyond the risk paradigm*. New York, NY: Routledge.

Putting risk factors in their place: an evolutionary-developmental approach to understanding risk

Russil Durrant

School of Social and Cultural Studies, Institute of Criminology, Victoria University of Wellington, Wellington, New Zealand

ABSTRACT

The assessment of criminal risk plays a prominent role in the criminal justice systems of many different countries and risk assessment is employed in a number of different domains. Given the importance of risk assessment tools in forensic contexts, and the amount of research devoted to evaluating their accuracy in predicting re-offending, it might be expected that risk assessment tools are grounded in our best theoretical understanding of the causal processes that give rise to criminal actions. However, it is not at all clear that this is the case. In this article, I will argue that one important area of neglect is the failure to fully engage with the literature in developmental and life-course criminology which also has directed an enormous amount of effort in to identifying risk factors for offending. At the heart of this neglect, I will claim, is the failure to fully recognise the key distinction between predicting offending and predicting *re*-offending. I will further argue that an evolutionary developmental perspective provides the theoretical resources to provide fully *explanatory* accounts of offending and re-offending, and in which risk factors can be appropriately located. I conclude by briefly considering some implications for theory, research, and practice.

Introduction

The assessment of criminal risk plays a prominent role in the criminal justice systems of many different countries (Singh, Grann, & Fazel, 2011). Risk assessment is employed in a number of different domains: it is used to make decisions regarding parole, bail, civil commitment and, increasingly in recent years, criminal sanctions (Monahan & Skeem, 2014; Skeem & Monahan, 2011). The assessment of risk also plays a pivotal role in the assignment of treatment and in decision-making concerning appropriate treatment targets (Andrews & Bonta, 2010). Risk assessment tools are also pressed in to service in research that aims to understand the key factors that lead to offender recidivism. There are now literally hundreds of different risk assessment tools that are employed in criminal justice contexts and a voluminous body of empirical research that has evaluated their efficacy in predicting re-offending (Singh et al., 2011; Singh, Sinnott-Armstrong, & Savlulescu, 2014).

Given the importance of risk assessment tools in forensic contexts, and the amount of research devoted to evaluating their accuracy in predicting re-offending, it might be expected that risk assessment tools are grounded in our best theoretical understanding of the causal processes that give rise to criminal actions. However, as a number of scholars have argued, this assumption is open to question (e.g. Skeem & Monahan, 2011; Ward, 2015; Ward & Beech, 2015). It is not at all clear that the risk factors identified in empirical research and which form the basis of risk assessment instruments are based on our best causal understanding of offending. In short, it is argued that there has been an overly narrow focus on prediction rather than explanation and a subsequent neglect of theoretical issues in the development and use of risk assessment tools (Douglas & Skeem, 2005; Ward & Beech, 2015). Ward and Beech (2015, p. 101) provide an apt summary of the field, as they see it:

> A key reason for the neglect of theoretical issues associated with risk assessment seems to be that there is little communication between researchers working in adjacent areas within the offending field. Individuals investigating risk assessment and those researching the causes of offending – or the features of offenders – do not appear to read papers outside their narrow area of speciality or, for that matter, believe they have anything useful to learn from each other.

In this article, I will argue that one important area of neglect is the failure to fully engage with the literature in developmental and life-course criminology which also has directed an enormous amount of effort in to identifying risk factors for offending. At the heart of this neglect, I will claim, is the failure to fully recognise the key distinction between predicting offending and predicting *re*-offending. I will further argue that an evolutionary developmental perspective provides the theoretical resources to provide fully *explanatory* accounts of offending and re-offending, and in which risk factors can be appropriately located.

I first briefly outline the nature of risk assessment in forensic contexts and discuss some of the key conceptual issues that have been raised concerning the nature of risk. I then discuss what I see as a key distinction between predicting offending and predicting re-offending and provide a comparative overview of risk factors identified in the forensic literature and in the literature on developmental and life-course criminology. I then locate these risk factors within an evolutionary developmental framework for understanding offending that offers to provide an appropriate explanatory framework for understanding risk. I conclude, by briefly considering some implications for theory, research, and practice.

On the nature of risk factors in criminology and criminal justice: Conceptual issues

Andrews, Bonta, and Wormith (2006) provide an overview of what they have described as four generations of risk assessment (see also Andrews & Bonta, 2010). First generation risk assessment largely consisted of clinical judgement concerning the perceived likelihood of re-offending, whereas second generation risk assessment was based on empirically validated tools that measured largely static or unchangeable risk factors for offending (e.g. the Static-99R). The addition of theoretically informed dynamic or changeable risk factors characterises third generation risk assessment tools (e.g. the LSI-R), while fourth generation risk assessment integrates risk/need assessment with case management strategies. The picture provided by Andrews et al. (2006) is largely upbeat: the historical development of offender assessment has furnished forensic practitioners with the tools to not only predict re-offending with some degree of accuracy, but also to effectively target dynamic risk factors (or 'criminogenic needs') in ways that can significantly reduce recidivism.

This optimism is to some extent warranted: both second and third generation risk assessment tools can successfully predict re-offending. For example, in a meta-analysis of nine risk assessment tools for violent offending Yang, Wong, and Coid (2010) concluded that all nine tools (with the exception of the PCL-R factor 1) successfully predicted violence, although there was little difference in the efficacy of the different instruments. Indeed, although there is a large body of empirical research that has investigated the efficacy of risk assessment tools it seems as though there is relatively little difference in the predictive validity of the different instruments (Singh & Fazel, 2010; Singh et al., 2011; Yang et al., 2010). It also seems that second generation risk assessment measures that focus on static risk factors such as age, gender, and criminal history variables perform as well if not better than third generation tools that incorporate dynamic risk factors, or criminogenic needs (Caudy, Durso, & Taxman, 2013). Nonetheless, there is considerable evidence that rehabilitation efforts that target dynamic risk factors can reduce re-offending (Andrews & Bonta, 2010), although the effects are somewhat modest and some scholars remain relatively pessimistic about the efficacy of psychological treatment for particular groups of offenders (e.g. Walton & Chou, 2015). In short, although significant progress has been made in the assessment and treatment of offenders, the predictive equivalence of most risk assessment tools, the greater predictive efficacy of static versus dynamic risk factors, and the scope for improvement in treatment outcomes suggests that there remain opportunities for improving the nature and process of risk assessment in forensic settings.

Of particular importance for many scholars is the way that risk factors are theoretically framed. As illustrated in Table 1 there is an – at times bewildering – diversity of ways of

Table 1. Risk factor taxonomies.

Taxonomy	Description	Source
Static risk factors	A risk factor that is not amenable to change (e.g. age)	Andrews and Bonta (2010)
Dynamic risk factors (Criminogenic needs)	A risk factor that is potentially amenable to change (e.g. antisocial attitudes)	
Fixed markers	A risk factor that is unchangeable (e.g. gender)	Kraemer et al. (1997); Monahan and Skeem (2014)
Variable markers	A risk factor that may change but not via intervention (e.g. age)	
Variable risk factors	A risk factor that is changeable via intervention (e.g. employment status)	
Causal risk factors	A risk factor that is changeable via intervention and which can reduce the risk of recidivism (e.g. antisocial cognitions)	
Stable dynamic risk factors	Risk factors that are relatively enduring characteristics of individuals (e.g. substance abuse problems)	Hanson and Harris (2000)
Acute dynamic risk factors	Risk factors that change more rapidly and may immediately precipitate offending (e.g. intoxication)	
Risk status	Inter-individual differences in risk based largely on static risk factors	Douglas and Skeem (2005)
Risk state	Intra-individual differences in risk based on current status of dynamic risk factors	
Psychologically meaningful risk factors	Propensities to offend that (a) play a causal role in offending; and (b) predict recidivism	Mann et al. (2010)

conceptualising risk factors. Broadly speaking a risk factor for re-offending is simply any characteristics of an individual that temporally precedes and is statistically correlated with recidivism (Kraemer et al., 1997). The most widely employed distinction is between static and dynamic risk factors: the former predict reoffending but are not amenable to change whereas the latter also predict re-offending but are amenable to change and hence can be targeted in a treatment context. Kraemer et al. (1997) subdivide statics risk factors in to those that are inherently unchangeable (e.g. gender) and those that change, but are not amenable to intervention (e.g. age, prior convictions). They also make a distinction between risk factors that can be changed via intervention but are not truly causal and those factors that are changeable and that bring about a change in recidivism and hence reflect underlying causal processes. Others have made a distinction between relatively enduring characteristics of individuals (stable dynamic risk factors) and those that change more rapidly and may precipitate an episode of offending (acute dynamic risk factors; Hanson & Harris, 2000; see also Taxman & Caudy's, 2015 notion of 'destabilising factors'). Finally, in the context of sexual offending, Mann, Hanson, and Thornton (2010) have argued for the importance of what they terms 'psychologically meaningful risk factors' or propensities to offend.

It is beyond the scope of this paper to provide a nuanced evaluation of the different ways that risk factors are conceptualised. Rather, I want to draw attention to the fact that regardless of how risk factors for re-offending are conceptualised, they remain just that: *characteristics of individuals that are statistically correlated with criminal recidivism*. As such, risk factors should not be confused for the underlying causal processes that bring about or result in offending (Durrant & Ward, 2015; Ward, 2015; Ward & Beech, 2015). This is obviously true for static risk factors. Age and gender are major correlates of offending, but neither can be plausibly conceptualised as *causes* of offending (although, as I argue below, due attention to age and gender can provide important insights in to underlying causal processes). Criminal history variables (e.g. the number and diversity of prior convictions) are best conceived of as *markers* for the diverse range of causal processes that give rise to offending (Beech & Wad, 2004) and, therefore, unsurprisingly, represent some of the best predictors of reoffending (offending predicts re-offending). However, dynamic risk factors, regardless of how they are conceptualised, also arguably fail to cleanly pick out the causal processes that underlie offending. For Ward and Beech (2015, p. 111) dynamic risk factors are 'hybrid concepts containing "symptom" or phenomena aspects and etiological aspects'. In short, they comprise a mix of descriptive and explanatory elements. In sum, although risk factors have demonstrable value in predicting re-offending, they have, by themselves, limited explanatory value.

The prediction of reoffending versus the prediction of offending

One reason for the failure of risk factors, as they have been conceptualised in the forensic psychology literature, to do any meaningfully explanatory work is because they have been almost exclusively derived from research that has focussed on predicting re-offending, not research that has focussed on predicting offending. There are a number of reasons why we should expect that the risk factors for re-offending may be different from the risk factors for offending. Most straightforwardly risk factors for re-offending are almost exclusively based on research with correctional populations. As such, the factors that are identified discriminate between offenders who are more likely to re-offend and offenders who are less likely to re-offend. These may or may not be the same factors that discriminate between individuals who offend and individuals who do not offend, as identified in community samples. A second reason to expect some divergence between risk factors for offending and risk factors for re-offending is that factors that predict re-offending are more likely to be downstream effects of specific developmental processes that play a key causal role in offending propensity. To take just one example, the experience of sexual abuse during childhood is a major risk factor for later sexual offending (Jespersen, Lalumière, & Seto, 2009; Simons, Wurtele, & Durham, 2008). There are several plausible causal pathways that can account for this finding: the experience of sexual abuse may negatively impact on attachment relations and result in problems in developing and maintaining intimacy, may lead to the development of distorted sexual scripts, and result in thinking patterns favourable to sexual offending. However, prior sexual abuse does not feature as a major risk factors for sexual recidivism, while intimacy deficits, cognitive distortions, and deviant sexual interests do (Hanson & Morton-Bourgon, 2005). By focussing only on the factors that predict reoffending there is, therefore, a relative neglect of the underlying causal processes that give rise to sexual offending against children.

Fortunately, just as there is an extensive literature on the risk factors for recidivism there is an equally extensive scholarly literature within developmental criminology on risk factors for offending based largely on longitudinal studies (Farrington, 2015). Although there are clearly offence specific risk factors in both domains, Table 2 highlights some of the most prominent risk factors for general offending and antisocial behaviour in both the forensic psychological and the developmental criminological literatures.

Table 2. Risk factors for re-offending vs. risk factors for offending.

Re-offending[a]	Offending[b]
Static	*Demographic*
Age	Age
Gender	Gender
Criminal history	Ethnicity
(Ethnicity)	
The 'Big four' and 'Central eight'	*Developmental risk factors*
History of antisocial behaviour	Conduct problems/externalising problems
	Low intelligence/school failure
Antisocial personality pattern	Low self-control/impulsiveness
Antisocial cognition	Low empathy/callous unemotional traits
Antisocial associates	Attention deficit/hyperactivity disorder
Family and/or marital	Antisocial parents, siblings and relatives
School and/or work	Parental conflict
Leisure and/or recreation	Child abuse and neglect
Substance abuse	Harsh or erratic parenting
	Lack of parental monitoring
	Low socio-economic status
	Association with delinquent peers
	Deprived neighbourhood community
	Factors relating to desistance[c]
	Marriage
	Parenthood
	Meaningful employment

[a]Andrews et al. (2006).
[b]Farrington (2015).
[c]Kazemian (2015).

As previously mentioned, static risk factors for re-offending include age, gender, and criminal offence history. Men, younger individuals, and those with a more extensive prior history of offending are statistically more likely to re-offend (Andrews & Bonta, 2010). Ethnic minority status is also a significant predictor of re-offending, although for a variety of reasons ethnicity does not generally feature in risk assessment tools. Age, gender, and ethnicity are also significant risk factors for offending. The relationship between age and offending is widely recognised by criminologists: the onset of offending tends to occur between the ages of 8 and 14, peaking during late adolescence and then declines thereafter (Loeber, 2012; Loeber & Farrington, 2012). The gender gap in offending is also a robust finding widely appreciated by criminologists: for virtually all types of offending men are overwhelmingly more likely to be perpetrators compared to women, with the magnitude of the gender gap largest for more serious violent and sexual offences (Daly & Wilson, 1988; Fagan, 2014). Finally, ethnicity – particularly in English-speaking Western societies – remains a significant predictor of offending and, in particular, arrest and incarceration). Gender, age, and ethnicity are clearly not, by themselves causal factors for offending or re-offending and are best conceptualised as markers for a combination of underlying biological, psychological, social, and cultural–historical processes. The importance, in particular, of gender and age as correlates of both offending and re-offending suggests that there is a need to more fully understand the causal processes that make age and gender important markers for criminal behaviour. Understanding the causal processes that make ethnicity an important marker for offending and reoffending is, in some respects, more complex, because ethnicity is typically entangled with a host of other risk factors that are related to socio-economic status and reflect the particular cultural–historical trajectories of countries and how this has impacted on the marginalisation and discrimination of specific ethnic minority groups.

According to Andrews and Bonta (2010) the 'big four' risk factors for reoffending are: (a) history of antisocial behaviour; (b) antisocial personality pattern; (c) antisocial cognition; and (d) antisocial associates. The first of these – a history of antisocial behaviour – has its counterpart in conduct problems and externalising problems in the developmental literature. As noted above, a history of antisocial behaviour is likely to largely reflect the operation of the various causal processes that give rise to antisocial behaviour rather than marking any unique causal pathway. The developmental literature clearly highlights the marked continuity in antisocial and problem behaviour from an early age through to adulthood (e.g. Caspi, 2000) suggesting that there are relatively enduring characteristics of individuals and their environments that continue to influence behaviour. Of course, we should not ignore the possibility that the simple act of engaging in antisocial actions makes future antisocial actions more likely due to reinforcement effects or through the criminogenic effects of involvement in the criminal justice system (Nagin, Cullen, & Johnson, 2009). The second of the 'big four' factors – antisocial personality pattern – is also clearly represented in the developmental literature. A substantial body of research has highlighted how hyperactivity, impulsivity, low empathy, and callous unemotional traits are significant predictors of antisocial and criminal behaviour (Farrington, 2015). Because both the forensic psychological literature and the developmental criminological literature on risk are largely concerned with explaining *individual differences* it is not surprising that antisocial personality characteristics are important in predicting why some individuals rather than others offend or re-offend, and are probably closely tied to underlying causal mechanisms relating to self-regulation and emotional responses to others. Having antisocial associates is also an important risk factor for re-offending, whereas association with delinquent peers is an important risk factor for antisocial behaviour in the developmental literature. The specific causal role of antisocial others remains more elusive and clearly there are both selection and peer influence effects on antisocial behaviour that need to be considered (Warr, 2002). The final 'big four' risk factor for re-offending – antisocial cognitions – does not have any clear counterpart in the developmental literature. However, individual differences in attitudes, values, beliefs, and norms regarding antisocial behaviour are likely to be the downstream effects of various developmental processes including being raised by antisocial parents, association with delinquent peers, low socio-economic status, and residence in deprived neighbourhoods.

Moving beyond the 'big four' risk factors for re-offending we see further similarities and differences with the main developmental risk factors for offending. First, in the developmental literature, family risk factors such as parental conflict, child abuse, harsh or erratic parenting, and lack of parental monitoring play a prominent role in predicting offending (Kerig & Becker, 2015; Pardini, Waller, & Hawes, 2015). Although family factors such as parental nurturance/caring and monitoring/supervision are listed as risk factors for re-offending, they are, arguably, afforded less prominence in predicting recidivism. Second, two of the 'central eight' risk factor for re-offending – family/marriage and school/work – do have their clear counterparts in the developmental literature although as factors that are related to *desistance* from offending and in this respect serve in the same way to (negatively) predict re-offending. Although there remains considerable discussion about the nature and magnitude of the relationship between employment, marriage, parenthood, and desistance from offending there is general agreement that gaining meaningful employment (Horney, Tolan, & Weisburd, 2012), getting married (Craig, Diamond, & Piquero, 2014; Theobald & Farrington, 2010), and becoming a parent (Theobald, Farrington, & Piquero, 2014) are all negatively associated with re-offending. However, there is little obvious place for socio-economic status and neighbourhood context in predicting re-offending although, these are important risk factors for the development of antisocial behaviour, and feature prominently in criminology theories of offending (Elliott, Dupéré, & Leventhal, 2015). Finally, although leisure and/or recreation and substance abuse feature as two of the 'central eight' risk factors for re-offending, neither are prominent in the developmental literature. For substance abuse, at least, this is because it is mainly viewed as part of the general *pattern* of antisocial behaviour rather than as a risk factor for its development.

The risk factors for re-offending as derived from the forensic psychological literature and the risk factors for offending that have emerged from longitudinal research that are displayed in Table 2 clearly do not exhaust all the factors that have emerged from relevant research and we need to recognise substantial literatures devoted to exploring risk factors for specific types of (re)offending (e.g. intimate partner violence, sexual offending) in addition to research that has explored how these risk factors may vary depending on ethnicity and gender (Craig, 2015; Piquero, 2015). In addition, we could add a substantial list of biological risk factors for offending such as resting heart rate (Portnoy & Farrington, 2015) and genetic and gene–environment interactions that may also serve to predict re-offending (see the articles in Singh et al., 2014).

However, many risk factors we compile, a central task for theorists is to embed these factors within a broader theoretical perspective that provides a causal account of how the risk factors are related to criminal behaviour. Furthermore, this causal account should essentially be the same, regardless of whether we are explaining offending or re-offending. Certainly, some processes may be more salient in explaining why someone becomes a persistent offender and other processes may be more salient for explaining why a persistent offender re-offends. However, ultimately the explanatory task is about explaining variations in offending (among individuals, within individuals, between communities, etc.) and thus, we should expect a core set of explanatory processes to be relevant. In the following section an outline of a plausible explanatory framework for embedding risk factors is presented.

Locating risk factors within an evolutionary developmental perspective

Criminologists cannot be accused of neglecting theory in their efforts to explain offending. Indeed, there are a large number of different theoretical approaches that have been developed to explain all aspects of offending, many of which are fully compatible with one another (Agnew, 2011). Andrews et al. (2006, p. 9) claim that 'The general personality and social psychology of crime, with special attention to social learning and/or social cognition theory, is now the prominent theoretical position in criminology'. However, this assertion is open to dispute, and it would be fairer to characterise the state of criminological theory as one of diversity with no substantive agreement concerning the best theoretical perspective (Agnew, 2011; Durrant & Ward, 2015). Durrant and Ward (2015) have argued that the best approach to understanding the diversity of theoretical perspectives in criminology is to endorse a version of *integrative pluralism* (Mitchell, 2009), which recognises that different theories have different *levels of analysis* and different *levels of organisation*. Levels of analysis refer to the specific *kinds* of explanation that can be provided for any given biological phenomenon. Tinbergen's (1963) influential framework highlights the importance of attention to four main levels of analysis, each of which emphasises a particular type of epistemic inquiry: (1) evolutionary history (how has the character or trait evolved over time?); (2) evolutionary function (what is the adaptive value of the character or trait?); (3) ontogeny (how has the character or trait developed during the lifespan of the organism; and (4) causation (what are the proximate physiological and psychological mechanisms that bring about the behaviour?). Levels of organisation, in contrast, refers largely to the fact that the world is organised in a hierarchically structured fashion with higher level entities (e.g. societies, individuals), composed of, but not reducible to, lower level entities and processes (e.g. cognitive sub-systems, neurobiological processes). Efforts should be made, therefore, to wherever possible forge links between theoretical explanations across different levels of analysis and different levels of organisation. Rather than leading to any grand theoretical perspective this approach emphasises the importance of developing what Ward (2013) calls a 'coalition of friendly theories' that are mutually consistent and which can address a range of different explanatory targets.

An example should help to clarify this approach. As noted above, gender is a significant risk factor for both offending and re-offending: men are more likely to engage in – especially serious violent and sexual – crime compared to women. The magnitude of this gender gap is substantial: for example, globally men account for 95% of all convictions for homicide (United Nations Office of Drugs and Crime, 2014). Standard criminological explanation for the gender gap in offending will emphasise the role of differential socialisation into social roles and the influence of culture (e.g. Fagan, 2014). Although these explanations are not doubt relevant, they provide an incomplete explanation. A more comprehensive explanation needs to consider how sexual selection processes have favoured men (more than women) who are willing to engage in a diverse range of risky behaviours, including aggression and violence, ultimately because males can increase their reproductive success through such behaviours, relative to women (Archer, 2009; Puts, 2010). These different selective pressures have favoured psychological characteristics in men such as less self-control, greater impulsivity, and lower levels of fear compared to women (Campbell, 2013), which are instantiated at the neurobiological level in terms of differences in the size and functioning of the pre-frontal cortex and the amygdala (Raine, 2013). Developmental experiences are likely to either amplify or dampen these differences depending on particular familial and cultural contexts. Gender is likely to remain a robust risk factor for offending and re-offending, therefore, because it is a marker for a diverse range of causal processes. Gender is, perhaps, less of an important risk factor for re-offending in the forensic psychological literature because the vast majority of offenders are male and, therefore, it adds little additional predictive power. However, understanding the causal processes that give rise to gender being a risk factor is useful because it can help us understand the role of other risk factors and why they may serve as markers for casual processes.

Life history theory as an organising framework for developmental criminology

An evolutionary developmental approach provides a useful place to locate risk factors for offending and for re-offending for a number of reasons. Consistent with the idea of integrative pluralism, a developmental approach provides a useful point of integration for a range of different theoretical perspectives in criminology because development entails complex interactions among biological, psychological, social, and cultural processes. It is, thus, a useful place to consider how theories that focus on different levels of analysis (evolution, function, development, causation), and different levels of organisation (intra-individual, individual, family, neighbourhood, society) might be related to one another. An evolutionary developmental approach, thus, provides an opportunity to consider how normative aspects of development are related to offending and how different developmental trajectories plausibly reflect different adaptive life history strategies in response to different developmental experiences (thus addressing issues of evolution and function). Risk factors that are identified in both the forensic psychological literature and the developmental criminological literature can also be embedded in the causal unfolding of life histories allowing for a clearer analysis of the relevant causal mechanisms that are in play (thus addressing questions that relate to proximate causal processes). Life history theory is centrally concerned with the way that developing organisms allocate finite resources to key developmental tasks such as growth, body maintenance, learning, mating, and parenting (Ellis et al., 2012; Hochberg & Belsky, 2013). Different stages in human development entail different trade-offs between these various tasks resulting in both characteristic life history patterns and in individual differences that arise due to different developmental experiences.

A useful place to start this analysis is by considering how many of the risk factors for offending (and re-offending) can be located within normative aspects of human development. Two important risk factors identified in both the forensic psychological literature and the developmental criminological literature are age and antisocial associates/deviant peers: offending/re-offending is more likely for adolescents and young adults than for older individuals, and individuals are more likely to offend/re-offend if they associate with deviant others. In the developmental literature these two risk factors are related: adolescents are more influenced by deviant peers than older individuals and are more likely to engage in co-offending. From a distal, evolutionary perspective, the association between age and offending reflects the importance of adolescence and early adulthood as a critical juncture in the life history of our species that is intimately related (for males in particular) to obtaining social status and competing successfully against intra-sexual competitors (Durrant & Ward, 2015; Ellis et al., 2012). The fact that the presence of peers tends to heighten risk-taking during adolescence more so than for older age groups reflects the importance of the social context in which intra-sexual aggression and risk-taking takes place. At a proximate level, it is plausible to suggest that selection has favoured neurodevelopmental processes that heighten sensitivity to reward while cognitive control systems are still maturing (Galván, 2013; Spear, 2013; Steinberg, 2010). These are manifest at the psychological level as greater sensation seeking and a still limited capacity for self-control, during a period where socially individuals are more oriented to peer rather than parental relationships. Adolescents and young adults are, therefore, more likely to offend/re-offend because they are more attracted to risk and less able to regulate behaviour and hence may be more likely to pursue criminal opportunities. From an evolutionary perspective, the desistance in offending that is related (albeit complexly) to getting married and having children reflects the relative orientation of males away from the mating and towards the parenting domain. This perspective highlights the importance of focussing on the *quality* of relationships to partners and children as it is the *investment* in intimate partners and offspring that are likely to signal a shift away from intra-sexual competition (mating effort) and towards offspring (parenting effort), rather than the simple fact of getting married or having children. Consistent with this perspective, and the idea that testosterone plays an important role in intra-sexual contests, emerging research has highlighted how levels of testosterone decrease when men get married (Gray, Ellison, & Campbell, 2007) and have children (Gettler, McDade, Feranil, & Kuzawa, 2011), but increase when they get divorced (Mazur & Michalek, 1998).

An evolutionary developmental perspective can, thus, locate some of the major risk factors for offending/-re-offending within the normative context of human development. Individual differences in the likelihood of offending/re-offending can also be explained in a way which helps to embed risk factors within a causal developmental framework. Although individual differences are likely to reflect a complex combination of genetic and gene–environment interactions, from a life history perspective at least some of the important individual difference that we see in the likelihood of offending reflect the adaptive calibration of individuals to either faster or slower life histories based on their exposure to critical features of the early environment (Bjorklund & Ellis, 2014; Durrant & Ward, 2015; Ellis et al., 2012). According to the adaptive calibration model of Ellis and colleagues (Ellis, Figueredo, Brumbach, & Schlomer, 2009) early exposure to harsh and/or unpredictable environments, characterised by cues indicating high levels of extrinsic morbidity/mortality signal to the developing child that the future is likely to be a risky, dangerous and unpredictable place. Under these circumstances, it is argued, that individuals shift to a relatively faster life history characterised by earlier puberty, more mating and less parenting effort, and a relative focus on short-term, immediate gains. The logic of this model is straightforward: In dangerous, unpredictable environments it makes sense for individuals to accelerate their reproductive effort and to invest more time and effort in to the mating rather than the parenting domain. Ellis and colleagues have highlighted the important mediating role of the stress response system in shifting individuals to relatively faster life histories. In dangerous and unpredictable environments, the stress response system develops in a way that leads individuals to adopt an agonistic behavioural pattern that involves hyper-vigilance to environmental threats, while under conditions of extreme stress the stress response system may become hypo-responsive resulting in low levels of fear and anxiety and relative unconcern about the harmful consequences of aggressive and antisocial behaviour (Ellis & Del Giudice, 2014).

How might some of the key risk factors for offending/re-offending embed within this causal developmental framework? Many of the important individual risk factors for offending (e.g. antisocial personality characteristics such as low self-control, impulsiveness, low empathy, callous unemotional traits) can be viewed, in part (and leaving aside genetically based individual differences) as a cluster of psychological characteristics, underpinned by neurobiological processes that reflect an orientation towards a faster life history strategy involving more risk-taking, aggression, and intra-sexual competition. These traits, in turn, can be viewed as the downstream consequences of a cluster of environmental factors relating to the familial and social environment that the child was exposed to. Thus, child abuse, harsh and erratic parenting, low socio-economic status, and a deprived community are all risk factors for later offending because they signal to the developing child a future environment which is risky, unpredictable, dangerous, and lacking long-term enduring relationships.

Although an evolutionary developmental perspective may suggest to some an overly deterministic approach to human development, its main value is in providing a functionally informed causal account of how environmental processes might shape later outcomes in the context of our species specific life history. There is clearly a role for both culture and human agency in this framework. The importance of social learning is widely recognised by human evolutionary scientists (Mesoudi, 2011), and clearly the specific beliefs, values, attitudes, and norms that individuals acquire are strongly influenced by their exposure to relevant familial and community models. Antisocial cognitions, therefore, are risk factors for re-offending because they reflect the belief systems that emerge in particular developmental contexts. Obviously, to the extent that antisocial behaviour is adaptive given particular developmental trajectories, individuals are likely to acquire beliefs, values, and norms that are favourable to antisocial behaviour and that are consistent with other life history traits.

Humans also obviously have the capacity to develop goals, form plans, and implement strategies that both influence and are influenced by internal (psychological, physiological) and external (social, physical, cultural) environments. In short, humans have the capacity for agency. Many of the risk factors that feature in both the forensic psychological and the developmental criminological literatures can be viewed as elements (both internal and external) that influence agentic processes (Durrant & Ward, 2015). For example, a young man might have the goal of becoming an important player in the local distribution of illegal drugs. He has gravitated towards this goal because his early developmental experiences (e.g. harsh family environment, deprived neighbourhood community) have resulted in fast life history traits characterised by low self-control (antisocial personality), the willingness to use violence to settle disputes (antisocial cognitions), and a focus on immediate rewards (antisocial personality), in an environment in which antisocial behaviour is normative (antisocial associates). Given available options in his local environment becoming a high-level drug dealer is an important avenue for social status and directs the implementation of specific strategies that are likely to realise these goals including the effective use of threats and violence. Re-orienting (rehabilitating) this particular individual away from criminal activities will require considering not only how his particular characteristics have been shaped by his developmental history, but will also require understanding how his high-end goals can be realised through non-criminal channels in ways that might be consistent with his underlying characteristics.

In sum, from an evolutionary developmental perspective, risk factors for offending/re-offending are a heterogeneous collection of markers, traits, and processes. Some, such as gender and age are important because they mark important underlying biological processes that are closely related to the broader domain of risk-taking, aggression, and antisocial behaviour which in turn reflect past selection for traits that can advance reproductive success. Others, such as antisocial personality and antisocial cognition capture proximate causal processes that result from the downstream effects of key developmental processes. Importantly, alongside genetic factors, exposure to early environments that signal unpredictable and dangerous future environments (e.g. parental abuse and neglect) lead to the 'adoption' of fast life history strategies that orient individuals to mating rather than parenting effort. These effects are likely to be mediated by a suite of psychophysiological processes involving the stress response system with links to hormonal and neurotransmitter functioning, alongside the acquisition of specific beliefs, values, and norms.

Summary: implications for theory, research, and practice

I would like to conclude by briefly teasing out some of the implications of the arguments presented in this article for theory, research and practice. At a theoretical level, an evolutionary developmental perspective should encourage the consideration of a wider range of causal processes than is typically considered within forensic psychological or criminological theory. Although the framework presented in this paper could, inevitably, be elaborated upon it highlights the usefulness in considering explanations that draw on a range of both distal and proximate causal processes. Humans, like all other species, have an evolutionary history and this history has shaped many of the specific psychological, physiological, and behavioural characteristics that we possess. Understanding, why humans engage in antisocial and criminal behaviour can, I argue, be substantially informed by this perspective. In terms of research, the evolutionary developmental approach should encourage researchers to explore the causal processes that underlie risk factors for offending/re-offending in more detail. To take just one example, although marriage and parenthood are important factors relating to desistance, recent reviews of the literature have highlighted the patchy results that typically emerge in the literature.

For example, desistance often precedes rather than follows marriage (Skardhamar, Savolainen, Aase, & Lyngstad, 2015), parenthood does not always result in desistance, and the effects of marriage and parenthood seem to vary by gender, age, and ethnicity (Craig, 2015). From an evolutionary developmental perspective marriage and parenthood are simply correlates of a shift (for men) away from mating effort and towards parenting effort with a concomitant reduction in risk-taking and intra-sexual competition and their importance in reducing crime will depend on the age of the individual (and their partners) and features of the local environment (such as the operational sex ratio). Future research might explore both how these evolutionarily relevant factors moderate the effect of marriage and parenthood along with a consideration of the causal processes, both psychological and physiological (e.g. levels of testosterone) that mediate it.

Finally, it is worth considering the practical implications of the approach taken in this paper. As noted in the introduction there are literally hundreds of risk assessment tools all of which seem to do a reasonably equivalent job at predicting risk for re-offending. Although it is perfectly reasonable to continue to make predictions about risk based on well-validated measures using largely a-theoretically derived variables, a better understanding of the causal processes that give rise to risk factors provides an opportunity to fine tune measures in ways that may improve their success in predicting offending. A consideration of the risk factors for offending and for re-offending may also prompt a more seamless suite of intervention strategies that span early developmental prevention programmes and efforts at adult rehabilitation located in correctional facilities. Once it is appreciated that many of the risk factors for re-offending are actually downstream effects of the processes initiated by risk factors for offending and that these can be understood as alternative life history strategies then there are opportunities for both coordinated efforts at changing early developmental environments alongside efforts to tailor interventions with adults in ways that enable the pursuit of individually meaningful goals.

Disclosure statement

No potential conflict of interest was reported by the author.

References

Agnew, R. (2011). *Toward a unified criminology: Integrating assumptions about crime, people, and society*. New York, NY: New York University Press.

Andrews, D. A., & Bonta, J. (2010). *The psychology of criminal conduct* (4th ed.). Newark, NJ: Anderson Publishing.

Andrews, D. A., Bonta, J., & Wormith, J. S. (2006). The recent past and near future of risk and/or needs assessment. *Crime and Delinquency, 52*(1), 7–27. doi:10.1177/0011128705281756

Archer, J. (2009). Does sexual selection explain human sex differences in aggression? *Behavioral and Brain Sciences, 32*(3–4), 249–311. doi:10.1017/S0140525X09990951

Beech, A. R., & Wad, T. (2004). The integration of etiology and risk in sexual offenders: A theoretical framework. *Aggression and Violent Behavior, 10*(1), 31–63. doi:10.1016/j.avb.2003.08.002

Bjorklund, D. F., & Ellis, B. J. (2014). Children, childhood, and development in evolutionary perspective. *Developmental Review, 34*(3), 225–264. doi:10.1016/j.dr.2014.05.005

Campbell, A. (2013). The evolutionary psychology of women's aggression. *Philosophical Transactions of the Royal Society B, 368*. doi:10.1098/rstb.2013.0078

Caspi, A. (2000). The child is father of the man: Personality continuities from childhood to adulthood. *Journal of Personality and Social Psychology*, *78*(1), 158–172.

Caudy, M. S., Durso, J. M., & Taxman, F. S. (2013). How well do dynamic needs predict recidivism? Implications for risk assessment and risk reduction. *Journal of Criminal Justice*, *41*, 458–466.

Craig, J. M. (2014). The effects of marriage and parenthood on offending levels over time among juvenile offenders across race and ethnicity. *Journal of Crime and Justice*, *38*(2), 163–182. doi:10.1080/0735648X.2014.884468

Craig, J. M., Diamond, B., & Piquero, A. R. (2014). Marriage as an intervention in the lives of criminal offenders. In J. A. Humphrey & P. Cordella (Eds.), *Effective interventions in the lives of criminal offenders* (pp. 19–37). New York, NY: Springer.

Daly, M., & Wilson, M. (1988). *Homicide.* Hawthorne, NY: Aldine.

Douglas, K. S., & Skeem, J. L. (2005). Violence risk assessment: Getting specific about being dynamic. *Psychology, Public Policy & Law*, *11*(3), 347–383. doi:10.1037/1076-8971.11.3.347

Durrant, R., & Ward, T. (2015). *Evolutionary criminology: Toward a comprehensive explanation of crime.* London: Academic Press.

Elliott, M. C., Dupéré, V., & Leventhal, T. (2015). Neighborhood context and the development of criminal and antisocial behaviour. In J. Morizot & L. Kazemian (Eds.), *The development of criminal and antisocial behaviour* (pp. 253–265). Dordrecht: Springer.

Ellis, B. J., & Del Giudice, M. (2014). Beyond allostatic load: Rethinking the role of stress in regulating human development. *Development and Psychopathology*, *26*, 1–20. doi:10.1017/S0954579413000849

Ellis, B. J., Dishion, T. J., Gray, P., Hawley, P. H., Volk, A. A., Del Giudice, M., … Wilson, D. S. (2012). The evolutionary basis of risky adolescent behaviour: Implications for science, polity and practice. *Developmental Psychology*, *48*(3), 598–623. doi:10.1037/a0026220

Ellis, B. J., Figueredo, A. J., Brumbach, B. H., & Schlomer, G. L. (2009). Fundamental dimensions of environmental risk: The impact of harsh versus unpredictable environments of the evolution and development of life history strategies. *Human Nature*, *20*(2), 204–268. doi:10.1007/s12110-009-9063-7

Fagan, A. A. (2014). Sociological explanations for the gender gap in offending. In K. M. Beaver, J. C. Barnes, & B. B. Boutwell (Eds.), *The nature versus biosocial debate in criminology* (pp. 10–24). Los Angeles, CA: Sage.

Farrington, D. P. (2015). The developmental evidence base: Psychosocial research. In D. A. Crighton & G. J. Towl (Eds.), *Forensic psychology* (2nd ed.). (pp. 162–181). Chichester: John Wiley & Sons.

Galván, A. (2013). The teenage brain: Sensitivity to rewards. *Current Directions in Psychological Science*, *22*(2), 88–93. doi:10.1177/096372143480859

Gettler, L. T., McDade, T. W., Feranil, A. B., & Kuzawa, C. W. (2011). Longitudinal evidence that fatherhood decreases testosterone in human males. *Proceedings of the National Academy of Sciences*, *108* (39), 16194–16199. doi:10.1073/pnas.1105403108

Gray, P. B., Ellison, P. T., & Campbell, B. C. (2007). Testosterone and marriage among Ariaal men of Northern Kenya. *Current Anthropology*, *48*(5), 750–755. doi:10.1086/522061

Hanson, R. K., & Harris, A. J. R. (2000). Where should we intervene? Dynamic predictors of sexual offence recidivism. *Criminal Justice and Behaviour*, *27*(1), 6–35.

Hanson, R. K., & Morton-Bourgon, K. E. (2005). The characteristics of persistent sexual offenders: A meta-analysis of recidivism studies. *Journal of Consulting and Clinical Psychology*, *73*(6), 1154–1163. doi:10.1037/0022-006X.73.6.1154

Hochberg, Z., & Belsky, J. (2013). Evo-devo of human adolescence: Beyond disease models of early puberty. *BMC Medicine*, *11*, 1–11. doi:10.1186/1741-7015-11-113

Horney, J., Tolan, P., & Weisburd, D. (2012). Contextual influences. In R. Loeber, & D. P. Farrington (Eds.), *From Juvenile Delinquency to Adult Crime: Criminal Careers, Justice Policy, and Prevention.* (pp. 86–117). Oxford: Oxford University Press.

Jespersen, A. F., Lalumière, M. L., & Seto, M. C. (2009). Sexual abuse history among adult sex offenders and non-sex offenders: A meta-analysis. *Child Abuse and Neglect*, *33*(3), 179–192.

Kazemian, L. (2015). Desistance from crime and antisocial behaviour. In J. Morizot & L. Kazemian (Eds.), *The development of criminal and antisocial behaviour* (pp. 295–312). Dordrecht: Springer.

Kerig, P. K., & Becker, S. P. (2015). Early abuse and neglect as risk factors for the development of criminal and antisocial behaviour. In J. Morizot & L. Kazemian (Eds.), *The development of criminal and antisocial behaviour* (pp. 181–193). Dordrecht: Springer.

Kraemer, H. C., Kazdin, A. E., Offord, D. R., Kessler, R. C., Jensen, P. S., & Kupfer, D. J. (1997). Coming to terms with the terms of risk. *Archives of General Psychiatry, 54*(4), 337–344.

Loeber, R. (2012). Does the study of the age-crime curve have a future? In R. Loeber & B. C. Welsh (Eds.), *The Future of Criminology* (pp. 11–19). Oxford: Oxford University Press.

Loeber, R., & Farrington, D. P. (2012). Introduction. In R. Loeber & D. P. Farrington (Eds.), *From Juvenile Delinquency to Adult Crime: Criminal Careers, Justice Policy, and Prevention* (pp. 3–13). Oxford: Oxford University Press.

Mann, R. E., Hanson, R. K., & Thornton, D. (2010). Assessing risk for sexual recidivism: Some proposals on the nature of psychologically meaningful risk factors. *Sexual Abuse: A Journal of Research and Treatment, 22*(2), 191–217. doi:10.1177/1079063210366039

Mazur, A., & Michalek, J. (1998). Marriage, divorce, male testosterone. *Social Forces, 77*(1), 315–330.

Mesoudi, A. (2011). *Cultural evolution: How Darwinian theory can explain human culture and synthesize the social sciences*. Chicago, IL: University of Chicago Press.

Mitchell, S. D. (2009). *Unsimple truths: Science, complexity, and policy*. Chicago, IL: University of Chicago Press.

Monahan, J., & Skeem, J. L. (2014). Risk redux: The resurgence of risk assessment in criminal sanctioning. *Federal Sentencing Reporter, 26*(3), 158–166. doi:10.1525/fsr.2014.26.3.158

Nagin, D. S., Cullen, F. T., & Johnson, C. L. (2009). Imprisonment and reoffending. *Crime and Justice, 38*, 115–200.

Pardini, D. A., Waller, R., & Hawes, S. W. (2015). Familial influences on the development of serious conduct problems and delinquency. In J. Morizot & L. Kazemian (Eds.), *The development of criminal and antisocial behaviour* (pp. 201–220). Dordrecht: Springer.

Piquero, A. R. (2015). Understanding race/ethnicity differences in offending across the life course: Gaps and opportunities. *Journal of Developmental and Life Course Criminology, 1*(1), 21–32. doi:10.1007/s40865-015-0004-3

Portnoy, J., & Farrington, D. P. (2015). Resting heart rate and antisocial behaviour: An updated systematic review and meta-analysis. *Aggression and Violent Behaviour, 22*, 33–45. doi:10.1016/j.avb.2015.02.004

Puts, D. A. (2010). Beauty and the beast: Mechanisms of sexual selection in humans. *Evolution and Human Behavior, 31*(3), 157–175. doi:10.1016/j.evolhumbehav.2010.02.005

Raine, A. (2013). *The anatomy of violence: The biological roots of crime*. New York, NY: Pantheon Books.

Simons, D. A., Wurtele, S. K., & Durham, R. L. (2008). Developmental experiences of child sexual abusers and rapists. *Child Abuse and Neglect, 32*(5), 549–560.

Singh, I., Sinnott-Armstrong, W. P., & Savlulescu, J. (Eds.), (2014). *Bioprediction, biomarkers, and bad behaviour: Scientific, legal and ethical challenges*. Oxford: Oxford University Press.

Singh, J. P., & Fazel, S. (2010). Forensic risk assessment: A metareview. *Criminal Justice and Behaviour, 37*(9), 965–988. doi:10.1177/0093854810374274

Singh, J. P., Grann, M., & Fazel, S. (2011). A comparative study of violence risk assessment tools: A systematic review and metaregression analysis of 68 studies involving 25,980 participants. *Clinical Psychology Review, 31*(3), 499–513. doi:10.1016/j.cpr.2010.11.009

Skardhamar, T., Savolainen, J., Aase, K. N., & Lyngstad, T. H. (2015). Does marriage reduce crime? *Crime and Justice*: *44*, 385–557. doi:10.1086/681557

Skeem, J. L., & Monahan, J. (2011). Current directions in violence risk assessment. *Current Directions in Psychological Science, 20*(1), 38–42. doi:10.1177/0963721410397271

Spear, L. P. (2013). Adolescent neurodevelopment. *Journal of Adolescent Health, 52*(2), S7–S13. doi:10.1016/j.jadolhealth.2012.05.006

Steinberg, L. (2010). A dual systems model of adolescent risk-taking. *Developmental Psychobiology, 52*, 216–224. doi:10.1002/dev.20445

Taxman, F. S., & Caudy, M. S. (2015). Risk tells us who, but not what or how: Empirical assessment of the complexity of criminogenic needs to inform correctional programming. *Criminology and Public Policy, 14*(1), 71–103. doi:10.1111/1745-9133.12116

Theobald, D., & Farrington, D. P. (2010). Why do the crime-reducing effects of marriage vary with age? *British Journal of Criminology, 51*(1), 136–158. doi:10.1093/bjc/azq060

Theobald, D., Farrington, D. P., & Piquero, A. R. (2014). Does the birth of a first child reduce the father's offending? *Australian and New Zealand Journal of Criminology*. doi:10.1177/0004865814537840

Tinbergen, N. (1963). On aims and methods in ethology. *Zeitschrift Für Tierpsychologie, 20*(4), 410–433.

United Nations Office of Drugs and Crime. (2014). *Global study on homicide 2013*. Vienna: United Nations Office of Drugs and Crime.

Walton, J. S., & Chou, S. (2015). The effectiveness of psychological treatment for reducing recidivism in child molesters: A systematic review of randomized and nonrandomized trials. *Trauma, Violence, & Abuse, 16*, 401–417. doi:10.1177/1524838014537905

Ward, T. (2013). The explanation of sexual offending: From single factor theories to integrative pluralism. *Journal of Sexual Aggression, 20*(2), 130–141. doi:10.1080/13552600.2013.870242

Ward, T. (2015). Detection of dynamic risk factors and correctional practice. *Criminology and Public Policy, 14*(1), 105–111. doi:10.1111/1745-9133.12115

Ward, T., & Beech, A. R. (2015). Dynamic risk factors: A theoretical dead-end? *Psychology, Crime & Law, 21*(2), 100–113.

Warr, M. (2002). *Companions in crime: The social aspects of criminal conduct*. Cambridge: Cambridge University Press.

Yang, M., Wong, S. C. P., & Coid, J. (2010). The efficacy of violence prediction: A meta-analytic comparison of nine risk assessment tools. *Psychological Bulletin, 136*(5), 740–767. doi:10.1037/a0020473

A conceptual kaleidoscope: contemplating 'dynamic structural risk' and an uncoupling of risk from need

Kelly Hannah-Moffat

Department of Sociology, Centre of Criminology and Sociolegal Studies, University of Toronto, Toronto, Canada

ABSTRACT

Recent calls for 'evidence-based' approaches have firmly positioned risk assessment as a promising path towards more efficient, unbiased, and empirically based offender management, in custody and in the community. Simultaneously, sociological and critical legal scholars have questioned the focus on individual needs at the expense of wider structural factors'. I will demonstrate the need to reconceptualise risk/need logics and the use of 'evidence'. I will argue that various criminal justice processes are themselves dynamic criminogenic risks that produce systemic conditions for recidivism and which, if modified, could make a measurable difference in recidivism and other correctional efficiencies. Finally, I will argue that the logic of dynamic risk is transferable to an analysis of socio-structural factors, and that this characterisation can alter the framing of penal subjects, governmental responsibilities, and potentially interrupt the systemically produced criminogenic pathways that perpetuate criminal involvement and marginalisation.

The science of risk assessment is rapidly advancing. Alongside, criminal justice and correctional jurisdictions worldwide are turning to risk/need practices as a way to treat, manage, and reduce criminal justice populations. Actuarial risk/need assessment has penetrated multiple criminal justice decision-making points, especially policies about the management of capacious and expensive penal populations. Actuarial risk assessment tools include clusters of individual 'risk and need factors' that are statistically correlated with recidivism. Researchers and practitioners are particularly interested in identifying and measuring dynamic risk factors or criminogenic needs because these factors identify the attributes or characteristics of an individual's life that are correlated with recidivism and are changeable through treatment (Hannah-Moffat, 2004), unlike static risk factors, which are also informative but are considered unalterable (e.g. age of first arrest, number of convictions, sex). Dynamic risks are often treated as 'causal factors' (Ward, 2016) and assessments of these factors are typically used to help practitioners categorise, prioritise, and identify programmes that target changeable, statistically determined attributes of offenders and thereby reduce the likelihood of recidivism.

Various forms of risk/need assessment have been used for years in forensic contexts. This technology has moved out of the realm of therapeutic intervention into policy-making, resource allocation, and daily practices of crime control and offender management. Practitioners with limited clinical training are employing the logic of dynamic risk to make a range of policy, managerial, punishing, and corrective treatment decisions (Hannah-Moffat, 2013). This shift necessitates a re-examination of, and dialogue about, how we understand and use risk assessment. To date, relatively little theoretical or critical work on risk has informed the empirical and highly statistical body of scholarship about risk assessment (Bushway et al., 2014; Ward & Beech, 2015). According to Ward and Beech (2015), this paucity of theoretical work is the result of the failure of researchers to engage in critical debate, a misguided reliance on empirical generalisations, and 'an inherent failure to critically evaluate prominent rehabilitation theories' (p. 2). Further, Ward (2016) shows that dominant theorisations of dynamic risk, although 'informed by psychological mechanisms', are not indicative of causal processes (p. X). Instead, Ward maintains that they should be understood as essentially normative multi-faceted predictive factors because 'they are conceptualised with reference to social, political, and legal institutions' (p. 6). While I agree with these insights, especially as they apply to the practice of risk, I would also argue that disciplinary boundaries and concerns about the preservation of particular types of individualised assessment and correctional programming also play a role in perpetuating how dynamic risk is problematically conceptualised, institutionalised, and positioned in policy.

To advance theorisations of risk in criminology, the causal assumptions informing concepts like dynamic and static risk need to be challenged, and researchers, practitioners, and policy-makers need to clarify how and when 'risk' can be defensibly and meaningfully used to inform policy and practice. In many sectors of the criminal justice system, there is a myopic emphasis on the predictive accuracy of actuarial risk versus clinical assessments of risk and unwavering actuarial faith in the capacity of actuarially derived tools to make neutral, unbiased decisions about risk (Andrews & Bonta, 2006; Skeem, 2012). Actuarial tools measuring static and dynamic risk levels have been promoted as being able to replace practitioners' discretionary decision-making with structured, quantitatively derived decision-making templates that rely on social scientific evidence – particularly about recidivism and correctional interventions that reduce criminal propensities and enhance public safety. This emphasis limits the ability of scholars to step back and question some of the central assumptions informing risk logics, and to explore the possibility of developing innovative policy using alternative ways of thinking about risk and need. This kind of focus also tends to prevent or silence wider debates about the appropriateness and misapplication of generic static and dynamic risk assessments, and can even prevent critical discussion about the nuanced, socio-cultural complexities of 'recidivism', which many tools purport to predict.

Recent calls for 'evidence-based' approaches have also firmly positioned risk assessment as a promising path towards more efficient, unbiased, and empirically based offender management in custody and in the community. Arguably, the call for evidence such approaches to risk management creates an opening for sociological and critical legal scholars to question the focus on individual risk and needs at the expense of gendered and racialised structural variables (Goddard, 2014; Hannah-Moffat & Maurutto, 2010) or what some scholars call 'destabilising factors' (Taxman & Caudy, 2015). Here, I will argue that a consideration of 'evidence' taken from a wider cross-disciplinary base can enrich our theorisation of dynamic risk and produce alternative policy and risk management options. I will argue that various policies and criminal justice processes are themselves dynamic criminogenic risks that produce systemic conditions for recidivism and which, if modified, could make a measurable difference in recidivism and other correctional efficiencies. Finally, I will argue that the logic of dynamic risk is transferable to an analysis of socio-structural factors, and that this characterisation can alter the framing of penal subjects and governmental responsibilities. It can also potentially interrupt the systemically produced criminogenic pathways that perpetuate criminal involvement and marginalisation.

First, I briefly outline the past and current assumptions about static and dynamic risk. Second, I show how the omission of socio-structural risks in most dialogues of dynamic risk can exaggerate the predictive power of assessments and obscure important structural features of recidivism. Specifically, I argue that by focusing on individual deficits and prediction, dynamic risk logic overlooks the social conditions and processes that are themselves criminogenic and dynamic or changeable: structural factors are more than 'destabilising factors' – they are actually key features of a dynamic risk prediction model. Therefore, theorisation of dynamic risk should include interactions between individual agency and structure and re-examine the conceptual value of criminogenic need.

Third, moving beyond the difficulties associated with prediction, I argue that the outcome of recidivism (which is precarious, nuanced, and difficult to measure) limits our ability to understand how individual needs (and thus the potential risks of unmet needs) can be meaningfully managed to minimise criminal involvement. I do not suggest that agency and individual responsibility are unimportant – just that there is also a need to empirically examine how socio-structural processes and factors interact with and inform agency. This type of analysis requires an analytical and practical decoupling of risk and need and a more complex, situated socio-structural understanding of how unmet needs can produce risk. I use the debate on gender, race, and risk to illustrate how an emphasis on generic forms of risk prediction limits our conceptual knowledge of risk, which is gendered and racialised as are its effects when incorporated into policy or treatment (Hannah-Moffat & O'Malley, 2007). A focus on individual deficits neglects the structural factors that can support desistance and compliance. Therefore, theoretical and practical dialogues should explore how gendered and racialised individuals interact with, and navigate, criminogenic socio-structural factors and the self-identified needs of offenders. It should be possible to develop structural risk assessments that assess the level of risk generated by particular laws, institutional practices, and social welfare policies. In conclusion, I argue for an extension of the logic of so called evidence-based risk-informed policy and practices that encompasses a socio-structural analysis of risk. I maintain that a focus on evidence-based, socio-structural factors provides a more comprehensive picture of 'risk' (which is dynamic insofar as it is alterable), redistributes responsibility, can encourage changes in interventions, and can create a space for critical analysis of policy (or service gaps) and various institutional risk/need management practices.

Theorising or operationalising risk?

The theoretical lineage of 'dynamic risk' can be traced back to the pivotal work of Canadian psychologists Don Andrews and Jim Bonta, who presented the Risk-Need-Responsivity

Model (RNR) in their book *The Psychology of Criminal Conduct* (Andrews & Bonta, 1994/2010).[1] This theoretical model outlines the causes of persistent criminal behaviour, identifies risk/need principles, and provides direction about methods for effective correctional rehabilitation. The model has been integrated into a variety of risk/need assessment instruments, correctional programming templates, and policy, and a vast body of literature has focused on the resulting correctional interventions (see e.g. Blanchette & Brown, 2006; Polaschek, 2012).[2] Although these issues are important, the main focus of this discussion is a related issue: how Andrews and Bonta's initial theorisation of RNR has led to a particular hegemonic conceptualisation of 'criminogenic need' or 'dynamic risk' as distinct from the 'static risk' that is largely taken for granted, empirically tested, operationalised, commercialised, and institutionalised with few substantive challenges to its underpinning logic (Hannah-Moffat, 2004, 2013; Ward & Beech, 2015).

In an effort to distinguish static (unalterable) risk factors from more malleable factors, and to identify prospective targets for correctional intervention and improved prediction, Andrews and Bonta (2006) coined the term 'dynamic risk factor' (criminogenic need) to label certain individual characteristics or 'needs' as criminogenic. A criminogenic 'need' refers to alterable individual behaviours or characteristics that are statistically correlated with recidivism, which if changed could affect the probability of recidivism. Dynamic risk factors are defined as an individual's psychological or behavioural characteristics (i.e. unstable lifestyle, relationships, substance use, employment) that are amenable to changes over time, unlike 'static risk factors' (i.e. criminal history measures, gender) that cannot be changed by the individual (Andrews & Bonta, 2006). Many practitioners and researchers find assessments of dynamic risk clinically useful for treating and monitoring individuals, particularly those identified as being at high risk of reoffending (Andrews & Bonta, 2006; Brown, St. Amand, & Zamble, 2009; Vitopoulos, Peterson-Badali, & Skilling, 2012). This framing of risk enables the continued emphasis on the capacity of offenders to change with targeted rehabilitative programming and interventions.

Decoupling risk and needs and decentring recidivism

Andrews and Bonta's initial theorisation of dynamic risk, which has been uncritically adopted by many, cannot adequately account for complex interactions between social contexts, agency, and changes over the life course. The initial theorisation of dynamic risk (criminogenic need) strategically aligned risk with narrowly defined conceptualisation of needs that shared two characteristics: they were statistically correlated with recidivism; and they could be addressed using correctional treatment (cognitive behaviour models). The later connection to treatment is quite problematic because factors that are predicative are not inherently causal or aetiological. Ward (2016) shows that within the RNR theorisation of dynamic risk, although 'informed by psychological mechanisms', dynamic risks are not indicative of causal processes (p. 6 of manuscript). Instead, they should be understood as multi-faceted predictive factors that are essentially normative because 'they are conceptualised with reference to social, political, and legal institutions' (Ward, 2016, p. 6). For the concept of dynamic risk to have more theoretical salience, it is important to consider how the term 'dynamic risk' is used as a euphemism for criminogenic need. This is more than a linguistic shift: the term criminogenic need, or dynamic risk, was deliberately coined to identify 'needs' that are statistically related to recidivism. Distinguishing between needs that are statistically correlated with recidivism and needs that are self-identified or are produced artificially prioritises the range of needs a person may have and suggests that they are causally linked to their criminal involvements.

The emphasis on statistical relationships between need variables and recidivism in programme development and assessment is also misinterpreted and causally linked to criminality. In this instance, the need variables shown to be correlated with recidivism on an aggregate level are erroneously ascribed to a decontextualised individual. This theoretical lineage of dynamic risk tends to minimise the complexities of offender personalities, personal agency, and socio-structural factors (Heffernan & Ward, 2015; Ward & Maruna, 2007). This basic assumption limits the value of this construct and its ability to capture the nuanced aspects of risk minimisation. The core criminogenic logic requires that these risk factors be rooted in individual, alterable, and robust statistical predictors of recidivism. Consequently, current conceptualisations of dynamic risk are unavoidably disconnected from wider social processes and contexts, and ensure that an offender's needs are distinct.

Decoupling risk from need can reveal how unmet needs can affect pathways into crime, limit alternative choices, and hamper desistance efforts. It can help redistribute social responsibility, whereby resources are provided in a way that meets the needs of individuals. Specifically, it can help meet the needs of individual that are identified as contributing to their criminal involvement, and can reveal how interactions between structural constraints and policy contexts (e.g. high unemployment, lifetime bans on welfare, access to affordable housing, access to mental health care) affect an individual's ability to make choices about meeting their basic needs (e.g. financial, housing, health). Because most research on effective correctional interventions currently uses the RNR characterisation of criminogenic need (dynamic risk), non-criminogenic needs (needs that are not empirically linked to recidivism and may be alterable) are devalued. Empirically based interventions currently target predefined sets of criminogenic needs (dynamic risks) that reportedly tend to reduce recidivism, and the needs connected to structural constraints are positioned as individual limitations that can be overcome (e.g. through job training, educational upgrading, medication compliance). If the concept of dynamic risk is to capture a wider range of social processes, self-defined, and self-prioritised needs, and have greater empirical relevance to treatment providers, it must focus on individual outcomes other than recidivism.

I have argued that hegemonic constructions of criminogenic or dynamic risk locate harm within the individual and unchallenged expectations about their past opportunities and choices. This individualisation of risk allows for a diagnosis of risk factors as individual deficits, which can be corrected with the right kind of intervention. The foundational RNR model identifies 'promising targets for change' (Andrews & Bonta, 1994/2010, p. 33) within the individual, precluding meaningful considerations of how social inequality shapes opportunities and choices, and how it is itself a risk to be managed. By responsibilising criminalised subjects and requiring them to implicitly navigate these structural limitations through 'good choices', 'prosocial decisions', and cognitive reorientations, governments, policy-makers, and criminal justice actors (police, judges, prosecutors, defence attorney, probation officers, etc.) are 'deresponsibilised'. Their collective and individual choices avoid scrutiny and are rarely framed as criminogenic, subject to change, or making a 'significant' difference. This is problematic for researchers who are interested in understanding and identifying statistically significant risk or need factors and devising correctional interventions. They tend to be somewhat dismissive of the role of social inequalities and social policy in the production of risk and in the development of alternative ways of managing risk.

Andrews and Bonta's initial theorisation of dynamic risk, which has been uncritically adopted by many, cannot adequately account for complex interactions between social contexts, agency, and changes over the life course. This is partly because their initial theorisation of dynamic risk was meant to identify predictive variables, and as such they represent a complex assemblage of social and individual factors (Ward, 2016). In the previous section I argued in favour of reconsidering the conceptual utility of aligning risk with need. An alternative understanding of dynamic risk ought to account for changes in behaviour beyond reoffending, as well as a wide range of empirical research that has demonstrated the significance of accommodating needs that are not statistically correlated with recidivism but are relevant to the aetiology of crime and desistance. I explore how the concept of dynamic risk can be applied and extended to analyses of socio-structural and policy contexts.

Dynamic risk must be disentangled from vague, aggregate recidivism outcomes. Presently, correctional interventions are tested and accredited partly on their ability to demonstrate a reduction in risk to reoffend, specifically that RNR measures of dynamic risk are lowered after the intervention. Empirical changes are clinically measureable through aggregated reductions in risk assessment scores among offenders being treated for the identified criminogenic need (Brooks Holliday, Heilbrun, & Fretz, 2012). However, it is not clear how these interventions help at the individual level in the 'real world' given the complexities of lives, needs, and social or jurisdictional contexts. When criminogenic need is framed and measured as interrelationships between needs identified as criminogenic, it makes it difficult to clarify and incorporate other needs prioritised by an individual, and how these interact with particular structural constraints as he or she navigates the precarious process of re-entry or criminal disengagement. Further, in RNR, a need is only deemed criminogenic by its association with recidivism, a negative and non-specific construct. This connection is perhaps more useful politically than conceptually. Politically, the linkage between some needs and related interventions and recidivism allows researchers and advocates of rehabilitation to identify 'what works' by way of correctional intervention and to empirically defend the continued albeit limited provision of services. This purposeful ideological linkage is historically important and useful in maintaining space for rehabilitative ideas, but it also limits how need, and by extension criminogenic need and dynamic risk, can be framed and may fundamentally restrict the theorisation of 'dynamic risk'.

The logic of criminogenic need versus non-criminogenic need must also be deconstructed and disentangled from the singular emphasis on risk of recidivism. A vast amount of risk-informed policy engages with generic notions of risk or recidivism, non-specific offence types or offenders, or the generic problem of recidivism without being precise. Reconsidering dynamic risk requires a broader contextual understanding of the pathways of an individual into and out of crime. Instead of focusing on recidivism as the outcome variable of interest, it may be worthwhile to think about how post-conviction (or post-prison) experiences are mediated and strengthened by personal, situational, and structural characteristics, including the individual's social environment of peers, family, community, and jurisdictional-level policies (cf. Visher & Travis, 2003). Research about re-entry, restorative approaches, and desistance stresses the importance of protective factors, strengths, and resiliencies, and how these can help reduce the likelihood of an individual's continued involvement in crime or vulnerability to breaches. This approach is compatible with the general idea of dynamic risk, but focuses more on changes beyond the individual, by revealing how social inequality, culture, personal characteristics, and policies all play a role in desistance. From this perspective, the discontinuation or continuation of criminal activity is a process rather than a discrete and measureable event, making it difficult to measure with precision. Additionally, the focus should not simply be on recidivism – it should be on identifying policies and resources that contribute to criminogenic structural disincentives to compliance (housing, employment, programme interruptions, extensive conditions, racial segregation, poverty, etc.) as well as strengths or resiliencies that support an individual's efforts to disengage with crime, and which may be supported through programmes and needs provisions. Here, the emphasis is on an individual's holistic needs and goals: needs are not statistical artefacts but are holistically and self-determined.

Going beyond binaries: the systemic importance of gender, race, and inequality

The criminological literature on risk is becoming more focused on risk and diversities. Many scholars argue that risk is a complex, fluid construct that is interpreted through gender, race, socio-economic, and regional diversities and has variable effects (Hannah-Moffat & Maurutto, 2010; Hannah-Moffat & O'Malley, 2007). Yet, the effect of diversities has been understudied in terms of how risk gets constructed. An extensive body of research has criticised RNR for using universal criminogenic need categories without comprehensive analysis of how needs differ among various subgroups, and how these categories affect how offender populations are defined, assessed, targeted, and managed (Hannah-Moffat, 2006, 2013, 2015; Hannah-Moffat & Maurutto, 2010; Harcourt, 2010; Holtfreter & Cupp, 2007; Raynor & Lewis, 2011; Taylor & Blanchette, 2009; Van Voorhis, 2012). Specifically, scholars have criticised RNR for not considering gender and race (Blanchette & Brown, 2006; Hannah-Moffat, 2004, 2006, 2009, 2013; Kreis, Schwannauer, & Gillings, 2014; Maurutto & Hannah-Moffat, 2006, 2007a, 2007b; Spiropoulos, Salisbury, & Van Voorhis, 2015; Taylor & Blanchette, 2009; Van Voorhis, 2012). In many ways, these conceptual and empirical critiques are misunderstood and often branded as methodological problems. Consequently, these critiques have generally resulted in some adjustments to dynamic risk categories to make them more inclusive, or adjustments to empirical tests to improve statistical reliability and validity across offender subpopulations. Many scholars have attempted to identify the predictive potency of various dynamic risks, refined their measurement and assessments, and explored how dynamic risk factors differ among subgroups of offenders, including women (Brown & Blanchette, 2009; Kreis et al., 2014; Taylor & Blanchette, 2009; Van Voorhis, 2012), sexual and violent offenders (Fortune, Bourke, & Ward, 2015), youth (Vitopoulos et al., 2012), and racialised groups (Spiropoulos et al., 2015). However, most research and theory on risk has focused on the official creation of abstract universal, 'gender-'and 'race-neutral' subjects such as members of offender risk categories. This work has not led to a fundamental rethinking of dynamic risk or how gendered, stratified, and racialised social structures mediate the types of needs subgroups have. Nor has it led to a change in direction about how differential social histories, pathways, and opportunities affect our aetiological understanding of criminal involvement. The conceptual validity of constructs used to measure dynamic risk need to meaningfully advance and account for well-established empirical differences between and among men and women.

Race, like gender is strongly co-related with crime, but few in the risk assessment field have attempted to understand how this co-relation is deeply affected by various forms of overt and systemic racism that lurk behind dynamic categories such as employment, education, marital family, substance use, etc. There is also an absence of meaningful theoretical discussion about how a particular risk variable functions as a proxy for race (see arguments by Hannah-Moffat & Maurutto, 2010; Harcourt, 2007). Forms of static and dynamic risk assessment have been critiqued for their lack of racial specificity and inability to account for racialised penal populations. Research that does directly investigate dynamic risk among racialised populations shows, for example, that racial minorities have different self-reported needs (Gavazzi, Yarcheck, & Lim, 2005; Mitchell, 2005), different experiences of victimisation and criminalisation (Ghandnoosh, 2014), and that race and ethnicity can influence how practitioners attribute risk factors to offenders (Harcourt, 2007, 2010; Hudson & Bramhall, 2005; Martel, Brassard, & Jaccoud, 2011). Dynamic risk scholarship has also not adequately theorised the importance of unique circumstances arising from or specific to Aboriginal heritage (e.g. marginalisation, residential school experiences, overt racism, chronic substance abuse in communities of origin, family or community background, isolation, community relocation, dislocation from aboriginal community given adoption and/or product of child welfare system). A similar gap exists in relation to the racialised experiences of African-Americans in the USA.

Some researchers have worked to validate assessment measures and develop protocols for various subpopulations (Holsinger, Lowenkamp, & Latessa, 2006; Salisbury, Van Voorhis, & Spiropoulis, 2009; Smith, Cullen, & Latessa, 2009; Van Voorhis, Wright, Salisbury, & Bauman, 2010). As a result, many gender-specific factors that were previously identified as 'needs' (e.g. past trauma, self-injury, early pregnancies, single parenting) have now been identified as 'risks'. Currently, researchers are divided: some argue that general dynamic domains (marital family, acquaintances, attitudes, employment/education, personal and emotional issues, etc.) are sufficient, and that factors such as gender and race matter more when treating an individual and developing effective interventions (see e.g. Andrews & Bonta, 1994/2010); others have called for more gender-specific assessments and precise understandings of how needs differ within general categories (i.e. differential impacts of sexual violence, or relationships; Kreis et al., 2014). As far as I know, no scholar has called for race-specific assessments, which would no doubt be a legally and politically contentious move, especially if the outcome of concern is recidivism.

Overall, this important empirical work on dynamic risk factors does not contribute to a deeper conceptual understanding of criminality, recidivism, or desistance. Ward (2016) shows that there are distinct differences between predictive and causal variables. The debates about gender and race exemplify this paradox. Current research is only marginally able to add to the theorisation of a dynamic risk. And when the logic of dynamic risk is unravelled, important theoretical concerns emerge about the relationships between race, gender, social inequality, and specific risk factors. The gendered and race-based critiques of risk assessment are not simply about the sample or the inclusion of sex and race variables in empirical assessments of risk or conducting more accurate statistical tests 'to hone in on targets for change and improve correctional practices' (Latessa, 2015, p. 68). They are about the decontextualised individualistic approach to the problem of risk. For the theorisation of dynamic risk to benefit from gender and race informed critiques, gender, race, and marginality need to be understood as complex social constructs that shape individuals, their experiences, and their opportunities. Some researchers have started to consider how gendered (or racial) pathways into crime differ and how such differences could impact how we think about dynamic risk. For example, Taylor and Blanchette's (2009) article discussed how debates about the suitability of the Level of Service Inventory-Revised for women have demonstrated that gendered pathways can provide a more detailed conceptual understanding of women's criminality and thus inform assessment and treatment. For example, they point to research by Owen (1998) that suggested, 'economic marginalisation is intertwined with women's individual propensities to move toward increased criminality' (as cited in Taylor & Blanchette, 2009, p. 224). Whereas, other researchers showed that 'poverty status was a more powerful predictor of recidivism among women offenders than the combined summary risk index of the LSI-R' (Holtfreter et al., 2004 as cited in Taylor & Blanchette, 2009, p. 225). This type of empirical evidence shows that structural variables are strong predictors of crime, that there is ample evidence that economic marginalisation is racialized and gendered, and that structural variables are relevant to pathways out of crime or desistance (Calverley, 2012). What it does not address is causality.

Despite their predictive value and usefulness in theorising dynamic risk, the use of such structural variables in current models has the effect of responsibilising offenders for social problems. Taking gender, race, and poverty seriously requires us to view the individual in the context of their socio-economic background. Nonetheless, dynamic risk as presently theorised positions offenders as members of statistical distributions rather than as unique cases. Individuals, in other words, are reduced to a series of risk categories and calculations that negate social context and structures that are in many instances beyond an individual's control (Quirouette, Hannah-Moffat, & Maurutto, 2015). This conceptual dissonance and commitment to recidivism restricts the capacity to shift debates about dynamic risk and create cross-disciplinary bridges.

Beyond the individual: 'dynamic structural risk'?

If analysis of dynamic risk was theorised with a different unit of analysis (jurisdictional policy related to parole, police, housing welfare, etc., or community stability), we could closely examine the variable risk of particular policies or community characteristics (level of racial/economic segregation, income disparities, availability of social services, employment, housing, education) producing the conditions for offending or recidivism. Here the work of desistance scholars can also be meaningfully integrated into thinking about dynamic risk by shifting our focus away from predicting probabilities of individual recidivism to considering what offenders need to succeed in their desistance efforts (Calverley, 2013; Ward & Maruna, 2007).

According to culture-based approaches to the study of risk, what is a 'risk' differs across time and space. Instead of exploring risk using an objective scientific process, this approach focuses on the logic and influence of institutions (Baker & Simon, 2002; Power, 2007). Although the concept of dynamic risk is linked with recidivism or repeat offending, it is possible to conduct a broader non-individualistic empirical analysis of factors that can be characterised as dynamic risks but are alterable and may reduce recidivism. Various policies and structural constraints can be considered forms of dynamic risk that can be altered and targeted. Most empirical analyses and applications of dynamic risk-based assessments neglect rigorous examinations and interpretations of the complex and nuanced ways in which dynamic needs are produced, mediated, and contingent upon malleable and criminogenic structural factors and jurisdictional policies. However, some scholars have produced equally robust and rigorous empirical evidence for how various structural factors may affect recidivism: McNeill (2003), Farrall, Bottoms, and Shapland (2010), and Farrall and Maruna (2003) emphasised desistence-based and strength-based approaches, which could help practitioners de-emphasise individual pathology by focusing on larger social contexts and the conditions required to support change.

A jurisdiction's criminal justice and social policy context can have significant effects on criminal pathways (and recidivism metrics). For example, policy around background and record-checking can marginalise large cohorts of people and limit their access to employment, housing, and volunteer and educational opportunities. Conditions placed on a supervision order can create a host of compliance complications, generating conditions for breaches that are administrative offences, but are considered as important as new criminal charges when assessing recidivism. For example, empirical evidence suggests that the number and types of conditions an offender is given on a bail, probation, or parole order is linked with recidivism (Thigpen, Beauclair, Keiser, & Banks, 2010). Additionally, the presence of a cognitive deficit, brain injury, or other relevant diagnosis may significantly affect compliance. Therefore, systemic changes may be required to develop condition recommendations, applications, and interventions aimed at enabling compliance.

Research conducted by scholars working in the field of desistance could lead to creative solutions for managing the static structural factors that impede meaningful change. However, these factors are largely dismissed in risk research, indiscriminately scored, and relegated to individual deficits in most dominant risk/need models. It could be more helpful to reinterpret dynamic risk to include social-structural risk, with the goal of ameliorating the effects of specific structural risks, instead of focusing on agency or enhancing personal competencies. By identifying, measuring, and assessing dynamic socio-structural and policy risks, along with interventions used to mitigate these, researchers could rethink questions of risk. This approach would yield empirical evidence that can redirect policy and institutional practices regarding how we respond to and prevent crime. Within this context, offenders would share the responsibility for disengaging with crime with their communities and governments, who would actively work to produce conditions that support desistance, such as affordable, accessible housing (Quirouette et al., 2015).

Although it is useful to identify the limitations of concepts like dynamic risk, static risk factors are equally important. Policy-makers and researchers should scrutinise all categorisations of risk and their practical applications. Statistics-based analyses of risk that use carefully vetted and meaningful risk variables will reveal statistically significant correlations, variances, associations, and probabilities, and in some cases, causations. Meanings of risk are fluid and interpretive, and researchers do not always share the same understandings of risk as practitioners, policy-makers, or the general public, who all routinely make risk-based decisions. Similarly, 'offenders', who are simultaneously objects of risk and members of the general public, must make a host of risk-based decisions about how to manage a range of 'risks' (homelessness, unemployment, addiction, health, etc.) that are not of central concern to policy-makers and others who regulate, treat, and manage them. This disconnect occurs in part because the framing of static and dynamic risk is epistemologically grounded in a view of the individual as a rational actor whose agency, cognitive skills, and choices determine criminality and deviance. The dominant understanding of static and dynamic risk neglects alternative framings of how structure and agency interact to produce risk, and are thus meaningful in the construction and interpretation of dynamic and static risk variables. The 'structure versus agency' debate is a long-standing problem in social science: practitioners and policy-makers understandably want to 'know what to do' with an individual who violates the law.

Conclusions: unpacking and bracketing causality

Ward (2016) observed that we still do not fully understand the interrelationship between dynamic risk factors and how or if clusters of dynamic factors can be attributed causal significance. The same may apply to static factors. Empirical research on risk, and ultimately the risk assessments they produce, only identifies (within their obvious limitations) who is more likely to reoffend, and the types of correctional programming that may reduce the likelihood of recidivism. In practical terms, however, dynamic risk assessments, which are de facto:

> quantifications of 'need' no longer serve as probability scores, but rather serve as a prescription for correctional treatment. The 'abstract' risk score is thus converted into a correctional artefact that enables the efficient management of offender populations and resources and defines a person's criminal justice experiences. (Hannah-Moffat, 2013, p. 9)

The statistical attributes of dynamic risk fundamentally limit its conceptual utility when it comes to the aetiology of crime. The pathways into and out of crime are complex and nuanced. Individual needs and agency are but one piece of the crime puzzle. A robust body of literature has focused on static and dynamic factors, particularly in the subfield of predicting violent and sexual recidivism, to understand how individual factors contribute to differential involvement in crime. At the same time, this scholarship is also necessarily limited and theoretically constrained.

New directions in risk research might alternatively consider the interrelationships between dynamic and static factors (which can also be proxies for socio-structural risk variables), how dynamic factors change over time, how nuances in dynamic factors vary with subgroups, and how dynamic factors interact with environmental factors (i.e. the release environment; Kraemer, Stice, Kazdin, & Kupfer, 2001; Scoones, Willis, & Grace, 2012; Taxman & Caudy, 2015). Framings of dynamic and static risk could explore how broader social policies (e.g. number and type of release conditions, availability of community resources, welfare or housing restrictions, racial profiling) and social inequalities (e.g. gender, race, ethnic, health, income) inform risk and its applicability to decisions that are informed by risk assessments, such as sentencing, imposition of conditions, release, or how these social structures inform risk (or need) variables. There are ample measures of social inequality and existing measures of community health that can be used. A more comprehensive dialogue about these issues could help identify and remedy criminogenic structures and assess the construct validity of risk variables. It could also lead to a reconsideration of the suitability of risk assessment in non-treatment settings and a different understanding of the consequences of having risk scores that may be invalid or misinterpreted. By repositioning institutional practices and socio-structural factors as potential dynamic risk factors, we can re-evaluate and situate individual-based dynamic factors and reconsider opportunities for corrective interventions.

More promising conceptual advances could emerge from building on the abundance of criminological and social science research available to identify 'dynamic structural risk' factors that, when situated in a particular historical or jurisdictional context, can yield alternative understandings of risk and forms of assessment. By combining structural and individual understandings of risk, it is possible to develop a more fluid, nuanced understanding of how social and individual factors interact and produce conditions for initial, continued, or discontinued involvement in criminal or criminalised activities. This kind of analysis can also reveal how conditions that are beyond an individual's control but are alterable, such as jurisdiction-specific policies, police, and bail or parole practices, can encourage or discourage recidivism. It can also shift attention away from recidivism to asking what helps offenders in the short and long term desist from crime (Maruna, 2001).

Notes

1. The book *Psychology of Criminal Conduct* (Andrews & Bonta, 1994/2010) has been revised on several occasions (1998, 2003, 2006, 2010).
2. For example, a robust debate has focused on the nuances of general personality and cognitive social learning theories, which inform offender rehabilitation (see e.g. Polaschek, 2012).

Acknowledgements

I would like to thank Tony Ward, Philip Goodman, Linn Clark, and reviewers for their instructive comments.

Disclosure statement

No potential conflict of interest was reported by the author.

References

Andrews, D. A., & Bonta, J. (1994/2010). *The psychology of criminal conduct*. Cincinnati, OH: Anderson.

Andrews, D., & Bonta, J. (2006). The recent past and near future of risk and/or need assessment. *Crime and Delinquency, 52*(1), 7–27.

Baker, T., & Simon, J. (2002). *Embracing risk: The changing culture of Insurance and responsibility*. Chicago, IL: University of Chicago Press.

Blanchette, K., & Brown, S. L. (2006). *The assessment and treatment of women offenders: An integrative perspective*. West Sussex: Wiley.

Brooks Holliday, S., Heilbrun, K., & Fretz, R. (2012). Examining improvements in criminogenic needs: The risk reduction potential of a structured re-entry program. *Behavioural Sciences and Law, 2012, 30*(4), 431–447.

Brown, S. L., St. Amand, M. D., & Zamble, E. (2009). The dynamic prediction of criminal recidivism: A three-wave prospective study. *Law and Human Behavior, 33*(1), 25–45.

Bushway, S., Krohon, M., Lizotte, A. J., Phillips, M. D., & Schmidt, N. (2014). Are risky youth less protectable as they age? The dynamics of protection during adolescence and young adulthood. *Justice Quarterly, 30*(101), 84–116.

Claverley, A. (2012). *Cultures of desistance: Rehabilitation, reintegration and ethnic minorities*, Abingdon: Routledge.

Farrall, S., Bottoms, A. & Shapland, J. (2010). Social structures and desistance from crime. *European Journal of Criminology*, 7(6), 546–570.

Farrall, S., & Maruna, S. (2003). Desistance-focused criminal justice policy research: Introduction to a special issue on desistance from crime and public policy. *The Howard Journal of Criminal Justice*, *43*(4), 358–367.

Fortune, CA., Bourke, P., & Ward, T. (2015). Expertise and child sex offenders. *Aggression and Violent Behavior*, *20*, 33–41.

Gavazzi, S. M., Yarcheck, C. M., & Lim, J. -Y. (2005). Ethnicity, gender, and global risk indicators in the lives of status offenders coming to the attention of the juvenile court. *International Journal of Offender Therapy and Comparative Criminology*, *49*(6), 696–710.

Ghandnoosh, N. (2014). *Race and punishment: Racial perceptions of crime and support for punitive policies*. Washington, DC: The Sentencing Project.

Goddard, T. (2014). The indeterminacy of the risk factor prevention paradigm: A case study of community partnerships implementing youth and gang violence prevention policy. *Youth Justice*, *14* (1), 3–21.

Hannah-Moffat, K. (2004). Criminogenic needs and the transformative risk subject: Hybridizations of risk/need in penality. *Punishment and Society*, *7*(1), 29–51.

Hannah-Moffat, K. (2006). Pandora's box: Risk/need and gender-responsive corrections. *Criminology and Public Policy*, *5*(1), 183–192.

Hannah-Moffat, K. (2009). Gridlock or mutability: Reconsidering 'gender' and risk assessment. *Criminology and Public Policy*, *8*(1), 209–219.

Hannah-Moffat, K. (2013). Actuarial sentencing: An 'unsettled' proposition. *Justice Quarterly*, *30*(2), 270–296.

Hannah-Moffat, K. (2015). Needle in a haystack: Logical parameters of treatment based on actuarial risk-needs assessments. *Criminology and Public Policy*, *14*(1), 113–120.

Hannah-Moffat, K., & Maurutto, P. (2010). Re-contextualizing pre-sentence reports. *Punishment and Society*, *12*(3), 262–286.

Hannah-Moffat, K., & O'Malley, P. (Eds.). (2007). *Gendered risks*. London: Routledge-Cavendish. Publishing.

Harcourt, B. E. (2007). *Against prediction: Profiling, policing and punishing in the actuarial age*. Chicago, IL: University of Chicago Press.

Harcourt, Bernard E. (2010). *Risk as a proxy for race criminology and public policy*. University of Chicago Law & Economics Olin Working Paper No. 535; University of Chicago Public Law Working Paper No. 323. Retrieved January 4, 2012, from SSRN, ssrn.com/abstract=1677654.

Heffernan, R., & Ward, T. (2015). The conceptualization of dynamic risk factors in child sex offenders: An agency model. *Aggression and Violent Behavior*, *24*, 250–260.

Holsinger, A. M., Lowenkamp, C. T., & Latessa, E. J. (2006). Exploring the validity of the level of service inventory-revised with Native American offenders. *Journal of Criminal Justice*, *34*(3), 331–337.

Holtfreter, K., & Cupp, R. (2007). Gender and risk assessment: The empirical status of the LSI-R for women. *Journal of Contemporary Criminal Justice*, *23*(4), 363–382.

Hudson, B., & Bramhall, G. (2005). Assessing the other: Constructions of Asianness in risk assessment by probation officers. *British Journal of Criminology*, *45*(5), 721–740.

Kraemer, H. C., Stice, E., Kazdin, A., & Kupfer, D. (2001). How do risk factors work together to produce an outcome? Mediators, moderators, independent, overlapping and proxy risk factors. *American Journal of Psychiatry*, *158*(6), 848–856.

Kreis, M. K. F., Schwannauer, M., & Gillings, K. (2014). Relational risk factors for reoffending in women: A systematic review. *International Journal of Forensic Mental Health*, *13*(4), 381–393.

Latessa, E. J. (2015). Taking risk to the next step. *Criminology and Public Policy*, *14*(1), 67–69.

Martel, J., Brassard, R., & Jaccoud, M. (2011). When two worlds collide: Risk management in Canadian aboriginal corrections. *British Journal of Criminology*, *51*(2), 235–255.

Maruna, S. (2001). *Making good: How ex-convicts reform and rebuild their lives*. Washington, DC: American Psychological Association Books.

Maurutto, P., & Hannah-Moffat, K. (2006). Assembling risk and the restructuring of penal control. *British Journal of Criminology*, *46*(3), 438–454.

Maurutto, P., & Hannah-Moffat, K. (2007a). Understanding risk in the context of the youth criminal justice act. *Canadian Journal of Criminology, 49*(4), 465–491.

Maurutto, P., & Hannah-Moffat, K. (2007b). Response to commentary: Cross-examining risk 'knowledge.' *Canadian Journal of Criminology, 49*(4), 543–550.

McNeill, F. (2003). Desistance-focused probation practice. In Wing Hong Chui & Mike Nellis (Eds.), *Moving probation forward*, (146–161). Harlow: Longman.

Mitchell, O. (2005). A meta-analysis of race and sentencing research: Explaining the inconsistencies. *Journal of Quantitative Criminology, 21*(4), 439–466.

Polaschek, D. L. L. (2012). An appraisal of the risk-need-responsivity (RNR) model of offender rehabilitation and its application in correctional treatment. *Legal and Criminal Psychology, 17*(1), 1–17.

Power, M. (2007). *Organized uncertainty: Designing a world of risk management.* Oxford: Oxford University Press. ISBN 9780199253944

Quirouette, M., Hannah-Moffat, K., & Maurutto, P. (2015). 'A precarious place:' Housing and clients of specialized courts. *British Journal of Criminology*. http://bjc.oxfordjournals.org/content/early/2015/06/02/bjc.azv050.full.pdf+html

Raynor, P., & Lewis, S. (2011). Risk-need assessment, sentencing and minority ethnic offenders in Britain. *British Journal of Social Work, 41*(7), 1357–1371.

Salisbury, E. J., Van Voorhis, P., & Spiropoulis, G. V. (2009). The predictive validity of a gender responsive risk/needs assessment. *Crime and Delinquency, 55*(4), 550–585.

Scoones, C. D., Willis, G. M., & Grace, R. C. (2012). Beyond static and dynamic risk factors. *Journal of Interpersonal Violence, 27*(2), 222–238.

Skeem, J. (2012). Risk technology in sentencing: Testing the promises and perils. *Justice Quarterly*. Advance online publication.

Smith, P., Cullen, F. T., & Latessa, E. J. (2009). Can 14,737 women be wrong? A meta-analysis of the LSI-R and recidivism for female offenders. *Criminology and Public Policy, 8*(1), 183–208.

Spiropoulos, G., Salisbury, E. & Van Voorhis, P. (2015). Moderators of correctional treatment success: An exploratory study of racial differences. *International Journal of Offender Therapy and Comparative Criminology, 58*(7), 835–860.

Taxman, F. S., & Caudy, M. S. (2015). Risk tells us who, but not what or how: Empirical assessment of the complexity of criminogenic needs to inform correctional programming. *Criminology and Public Policy, 14*(1), 71–103.

Taylor, K. N., & Blanchette, K. (2009). The women are not wrong: It is the approach that is debatable. *Criminology and Public Policy, 8*(1), 221–229.

Thigpen, M., Beauclair, T., Keiser, G., & Banks, C. (2010). *Parole essentials: Practical guides for parole leaders*. Washington, DC: Department of Justice, National Institute of Corrections.

Van Voorhis, P. (2012). On behalf of women offenders. *Criminology and Public Policy, 11*(2), 111–145.

Van Voorhis, P., Wright, E., Salisbury, S., & Bauman, A. (2010). Women's rick factors and their contributions to existing risk/needs assessment: The current status of gender responsive assessment. *Criminal Justice and Behavior, 37*(3), 261–288.

Vitopoulos, N., Peterson-Badali, M., & Skilling, T. (2012). The relationship between matching service to criminogenic need and recidivism in male and female youth: Examining the RNR principles in practice. *Criminal Justice and Behavior, 39*(8), 1025–1041.

Visher, C. A., & Travis, J. (2003). Transitions from prison to community: Understanding individual pathways. *Annual Review of Sociology, 29*(1), 89–113.

Ward, T. (2016). Dynamic risk factors: Scientific kinds or predictive constructs. *Psychology, Crime & Law, 22*(1–2), 2–16.

Ward, T., & Beech, A. R. (2015). Dynamic risk factors: A theoretical dead-end? *Psychology, Crime & Law, 21*(2), 100–113.

Ward, T., & Maruna, S. (2007). *Rehabilitation: Beyond the risk paradigm.* New York, NY: Routledge.

Dysfunctional expertise and its relationship with dynamic risk factors in offenders

Zarah Vernham and Claire Nee

Psychology Department, University of Portsmouth, Portsmouth, UK

ABSTRACT

Predicting the risk an offender poses is vital for protecting the public and/or the offender themselves; thus reducing recidivism rates. Dynamic risk factors are useful for informing treatment programmes because of their changeability. However, the current conceptualisation of dynamic risk factors has recently been under scrutiny within the rehabilitation literature, because their categorical nature lacks description and cannot explain the underlying causal mechanisms of offending behaviours. Expertise is a new area within the rehabilitation literature that examines the decision-making processes involved across the offending episode (prior, during, and after a crime). It is one example of how looking more closely at the processes the offender employs across the offending episode might help to understand more clearly some of the mechanisms underlying dynamic risk factors. This article first discusses the literature and theoretical models that have been proposed with regard to risk prediction and offender expertise, before exploring the links between the two. Using a theoretical framework, which moves away from a deficit-based focus to one in which emphasis is placed on the offender's own personal agency, the authors describe how the competencies underpinning cognition can be used as a starting point for positive change. Implications for offender treatments are discussed.

Academics and practitioners in the area of forensic psychology, specifically the explanation, assessment, and rehabilitation of offenders, frequently focus on the importance of predicting and measuring risk of offending. Differentiating high-risk offenders from low risk offenders is important for not only protecting the public and the offenders themselves, but also for police, courts, and those working within correctional facilities (Andrews & Bonta, 2003). The risk that someone poses is important to measure as it allows for interventions to be tailored towards the offender's specific needs (e.g. in terms of risk level and type/cause of offending), which subsequently contributes to the prevention of future offences. However, predicting risk is a difficult task that still needs a great deal of attention, particularly with regard to those factors that can be changed (i.e. dynamic risk factors, such as substance abuse and unemployment) and the impact that such factors can have on treatment success and reoffending rates.

Currently, the prediction of risk of reoffending is based upon clusters of dynamic risk factors that correlate with recidivism (Heffernan & Ward, 2015). As a result, the underlying psychological mechanisms of these factors and how they explain or cause offending behaviours have been neglected. Additionally, the link between offender expertise (i.e. the necessary mechanisms, skills, and knowledge that the offender acquires through practice to be able to fulfil their crime; Nee & Ward, 2015) and risk prediction has not been explored, yet an understanding of the mechanisms underpinning expertise could contribute to a better understanding of what dynamic risk factors are and how they should be conceptualised. If the conceptualisation of dynamic risk factors is re-examined then the interventions available for offenders should have a larger impact and ultimately recidivism rates should decrease. Therefore, in this article the aim is to explore how awareness of expertise and competency in offenders can contribute to a deeper understanding of dynamic risk factors. The article will first provide an overview of dynamic risk factors and the debate that currently exists within this area before describing the literature surrounding expertise in offenders. The article will then turn to a more detailed examination of expertise and how it interlinks with various domains of dynamic risk factors in acquisitive offenders (specifically burglars) and more briefly in child sexual offenders.[1] These two types of offending have arguably the most developed accounts of expertise in correctional psychology. Finally, the implications for treatment will be discussed.

Overview of the debate surrounding dynamic risk factors

Risk assessments are an essential part of clinical and/or forensic practice, and therefore researchers and practitioners have focused on identifying those factors that accurately measure and predict risk (referred to as risk factors). Risk factors can vary in changeability, with static factors being historical, unchangeable features, such as number of previous convictions or age at first conviction, and dynamic factors being changeable features, such as emotional state or poor coping strategies (Bonta, 1996). Dynamic risk factors can additionally vary in terms of duration: stable (relatively enduring problems, e.g. alcoholism) versus acute (rapidly changing problems, e.g. emotional collapse; Hanson & Harris, 2000). Although static risk factors have strong predictive validity and are easy to measure, their lack of changeability means that they cannot be the focus of treatment programmes nor can they be altered to help reduce recidivism rates (Andrews & Bonta, 2006). Conversely, whilst dynamic risk factors are difficult to reliably measure and generally have poorer predictive validity than static risk factors (Craig, Browne, & Beech, 2008), they can be modified and consequently are more useful for informing treatment programmes. As a result, it is the dynamic risk factors that, if dealt with appropriately in treatment, should help to reduce recidivism. Nevertheless, whilst there seems to be a clear distinction between static and dynamic factors in terms of risk prediction, there is not necessarily such a distinction between the two types of factors when it comes to understanding different types of crime. This is because static factors (e.g. criminal convictions) can be seen as outcomes of dynamic factors (e.g. anti-social attitudes; Beech & Craig, 2012; Beech & Ward, 2004).

Additionally, although risk factors predict crime, it is important to note that protective factors can promote desistance; thus can also be predictive of recidivism (Thornton, 2013). Protective factors are those variables that mitigate or eliminate risk, such as school achievement, supportive family, or positive peer groups. By monitoring the presence or absence of protective factors, one can learn what factors were in place when the offender did not offend and what factors were not in place when the offender did offend (Rogers, 2000). Consequently, it is important to introduce and maintain protective factors in the offenders' life to help reduce the risk of reoffending. However, cause and effect cannot be established and so it is difficult to determine whether it is protective factors that cause the reduction in reoffending, or the result of other confounding factors, such as maturational effects.

The Risk–Need–Responsivity (RNR) model (Andrews & Bonta, 2003; Andrews, Bonta, & Hoge, 1990) is undoubtedly the most influential risk-orientated model of offender rehabilitation. It has significantly contributed to the understanding and prediction of risk by emphasising the need to distinguish between static and dynamic risk factors. The RNR model is based on three principles that help to understand the prediction of risk and the classification of offenders for treatment: (1) *Risk*, which refers to matching the offenders level of intervention to their risk of reoffending; (2) *Need*, which refers to assessing the dynamic risk factors or criminogenic needs and targeting them in treatment; (3) *Responsivity*, which refers to how the treatment is provided, emphasising the need for the intervention to be tailored to the individual characteristics of each offender (e.g. learning style or level of motivation). Andrews and Bonta (1995) used the three principles of the RNR model to create an actuarial criminogenic risk–need assessment tool known as the Level of Service Inventory-Revised (LSI-R). The LSI-R is a 54-item measure that addresses 10 domains (including both static and dynamic factors) associated with offending behaviours: criminal history, education/employment, financial, family/marital, accommodation, leisure/recreation, companions, alcohol/drug problems, emotional/personal, and attitudes/orientation. Higher scores on this assessment indicate a higher propensity to commit further criminal acts, and it has been found to have good predictive validity (around 65%; Raynor, Kynch, Roberts, & Merrington, 2000). Measures of risk, such as the LSI-R, are used to allocate individuals to treatment programmes and to determine the necessary intensity of the treatment. Despite the RNR model; (i) being theoretically based (e.g. the Psychology of Criminal Conduct, General Personality and Social Psychological Perspective on Criminal Conduct, and Personal Interpersonal Community-Reinforcement Perspective); (ii) obtaining strong empirical support (e.g. Andrews & Bonta, 2006; Bonta & Andrews, 1993; Dowden & Andrews, 2003, 2004; Hanson, Bourgon, Helmus, & Hodgson, 2009); and (iii) leading to a wide range of research in the area of offender assessment and treatment (e.g. Heffernan & Ward, 2015; Ward, Melser, & Yates, 2007), it has been highly criticised with regard to its focus on dynamic risk factors, lack of scope, and lack of theoretical and practical implications (e.g. Ward & Beech, 2015; Ward & Brown, 2004).

Based on the initial research into risk prediction, it is apparent that dynamic risk factors are merely interpreted as a list of features or vague descriptions based on those variables that have been found to correlate with offending behaviours (e.g. substance misuse, lack of employment, and no stable accommodation; Brunton-Smith & Hopkins, 2013). This suggests that dynamic risk factors have been inadequately defined and that current conceptualisations overlook the highly varying nature of these variables, ignoring the need to consider their internal structure (Ward & Beech, 2015). That is, there is a lack of theoretical underpinnings within the conceptualisation of dynamic risk factors which means that such factors do not explain the causal psychological mechanisms, or maintenance, of offending behaviours (Mann, Hanson, & Thornton, 2010). These issues with measuring and conceptualising dynamic risk factors have led to much debate within the offender rehabilitation literature. This has therefore resulted in many researchers and practitioners exploring ways in which dynamic risk factors can be better understood in order to; prevent the literature from purely focusing on prediction at the expense of explanation, improve risk assessments, and successfully treat individuals (Ward, 2014; Ward & Beech, 2015).

Risk domains often form the basis of offender risk assessments (e.g. the LSI-R (Andrews & Bonta, 1995), Static-99 (Hanson & Thornton, 2000), or Violence Risk Appraisal Guide (Quinsey, Harris, Rice, & Cormier, 2006)), and research supports the notion that there are at least four major domains of risk: cognition (cognitive skill deficits or offense-supportive beliefs), self-regulation (negative affect or poor self-management), interpersonal functioning (social skill and intimacy deficits), and sexual (sexual deviance and preoccupation; Hanson & Harris, 2000; Thornton, 2002). However, it is important to note that these particular domains may differ slightly depending on the type of crime. For example, sexual offenders may have all four to varying degrees, but there may be no sexual domain for acquisitive or violent offending; instead, other domains may be more prominent (e.g. the cognition domain will probably be more prominent for acquisitive offenders and the self-regulation domain more prominent for violent offenders). Nevertheless, regardless of the exact crime type or risk domain categories, it is unclear how the risk domains function to cause specific offending behaviours.

Beech and Ward (2004) were the first to explore the possible conceptual and causal relationships between aetiological theories and risk factors. They developed the Aetiological Model of Risk, which outlines the offence process and considers; developmental variables (e.g. abuse), vulnerabilities (measured by static risk factors, e.g. psychosocial problems, and stable dynamic risk factors, e.g. self-regulation problems), triggering events or contextual risk factors (e.g. access to victims), and dynamic acute risk factors (e.g. arousal). Despite the important theoretical developments since this model was proposed, the significance of the link between risk and aetiology has been neglected, and so more is needed to create a conceptual bridge between risk assessment and aetiological theory.

The research by Beech and Ward (2004) challenges the static/dynamic distinction because Beech and Ward claim that static risk factors only have significant predictive validity because they act as markers of past actions of dynamic risk factors. Mann et al. (2010) also challenged the static/dynamic distinction. They developed a list of psychologically meaningful risk factors based on what factors had the highest predictability of reoffending. Mann et al. conceptualised dynamic risk factors as propensities to offend that are triggered in certain contexts, and so dynamic risk factors are vulnerabilities that may or may not lead to an offence. However, this conceptualisation is unclear because the causal mechanisms that mediate the relationship between the risk factors and offending have not been established.

Heffernan and Ward (2015) explored the nature and function of dynamic risk factors in their ability to explain sexual offending and guide treatment. They argued that when risk domains are labelled as deficits or risk factors that there is the tendency to undermine the offenders perceived agency (i.e. to remove responsibility for the actions away from the offender). Therefore, Heffernan and Ward (2015) referred to dynamic risk factors as composite constructs and developed a new aetiological model: The Agency

Model of Risk (AMR). The AMR proposes three levels of agency; (1) *personal level*, which refers to what the individual believes about themselves (e.g. personal values, priorities, norms); (2) *social level*, which refers to the self in relation to others (e.g. interpersonal interactions and reinforcement); and (3) *systems level*, which refers to the physical states that influence offending (e.g. biological needs). These three agency levels can influence one another and are each associated with a distinct set of goals (values that direct behaviour), plans, and strategies (the actions or skills that need to be implemented in order to achieve the goals), action implementation (offending behaviours), and self-monitoring and reflection. It is believed that dynamic risk factors and protective factors are the psychological and social processes that refer to the components of agency (i.e. goals, plans, strategies, action implementation, self-reflection), and consequently, they impair normal functioning within the individuals' social, cultural, and physical environments. That is, dynamic risk factors are the mechanisms that influence someone's ability to act in a prosocial or goal-directed manner. Four risk domains are distributed across the components of the AMR: intimacy deficits, general self-regulation problems, cognitive distortions, and sexual deviance. The AMR has contributed to the literature on predicting risk by attempting to explain offending behaviour rather than predict it. It highlights the complex nature present in the link between dynamic risk factors and offending, demonstrating the important roles of human agency and values that motivate behaviour. The AMR emphasises the need to be cautious when viewing risk factors as causal factors of offending.

To summarise, the reliance on measuring dynamic risk factors as correlates of recidivism has been found to be misleading. Therefore, much debate within the correctional literature has focused on exploring alternative ways of conceptualising dynamic risk factors. The need to stop viewing dynamic risk factors as causal entities of offending is clear (Ward & Beech, 2015), and several researchers are now proposing new conceptualisation systems of risk factors that no longer distinguish between static and dynamic, and that attempt to improve the explanatory power of dynamic risk factors (e.g. Heffernan & Ward, 2015). A better understanding of dynamic risk factors would help to improve the success of treatment programmes, and ultimately increase the predictive validity of dynamic risk factors; thus reducing reoffending rates. However, it is important to note that research into dynamic risk factors has focused on sexual offenders, and whilst it is likely that this research can also be applied to other types of offending, further research needs to be conducted with regard to the risk domains of other crime types before any firm conclusions can be made.

Expertise in offenders

Recently, a number of researchers within the field of offending behaviours and rehabilitation have attempted to study the decision-making processes (*cognitive operations*) involved in committing a crime. However, the focus should not just be on the commission of the crime itself, but on the entire decision-chain (i.e. the decisions made prior to the crime, during the crime, and after the crime; Nee & Ward, 2015). Within this area of decision-making is the notion of *expertise* and whether offenders are experts at making decisions related to their specific criminal acts (e.g. burglary, sexual offending, drug dealing, arson). Expertise can be defined as

> the acquisition of cognitive processes and consequent behaviour that are demonstrably superior to those new to a given domain, in the sense that they are faster, more cognitively economical, are triggered automatically in relevant environments and are based on considerable experience and honing of skills over time. (Nee & Ward, 2015, p. 2)

Expertise or skill level can facilitate offending behaviours and therefore a better understanding of expertise and its cognitive, behavioural, and affective mechanisms would be useful for understanding the commission of an offence and how future offences can be prevented (Ward, 1999).

Each offence that an individual commits, results in that individual acquiring new knowledge that is processed in accordance with his existing implicit schema (Ward, 1999). Offence scripts (often thought to manifest themselves within dynamic risk factors, e.g. offence-supportive beliefs; Bourke, Ward, & Rose, 2012) aid the decision-making process for committing an offence. Thus, any new knowledge obtained during the offence process will amend these scripts causing the individual to conduct their next offence in a different manner, depending on what the offender has previously learnt and experienced (Fortune, Bourke, & Ward, 2015). Every offence committed can therefore be viewed as a learning curve that improves the individuals' offence-related strategies, competencies and skills, enhancing their capabilities in that particular domain (crime). As the offender becomes more competent, the outcomes of his actions increase and the chance of him being apprehended reduces. Hence, increased competencies facilitate the ability for the offender to detect offence opportunities and navigate his way past any barriers that may be preventing him from committing an offence. Those offenders who avoid detection are thought to be experts who have refined their offending skills and offence-related strategies (Bourke et al., 2012; Ward, 1999).

Expertise, as a general concept, lies on a continuum from novices to masters (Ericsson, 2006; Hoffman, Shadbolt, Burton, & Klein, 1995), and it is believed that knowing the extent of the shift from where an offender currently lies on the expertise continuum compared to where they started prior to their offending career is indicative of their vulnerabilities (which are likely to be associated with dynamic risk factors; Beech & Ward, 2004). The task for most researchers is to understand why some offenders are more capable of their crimes than others. One possible way of understanding this it to consider the differences between how knowledge is organised and structured in experts compared to non-experts. Research has shown that experts compared to non-experts perceive the environment of their crimes differently (*perceptual skills*) and that this perception is directly related to superior offending knowledge and better skills for committing the offence (*procedural skills*; Nee & Meenaghan, 2006; Topalli, 2005). Consequently, experts develop, maintain, and use their cognitive abilities to assess their targets in different ways to non-experts, becoming specialised in their offending behaviours. Four cognitive mechanisms have been put forward as crucial to becoming an expert in a particular domain; (1) *chunking in memory* (through practice/experience and trial and error, the expert (offender) stores cues and patterns (schemas) in his long-term memory, which means he can respond to his environment more proficiently); (2) *automaticity* (offence process, including decision-making, occurs instantly and unconsciously); (3) *situational awareness and selective preconscious attention* (an expert preconsciously scans the environment, increasing his ability to automatically attend to, and prioritise, meaningful cues; thus the offender can make useful inferences based on small amounts of information); (4) *multi-tasking* (the automatic nature of making decisions means that the expert has free space for more conscious deliberations needed for his working memory). The notion of a continuum of expertise and that expertise has underlying cognitive mechanisms has been supported in many studies including those investigating sexual offences (of children; Bourke et al., 2012, and adults; O'Ciardha, 2015), and burglary (Nee, 2015).

Typically, expertise implies someone being exceptionally talented at a socially accepted domain, such as chess or medicine. However, as is clear from what has already been mentioned in the current review, this is not always the case. Someone can be an expert within any domain, including offending. Nee and Ward (2015) propose the model of *dysfunctional expertise* to help explain the decisions made by an offender in and around the crime scene. They suggest four stages of decision-making that an experienced offender undergoes: (1) Automatic, unintentional, and preconscious appraisal of the environment that cannot be switched off; (2) Superior and automatic recognition of the environment and offence-related cues that are meaningfully related to the expertise domain; (3) Activation of complex cognitive schemas, built up through practice, which allows for instant access to a number of exemplars and heuristics; (4) Speedy responses to environmental cues that have worked in the past and helped form offence scripts that allow for automatic commission of the offence. Nee and Ward (2015) suggest that there is the possibility for the behaviour to become more conscious and controllable at stages three and four, but that this depends on the complexity of the task and the particular individual undertaking the task. This approach helps to explain the offence process and the cognitive mechanisms that underlie the offence decision-chain, for example, the automatic and unconscious ability to attend to cues within the environment over time. Additionally, the approach has been used to help explain a variety of crimes including; burglary (Nee, 2015), drug-related offending (Casey, 2015), sexual offending (O'Ciardha, 2015), identity theft (Vieraitis, Copes, Powell, & Pike, 2015), firesetting (Butler & Gannon, 2015), intimate partner violence (Day & Bowen, 2015), homicide (Brookman, 2015), and carjacking (Topalli, Jacques, & Wright, 2015).

Despite the advantageous development of cognitive processes within experts, such processes can have limitations. First, as a result of the automaticity and effortless nature of making a decision, errors can be made, especially in stressful situations (Klein, 2009), and consequently crimes can go wrong. Second, as a result of the repeated learning and habitual nature of the offence process, the ability to be flexible and to problem solve effectively when confronted with completely unexpected situations is blocked or hindered (Woollett & Maguire, 2010). Although these are negative consequences of an expert's cognitive processes, they are the processes that law enforcement should exploit if they are to increase the chances of apprehending expert criminals.

It is clear that understanding offender expertise has enabled researchers in the field to assess the psychological processes involved in the decision-making of an offence. However, there are many limitations within the expertise literature. First, offenders (regardless of type, e.g. violent versus sexual) are not a homogeneous group (Harris & Rice, 1997; Kemshall, 2001; Sample & Bray, 2006), and therefore there are likely to be some individual differences between offenders in terms of their offence process (or decision-making chain). Second, most of the work on offender expertise has been conducted with burglars (e.g. Nee, 2015) and sexual offenders (e.g. Bourke et al., 2012), and whilst (based on the theory in which expertise is grounded) no significant differences are expected for expertise based on the type of crime committed, more research is needed to explore expertise within other crime types. Third, knowledge and understanding of expertise for offenders has mostly been based on those offenders that have been detected, and more research is required on those offenders who have not been caught (e.g. Topalli, 2006 on violent street offenders, and Wright & Decker, 1994 on burglars). This information would be beneficial for enhancing the understanding of offender expertise amongst those who are likely to be the most skilled. Fourth, the information available on offender expertise is only based on consciously accessed knowledge from those offenders who are willing to talk. There may well be a considerable proportion of information that is not accessible, e.g. due to the unconscious nature of being an expert at a particular domain. Additionally, the literature assumes that the offender is recalling information truthfully: offenders may deliver false information that does not actually reflect their offence process in order to deceive practitioners or researchers. Fifth, more research is needed to learn about the amount of experience and level of practice required to become an expert (Nee & Ward, 2015). Finally, whilst it is clear that understanding expertise within offenders contributes to understanding the 'how' of offending (i.e. the skills, schemas, heightened awareness of contexts, and automaticity that aid offending), it does not contribute to understanding the 'why' of offending (i.e. the states, traits, core beliefs, or self-regulation that has been found to be associated with offending).

To summarise, expertise can develop within any domain, including offender behaviours. By looking at differences in offender experience, knowledge, and skill acquisition, cognitive mechanisms can be identified that aid the offence process. Thus, these mechanisms, at minimum, should be the focus of treatment programmes if recidivism rates are to decrease. However, due to the accumulated nature of expertise, expert offenders may be more difficult to treat, and therefore treatment for these offenders will need to be slower and more intricate, providing alternative ways of thinking so that the offenders replace their existing anti-social schemata with more prosocial schemata (Nee & Ward, 2015). As previously stated, the aim of this article is to examine the links between offender expertise and dynamic risk factors. The remaining sections of this review will consider this link as well as discussing treatment implications.

Dynamic risk factors, dysfunctional expertise, and acquisitive crime

In the quest to further elucidate the causal processes underlying offending behaviour, this review takes a more focused look at how the components of dysfunctional expertise in offenders are linked to dynamic risk factors in particular types of offending behaviour. As previously stated, the focus will be on burglary and, to some extent, child sexual offending as these have obtained the most developed theoretical explanations in relation to offender expertise. The AMR (Heffernan & Ward, 2015) and the model of dysfunctional expertise (Nee & Ward, 2015) will be referred to as general frameworks for guiding the author's explorations. This is because both of these models explored in a detailed way the underpinning psychological, biological and social mechanisms involved in offending behaviour.

What are the dynamic risk factors that may be associated with acquisitive offending?

To begin, a closer look at the ways in which dynamic risk factors may be associated with the 'why' of acquisitive offending, specifically for burglars, will be undertaken. Subsequently, the 'how' of offending, the cognitive and self-regulatory components (e.g. skills, knowledge, competencies, planning, and time management) will be examined. The authors feel it is in the doing of the crime in which the most useful links between competencies and risk/protective factors will be found, which will improve the understanding of the topic more thoroughly and ultimately help to reduce offending behaviour more effectively. To do this, different parts of the decision-chain will be examined consecutively: initial decisions, journey to crime, commission of the crime, and after the crime, as it is suspected that the nature of action and reflection might vary during these phases. In other words, offenders may prioritise one of the three levels of agency described by Heffernan and Ward (2015): systems level, personal level, and social level at different points of the process.

What is meant by acquisitive offenders?

Acquisitive offenders (a category which usually includes all types of theft, burglary, fraud, and criminal damage) are very common. In the UK, for instance, they make up around 80% of all recorded incidents of victim-based crime (Office for National Statistics, 2014) and this is likely to be similar in other countries. Those convicted of burglary in any one year make up a sizable chunk of this population. It is also know that acquisitive offenders tend to carry out a mixture of the above crimes (Tarling, 1993), so experienced burglars are likely to have expertise in other acquisitive crimes and vice versa.

The why

As a 'typical' male offender,[2] a burglar's background is likely to strongly reflect the empirically based risk factors underpinning traditional risk models of offending (e.g. Andrews & Bonta, 2010). However, in line with the underlying ethos of this article, how useful is it to list a number of broad categories associated with offending behaviour which are simply correlated with risk? It is perhaps of very little value for intervention and rehabilitation. As noted earlier, dynamic risk factors are merely descriptions, void of any explanatory value, that act as markers of deeper problems associated with the risk of reoffending. Underneath these risk factors lie individual stories, which are often infused with a range of obstacles and challenges that have made it difficult to develop prosocial agency and autonomy (Nee & Ioannou, in press). These life stories may also, however, offer possibilities for developing resilience and reflection. For instance, plumbing down from the risk factor 'lack of educational attainment' it is likely that attachment problems in childhood as a result of a substance misusing, young, single parent, will be found. Competencies in intelligence not translating into achievement as a result of anger and rejection from school peers due to lack of social skills may also be found. The risk factor paradigm paints a very bleak picture for rehabilitation, with no emphasis at all on any positive features that can be nurtured, such as the ability to plan and appraise, which might eventually support a greater sense of prosocial agency and governance (Gannon & Ward, 2014). More useful might be to look at the competencies involved in the offender's day-to-day life, and how dysfunctional expertise might be translated into something prosocial.

The how

The initial decision to offend. It is well known from a variety of sources that many offenders lead comparatively chaotic lives (e.g. Maruna, 2001). However, when it comes to the commission of the act, very few burglars act indiscriminately or impulsively, nor do they heavily plan their crimes (Bennett & Wright, 1984; Nee, 2015; Nee & Meenaghan, 2006; Wright & Decker, 1994). Instead, they seem to act with the automaticity characteristic of someone experienced and practised at what they do (Nee & Meenaghan, 2006). Their initial, relatively conscious decision to undertake a burglary is usually away from the scene of the eventual crime (Nee & Taylor, 2000) hours or even days before the crime occurs (Wright & Decker, 1994). This decision is likely to occur as a result of two processes: internal needs and awareness of opportunities.

Basic internal needs arise in the agent for 'primary goods' (Ward & Maruna, 2007). These could be emotional, biological, or cognitive and might include; a need to provide for the basic needs of self and family (food, clothing, accommodation) through the secondary goods of money (Nee & Taylor, 1988); a need to restore well-being, either in the self (servicing an addiction or through a sense of mastery); or with peers (via friendship, social interaction, and recreation; Shover, 1973, 1996; Wright & Decker, 1994). Alongside this there is likely to be a heightened, semi-conscious awareness in working memory of recent environmental cues indicating attractive burglary targets (Nee, 2015; Nee & Meenaghan, 2006). It is well established in the dual-processing paradigm that much of people's decision-making and environmental awareness is below consciousness (Kahneman, 2011). Burglars, in line with anyone else who is experienced at what they do, will recognise cues in the environment linked to potential reward and positive affect in memory. These will increase motivation and allow goals to be activated unconsciously (Chartrand & Bargh, 2002). Preconscious scanning of the environment for cues related to reward and well-being (as well as threat) are automatic and cannot be turned off (see Nee & Ward, 2015 for a fuller description). Bargh (1994, p. 5) refers to this as 'eternal vigilance'. Thus, a mixture of internal and external needs, facilitated by particular contexts and environments result in goal-setting, motivation, and the initial decision to offend. The latter may comprise a relatively conscious moment in an otherwise semi-conscious and unconscious context, but as noted elsewhere (Bargh, 1994), practised behaviour may begin with a deliberative initial decision to act, and very quickly become automatic (e.g. driving a car) by triggering schemas in memory about what to do in given situations (Shanteau, 1992).

The description above might suggest that the systems level (biological need) and personal level ('offending is acceptable and I have the skills to do it') of agency are salient in these processes. Goals are set, and with them come plans and strategies. Plans might involve when (and with whom) to undertake the crime and in which neighbourhood (Nee & Taylor, 2000). Strategies at this stage might involve activating schemas about how to navigate to a potential locale of the crime successfully without being noticed by residents and passers-by (Nee, 2015).

The aim of this article is to understand more clearly the underpinnings of dynamic risk factors. The internal needs described above, combined with relatively unconscious responses from long-term memory to external cues, comprise characteristics of the offender that clearly increase their likelihood of reoffending. Exploring the process of offending with experienced offenders in this way represents an example of how researchers can uncover the mechanisms underpinning risk factor categories, which is found in risk assessment tools. Findings can contextualise and make meaningful, how risk might increase and decrease in given contexts. This will give us clues as to how to approach intervention more effectively, with greater significance for the offender. This will be revisited in the implications section below.

The journey to crime (the implementation of strategies and plans). As noted above, the burglar's heightened situational awareness of environmental cues linked in memory with positive affect and reward will have allowed him to recognise opportunities for future criminal activity (such as, a neighbourhood that seems relatively unoccupied at particular times, and also signals a number of profitable outcomes). With these ideas driving his plans and intentions, the burglar begins his journey to the actual crime. En route the burglar will continue to appraise the environment, implementing his tried and tested strategies with ease and an implicit belief in his ability to carry out the crime. The social level of agency will play a role in his ability to perceive how others are judging him in potentially new environments, so as not to stand out. To support this, research shows that the routes taken within and around the burglary target are notably 'cleaner' and more systematic than by inexperienced control groups (Nee et al., 2015; Taylor & Nee, 1988). The environmental criminology literature also supports that the journeys to the locale of the crime are more careful and systematic too (Bernasco & Luykx, 2003; Rengert & Wasilchick, 2000). The accounts of experienced burglars on their journey to the crime site indicate versatility (likely to be a result of rich, interconnected schemas which allow instantaneous solutions when somewhat unexpected contexts arise). They may therefore become aware of a new locale that partially meets their needs, en route. Clare (2011) noted that increasing expertise in burglars allowed for a greater sense of self-efficacy and belief in their ability to make inferences from only partially familiar information. This locale may be revisited if the originally intended neighbourhood proves too risky on that occasion. This personal level of agency (Heffernan & Ward, 2015) that is driven by the beliefs, values and norms that the offender has accrued over time, will be increasingly supplemented by the systems level: excitement, anxiety, and imminent reward playing an increasingly strong and inextricable role in the drive to commit the crime as the target becomes closer. These internal emotional drivers (or 'acute dynamic risk factors' as described by Beech and Ward (2004) in one of the first attempts to deconstruct these features) and the extent to which they build as the crime becomes closer, are in desperate need of robust examination through research. These earlier phases of the offending cycle (i.e. before the offender arrives at the actual scene) may offer the best chances in terms of working with the offender to bring these processes to consciousness, so that the offender can reflect on his behaviour and re-evaluate the consequences.

Self-monitoring and evaluation, an important element of any model which emphasises agency and self-governance (Heffernan & Ward, 2015), are rarely explicitly discussed in the offender expertise literature. However, adoption of new strategies when faced with an interesting opportunity or an unexpected constellation of external cues, are surely done as a result of reflecting (even if automatically) on one's analysis of internal and external cues. Unfortunately, for those trying to intervene (and for the offender motivated to change) it is very likely that these mechanisms are unconscious (Nee & Ward, 2015). Once in a vicinity recognised by the offender as the potential locale of the crime, it is likely that preconscious scanning gives way to a more acute and evaluative appraisal (Nee, 2015), which is still nevertheless automatic.

Underlying processes in target selection and the commission of burglary

Previous research has shown that, once the burglar's attention is drawn to a potential target, he will instantaneously appraise a number of aspects with ease and speed in comparison to those without this expertise (Logie, Wright, & Decker, 1992; Nee & Taylor, 2000; Wright, Logie, & Decker, 1995). Burglars will assess relative gain, access, occupancy, and security features within seconds (see Nee, 2015 for a more detailed account), and experimental work has indicated that fewer cues are needed to reach a decision with experience as the offender employs efficient, compensatory mental strategies (Garcia-Retamero & Dhami, 2009; Homel, Macintyre, & Wortley, 2014; Snook, Dhami, & Kavanagh, 2011). In terms of self-regulation, physiological arousal associated with optimal performance and reward are now likely to be at their peak and continue to be as the burglar enters and undertakes the crime. This has never been studied, but it is believed that alpha desynchronisation does not occur in the brains of experts when doing tasks related to their expertise, and that anxiety is reportedly lower in experienced burglars (Wright & Decker, 1994). Consequently, measures are expected to reflect this. Once inside, the burglar engages in a more or less automated sequence, especially if the layout and general interior of the property is as expected. He will take a practised route to maximise gain and limit risk, gathering high value items in a discriminate way (Nee & Meenaghan, 2006; Nee et al., 2015; Wright & Decker, 1994). As long as self-regulatory feedback, based on arousal and personal values about what is expected and what is the norm, is as anticipated, the burglary continues to its conclusion with the burglar exiting and leaving the scene, either on foot or in a vehicle. Very little is known about what happens next in the cognitive and emotional world of the burglar, other than that the offender will be keen to convert goods into cash or other 'secondary goods' (Ferrante & Clare, 2006; Wright & Decker, 1994). There is some suggestion in early studies that a feeling of elation and relief ensues (Katz, 1988; Wright & Decker, 1994) and that the offender returns to his more chaotic lifestyle (Clare, 2011). However, whether the offender becomes more reflective at this stage (as has been noted in studies of child sexual offenders; Bourke et al., 2012; Fortune et al., 2015) has not been studied, and may play a strong role in intervention. In line with contemporary models of human agency (Bratman, 1999), reflection on performance, which is not necessarily deliberative or fully conscious, may result in a subtle revision of goals, plans, and strategies for future actions (Heffernan & Ward, 2015; Ward, 2015). More knowledge about this phase of the offending cycle could be recruited in future rehabilitation strategies.

Dysfunctional expertise and dynamic risk factors in child sexual offenders

As previously mentioned in this article, alongside the cognitive and self-regulatory domains of risk characteristic of acquisitive offenders, additional vulnerabilities regarding intimacy and sexual deviance have been noted in child sexual offenders (Hanson & Harris, 2000; Mann et al., 2010; Thornton, 2013). Given the right contexts (which might arise through practised planning), these vulnerabilities may result in criminal behaviour. Over the years (Bourke et al., 2012; Deslauriers-Varin & Beauregard, 2010; Fortune et al., 2015; Leclerc, Carpentier, & Proulx, 2006; Ward, 1999; Ward & Hudson, 2000), a picture of the cognitive processes of the experienced sexual offender has emerged that, like those of acquisitive offenders, fit well with Nee and Ward's (2015) four stage model of dysfunctional expertise. Experienced child sexual offenders appear to have superior, automatic recognition of cues relating to vulnerable targets and contexts; and access to rich schemas in memory including a variety of exemplars and behavioural scripts that will play out with ease depending on the context. From an agency point of view (Heffernan & Ward, 2015), these competencies will include implicit plans, skills and strategies for befriending and developing what appear to be mutually rewarding relationships with children (for instance, through gift buying and sharing of feelings to strengthen emotional bonds). Importantly, the offender themselves may not be fully aware of when acceptable boundaries have been crossed. Moreover, strategies to prevent and avoid detection are more important to the sexual offender (than, for example, the burglar) due to the interpersonal nature of the crime. Reflection and honing of skills over time results in considerable knowledge about how to avoid detection in terms of planning the location, deceiving others close to the offender and the victim, maintaining a good level of outward self-regulation, intimidating the victim and leading a seemingly normal life (Fortune et al., 2015; Ward, 1999). Personal norms and values, developed through dysfunctional experiences in childhood and adolescence might include a sense of entitlement to sex and that sex with children is acceptable. On a systems level, sexual needs may be heightened, especially if substance misuse or alcohol are present.

A somewhat different array of competencies emerge for the child sexual offender in comparison to the burglar. Interpersonal skills in relation to grooming the child without arousing suspicion, planning (to avoid detection), and reflection post the offence to refine skills, point to a more contemplative offender (though in line with mainstream explanations of expertise, planning, and reflection reduce once automatic schemas of how to undertake crimes build up; Bourke et al., 2012). One explanation for this is that this is an interpersonal crime (burglars, in contrast, prefer not to meet their victims; Coupe & Blake, 2006; Cromwell, Olson, & Avary, 1991; Hearndon & Magill, 2004; Nee & Meenaghan, 2006; Wright & Decker, 1994) and is therefore inherently more risky, with increased chance of detection through disclosure by the victim.

All-in-all, these explanations of the often dysfunctional goals, strategies, and behaviour of offenders, derived from analysis of the offender's description of what he does, assist in providing insight into the mechanisms underpinning what are traditionally called 'dynamic risk factors'. In approaching the reduction of crime, these explanations provide a greater depth of understanding and a more individualised account of the process of crime from start to finish, instead of simply badging an individual as a collection of deficits. Therefore, a greater depth of understanding should significantly help in rehabilitation.

Implications for treatment

The vulnerabilities or 'risks' associated with expertise in offending are the result of hundreds of repetitions of the behaviour in question (in the case of the child sexual offender this may be through mental rehearsal as the actual offending rate is lower) and are particularly difficult to challenge as they are deeply entrenched, interconnected, automatic, and likely to be below consciousness (Nee & Ward, 2015). Ways of addressing this might be; (i) by working with the offender's sense of personal agency and competence; (ii) by replacing dysfunctional automatic scripts with functional ones; or (iii) as a result of both of these processes, by fostering a more reflective outlook.

Agency and competence

The underlying principle of strength's based models of offender rehabilitation, such as the Good Lives Model (Ward & Maruna, 2007) and the AMR (Heffernan & Ward, 2015), is that the offender should be engaged in, and eventually take control of, their journey to a crime free life. Rather than a didactic or instructive relationship between the correctional professional and the offender, the idea is to work in Socratic, shared-agency in order to motivate the offender towards a less destructive (and hopefully fulfilling) life of their own choosing and of their own volition. It is important to note that the underpinning goals which may have originally driven the offender's behaviour (e.g. to look after one's needs; to achieve self-esteem, mastery, and intimacy) are often not negative in themselves and this can be used as a starting point (Ward & Stewart, 2003). Within this framework the idea would be to recruit the functional, positive aspects of competency and agency to reduce offending behaviour. In RNR terminology, the ability to accrue expertise and the sense of mastery, self-efficacy, and 'normality' persistent criminal activity might be seen as increasing the risk of reoffending, rather than being seen as competencies. However, an awareness of these aspects could be used in the motivated offender to foster a sense of prosocial possibility – 'I have capacities and competencies'; 'I can have the life I want without resorting to crime but I have to retrain these capacities and build a different sense of self-identity and self-governance.' Intervention, even with the motivated offender however, may be extensive and challenging, given that 'successful' offending is likely to represent the greatest sense of mastery and reward in the offender's life until now. Learning to recognise patterns in behaviour and becoming more aware of the internal and external triggers at different points on the decision-chain would be a valuable early lesson (such as the 'seemingly unimportant decisions' of sexual offenders (Ward & Hudson, 2000) and the 'pre-conscious scanning' of the environment in burglars (Nee, 2015)). Much more research is needed on the different phases that make up the entire offending cycle (as outlined above for burglars) on different types of crime in order to support interventions. This should ideally use simulated criminogenic environments and neuro-phenomenological methods in order to reinstate the context of crime in an ethical way and to consequently understand the offender's lived experience of undertaking the crime. What is already clear from the preliminary studies conducted on competencies in child sexual offenders and burglars is that the mechanisms underlying risk categories are more complex and composite than a standard risk assessment might suggest, and that they clearly vary from offence to offence (and from offender to offender).

Retraining automaticity

Several areas of psychological research and therapy have produced evidence that dysfunctional automatic responses to meaningful triggers can be replaced by functional ones. Three areas will briefly be referred to here; (1) interventions reducing prejudiced responses; (2) interventions for eating behaviour; and (3) interventions for depression and anxiety. Much research in the field of social psychology (Bargh, 1994; Blair & Banaji, 1996; Devine, 1989) has demonstrated that stereotypes are automatic, cognitive shortcuts that help us make sense of the world in a resource-efficient way. However, these can quickly develop into negative, instant prejudices in particular contexts. In experimental settings, these scholars have shown how stereotypes can be automatically and unconsciously activated through priming techniques. Devine (1989) demonstrated that once activated and some level of awareness is reached, one can be taught to automate a habit of *non-stereotyping* (e.g. a script of fairness) which becomes instantly activated immediately after the original stereotypical thought is invoked. This process is likely to happen naturally when some level of awareness and reflection are typically present in an individual's repertoire. However, these elements are less likely to be prioritised in the more automatic, reward-driven type of decision-making characteristic of offenders. This priming type of intervention, therefore, could be piloted with motivated offenders as it is characteristic of the following two interventions also.

Changing health-harming behaviours in the general public, such as over-eating and smoking, by raising awareness of risk are not notably successful, except in small numbers of highly motivated individuals (Marteau et al., 2010; Webb & Sheeran, 2010). Eating (and therefore over-eating), for instance, is strongly governed by automatic scripts triggered by environmental cues which are rarely overridden by more reflective processes. In order to do this, one needs the requisite resources such as energy, attention, motivation, and awareness. More recent developments in this field (Marteau, Hollands, & Fletcher, 2012), have advocated interventions that target automatic (rather than reflective) processes to activate, inhibit, or create new associations through priming (e.g. learning to associate positive outcomes with healthier food), so that the agent behaves differently when presented with the cue (Papies, 2012; Roberto, Baik, Harris, & Brownell, 2010). This approach also concurs with recent interventions for depression and anxiety known as cognitive bias modification (CBM). Large bodies of research indicate that those with depression tend to automatically process neutral external stimuli as negative (Holmes, Lang, & Shah, 2009) whilst anxious individuals process neutral stimuli as threatening (Macleod & Mathews, 1988). CBM utilises computer based tasks and games involving hundreds of repetitions over two to four weeks. Participants are required to replace 'threatening' or 'negative' stimuli (such as faces or words) with neutral ones and are rewarded for doing so. Although, still in the early stages of evidence, participants over numerous and varied samples have shown reductions in self-reported and psychometric follow-up measures of depression and anxiety, with effect sizes comparable to those of traditional cognitive behaviour therapy (Beard, 2011; Watkins, Baeyens, & Read, 2009). These interventions suggest the potential to retrain automaticity in offenders in line with mutually beneficial (prosocial) goals, or at least replace automatic early stages of the decision-chain (initial decisions and on journey to crime) with an automatically triggered re-evaluation of the consequences of crime.

Fostering a more reflective outlook

Impulsivity is one of the most stable characteristics of the general offender population, and promoting a more reflective outlook has been an aim of offender rehabilitation programmes since they began in earnest in the 1980s (McGuire, 1995). As a result of the often impoverished backgrounds from which many offenders come, many of the conditions necessary for the development of self-control (nutrition, rest, security, consistent parenting, a stimulating and loving environment; Tarullo, Obradovic, & Gunnar, 2009) are absent and instead a survival mentality is fostered (Nee & Ioannou, in press). Given that much of human behaviour is largely habit-driven and routine (Marteau et al., 2012; Strack & Deutsch, 2004), coaching this population to prioritise reflection over reward-driven, automatic processes will be no easy task. Mindfulness techniques may assist, and retraining automaticity as described above, may paradoxically improve awareness through discussion of the intended outcomes of the intervention. Furthermore, an agency-based approach to intervention is more likely to foster a sense of self-governance, self-efficacy, and reflection than traditional deficit-based approaches to rehabilitation, such as Reasoning and Rehabilitation (Ross & Fabiano, 1985), which developed as part of the RNR model. It has been noted, here, that different parts of the offending process appear more conducive to reflection (namely, the early phases before reward is very strongly influencing behaviour near the scene of the crime, and post-crime) though this is speculative at present in the absence of a robust body of research. The authors hope that in time the gaps in knowledge both here and in the proposed interventions above will be resolved and will assist in these aims.

Conclusion

To conclude, it is clear that the current conceptualisation of dynamic risk factors as merely a list of features that correlate with offending behaviours is minimalistic. Not only does it lack description and the inherent variation within these features, but it neglects the underlying psychological mechanisms that lead to and maintain offending behaviours. Therefore, other conceptualisation models, such as the AMR (Heffernan & Ward, 2015), are required to further the understanding of risk and ultimately reduce recidivism rates. Furthermore, the three phases of the offence chain (i.e. prior, during, and after a crime) need to be explored if researchers and practitioners are to accurately enhance their knowledge of the decisions that offenders make at each offence stage, as well as have awareness of expertise levels and the vulnerabilities that are present, which can increase the risk of the offence being committed again. To date, dynamic risk factors and their relationship with dysfunctional expertise, in offending populations, has never been examined. However, this review has shown that studying expertise in offenders is one example of how one can understand much more about the offending process and what underpins the various domains of dynamic risk factors, particularly in acquisitive and/or sexual offenders. Consequently, a more in-depth examination of these and other types of offending would contribute significantly to the offender rehabilitation literature and have significant implications for treatment. Further research is needed into the link between offender expertise, risk and rehabilitation, with more elaborate models being established to help explain the decision-chain of offending and the underlying mechanisms that cause individuals to commit crime.

Notes

1. Links between child sexual offending and dynamic risk factors will be covered in more depth in other articles within this special issue.
2. Burglary is an overwhelmingly male crime, hence why this review refers to the offender being male in the examples. However, for an unusual insight into the role of women in the undertaking of the crime, see Mullins and Wright (2003).

Disclosure statement

No potential conflict of interest was reported by the authors.

References

Andrews, D. A., & Bonta, J. (1995). *The level of service inventory – Revised.* Toronto: Multi-Health Systems.

Andrews, D. A., & Bonta, J. (2003). *The psychology of criminal conduct* (3rd ed.). Cincinnati, OH: Anderson.

Andrews, D. A., & Bonta, J. (2006). *The psychology of criminal conduct* (4th ed.). Newark, NJ: LexisNexis.

Andrews, D. A., & Bonta, J. (2010). Rehabilitation through the lens of the Risk-Needs-Responsivity model. In F. McNeil, P. Raynor, & C. Trotter (Eds.), *Offender supervision: New directions in theory, research and practice* (pp. 19–40). Cullompton: Willan.

Andrews, D. A., Bonta, J., & Hoge, R. D. (1990). Classification for effective rehabilitation: Rediscovering psychology. *Criminal Justice and Behavior, 17*(1), 19–52. doi:10.1177/0093854890017001004

Bargh, J. (1994). The four horsemen of automaticity: Awareness, intention, efficiency, and control in social cognition. In R. Wyer & T. Srull (Eds.), *Handbook of social cognition* (pp. 1–40). Hillsdale, NJ: Lawrence Erlbaum Associates.

Beard, C. (2011). Cognitive bias modification for anxiety: Current evidence and future directions. *Expert Review of Neurotherapeutics, 11*(2), 299–311. doi:10.1586/ern.10.194

Beech, A. R., & Craig, L. A. (2012). The current status of static and dynamic factors in sexual offender risk assessment. *Journal of Aggression, Conflict and Peace Research, 4*(4), 169–185. doi:10.1108/17596591211270671

Beech, A. R., & Ward, T. (2004). The integration of etiology and risk in sexual offenders: A theoretical framework. *Aggression and Violent Behavior, 10*(1), 31–63. doi:10.1016/j.avb.2003.08.002

Bennett, T., & Wright, R. (1984). *Burglars on burglary: Prevention and the offender.* Aldershot: Gower.

Bernasco, W., & Luykx, F. (2003). Effects of attractiveness, opportunity and accessibility to burglars on residential burglary rates of urban neighborhoods. *Criminology, 41*(3), 981–1002. doi:10.1111/j.1745-9125.2003.tb01011.x

Blair, I., & Banaji, M. (1996). Automatic and controlled processes in stereotype priming. *Journal of Personality and Social Psychology, 70*(6), 1142–1163. doi:10.1037//0022-3514.70.6.1142

Bonta, J. (1996). Risk-needs assessment and treatment. In A. T. Harland (Ed.), *Choosing correctional options that work: Defining the demand and evaluating the supply* (pp. 18–32). Thousand Oaks, CA: Sage.

Bonta, J., & Andrews, D. A. (1993). The level of supervision inventory: An overview. *IARCA Journal, 5,* 6–8.

Bourke, P., Ward, T., & Rose, C. (2012). Expertise and sexual offending: A preliminary empirical model. *Journal of Interpersonal Violence, 27*(12), 2391–2414. doi:10.1177/0886260511433513

Bratman, M. E. (1999). *Faces of intention: Selected essays on intention and agency.* New York, NY: Cambridge University Press.

Brookman, F. (2015). Killer decisions: The role of cognition and affect in homicide. *Aggression and Violent Behavior, 20,* 42–52. doi:10.1016/j.avb.2014.12.007

Brunton-Smith, I., & Hopkins, K. (2013). *The factors associated with proven re-offending following release from prison: Findings from Waves 1 to 3 of Surveying Prisoner Crime Reduction (SPCR).* Ministry of Justice Analytical Series. Retrieved from https://www.gov.uk/government/uploads/system/uploads/attachment_data/file/261620/re-offending-release-waves-1-3-spcr-findings.pdf

Butler, H., & Gannon, T. (2015). The scripts and expertise of firesetters: A preliminary conceptualization. *Aggression and Violent Behavior, 20,* 72–81. doi:10.1016/j.avb.2014.12.011

Casey, S. (2015). Drug-related offending: Expertise and decision making. *Aggression and Violent Behavior, 20,* 82–91. doi:10.1016/j.avb.2014.12.010

Chartrand, T. L., & Bargh, J. A. (2002). Nonconscious motivations: Their activation, operation, and consequences. In A. Tesser, D. Stapel, & J. Wood (Eds.), *Self and motivation: Emerging psychological perspectives* (pp. 13–41). Washington, DC: American Psychological Association.

Clare, J. (2011). Examination of systematic variations in burglars' domain-specific perceptual and procedural skills. *Psychology, Crime & Law, 17*(3), 199–214.

Coupe, T., & Blake, L. (2006). Daylight and darkness targeting strategies and the risks of being seen at residential burglaries. *Criminology, 44*(2), 431–464. doi:10.1111/j.1745-9125.2006.00054.x

Craig, L. A., Browne, K. D., & Beech, A. R. (2008). *Assessing risk in sex offenders: A practitioner's guide.* Chichester: Wiley.

Cromwell, P., Olson, J., & Avary, D. (1991). *Breaking and entering: An ethnographic analysis of burglary.* Newbury Park, CA: Sage.

Day, A., & Bowen, E. (2015). Offending competency and coercive control in intimate partner violence. *Aggression and Violent Behavior, 20*, 62–71. doi:10.1016/j.avb.2014.12.004

Deslauriers-Varin, N., & Beauregard, E. (2010). Victims' routine activities and sex offenders' target selection scripts: A latent class analysis. *Sexual Abuse: A Journal of Research and Treatment, 22*, 315–342. doi:10.1177/1079063210375975

Devine, P. (1989). Stereotypes and prejudice: Their automatic and controlled components. *Journal of Personality and Social Psychology, 56*(1), 5–18. doi:10.1037/0022-3514.56.1.5

Dowden, C., & Andrews, D. A. (2003). Does family intervention work for delinquents? Results of a meta-analysis. *Canadian Journal of Criminology and Criminal Justice, 45*(3), 327–342. doi:10.3138/cjccj.45.3.327

Dowden, C., & Andrews, D. A. (2004). The importance of staff practices in delivering effective correctional treatment: A meta-analysis of core correctional practices. *International Journal of Offender Therapy and Comparative Criminology, 48*(2), 203–214. doi:10.1177/0306624X03257765

Ericsson, K. A. (2006). An introduction to the Cambridge handbook of expertise and expert performance: Its development, organisation and content. In K. Ericsson, N. Charness, P. Feltovich, & R. Hoffman (Eds.), *The Cambridge handbook of expertise and expert performance* (pp. 3–20). Cambridge: Cambridge University Press.

Ferrante, A., & Clare, J. (2006). *'Known' burglars and the stolen goods market in Western Australia (Research Report)*. Perth: Office of Crime Prevention, Western Australian Department of Premier and Cabinet.

Fortune, C., Bourke, P., & Ward, T. (2015). Expertise and child sex offenders. *Aggression and Violent Behavior, 20*, 33–41. doi:10.1016/j.avb.2014.12.005

Gannon, T., & Ward, T. (2014). Where has all the psychology gone? A critical review of evidence-based psychological practice in correctional settings. *Aggression and Violent Behavior, 19*(4), 435–446. doi:10.1016/j.avb.2014.06.006

Garcia-Retamero, R., & Dhami, M. K. (2009). Take-the-best in expert-novice decision strategies for residential burglary. *Psychonomic Bulletin & Review, 16*(1), 163–169. doi:10.3758/PBR.16.1.163

Hanson, R. K., Bourgon, G., Helmus, L., & Hodgson, S. (2009). The principles of effective correctional treatment also apply to sexual offenders: A meta-analysis. *Criminal Justice and Behavior, 36*(9), 865–891. doi:10.1177/0093854809338545

Hanson, R. K., & Harris, A. J. R. (2000).Where should we intervene? Dynamic predictors of sexual offense recidivism. *Criminal Justice and Behavior, 27*(1), 6–35. doi:10.1177/0093854800027001002

Hanson, R. K., & Thornton, D. (2000). Improving risk assessments for sex offenders: A comparison of three actuarial scales. *Law and Human Behavior, 24*(1), 119–136. doi:10.1023/A:1005482921333

Harris, G. T., & Rice, M. E. (1997). Mentally disordered offenders: What research says about effective service. In C. D. Webster & M. A. Jackson (Eds.), *Impulsivity: Theory, assessment, and treatment* (pp. 361–393). New York, NY: The Guilford Press.

Hearndon, I., & Magill, C. (2004). *Decision-making by house burglars: Offenders' perspectives* (Home Office Research Findings No. 249). London: Home Office.

Heffernan, R., & Ward, T. (2015). The conceptualization of dynamic risk factors in child sex offenders: An agency model. *Aggression and Violent Behavior, 24*, 250–260. doi:10.1016/j.avb.2015.07.001

Hoffman, R., Shadbolt, N., Burton, A., & Klein, G. (1995). Eliciting knowledge from experts: A methodological analysis. *Organizational Behavior and Human Decision Processes, 62*(2), 129–158. doi:10.1006/obhd.1995.1039

Holmes, E. A., Lang, T. J., & Shah, D. M. (2009). Developing interpretation bias modification as a "cognitive vaccine" for depressed mood: Imagining positive events makes you feel better than thinking about them verbally. *Journal of Abnormal Psychology, 118*(1), 76–88. doi:10.1037/a0012590

Homel, R., Macintyre, S., & Wortley, R. (2014). How burglars decide on targets: A computer based scenario approach. In B. LeClerc & R. Wortley (Eds.), *Cognition and crime: Offender decision making and script analyses* (pp. 26–47). Oxford: Routledge.

Kahneman, D. (2011). *Thinking, fast and slow*. New York, NY: Farrar, Strauss, Giroux.

Katz, J. (1988). *Seductions of crime: Moral and sensual attractions in doing evil* (5th ed.). New York, NY: Basic Books.

Kemshall, H. (2001). *Risk assessment and management of known sexual and violent offenders: A review of current issues* (Home Office Police Research Series Paper 140). London: Home Office.

Klein, G. (2009). *Streetlights and shadows: Searching for the keys to adaptive decision making*. Cambridge: MIT Press.

Leclerc, B., Carpentier, J., & Proulx, J. (2006). Strategies adopted by sexual offenders to involve children in sexual activity. In R. Wortley & S. Smallbone (Eds.), *Situational prevention of child sexual abuse, crime prevention studies* (Vol. 19, pp. 251–270). Monsey, NY: Criminal Justice Press.

Logie, R. H., Wright, R. T., & Decker, S. H. (1992). Recognition memory performance and residential burglary. *Applied Cognitive Psychology, 6*(2), 109–123. doi:10.1002/acp.2350060203

Macleod, C., & Mathews, A. (1988). Anxiety and the allocation of attention to threat. *The Quarterly Journal of Experimental Psychology Section A: Human Experimental Psychology, 40*(4), 653–670. doi:10.1080/14640748808402292

Mann, R. E., Hanson, R. K., & Thornton, D. (2010). Assessing risk for sexual recidivism: Some proposals on the nature of psychologically meaningful risk factors. *Sexual Abuse: A Journal of Research and Treatment, 22*(2), 191–217. doi:10.1177/1079063210366039

Marteau, T. M., French, D. P., Griffin, S. J., Prevost, A. T., Sutton, S., Watkinson, C., … Hollands, G. J. (2010). Effects of communicating DNA-based disease risk estimates on risk-reducing behaviours. *The Cochrane Database of Systematic Reviews* (10), CD007275. doi:10.1002/14651858.CD007275.pub2

Marteau, T. M., Hollands, G. J., & Fletcher, P. C. (2012). Changing human behaviour to prevent disease: The importance of targeting automatic processes. *Science, 337*, 1492–1495. doi:10.1126/science.1226918

Maruna, S. (2001). *Making good: How ex-convicts reform and rebuild their lives*. Washington, DC: American Psychological Association.

McGuire, J. (1995). *What works: Reducing reoffending. Guidelines from research and practice*. (J. McGuire, Ed.). Chichester: John Wiley.

Mullins, C. W., & Wright, R. (2003). Gender, social networks, and residential burglary. *Criminology, 41* (3), 813–840. doi:10.1111/j.1745-9125.2003.tb01005.x

Nee, C. (2015). Understanding expertise in burglars: From pre-conscious scanning to action and beyond. *Aggression and Violent Behavior, 20*, 53–61. doi:10.1016/j.avb.2014.12.006

Nee, C., & Ioannou, S. (in press). What have neuroscientific approaches to research taught us about acquisitive offenders?

Nee, C., & Meenaghan, A. (2006). Expert decision-making in burglars. *British Journal of Criminology, 46* (5), 935–949. doi:10.1093/bjc/azl013

Nee, C., & Taylor, M. (1988). Residential burglary in the Republic of Ireland: A situational perspective. *Howard Journal, 27*(2), 105–116. doi:10.1111/j.1468-2311.1988.tb00609.x

Nee, C., & Taylor, M. (2000). Examining burglars' target selection: Interview, experiment, or ethnomethodology? *Psychology, Crime & Law, 6*(1), 45–59.

Nee, C., & Ward, T. (2015). Review of expertise and its general implications for correctional psychology and criminology. *Aggression and Violent Behavior, 20*, 1–9. doi:10.1016/j.avb.2014.12.002

Nee, C., White, M., Woolford, K., Pascu, T., Barker, L., & Wainwright, L. (2015). New methods for examining expertise in burglars in natural and simulated environments: Preliminary findings. *Psychology Crime and Law, 21*(5), 507–513. doi:10.1080/1068316X.2014.989849

O'Ciardha, C. (2015). Experts in rape: Evaluating the evidence for a novice-to-expert continuum in the offense behavior and cognition of sexual offenders. *Aggression and Violent Behavior, 20*, 26–32. doi:10.1016/j.avb.2014.12.003

Office for National Statistics. (2014). Crime in England and Wales, year ending December 2013. *Statistical Bulletin*. Retrieved from http://www.ons.gov.uk/ons/dcp171778_360216.pdf

Papies, E. K. (2012). Goal priming in dieters: Recent insights and applications. *Current Obesity Reports, 1*(2), 99–105. doi:10.1007/s13679-012-0009-8

Quinsey, V. L., Harris, G. T., Rice, M. E., & Cormier, C. A. (2006). *Violent offenders: Appraising and managing risk* (2nd ed.). Washington, DC: American Psychological Association.

Raynor, P., Kynch, J., Roberts, R., & Merrington, S. (2000). *Risk and need assessment in probation services: An evaluation* (Home Office Research Study 211). London: Home Office.

Rengert, G. F., & Wasilchick, J. (2000). *Suburban burglary: A tale of two suburbs.* Chicago, IL: Thomas.

Roberto, C. A., Baik, J., Harris, J. L., & Brownell, K. D. (2010). Influence of licensed characters on children's taste and snack preferences. *Pediatrics, 126*(1), 88–93. doi:10.1542/peds.2009-3433

Rogers, R. (2000). The uncritical acceptance of risk assessment in forensic practice. *Law and Human Behavior, 24*(5), 595–605. doi:10.1023/A:1005575113507

Ross, R. R., & Fabiano, E. A. (1985). *Time to think: A cognitive model of delinquency prevention and rehabilitation.* Johnson City, TN: Institute of Social Sciences and Arts.

Sample, L. L., & Bray, T. M. (2006). Are sex offenders different? An examination of rearrest patterns. *Criminal Justice Policy Review, 17*(1), 83–102. doi:10.1177/0887403405282916

Shanteau, J. (1992). How much information does an expert use? Is it relevant? *Acta Psychologica, 81* (1), 75–86. doi:10.1016/0001-6918(92)90012-3

Shover, N. (1973). The social organization of burglary. *Social Problems, 20*(4), 499–514. doi:10.2307/799711

Shover, N. (1996). *Great pretenders: Pursuits and careers of persistent thieves.* Boulder, CO: Westview Press.

Snook, B., Dhami, M. K., & Kavanagh, J. (2011). Simply criminal: Predicting burglars' occupancy decisions with a simple heuristic. *Law and Human Behavior, 35*(4), 316–326. doi:10.1007/s10979-010-9238-0

Strack, F., & Deutsch, R. (2004). Reflective and impulsive determinants of social behaviour. *Personality and Social Psychology Review, 8*(3), 220–247. doi:10.1207/s15327957pspr0803_1

Tarling, R. (1993). *Analysing offending: Data, models and interpretations.* London: HMSO.

Tarullo, A. R., Obradovic, J., & Gunnar, M. R. (2009). Self-control and the developing brain. *Zero to Three, 29*, 31–37. Retrieved from http://web.stanford.edu/group/sparklab/pdf/Tarullo,20Obradovic,20Gunnar20(2009,200-3)20Self-Control20and20the20Developing%20Brain.pdf

Taylor, M., & Nee, C. (1988). The role of cues in simulated residential burglary: A preliminary investigation. *British Journal of Criminology, 28*, 396–401. Retrieved from http://bjc.oxfordjournals.org/content/28/3/396.full.pdf

Thornton, D. (2002). Constructing and testing a framework for dynamic risk assessment. *Sexual Abuse: A Journal of Research and Treatment, 14*, 137–151. doi:10.1177/107906320201400205

Thornton, D. (2013). Implications of our developing understanding of risk and protective factors in the treatment of adult male sexual offenders. *International Journal of Behavioral Consultation and Therapy, 8*(3–4), 62–65. Retrieved from http://www.baojournal.com/IJBCT/IJBCT-8_3-4/A12.pdf

Topalli, V. (2005). Criminal expertise and offender decision-making: An experimental analysis of how offenders and non-offenders differentially perceive social stimuli. *British Journal of Criminology, 45* (3), 269–295. doi:10.1093/bjc/azh086

Topalli, V. (2006). The seductive nature of autotelic crime: How neutralization theory serves as a boundary condition for understanding street crime. *Sociological Inquiry, 76*(4), 475–501. doi:10.1111/j.1475-682X.2006.00167.x

Topalli, V., Jacques, S., & Wright, R. (2015). "It takes skills to take a car": Perceptual and procedural expertise in carjacking. *Aggression and Violent Behavior, 20*, 19–25. doi:10.1016/j.avb.2014.12.001

Vieraitis, L., Copes, H., Powell, Z., & Pike, A. (2015). A little information goes a long way: Expertise and identity theft. *Aggression and Violent Behavior, 20*, 10–18. doi:10.1016/j.avb.2014.12.008

Ward, T. (1999). Competency and deficit models in the understanding and treatment of sexual offenders. *Journal of Sex Research, 36*(3), 298–305. doi:10.1080/00224499909552000

Ward, T. (2014). The explanation of sexual offending: From single factor theories to integrative pluralism. *Journal of Sexual Aggression, 20*(2), 130–141. doi:10.1080/13552600.2013.870242

Ward, T. (2015). Detection of dynamic risk factors and correctional practice. *Criminology & Public Policy, 14*(1), 105–111. doi:10.1111/1745-9133.12115

Ward, T., & Beech, A. R. (2015). Dynamic risk factors: A theoretical dead-end? *Psychology, Crime & Law, 21*(2), 100–113.

Ward, T., & Brown, M. (2004). The good lives model and conceptual issues in offender rehabilitation. *Psychology, Crime, and Law, 10*(3), 243–257. doi:10.1080/10683160410001662744

Ward, T., & Hudson, S. M. (2000). Sexual offenders' implicit planning: A conceptual model. *Sexual Abuse: A Journal of Research and Treatment, 12*, 189–202. doi:10.1023/A:1009534109157

Ward, T., & Maruna, S. (2007). *Rehabilitation: Beyond the risk assessment paradigm*. London: Routledge.

Ward, T., Melser, J., & Yates, P. (2007). Reconstructing the Risk-Need-Responsivity model: A theoretical elaboration and evaluation. *Aggression and Violent Behavior, 12*(2), 208–228. doi:10.1016/j.avb.2006.07.001

Ward, T., & Stewart, C. A. (2003). The treatment of sex offenders: Risk management and good lives. *Professional Psychology: Research and Practice, 34*(4), 353–360. doi:10.1037/0735-7028.34.4.353

Watkins, E. R., Baeyens, C. B., & Read, R. (2009). Concreteness training reduces dysphoria: Proof-of-principle for repeated cognitive bias modification in depression. *Journal of Abnormal Psychology, 118*(1), 55–64. doi:10.1037/a0013642

Webb, T. L., & Sheeran, P. (2010). A viable, integrative framework for contemporary research in health psychology: Commentary on Hall and Fong's temporal self-regulation theory. *Health Psychology Review, 4*(2), 79–82. doi:10.1080/17437191003717497

Woollett, K., & Maguire, E. (2010). The effect of navigational expertise on wayfinding in new environments. *Journal of Environmental Psychology*, 30(4), 565–573. doi:10.1016/j.jenvp.2010.03.003

Wright, R. T., & Decker, S. H. (1994). *Burglars on the job: Streetlife and residential break-ins*. Boston, MA: Northeastern University Press.

Wright, R. T., Logie, R. H., & Decker, S. H. (1995). Criminal expertise and offender decision making: An experimental study of the target selection process in residential burglary. *Journal of Research in Crime and Delinquency, 32*(1), 39–53. doi:10.1177/0022427895032001002

Problems in the measurement of dynamic risk factors in sexual offenders

Anthony R. Beech[a], Helen C. Wakeling[b], Filip Szumski[c] and Nick Freemantle[d]

[a]Centre for Forensic and Criminological Psychology, University of Birmingham, Birmingham, UK; [b]Commissioning Strategies Group, National Offender Management Service, London, UK; [c]Institute of Psychology, Adam Mickiewicz University, Poznań, Poland; [d]Department of Primary Care and Population Health, University College London, London, UK

ABSTRACT

Having valid and reliable tools to measure 'dynamic' risk factors and minimising assessor bias is said to be critical in helping to make decisions regarding how individuals convicted of committing crime should be managed and treated, and how resources within the Justice System should be prioritised. This article outlines the problems and issues associated with the measurement of such putative dynamic risk factors (see Ward, 2015 [Dynamic risk factors: Scientific kinds or predictive constructs. *Psychology, Crime and Law.*, *22*(1–2), 2–16], this volume for a critique of current conceptions of these), and suggests ways of ensuring that measurement is conducted in the most appropriate way for the population being dealt with. Specifically, we would note that the evidence suggests that psychometric analysis, and structured professional judgment can be used to measure dynamic psychological problems using *some* tools within *some* samples. However, their use can be hindered by a number of conceptual factors including how the tests are designed and used, their reliability and validity, the context in which they are used, and the samples used. Finally, we would note that interviews are also an important part in the process of dynamic assessment.

Introduction

The ability to measure those risk factors that are likely to raise, or reduce, an individual's likelihood of committing further crime is crucial if the Criminal Justice System is to be successful in reducing recidivism. Within the forensic field, two main types of features are employed in this approach, referred to as static, and dynamic, risk factors (Andrews & Bonta, 2010). Static risk factors are relatively fixed features, which cannot be deliberately changed and have been found to have a reliable relationship with sexual re-offending (e.g. Hanson & Morton-Bourgon, 2009), examples here include criminal history and age. Such items in the Criminal Justice System are typically been pooled together into actuarial assessments, which are statistically derived tools designed to predict the likelihood of a future risky behaviours (Beech, Fisher, & Thornton, 2003). In terms of assessing 'dangerousness' these tools put individuals into risk groups who differ reliably in their rates of reconviction. The term 'mechanical tools' (Hanson & Morton-Bourgon, 2009) is used to describe tools that have a defined set of items, and a defined (actuarial) method for producing an overall risk level. Such actuarial risk assessment tools in general are good predictors of reconviction and outperform other forms of risk assessment (Hanson & Morton-Bourgon, 2009).

However, due to the fact that such tools are based on fixed, static risk factors, they cannot tell us whether a psychological or behavioural change on other 'changeable' risk factors is meaningful in terms of reducing or increasing the chances of further offending. Some have said that these, therefore, lack practical utility in assessing treatment change (e.g. Douglas & Kropp, 2002). In contrast, dynamic risk factors have the potential to change, and are associated with a reduction or increase in recidivism rate when changed (Hanson, 1998). Such risk factors are also often described as *criminogenic needs* (see Ward, 2015, for a critique of current conceptions of dynamic risk factors). These are often pooled together into structured professional judgment (SPJ) approaches, or guided clinical judgment tools, to provide frameworks with which to assess those who have been convicted of committing crime. Within such tools, the judgment of clinicians is aided by guidelines designed to support clinical judgment (Tully, Chou, & Browne, 2013). While in the sexual offender field, there are also examples of semi-actuarial instruments of dynamic risk factors (e.g. the Sex Offender Need Assessment Rating, SONAR, Hanson & Harris, 2000; and the STABLE and ACUTE-2007, Hanson, Harris, Scott, & Helmus, 2007).

A variety of different methodologies have been employed to measure the presence of dynamic risk factors in sexual offenders in the forensic literature (see Craissati & Beech, 2003). These include examining information obtained from self-report psychometric measures (e.g. Hudson, Wales, Bakker, & Ward, 2002), using SPJ (i.e. subjective ratings of presence of risk factors rated by clinicians; Olver, Wong, Nicholaichuk, & Gordon, 2007), interview (Beech, 2001), or using a triangulation of these methods. Each of these has associated conceptual problems. Hence, the measurement of dynamic risk factors is a complex process, and one that we do not aim to untangle in the present article. Instead we wish to describe the issues associated with measurement, and offer ways of ensuring that measurement is conducted in the most appropriate way for the populations being dealt with. We will now discuss various methods in turn, and highlight the conceptual issues associated with these different methods of measurement of dynamic risk factors in sexual offenders.

Psychometric measurement of dynamic risk factors

The most frequently used tools within the field of applied psychology are psychometric measures. Psychometrics is the field of study relating to the development and refinement of theoretical approaches to measurement and the construction of instruments and procedures for measurement (Michael & Li, 2010). Self-report psychometric measures are used to tap unobservable (latent) variables, and measure personality traits, abilities, attitudes and knowledge. The most commonly applied psychometric theory in the field of psychology is classical test theory (CTT). CTT relates to the breaking down of an individual's observed score on a test into what is deemed a true score component, that is free from error (internal or external). The aim of CTT is to understand and improve the reliability of psychological tests, by examining sources of error one at a time.

Item Response Theory (IRT) is a more recent psychometric theory or set of theories, which examines the responses on psychometric measures as patterns (Nunnally & Bernstein, 1994). IRT applies mathematical models to data gathered from psychometric measures in order to measure the latent variables. This theory assumes that there is a correlation between an individual's response on one item and their overall ability on the latent trait being assessed. Therefore, the assumption behind the most basic IRT model is that items vary only with respect to their difficulty. Whichever of these theories is utilised, researchers and developers of psychometric tools must demonstrate that the tools they use are reliable and valid, which are the most important aspects of a psychometric test (Rust & Golombok, 1999). The types of reliability and validity considered in such tests are shown in Table 1.

Psychometric measures assess latent variables, or in other words, dynamic risk factors, in forensic settings. Within offending behaviour treatment programmes they are used primarily to measure those dynamic risk factors (treatment need areas), which are targeted in those programmes. They are usually completed before the start, and typically at the end, of treatment. Hence, psychometrics tools are often used for evaluation purposes determining the short-term impact of treatment programmes delivered to offenders in prison and community settings (see Wakeling & Travers, 2010). They are also used to help identify areas of treatment need and to help determine individual treatment change (e.g. Wakeling & Barnett, 2014). However, in order to have confidence in the use of such assessment

Table 1. Reliability and validity assessment.

Reliability assessments refers to the accuracy of the tool in question, it can be measured in the following ways:

(1) The **internal consistency** of a scale examines the level to which the items are all measuring the same characteristic or latent variable of interest. It assesses the precision between items of a scale by assessing the inter-correlation between items. If the items of a scale are measuring the same overall construct, then you would expect the scores on each of the items to correlate both with each other, and the overall scale. Cronbach's alpha (Cronbach, 1951; Kline, 1993, 2000) is often regarded to be the preferred measure of internal consistency;

(2) **Test-retest reliability** of a scale measures how stable the test is over time. If the correlation between scores at two different time points is high, then the test can be regarded as being potentially useful;

(3) **Split half reliability** of the scale estimates reliability based on the correlation of two equivalent forms of a measure. Again if correlations are high, the reliability of the tool can be regarded as useful;

(4) The **Inter-rater reliability** of the measure assesses the correlation of scores between or among two, or more raters, who rate the same item, scale or tool. Many guidelines for interpreting reliability estimates exist in the literature. For research purposes, Nunnally and Bernstein (1994) suggest that .70 is the minimum sufficient reliability estimate. However, others have proposed that if psychometric scores are being used for clinical purposes, that a reliability of .85, or higher is required (Rosenthal & Rosnow, 1991) to ensure a tool is useful.

Validity assessment refers to how well the tools measure what they intend to measure. Measures cannot be valid without being reliable: that is the reliability of a measure is a necessary, but not sufficient, condition for validity. The main forms of validity are:

(1) **Face validity** which refers to an appraisal of whether the tool appears to be a credible and whether the items contain plausible content of the construct under scrutiny;

(2) **Content validity** which refers to how well the tool can sample the content in the domain of interest, in relation to theory. Both face and content validity involve examining the tool's items in detail, and qualitatively reviewing their suitability in terms of what they appear to measure (face), and in accordance with the theoretical background of the construct (content);

(3) **Construct validity** which can be examined using convergent and discriminant validity. ***(3a) Convergent validity*** measures the extent to which the construct of interest is similar to other theoretically related constructs;
(3b) Discriminant validity examines the extent to which the construct of interest is unrelated to other constructs, which are assumed to be largely independent. Discriminant validity can also be examined in terms of the measures ability to discriminate between groups who should score differently on the construct in question;

(4) **Criterion validity** evaluates the comparison of the measure with some other standard. Criterion validity can be examined by looking at the concurrent validity and the predictive validity. Concurrent validity compares the psychometric test with another test that already exists, that is another measure of the same latent variable, whereas predictive validity examines the extent to which the construct can predict some type of criterion to be tested in the future, such as for example, future recidivism.

measures (within research and/or clinical practice), researchers and clinicians need to be certain that the measures employed are both valid and reliable (see Table 1), are measuring what they purport to measure, and are related to the outcome of interest (Grady, Broderson, & Abramson, 2011). Of utmost importance is the need for psychometrics to have good discriminant and predictive validity. That is, they must have a demonstrated relationship with the main outcome of interest – future reconviction. Decisions about treatment need and progress may have a direct impact on an individual's progression through the criminal justice system, and therefore there are ethical considerations regarding the selection of tests, their reliability and validity, and their use within resource allocation, treatment and risk assessment. Table 2 provides a brief summary of the benefits and drawbacks of the use of psychometrics tools in practice.

Issues in using psychometric measurement to assess dynamic risk

The literature generally indicates that psychometrics can have good levels of reliability, particularly internal consistency and inter-rater reliability. What is less clear and often more problematic, is how *valid* psychometrics are, particularly their levels of discriminative and predictive validity. In order to be accurate measures of dynamic risk factors, these validity checks are of the utmost importance. Walters (2006) conducted a review on the ability of dynamic risk assessment tools, and a number of self-report psychometrics, to predict general reconviction and violence. The main finding was that psychometric scores could predict outcome as well as other risk assessment tools, but only as long as the psychometrics used were designed to measure those constructs that were empirically related to risk of reoffending.

In a review of the available psychometric measures to use with sexual offenders and to measure appropriate dynamic risk factors, Grady et al. (2011) conclude that there are few valid and reliable instruments available to researchers and clinicians to accurately measure

Table 2. Benefits and shortcomings of using psychometric measures.

Benefits

- They are objective measures, and have clear methods to follow to produce an overall score.
- There are also usually structured guidelines for how to both produce and interpret a score, thereby reducing the possibility of introducing subjectivity into the production and interpretation of scores. As such, assessor bias should not interfere with the use of a psychometric (though this does not mean that bias in interpretation cannot be observed).
- They are economical to administer, as they can be conducted in group settings, and are therefore a convenient method of gathering information with minimal possibility of assessor biases.

Shortcomings

- The results depend upon individuals possessing a level of personal reflection and insight, which may not always be present in offender populations.
- Self-report measures have been criticised in the criminological literature for being particularly susceptible to individuals lying, faking, and/or responding in a socially desirable way (e.g. Holden, Kroner, Fekken, & Popham, 1992; Schretlen & Arkowitz, 1990; Tierney & McCabe, 2001).
- Individuals filling out such measures in way to protect their personal identities, and to reduce feelings of shame and guilt associated with their offending. However, this might be a healthy stance for offenders to take, particularly in light of the desistance literature (e.g. Maruna, 2001), which indicates that development of a pro-social and positive identify is key to desisting from crime.
- All of the problems associated with the general use of psychometrics may in fact be exacerbated in an offender population, due to the fact that an individual's progression through the criminal justice system may, in part, depend on the outcome of psychometric testing.

sexual offenders' areas of deficits (see Wakeling & Barnett, 2014, for a review of studies specific to sexual offenders). Hence there is a need to identify specific instruments that can be used and are validated with sexual offenders. Such an approach will enable a better understanding of the dynamic risk factors of sexual offenders. Selection of the appropriate measures is therefore critical, alongside the need for more research to fully validate appropriate measures to use with sexual offenders.

Some studies in the literature have found psychometrics to have good predictive validity in a number of forensic areas (e.g. Loza et al., 2004; Loza & Loza-Fanous, 2000, 2003; Mills, Loza, & Kroner, 2003), other studies have found the opposite to be true (e.g. Bowen, Gilchrist, & Beech, 2005; Hanson, Cox, & Woszczyna, 1991; Hanson, Steffy, & Gauthier, 1993; Hanson & Wallace-Capretta, 2000; Wilkinson, 2005). While in part this may be to do with the psychometric measures not measuring factors relevant to risk, the discrepancy observed could also be due to the use of out-dated, or non-standardised, tests in some of the studies, or the use of tests not specifically designed/validated with offenders (e.g. Proulx et al., 1997).

Hence, not only do psychometric measures need to reflect the constructs thought to be related to risk factors in order to be useful as measurement tools, but they also need to reflect modern societal views and language, and they need to be validated with the specific population they intend to be used with. This latter point includes ensuring tools are validated with particular subsets of the offending population. Just because a particular tool is validated with an adult offender population, this does not mean, for example, that it will necessarily be valid with a young offender population. It is also important to ensure tools are validated with the specific population of interest. This includes paying attention to factors such as gender, age, offending type, and literacy level. This latter point is of particular importance, due to the higher levels of intellectual difficulty observed in the offender population in comparison to the non-offender populations (e.g. Hayes, Shackell, Mottram, & Lancaster, 2007; Mason & Murphy, 2002).

The way the psychometrics data are gathered may have a significant impact on their results. Additionally, how they are introduced to the individual, how consent is gained, how questions regarding completion of the measure in question are responded to, and practice effects (i.e. how often an individual has been asked to complete a test), can all have an impact on the results obtained. Most importantly, if psychometrics are collected as part of a research context, and individuals are told that the results will have no bearing on them or their progression, they might produce very different results to the same psychometric used in a clinical context, when the individuals know that the results will feed into risk reports and/or their progression through the criminal justice system. Therefore, there are likely differences between the reliability and validity of psychometrics when used for research as opposed to when used in real clinical settings. This is not only because the methods used to gather these data are often different for these two contexts, but the impact the findings may have on the offender may also differ. This provides difficulties for the field, as it is often hard to generalise about various measurement methodologies from research studies to routine use. It is thus extremely important to assess the reliability and validity of a tool in the *context* in which it is going to be used.

There are also ethical issues in administering psychometrics that need to be mentioned, and which may also have a bearing on the results produced. Individuals must provide their informed consent for assessment, which necessitates them having: (1) the knowledge required to make an informed decision about whether or not to do an assessment; (2) having the rationality and the ability to understand the proposed assessment; (3) not being under any sort of coercion or influence to take part in the assessment (Lyden & Peters, 2004).

All of the above are difficult in a forensic setting, particularly when individuals are often required to undertake psychometrics as part the assessment process for interventions and when it might appear to hinder progression if they are not willing to comply with psychologist or professional requests for assessment. As such, individuals might consent to taking part in a psychometric assessment, but at the same time might feel under pressure to do so. Evidence also indicates that psychometric measure results are more valid indicators of risk of reoffending, when not gathered for risk assessment purposes (Mann, Ware, & Fernandez, 2011). When individuals believe that their risk is being examined, it seems that their responses become less valid. This is often believed to be because they want to present themselves in a favourable way and show a reduction in their risk. Indeed, socially desirable responding is a particular issue with psychometric assessment, which is difficult to quantify, particularly with offender populations. We will now examine the structured assessment approach to examining dynamic risk factors.

SPJ assessment of dynamic risk factors

SPJ tools are commonly used as measurement tools for dynamic risk factors (either with or without the addition of psychometric data). Such tools assess a list of risk factors which are specified in advance, and which are known to relate to risk of offending, examples include antisocial behaviour, violent attitudes. The overall evaluation of risk relies on the risk assessor/evaluator. As such there are usually no set rules for combining the information to produce an overall risk classification. Well-known examples of such tools include the Historical-Clinical-Risk Management-20 (HCR-20; Douglas et al., 2014), the Sexual Violence Risk-20 (SVR-20: Boer, Hart, Kropp, & Webster, 1997), and the Risk for Sexual Violence Protocol (RSVP: Hart, Kropp, & Laws, 2003).

Research indicates that SPJ tools are better predictors of outcome than unstructured clinical judgment (Hanson & Morton-Bourgon, 2009). That is to say, assessing dynamic risk factors using a specified list of factors for determining the presence or absence of these risk factors, provide better estimates of future reconviction, than the clinician using his/her own judgment about risk. Hanson and Morton-Bourgon (2009) provide good evidence of this occurring in their meta-analysis, where they examined the accuracy of adjusting actuarial assessment. Here, three studies were identified where professionals to take into account factors external to the static risk assessment adjusted actuarial assessments. Across these studies, with all types of assessors, tools and offence outcomes, the adjusted actuarial scores were worse at predicting reoffending than the unadjusted scores. Hence, this is an argument to say that introducing subjective opinion into the assessment, made the assessment less valid.

Issues in measuring dynamic risk using SPJ

It is important that the tools selected have been shown to have good inter-rater reliability, and good test-retest reliability (see Table 1). That is to say that if two assessors use the same tool on the same person being assessed, the same risk assessment conclusions should be reached. While, if an assessor conducted two assessments on the same individual being assessed over a short time period (with no intervening intervention) then the results should be broadly similar. Additionally, having predictive validity is again important; as well as ensuring the tools being used have been validated with the specific population of interest. For example, a tool that has been developed and tested with adult male offenders may not be suitable to be used with adult female offenders.

When using SPJ tools, the reliability and validity of the outcome can be affected by the sources of information that are examined. Therefore, it is important that a variety of different sources are examined and that final decisions are based on all sources; and that consideration has been given to all of the evidence, not simply, for example, what an individual has said during an interview. This corroborating or counter evidence helps to ensure a fair and balanced assessment process. Sources of evidence should also include information from others who know the offender well, such as hostel staff, wing staff, personal officers, file review and previous reports. It should be noted however, that simply asking observers for their opinion might not be sufficient. They may not understand the significance or relevance of what they observe and their opinion may be biased. As such, it is important to formulate indicators of risk and progress for the offender and ask others to rate these items in a more objective manner, if possible.

Assessor bias is also an issue with SPJ tools. There are a number of ways in which assessor bias can be reduced. Principally, professionals need to be aware of their own biases, and any tendency they have towards over, or underestimating, risk level. Mills and Kroner (2006), for example, have shown that assessors tend to overestimate recidivism rates attached to descriptive risk categories (low, medium and high), regardless of whether they have information on base rates of offending. These researchers found that personal fear of violence, age, gender and years of practice also influence assessors' perceptions of risk. Monahan (1981) presents a number of theorised reasons for the over-prediction of risk, as follows:

(1) assessors are particularly vulnerable to erring on the side of caution. They may tend to judge someone as risky because of the seriousness of the consequences of an individual committing a further offence. Some suggest that in recent times there has been a real, and general, shift towards public protection concerns over the rights of the offender, who may be wrongly classified as at high risk of committing another offence (Snacken, 2006);
(2) assessors may be prone to making illusory correlations: that is to link factors not related to risk, to their assessment of an individual. An example includes determining that someone is more risky because they do not possess good levels of victim empathy, or they do not accept responsibility for their offending;
(3) assessors may also tend to associate riskiness to cultural issues, which they might not fully understand. For example, where there might exist cultural differences between the offender and the assessor, the assessor may have trouble understanding the context in which the offender lives and operates, which may in turn lead the assessor to overestimate risk by placing too much relevance on these different cultural backgrounds. Such differences can also cause difficulty in establishing rapport between

the offender and the assessor, and as such may reduce the quality of information obtained during interview;

(4) finally, there is a tendency for assessors to see riskiness as a trait, and in doing so assessors may exclude other variables that might have a positive influence on the offender, such as social support or positive peer influences. It is important that when using SPJ tools, assessors follow the guidance provided with the tool as best they can, and attempt to reduce their assessor bias as best they can. Being aware of the notion of assessor bias is a good starting point. We will now examine the semi-actuarial measurement of dynamic risk factors stressing the similarities, and differences, between that approach and the SPJ.

Semi-actuarial measurement of dynamic risk factors

Semi-actuarial instruments of dynamic risk factors, which have been shown to have good inter-rater reliability, and predictive validity include: the SONAR (Hanson & Harris, 2000); and the STABLE and ACUTE-2007, Hanson, Harris, Scott, & Helmus, 2007). These instruments cannot be considered as 'completely actuarial', because their items refer to psychological characteristics and assessing them is much more subjective than assessing the presence of the static risk factors. Although, they are intended to identify the presence of dynamic risk factor in an actuarial way, they are what Hanson and Morton-Bourgon (2009) labelled as 'mechanical measures'. Using instruments belonging to this group is a similar process to using other to SPJ tools. However, there are a few differences that make the process less clinical and more actuarial. The lists of specified factors are shorter, the assessment process has more structure, and the factors are not as general, and time demanding, to score as in SPJ tools (like, for example the 'major mental illness' factor in HCR-20 and RSVP). There is limited evidence that the semi-actuarial measurement of dynamic risk add incremental validity when they are combined with actuarial measurement of static risk factors (Eher, Matthes, Schilling, Haubner-Maclean, & Rettenberger, 2012; Looman & Abracen, 2012). But these semi-actuarial tools are less subjective than other SPJ instruments.

Issues in semi-actuarial measurement of dynamic risk factors

The validity of semi-actuarial instruments is impacted by how they are used in the criminal justice system. Originally they were intended for use, like other actuarial tools, by not only mental health professional, but also by others involved in criminal justice systems, specifically prison officers. Harris and Hanson (2010) report that some officers, in their study, showed reduced motivation in the assessment process and thus their predictive accuracy is only marginally better than chance. The reduced motivation in non-mental health professionals might be due to two reasons: (1) the officers perceive the assessment as an additional duty which distracts them from their primary obligations; (2) lack of psychological knowledge may lead to perceiving psychological characteristics that are assessed as considerably less complex than they are and therefore perceiving the assessment of them as of low importance. Once the motivation is lowered, the officers are more prone to be biased and more careless in making their assessment decision.

We believe that the answer to this issue is not limiting the usage of semi-actuarial instruments, but comprehensive training and, especially, evaluating the performance before attempting risk assessments that may affect human lives. The abovementioned remarks concern the importance of the tool selection and evidence corroboration in SPJ measurement of dynamic risk factors. The stronger structure of semi-actuarial measurement of dynamic risk factors is intended to make the measurement less biased. On the downside, following such a strict procedure may divert attention from corroborating the evidences.

Assessment of dynamic risk by interview

This review will not be complete without a brief review of issues involved in the interview process often involved as part of the risk assessment process, which is outlined below (see Beech, 2001). The process of interview can be a necessary, but not sufficient, component of a dynamic risk assessment, therefore it is important that assessor's adapt their style to the individual with whom they are working. The approach and style used can have a significant impact on the quality and reliability of a risk assessment. The forum in which this is most relevant is in the risk assessment interview or the information gathering process. In order to get the most out of the interview, assessors should consider how best to build rapport, structure the interview and present the questions they wish to ask. Anxiety impedes performance and, as such, it is really important that any assessment starts with rapport building exercises.

The order in which questions are asked can also impact on the information received; commencing an interview with positive protective factors, can for example help with getting individuals to open up and get used to the process, before they move on to talk about more difficult topics, such as their risk factors. It is also essential to ensure use of the approaches and techniques that might work best for the individual in question. For example, the use of visual, auditory and kinaesthetic methods in interview may be really helpful. Research suggests that individuals with intellectual disabilities benefit when material is presented using multi-modal communication methods for example (Hurley, DesNoyers, Daniel, & Pfadt, 1998). There are several ways that the relevance and reliability of the information gathered can be affected: (1) if the offender does not understand what is being assessed and why, then the information obtained during interview can be severely compromised; (2) being aware that the assessment is a collaborative process, that is more accurate assessments will be produced if the assessor gets the offender 'on board' with the process from the outset; (3) being responsive to the needs of the offender and treating them as an individual can really help in building rapport and communicating effectively. In the final section of the paper we will briefly discuss changes in the level of dynamic risk in treatment.

Measurement of change in dynamic risk in sexual offenders

Similar to the measurement of the presence of dynamic risk factors, the identification of treatment change, or within-treatment outcome, can also be determined using different methods across research and clinical settings, and can be measured in a variety of different ways (Beggs, 2010), again these come with their own conceptual issues. Psychometrics tools have also frequently been used to measure *change* in offenders undergoing treatment. In a recent review of the use of psychometric measures with adult sexual offenders conducted, by Grady et al. (2011), the authors suggest that within sexual offender treatment provision, often there is a big gap between the main outcome of interest (recidivism) and the proximal outcome (changes in dynamic risk factors). They suggest that we need to focus our efforts on understanding treatment change, using measures which are reliable and valid, and which are effective measures of specific areas identified as dynamic risk factors (Fanniff & Becker, 2006). The use of valid psychometric tests to do this will enable researchers and clinicians to determine whether offenders who complete treatment are demonstrating changes in the core treatment need areas addressed on the programme. In turn this also presents a practical alternative for evaluating treatment programmes (Beggs, 2010), the problems of which have been well documented elsewhere (e.g. Hollin, 2008). It could be for example that linking short-term outcomes in the form of psychometric change, with long-term reconviction may be a more accurate method of examining the impact of a treatment programme (Friendship, Falshaw, & Beech, 2003).

Serin, Lloyd, Helmus, Derkzen, and Luong (2013) provide a comprehensive review of studies linking individual change scores to recidivism in areas of cognition, violence and substance misuse following treatment. Of the 49 studies examined, changes were shown to relate to recidivism in areas of antisocial attitudes, antisocial beliefs, antisocial personality, social support and substance misuse. The authors conclude that although there are promising links between change and recidivism, further high-quality studies are required.

As for an evidence-base for sexual offender therapy, Beggs (2010), in a review of within-treatment outcome studies, identified a number of studies detecting a positive change (or reduction) in the level of dynamic risk following treatment (e.g. Bakker, Hudson, Wales, & Riley, 1998; Beech & Hamilton-Giachritsis, 2005; Beggs, 2010; Bickley & Beech, 2003; Hudson et al., 2002; Marshall et al., 2002, 2003; Nunes, Babchishin, & Cortoni, 2011; Quinsey, Khanna, & Malcolm, 1998; Wakeling, 2007; Webster, Mann, Thornton, & Wakeling, 2007).

Within the sexual offender literature there is support for the notion that psychometrics can detect a positive change (or reduction) on dynamic risk following treatment (e.g. Bakker et al., 1998; Beech, Erikson, Friendship, & Ditchfield, 2001; Beech & Hamilton-Giachritsis, 2005; Bickley & Beech, 2003; Hedderman & Sugg, 1996; Hudson et al., 2002; Marshall et al., 2002, 2003, 2005; Nunes et al., 2011; Quinsey et al., 1998; Wakeling, 2007; Webster et al., 2007), when the psychometrics are empirically related to risk, and are targeted in the treatment programme (Beggs, 2010), and using a variety of different methodologies to assess change. However, it should be noted that other studies have found no relationship between psychometric change and recidivism (e.g. Hanson & Wallace-Capretta, 2000; Wilkinson, 2005).

While some studies use pre- to post-psychometric change, as noted above, others have evaluated changes in risk through the use of structured dynamic risk assessment tools (e.g. Olver et al., 2007; Wong & Gordon, 2006). Tools have also been specifically developed to assess treatment progress, such as the Goal Attainment Scale (Hogue, 1994), the Treatment Readiness Scale (Serin & Kennedy, 1997), and the Sex Offender Treatment Intervention and Progress Scale (McGrath, Lasher, & Cumming, 2012). Other approaches use structured professional clinical judgments of treatment progress (e.g. Looman, Abracen, Serin, & Marquis, 2005; Scalora & Garbin, 2003).

Issues in the measurement of change in dynamic risk in sexual offenders

It would appear that the use of different methodologies to examine psychometric change could have an impact on how well different tools appear to behave, and may in part explain the mixed results of treatment studies. Clinically significant change methodology has been used for example to examine the link between treatment change and recidivism outcome with some success in sexual offender treatment studies (e.g. Beech & Ford, 2006; Wakeling, Beech, & Freemantle, 2013), while other researchers have used this, plus other types of statistical methodology, such as the assessment of post-treatment ratings on the Standard Goal Attainment Scaling for Sex Offenders (e.g. Beggs & Grace, 2011).

Recent studies provide some evidence that the methodology employed to determine the predictive validity of psychometric measures may have a significant impact on the findings, with differing levels of predictive validity found for different methodologies used to determine change. Olver, Kingston, Nicholaichuk, and Wong (2014), for example, found that within-treatment change bore little relationship to outcome. However, when statistically corrected for pre-treatment score the relationship of treatment change to outcome frequently improved, even after controlling for the level of static risk.

As noted above, treatment progress has also been assessed through the use of structured dynamic risk assessment tools, or structured professional clinical judgments of treatment progress. These various methods may produce differential results in terms of both the identification of need and the amount of change observed, which complicates any attempts to assimilate evidence on dynamic risk factors. Given that the level of static risk accounts for the most prediction in risk, change in the level of dynamic risk is hard to demonstrate as being related to reduced recidivism in many studies (see Nunes et al., 2011). Although some tools have shown to be valid and reliable, similar to issues with SPJ tools, the biggest issue associated with such rating scales may be their subjective nature. Ratings of change may be affected by the relationship the assessor has with the individual in question, the importance the assessor places on various aspects of change, and their personal opinion of the individual. There is also difficulty for evaluators in stating that individuals have changed, or reduced their risk. Evaluators may be afraid of litigation for getting this wrong, and may, as a consequence, be likely to err on the side of caution and underestimate change and/or progression.

Conclusions

Further evidence is required in order to confirm how best to measure dynamic risk factors, and to confirm the notion that changes on dynamic risk factors are associated with meaningful reductions in offenders' recidivism risk (Beech et al., 2003). This article has outlined some of the prominent conceptual issues associated with the measurement of dynamic risk factors, including the problems associated with using psychometrics, using SPJ tools and other methods, such as rating scales. Ways in which we can improve our measurement of dynamic risk factors include selecting appropriate tools, validating the tools we are using for the specific population we are interested in, ensuring we gather the information appropriately and making every effort to minimise assessor bias. It is our view that perhaps the most appropriate way to measure dynamic risk factors is to triangulate evidence, using those tools, which have been shown to have reliability and validity alongside observation by trained clinicians. When assessing dynamic risk as clinicians, we advise following the recommendations set out by Prentky and Burgess (2000) to give us the best chance of doing this in a reliable way, that is, to: (1) draw conclusions and opinions which do not go beyond what the data supports; (2) only use instruments and procedures which are supported by the empirical literature; (3) where possible, conclusions should be drawn from multiple data sources; and (4) the conclusions drawn should be no stronger than the weakest link in the chain of data sources.

Disclosure statement

No potential conflict of interest was reported by the authors.

References

Andrews, D. A., & Bonta, J. (2010). *The psychology of criminal conduct* (5th ed.). New Providence, NJ: LexisNexis.

Bakker, L., Hudson, S., Wales, D., & Riley, D. (1998). *And there was light: Evaluating the Kia Marama treatment programme for New Zealand sex offenders against children* (Psychological Service Report). Department of Corrections, Wellington, New Zealand.

Beech, A. R. (2001). Case material and interview. In C. Hollin (Ed.), *Handbook of offender assessment and treatment* (pp. 123–138). Chichester: Wiley.

Beech, A. R., & Ford, H. (2006). The relationship between risk, deviance, treatment outcome and sexual reconviction in a sample of child sexual abusers completing residential treatment for their offending. *Psychology, Crime and Law, 12*, 685–701. doi:10.1080/10683160600558493

Beech, A. R., & Hamilton-Giachritsis, C. E. (2005). Relationship between therapeutic climate and treatment outcome in group-based sexual offender treatment programs. *Sexual Abuse: A Journal of Research and Treatment, 17*, 127–140. doi:10.1177/107906320501700204

Beech, A. R., Erikson, M., Friendship, C., & Ditchfield, J. (2001). *A six-year follow-up of men going through probation-based sex offender treatment programmes*. Research Findings, 144. Home Office Research, Development and Statistics Directorate.

Beech, A. R., Fisher, D. D., & Thornton, D. (2003). Risk assessment of sex offenders. *Professional Psychology: Research and Practice, 34*, 339–352. doi:10.1037/0735-7028.34.4.339

Beggs, S. (2010). Within-treatment outcome among sexual offenders: A review. *Aggression and Violent Behavior, 15*, 369–379. doi:10.1016/j.avb.2010.06.005

Beggs, S., & Grace, R. C. (2011). Treatment gain for sexual offenders against children predicts reduced recidivism: A comparative validity. *Journal of Consulting and Clinical Psychology, 79*, 182–192. doi:10.1037/a0022900

Bickley, J. A., & Beech, R. (2003). Implications for treatment of sexual offenders of the Ward and Hudson model of relapse. *Sexual Abuse: A Journal of Research and Treatment, 15*, 121–134. doi:10.1177/107906320301500203

Boer, D. P., Hart, S. D., Kropp, P. R., & Webster, C. D. (1997). *Manual for the Sexual Violence Risk-20: Professional guidelines for assessing risk of sexual violence*. Vancouver, BC: The Mental Health, Law, and Policy Institute.

Bowen, E., Gilchrist, E. A., & Beech, A. R. (2005). An examination of the impact of the community-based rehabilitation on the offending behaviour of male domestic violence offenders and the characteristics associated with recidivism. *Legal and Criminological Psychology, 10*, 189–209. doi:10.1348/135532505X36778

Craissati, J., & Beech, A. R. (2003). A review of dynamic variables and their relationship to risk prediction in sex offenders. *Journal of Sexual Aggression, 9*, 41–55. doi:10.1080/355260031000137968

Cronbach, L. J. (1951). Coefficient alpha and the internal structure of tests. *Psychometrika, 16*, 297–334. doi:10.1007/bf02310555

Douglas, K. S., Hart, S. D., Webster, C. D., Belfrage, H., Guy, L. S., & Wilson, C. M. (2014). Historical-Clinical-Risk Management-20 (HCR-20 v3): Development and overview. *International Journal of Forensic Mental Health, 13*, 93–108. doi:10.1080/14999013.2014.906519

Douglas, K., & Kropp, P. R. (2002). A prevention-based paradigm for violence risk assessment: Clinical and research applications. *Criminal Justice and Behavior, 29*, 617–658.

Eher, R., Matthes, A., Schilling, F., Haubner-Maclean, T., & Rettenberger, M. (2012). Dynamic risk assessment in sexual offenders using STABLE-2000 and the STABLE-2007: An investigation of predictive and incremental validity. *Sexual Abuse: A Journal of Research and Treatment, 24*, 5–28. doi:10.1177/1079063211403164

Fanniff, A. M., & Becker, J. V. (2006). Specialized assessment and treatment of adolescent sex offenders. *Aggression and Violent Behavior, 11*, 265–282. doi:10.1016/j.avb.2005.08.003

Friendship, C., Falshaw, L., & Beech, A. R. (2003). Measuring the real impact of accredited offending behavior programmes. *Legal and Criminological Psychology, 8*, 115–127. doi:10.1348/135532503762871282

Grady, M. D., Broderson, M., & Abramson, J. M. (2011). The state of psychological measures for adult sexual offenders. *Aggression and Violent Behavior, 16*, 227–240. doi:10.1016/j.avb.2011.03.001

Hanson, R. K. (1998). What do we know about sexual offender risk assessment. *Psychology, Public Policy, and Law, 4*, 50–72. doi:10.1037/1076-8971.4.1-2.50

Hanson, R. K., & Harris, A. (2000). *The Sex Offender Need Assessment Rating (SONAR): A method for measuring change in risk levels*. Public Safety Canada. Retrieved from http://www.publicsafety.gc.ca/cnt/rsrcs/pblctns/sx-ffndr-nd/sx-ffndr-nd-eng.pdf

Hanson, R. K., Harris, A. J. R., Scott, T-L., & Helmus, L. (2007). *Assessing the risk of sexual offenders on community supervision: The Dynamic Supervision Project Ottawa*. Public Safety Canada. Retrieved from http://www.publicsafety.gc.ca/cnt/rsrcs/pblctns/ssssng-rsk-sxl-ffndrs/ssssng-rsk-sxl-ffndrs-eng.pdf

Hanson, R. K., Cox, B. J., & Woszczyna, C. (1991). Assessing treatment outcome for sexual offenders. *Annals of Sex Research, 4*, 177–208. doi:10.1007/BF00850052

Hanson, R. K., & Morton-Bourgon, K. E. (2009). The accuracy of recidivism risk assessments for sexual offenders: A meta-analysis of 118 prediction studies. *Psychological Assessment, 21*, 1–21. doi:10.1037/a0014421

Hanson, R. K., Steffy, R. A., & Gauthier, R. (1993). Long-term recidivism of child molesters. *Journal of Consulting and Clinical Psychology, 61*, 646–652. doi:10.1037//0022-006X.61.4.646

Hanson, R. K., & Wallace-Capretta, S. (2000). *Predicting recidivism among male batterers*. Toronto: Public Works and Government Services Canada.

Harris, A. J. R., & Hanson, R. K. (2010). Clinical, actuarial and dynamic risk assessment of sexual offenders: Why do things keep changing? *Journal of Sexual Aggression, 16*, 296–310. doi:10.1080/13552600.2010.494772

Hart, S. D., Kropp, P. R., & Laws, D. R. (2003). *Risk for Sexual Violence Protocol (RSVP): Structured professional guidelines for assessing risk of sexual violence*. Burnaby, BC: The Mental Health, Law and Policy Institute, Simon Fraser University.

Hayes, S., Shackell, P., Mottram, P., & Lancaster, R. (2007). The prevalence of intellectual disability in a major UK prison. *British Journal of Learning Disabilities, 35*, 162–167. doi:10.1111/j.1468-3156.2007.00461.x

Hedderman, C., & Sugg, D. (1996). *Does treating sex offenders reduce reoffending*? Research Findings, 45. Home Office Research, Development and Statistics Directorate. Retrieved from www.homeoffice.gov.uk/rds/pdfs/r45.pdf

Hogue, T. E. (1994). Goal attainment scaling: A measure of clinical impact and risk assessment. *Issues in Criminological and Legal Psychology, 21*, 96–102. doi:10.1177/107906320101300201

Holden, R. R., Kroner, D. G., Fekken, G. C., & Popham, S. M. (1992). A model of personality test item response dissimulation. *Journal of Personality and Social Psychology, 63*, 272–279. doi:10.1037/0022-3514.63.2.272

Hollin, C. (2008). Evaluating offending behavior programs: Does only randomization glister? *Criminology and Criminal Justice*, *8*, 89–106. doi:10.1177/1748895807085871

Hudson, S. M., Wales, D. S., Bakker, L., & Ward, T. (2002). Dynamic risk factors: The Kia Marama evaluation. *Sexual Abuse: A Journal of Research and Treatment*, *14*, 103–119. doi:10.1023/A:1014616113997

Hurley, A., DesNoyers, T., Daniel, J., & Pfadt, A. G. (1998). Individual and group psychotherapy approaches for persons with mental retardation and developmental disabilities. *Journal of Developmental and Physical Disabilities*, *10*, 365–386. doi:10.1023/A:1021806605662

Kline, P. (1993). *The handbook of psychological testing*. London: Routledge.

Kline, P. (2000). *The handbook of psychological testing* (2nd ed.). London: Routledge.

Looman, J., & Abracen, J. (2012). *Long-term follow up of two groups of sex offenders*. Presentation at the annual research and treatment conference of the Association for the Treatment of Sexual Abusers, Denver. Retrieved from http://saratso.org/docs/Looman_ATSA_2012_twoGroupsLongTermFollowup.pdf

Looman, J., Abracen, J., Serin, R., & Marquis, P. (2005). Psychopathy, treatment change, and recidivism in high-risk, high-need sexual offenders. *Journal of Interpersonal Violence*, *20*, 549–568. doi:10.1177/0886260504271583

Loza, W., Cumbleton, A., Shahinfar, A., Neo, L. H., Evans, M., Conley, M., & Summers, R. (2004). Cross-validation of the Self-Appraisal Questionnaire (SAQ): An offender risk and need assessment measure on Australian, British, Canadian, Singaporean, and American Offenders. *Journal of Interpersonal Violence*, *19*, 1172–1190. doi:10.1177/0886260504269180

Loza, W., & Loza-Fanous, A. (2000). Predictive validity of the Self-Appraisal Questionnaire (SAQ): A measure for assessing violent and nonviolent release failures. *Journal of Interpersonal Violence*, *15*, 1183–1191. doi:10.1177/088626000015011005

Loza, W., & Loza-Fanous, A. (2003). More evidence for the validity of the Self-Appraisal Questionnaire (SAQ) for predicting violent and nonviolent recidivism: A five year follow up study. *Criminal, Justice and Behavior*, *30*, 709–721. doi:10.1177/0093854803256448

Lyden, M., & Peters, M. (2004). Assessing capacity for informed consent: A rationale and protocol. *Mental Health Aspects of Developmental Disabilities*, *7*, 97–106.

Mann, R. E., Ware, J., & Fernandez, Y. M. (2011). Managing sex offender treatment programs. In R. Eher, M. H. Miner, F. Pffafflin, D. Boer, & L. A. Craig (Eds.), *International perspectives on the assessment and treatment of sexual offenders: Theory, practice and research* (pp. 331–354). Chichester: Wiley Blackwell.

Marques, J. K., Wideranders, M., Day, D. M., Nelson, C., & van Ommeren, A. (2005). Effects of a relapse prevention program on sexual recidivism: Final results from California's Sex Offender Treatment and Evaluation Program (SOTEP). *Sexual Abuse: A Journal of Research and Treatment*, *17*, 79–107. doi:10.1177/107906320501700108

Marshall, W. L., Serran, G. A., Fernandez, Y. M., Mulloy, R., Mann, R. E., & Thornton, D. (2003). Therapist characteristics in the treatment of sexual offenders: Tentative data on their relationship with indices of behaviour change. *Journal of Sexual Aggression*, *9*, 25–30. doi:10.1080/355260031000137940

Marshall, W. L., Serran, G. A., Moulden, H., Mulloy, R., Fernandez, Y. M., Mann, R. E., & Thornton, D. (2002). Therapist features in sexual offender treatment: Their reliable identification and influence on behaviour change. *Clinical Psychological and Psychotherapy*, *9*, 395–405. doi:10.1002/cpp.335

Maruna, S. (2001). *Making good: How ex-convicts reform and rebuild their lives*. Washington, DC: American Psychological Association.

Mason, J., & Murphy, G. H. (2002). People with intellectual difficulties in the criminal justice system: Developing an assessment tool for measuring prevalence. *British Journal of Clinical Psychology*, *41*, 315–320. doi:10.1348/014466502760379163

McGrath, R. J., Lasher, M. P., & Cumming, G. (2012). The Sex Offender Treatment Intervention and Progress Scale (SOTIPS): Psychometric properties and incremental predictive validity with the Static-99R. *Sexual Abuse: A Journal of Research and Treatment*, *24*, 431–458.

Michael, P. G., & Li, S. T. (2010). Psychometrics. In J. C. Thomas & M. Hersen (Eds.), *Handbook of clinical psychology competencies* (pp. 343–365). New York, NY: Springer.

Mills, J. F. & Kroner, D. G. (2006). The effect of discordance among violence and general recidivism risk estimates on predictive accuracy. *Criminal Behaviour and Mental Health, 16*, 155–166. doi:10.1002/cbm.623

Mills, J. F., Loza, W., & Kroner, D. G. (2003). Predictive validity despite social desirability: Evidence for the robustness of self-report among offenders. *Criminal Behaviour and Mental Health, 13*, 140–150. doi:10.1002/cbm.536

Monahan, J. (1981). *The clinical prediction of violent behavior*. Washington, DC: Government Printing House.

Nunes, K. L. Babchishin, K. M., & Cortoni, F. (2011). Measuring treatment change in sex offenders: Clinical and statistical significance. *Criminal Justice and Behavior*, 38, 157–173.

Nunnally, J. C., & Bernstein, I. H. (1994). *Psychometric theory* (3rd ed.). New York, NY: McGraw-Hill.

Olver, M. E., Kingston, D. A., Nicholaichuk, T. P., & Wong, S. C. P. (2014). A psychometric examination of treatment change in a multisite sample of treated Canadian federal sexual offenders. *Law and Human Behavior, 38*, 544–559. doi:10.1037/lhb0000086

Olver, M. E., Wong, S. C. P., Nicholaichuk, T. P., & Gordon, A. E. (2007). The validity and reliability of the Violence Risk Scale – Sexual Offender Version: Assessing sex offender risk and evaluating therapeutic change. *Psychological Assessment, 19*, 318–329. doi:10.1037/1040-3590.19.3.318

Prentky, R. A., & Burgess, A. W. (2000). *Forensic management of sexual offenders*. New York, NY: Kluwer Academic/Plenum Publishers.

Proulx, J., Pellerin, B., Paradis, Y., McKibben, A., Aubut, J., & Ouimet, M. (1997). Static and dynamic predictors of recidivism in sexual aggressors. *Sexual Abuse: A Journal of Research and Treatment, 9*, 7–27.

Quinsey, V. L., Khanna, A., & Malcolm, P. B. (1998). A retrospective evaluation of the regional treatment centre sex offender treatment program. *Journal of Interpersonal Violence, 13*, 621–644. doi:10.1177/088626098013005005

Rosenthal, R., & Rosnow, R. L. (1991). *Essentials of behavioral research: Methods and data analysis* (2nd ed.). New York, NY: McGraw-Hill.

Rust, J., & Golombok, S. (1999). *Modern psychometrics: The science of psychological assessment* (2nd ed.). New York, NY: Routledge.

Scalora, M. J., & Garbin, C. (2003). A multivariate analysis of sex offender recidivism. *International Journal of Offender Therapy and Comparative Criminology, 47*, 309–323. doi:10.1177/0306624X03047003005

Schretlen, D., & Arkowitz, H. (1990). A psychological test battery to detect prison inmates who fake insanity or mental retardation. *Behavioral Sciences and the Law, 8*, 75–84. doi:10.1002/bsl.2370080109

Serin, R. C., & Kennedy, S. (1997). *Treatment readiness and responsivity: Contributing to effective correctional programming* (Research Report. R-54). Ottawa: Correctional Services of Canada.

Serin, R. C., Lloyd, C. D., Helmus, L., Derkzen, D. M., & Luong, D. (2013). Does intra-individual change predict offender recidivism? Searching for the Holy Grail in assessing offender change. *Aggression and Violent Behavior, 18*, 32–53. doi:10.1016/j.avb.2012.09.002

Snacken, S. (2006). A reductionist penal policy and European human rights standards. *European Journal of Criminal Policy and Research, 12*, 143–164. doi:10.1007/s10610-006-9014-3

Tierney, D. W., & McCabe, M. P. (2001). An evaluation of self-report measures of cognitive distortions and empathy among Australian sex offenders. *Archives of Sexual Behavior, 30*, 495–519. doi:10.1023/A:1010239217517

Tully, R. J., Chou, S., & Browne, K. D. (2013). A systematic review on the effectiveness of sex offender risk assessment tools in predicting sexual recidivism of adult male sex offenders. *Clinical Psychology Review, 33*, 287–316. doi:10.1016/j.cpr.2012.12.002

Wakeling, H. C. (2007). The psychometric validation of the Social Problem-Solving Inventory-Revised with UK incarcerated sexual offenders. *Sexual Abuse: A Journal of Research and Treatment, 19*, 217–236. doi:10.1177/107906320701900304

Wakeling, H. C., & Barnett, G. D. (2014). The relationship between psychometric test scores and reconviction in sexual offenders undertaking treatment. *Aggression and Violent Behavior, 19*, 138–145. doi:10.1016/j.avb.2014.01.002

Wakeling, H. C., Beech, A. R., & Freemantle, N. (2013). Investigating treatment change and its relationship to recidivism in a sample of 3773 sex offenders in the UK. *Psychology, Crime and Law, 19*, 233–252. doi:10.1080/1068316X.2011.626413

Wakeling, H. C., & Travers, R. (2010). Evaluating offending behaviour programmes in prison. In J. M. Brown & E. A. Campbell (Eds.), *The Cambridge handbook of forensic psychology* (pp. 820–829). Cambridge: Cambridge University Press.

Walters, G. D. (2006). Risk-appraisal versus self-report in the prediction of criminal justice outcomes. *Criminal Justice and Behavior, 33*, 279–304. doi:10.1177/0093854805284409

Ward, T. (2015). Dynamic risk factors: Scientific kinds or predictive constructs. *Psychology, Crime and Law*, 22(01-02), 2–16.

Webster, S., Mann, R. E., Thornton, D., & Wakeling, H. C. (2007). Further validation of the Short Self-esteem Scale with sexual offenders. *Legal and Criminological Psychology, 12*, 207–216. doi:10.1348/135532506X114347

Wilkinson, J. (2005). Evaluating evidence for the effectiveness of the Reasoning and Rehabilitation Programme. *The Howard Journal, 44*, 70–85. doi:10.1111/j.1468-2311.2005.00356.x

Wong, S. C. P., & Gordon, A. (2006). The validity and reliability of the Violence Risk Scale: A treatment friendly Violence Risk Assessment Scale. *Psychology, Public Policy and Law, 12*, 279–309. doi:10.1037/1076-8971.12.3.279

Challenges for the theory and application of dynamic risk factors

Jacinta R. Cording, Sarah M. Beggs Christofferson and Randolph C. Grace

Department of Psychology, University of Canterbury, Christchurch, New Zealand

ABSTRACT
The inclusion of dynamic factors in risk assessment measures used with forensic populations has largely been considered an improvement in both the accuracy and utility of these assessments in informing treatment and sentencing. However, there are important challenges associated with the current approach to the conceptualisation, identification, and use of dynamic factors in risk assessment. Whereas some of these challenges relate to applied settings (such as the use of measures with different offender populations), there are also deeper questions regarding the construct validity of dynamic risk measures and the methodological strategies used to identify them. More emphasis on theoretically driven research is needed, to identify causal and explanatory relationships between dynamic risk factors and recidivism. We hope that highlighting these challenges can help to build a consensus on a future research agenda for dynamic risk factors.

The accurate measurement of offender risk is becoming an increasingly important focus of forensic research, due in part to the major implications that offender risk level can have for sentencing, custodial and community living arrangements, and the decision to indefinitely detain certain high-risk offenders. In addition to informing these decisions, risk assessment plays an important role in determining appropriate treatment for offenders in that there is now a large empirical base to suggest that the level of intervention should match the level of risk posed by an offender (Andrews & Bonta, 2010). Risk assessment has undergone a stark transformation from the first generation practice of relying largely upon unstructured clinical judgement (Bonta, 1996). First was the development of the empirically based second generation tools based on static risk factors, followed by third generation measures that placed a greater emphasis on dynamic risk factors (also referred to as criminogenic needs) and were more theoretically informed. These third generation measures are the primary focus of the current article. Table 1 lists selected dynamic risk measures that have been developed with adult offender populations, including information about predictive validity and the samples used. As Table 1 shows, these dynamic risk measures have generally high levels of predictive accuracy that are at least on par with static measures of risk.

Table 1. Predictive validity and validation study demographics for a selection of dynamic risk measures.

Measure	Prediction of sexual recidivism	Prediction of violent recidivism	Prediction of general recidivism	Countries validated in	Offender types validated on
VRS-SO Version (Wong, Olver, Nicholaichuk, & Gordon, 2003)	AUC = .72, r = .34	AUC = .57 r = .11	N/A	Canada, New Zealand	Incarcerated male rapists and child molesters
STABLE 2007 (Hanson, Harris, Scott, & Helmus, 2007)	AUC = .67	AUC = .66	AUC = .66	Austria, Canada, New Zealand, and the USA	Male adult parolees/ probationers; rapists, child molesters and non-contact offenders
VRS (Wong & Gordon, 1999–2003)	N/A	AUC = .75 r = .40	AUC = .75 r = .43	Canada, New Zealand, The Netherlands	Incarcerated male offenders, forensic psychiatry inpatients, and personality-disordered offenders
LSI-R (Andrews & Bonta, 1995)	N/A	r = .26	r = .37	Nine countries, including Singapore, the USA, China, and Australia	Aboriginal, Asian, Black, and Hispanic offenders; Female and male offenders
Self-Appraisal Questionnaire (SAQ; Loza, 2005)	N/A	r = .32	r = .49	Australia, Canada, England, Singapore, and the USA	Female and male offenders; Asian, African-American, Hispanic and Aboriginal Australian offenders
DRAOR (Serin et al., 2012)	N/A	ns	AUC = .62	New Zealand	Male and female offenders

Note: Predictive validity scores are sourced from the first validation studies for each measure, apart from the LSI-R for which a meta-analysis was the source (Gendreau, Goggin, & Smith, 2002).

Although their causative and explanatory nature is still not clearly understood (Heffernan & Ward, 2015; Ward, 2015), dynamic risk factors are generally defined as situational and personal characteristics that are both empirically linked to an increased chance of future offending and are, theoretically at least, able to change (Andrews & Bonta, 2010). Although dynamic factors have received overall less attention than static factors (risk factors that are not amenable to change, e.g. age at first criminal offence) in research on risk assessment, they remain highly promising not only with regards to the accurate prediction of recidivism, but also in identifying useful and effective treatment targets for offenders.

The growing information on dynamic risk factors has enabled the development of a number of measures containing either exclusively dynamic risk factors, or a combination of both static and dynamic factors. This change in the focus of risk assessment measures has been justified by findings that dynamic measures are able to provide incremental predictive validity beyond static factors in the measurement of future reoffending rates (Craissati & Beech, 2003; Gendreau, Little, & Goggin, 1996; Hanson & Harris, 2000). The proliferation of risk assessment measures for different offender populations has greatly improved the ability of professionals to provide informed judgements about the risk posed by individual offenders.

However, there remain a number of concerns about the measurement of dynamic risk that have important implications for assessment in applied settings; our goal in this paper is to identify these problems, both theoretical and practical, so that we might help to generate discussion and build a consensus on a future research agenda. We begin with a consideration of current evidence for the reliability and validity of various risk assessment tools, extending this assessment to the application of risk assessment with different populations of offenders, and the use of tools in applied contexts. Next we discuss the difficulties that arise as a result of the multi-faceted and indistinct nature of many dynamic risk factors, and the issues posed by a data-driven, rather than theory-driven, approach to the identification and conceptualisation of dynamic risk. We discuss possible solutions, such as a greater focus on confirmatory factor analysis and causal modelling in theory construction and testing. Third, we discuss the challenges faced in applying risk assessment in practice contexts, including the assessment of offender change. Finally, we consider the implications of socially desirable responding (SDR) for the accuracy of dynamic risk assessment based upon self-report measures.

The validity of dynamic risk assessment

Construct validity

The most common interpretation of construct validity, as applied to dynamic risk factors, relates to whether the particular measure represents or measures what it is supposed to; this has been referred to as 'fundamental' construct validity (Colliver, Conlee, & Verhulst, 2012). As such, much research has focused on determining the concurrent validity – the extent to which a particular measure correlates with existing measures of the same constructs – and the predictive validity – the extent to which a measure accurately predicts a specific relevant outcome measure – of dynamic risk assessments. Overall, research has supported the concurrent validity of common dynamic risk assessment tools, in that offenders who are categorised as high risk on one particular measure are likely to also be categorised as high risk on other measures (Beggs & Grace, 2010; Loza, Dhaliwal, Kroner, & Loza-Fanous, 2000; Nunes & Babchishin, 2012). Thus, on the surface it appears as if there is a strong empirical basis for the construct validity of dynamic risk assessment. However, scholars have recently questioned the idea that concurrent and predictive validity are the two most important measures of construct validity (Borsboom, Mellenbergh, & van Heerden, 2004; Colliver et al., 2012; Haig, 2012). Instead, they argue that a given measure should be considered to have good construct validity if it is able to demonstrate a causal or explanatory link between the attributes it measures and the outcome of interest (Borsboom et al., 2004).

The implication is that dynamic risk assessment could be considered to have good construct validity only if researchers are able to demonstrate a causative or explanatory link between dynamic risk measures and recidivism. In order to assess whether this is possible given the current evidence base, we first must take a step back and ask an important question: what *are* dynamic risk factors? As defined by Andrews and Bonta (2010, p. 7), dynamic risk factors are theoretically changeable factors that are 'predictors of the criminal futures of individuals', and that with changes, 'we see changes in the chances of criminal activity' (p. 48). While this conceptualisation of dynamic risk factors, and therefore the assessment of dynamic risk, appears to at least theoretically meet the explanatory requirement of construct validity, there has been some recent doubt cast on whether the current reliance on correlational analyses and significance testing is a valid method of identifying truly causal factors relating to recidivism risk (Haig, 2012; Heffernan & Ward, 2015; Ward & Beech, 2014).

Ward (2015) discusses this issue in more depth; suffice to say, it is unclear whether the current conceptualisation of what constitutes as a 'risk factor' is demonstrably valid in a more meaningful sense of the term.

A further problem with validity in the area of risk assessment relates to the multi-dimensional and indistinct nature of many dynamic risk factors (Heffernan & Ward, 2015). 'Cognitive distortions' provides a good example. Typically, cognitive distortions are conceived of as non-normative belief structures that include justifications and rationalisations for sexual offending, and are regarded as a dynamic risk factor (Gannon, Ward, & Collie, 2007). However, Ó Ciardha and Gannon (2011) noted that 'cognitive distortions' has been applied to a multitude of different constructs including 'maladaptive beliefs' (Ward, Hudson, Johnston, & Marshall, 1997), 'defensiveness' (Rogers & Dickey, 1991), 'rationalisations' (Neidigh & Krop, 1992), 'incorrect or deviant cognitive practices' (Ward & Casey, 2010), and 'etiological cognitions' (Ó Ciardha & Gannon, 2011). Although definitions may play a larger role in the conceptualisation of scientific phenomena than perhaps they should (Haig, 2012), the degree of variation in how 'cognitive distortions' are defined poses a significant problem for developing valid measures of dynamic risk. Without clear definitions of risk factors, it is uncertain which features of each factor are linked to recidivism, and how to create clear scoring guidelines. Such uncertainty will not only potentially degrade the accuracy and discriminative validity of a measure, but also inter-rater and test–retest reliability. It also has implications for construct validity – how can we be sure that we are measuring what we want to measure, when we are unable to define clearly what that is?

Predictive validity

Predictive validity in the area of offender risk assessment is the extent to which risk scores derived from risk assessment methods or tools predict offender outcomes, typically in the form of reoffending or reconviction rates post release from custody. Because the prevention of reoffending is a major goal for offender treatment and the justice system as a whole, developing tools or assessment methods that can accurately predict recidivism has understandably been a key research focus.

A strong empirical base has developed over recent years which supports the view that measures of dynamic risk can significantly improve the accuracy of risk prediction over and above the ability of static risk alone (Beggs & Grace, 2010; Hanson & Harris, 2000). In general, studies indicate that empirically derived actuarial measures (i.e. measures with pre-determined items identified as risk factors in previous literature, and structured methods of calculating total risk) are significantly more predictive of reoffending compared to both structured clinical judgement (i.e. measures with pre-determined items but with no set method for calculating level of risk) and unstructured clinical judgement (Gendreau et al., 1996; Hanson & Morton-Bourgon, 2009). Somewhat unsurprisingly, studies have also found that the predictive accuracy of a particular measure changes depending on the match between the target behaviour being predicted and the type of behaviour the measure was developed to predict; for instance, a measure developed to measure risk of future sexual reoffending is typically more predictive of sexual recidivism than violent or general recidivism (Hanson & Morton-Bourgon, 2009). With this condition in mind, most common actuarial measures containing a large focus on dynamic items appear to perform relatively similarly in terms of predictive validity, with moderate rates of predictive validity for these measures in predicting sexual, violent, and general recidivism (Campbell, French, & Gendreau, 2009; Hanson & Morton-Bourgon, 2009).

While the predictive validity of dynamic risk measures has been clearly demonstrated in previous studies, questions remain about the generalisability of these measures to different groups, such as female, young, or aboriginal offenders. Research focusing on the identification of important dynamic risk factors, and the development and validation of related risk assessment tools, is overwhelmingly conducted using samples of adult male offenders (Reisig, Holtfreter, & Morash, 2006; Schwalbe, 2008) under the general assumption that dynamic risk factors are broadly consistent across gender and age (for discussion of the theory underlying this, see Andrews, Bonta, & Wormith, 2006). This view has been described by Yesberg and colleagues as the 'gender-neutral' assumption (Yesberg, Scanlan, Hanby, Serin, & Polaschek, 2015) and is currently the predominant view within the area of offender risk assessment. However, a number of scholars have rejected the gender-neutral assumption, instead asserting that there are a number of important differences between men and women which challenge the idea that dynamic risk factors – and therefore measures of dynamic risk – informed solely by male populations are equally valid for females. These include differences in motivations for offending (Veysey & Hamilton, 2007), experiences of victimisation (Reisig et al., 2006), base rates of offending (Odgers, Moretti, & Reppucci, 2005), and pathways to crime (Belknap, 2014; also see Yesberg et al., 2015). A meta-analysis that investigated the predictive validity of the Level of Service Inventory-Revised (LSI-R; a widely used dynamic risk measure in North America) for both male and female samples provided support for this view (Holtfreter & Cupp, 2007). They found that although the LSI-R performed moderately well for women, the measure was often more accurate for male offenders, and the predicted risk for female offenders was commonly too high; this was particularly true in cases where females had followed a pathway into crime that was dissimilar from typical male offenders (e.g. women with high levels of abuse and/or neglect, poverty, and victimisation), highlighting the importance of considering risk factors that are unique to female offenders.

Although Holtfreter and Cupp's (2007) results challenged the assumption of gender-neutral risk assessment, this conclusion is not straightforward because other studies with Level of Service (LS) risk measures have reported contradictory results. One recent meta-analysis found that LS tools in fact had greater predictive validity for female offenders (mean effect size = 0.53) than for male offenders (mean effect size = 0.39), for both adult and youth populations (Andrews et al., 2012). Support for the gender-neutral assumption has also been found with risk assessment tools developed for offenders in community settings, again with researchers finding that the predictive validity of the Dynamic Risk Assessment for Offender Re-entry (DRAOR; Serin, Mailloux, & Wilson, 2012) was greater for female offenders than for male offenders (Yesberg et al., 2015). The mixed results in research on gender and risk assessment highlight the need for further research in this area. Although overall results support the view that risk assessment tools are equally valid for males and females, it is important to investigate whether the inclusion of gender-specific items would further improve the predictive ability of risk assessment measures for females (Yesberg et al., 2015). It is also important to acknowledge that the generalisation of risk assessment measures to other minority offender populations, such as different ethnic groups, has also been challenged by the results of various studies that suggest a reduction in the accuracy of risk assessment tools for non-White populations within North America (Chenane, Brennan, Steiner, & Ellison, 2015; see Shepherd, Luebbers, & Dolan, 2013, for review).

We suggest that one of the major reasons for the lack of research on validating dynamic risk measures with different offender groups is because of the data-driven nature of research of dynamic risk factors and assessment. This leads to an over-reliance on empirical evidence that is available to researchers – which may be affected by particular choices of questionnaires or measures used as dynamic risk indicators – and under-reliance on theory or aetiology to guide our understanding of dynamic risk factors as scientific phenomena, and how these factors might be combined into an overall meaningful measure of risk; as explained by Haig (2013, p. 137), '[d]ata themselves are of scientific interest and importance only because they serve as evidence for the phenomena under investigation'. We consider the implications of the data-driven approach in the next section.

The data-driven approach to dynamic risk

Over-reliance on the hypothetico-deductive methodology in psychological research, where empirical data are used to identify, describe, and/or discover correlates of constructs to inform theory, has long been criticised (e.g. Cohen, 1994; Falk & Greenbaum, 1995; Rozeboom, 1960, 1997). By contrast, the abductive method may represent a more meaningful and valid approach to research (Borsboom et al., 2004; Haig, 2005, 2009, 2014). Haig (2014) describes the abductive approach as 'reasoning from factual premises to *explanatory* conclusions' (p. 60), noting that 'phenomena, not data, serve as evidence for the abducted theories' (p. 61). This differs from a purely inductive approach, whereby conclusions or theories are the 'same in kind' as the data used to generate them, meaning that they are more descriptive than explanatory in nature (Haig, 2014). As such, in using an abductive approach to theory generation, we are more likely to develop meaningful knowledge about the phenomena of interest, including an understanding of aetiology, causal networks, and the potential for change or adaptation.

The abductive critique of the hypothetico-deductive method is clearly applicable to prior research on dynamic risk assessment, which has been largely data-driven, attempting to identify the best predictors of recidivism among a set of candidate measures using regression-based statistical methods, rather than theory-driven (Heffernan & Ward, 2015; Ward, 2015). One could argue that variables which were studied as potential dynamic risk factors – such as lack of empathy for victims – were selected based on prior theoretical grounds (e.g. Marshall, Hamilton, & Fernandez, 2001); however, acceptance of these dynamic risk factors was reliant largely on evidence of their ability to predict recidivism, ideally beyond the contribution made by static factors. For example, an influential series of articles by Beech and colleagues showed that cluster analysis (a data-driven exploratory technique) could be used to classify sexual offenders as 'high deviance' or 'low deviance', and the deviance classification was subsequently shown to predict recidivism beyond the Static-99 (Beech, 1998; Beech, Friendship, Erikson, & Hanson, 2002; Fisher, Beech, & Browne, 1999).

Recent conceptualisations of validity suggest that a construct (or attribute) is valid only insofar as it is shown to relate causally to a criterion (Borsboom, 2005; Borsboom et al., 2004).

However, data-driven approaches which demonstrate that dynamic risk factors are correlated with recidivism fall short of providing evidence of a causal linkage. This is likely to result in an incomplete picture of the risk posed by an individual offender, and lacking in an explanation of the aetiology or maintenance of behaviour. Consequently, implications for treatment formulation in terms of the most important needs to target to reduce risk are compromised. A greater understanding of the aetiology of serious offending would allow us to develop more effective strategies for early intervention, ideally to reduce first-time sexual and violent offending rather than reoffending.

Reasons for the data-driven approach are understandable when one considers the definition of dynamic risk factors that was outlined above: risk factors are predictors of increased criminal behaviour (Andrews & Bonta, 2010). Thus, it is logical to identify risk factors by their ability to predict reoffending beyond the static, actuarial factors that had already been shown to have predictive validity. Leaving aside the issue of reliance on statistical significance testing (see Cumming, 2012), there are two major potential problems with the data-driven approach for dynamic risk: (1) there is no guarantee that the risk factors are clinically meaningful in the sense that they can be used to explain the aetiology or maintenance of offending (Heffernan & Ward, 2015; Mann, Hanson, & Thornton, 2010); and (2) the identification of important risk factors is reliant upon the data or measures available to a given researcher.

The variability in the identification of risk factors caused by differences between the information contained in different datasets is displayed clearly by the emergence of competing 'second-order' risk domains – composite risk factors that are predictive of reoffending, usually obtained by exploratory factor analysis on data from a psychometric battery. One example of this approach from the sex offender literature is from Allan, Grace, Rutherford, and Hudson (2007). These authors used exploratory factor analysis to identify dynamic risk factors from a large psychometric battery (a total of 20 different measures, including multiple sub-scales for some measures) that had been completed by a sample of sexual offenders against children prior to undergoing prison-based treatment. Four risk domains were identified that were each significantly predictive of sexual recidivism: social inadequacy (containing measures relating to low social competence and negative mood); sexual interests (containing measures relating to levels of sexual fantasies); anger/hostility (containing measures relating to anger expression and regulation); and pro-offending attitudes (containing measures relating largely to distorted cognitions and attitudes). Allan et al. combined these risk factors into a measure of 'Overall Deviance' which was shown to increase the predictive accuracy for recidivism beyond the Static-99. Previous researchers had also taken this approach for the development of general risk domains, however with slightly different results. For example, Olver, Nicholaichuk, and Wong (2014) identified three domains of dynamic risk for sexual offenders – socioemotional functioning, anger/hostility, and misogynist attitudes; Beech (1998) also identified three risk domains in his analysis of a psychometric battery, although these domains assessed conceptually different types of functioning: social competency, pro-offending attitudes, and sexual interests. Although there is evidence of some overlap between these factors, it is clear that the identification of relevant measures of risk for a given offender population varies depending on the measures available to a given researcher.

Moving beyond a data-driven approach will require different ways to identify risk factors, and possibly in how we conceptualise them. One approach that has been suggested elsewhere (Haig, 2005, 2012) is to modify our research methodologies to be more in line with an abductive approach to science, whereby theories are formed to explain patterns identified within the data (also called 'phenomena'), rather than data analysis being used to directly generate theories. In terms of research into dynamic risk assessment, this would require increased utilisation of techniques such as confirmatory factor analysis, which can be used to test proposed models for dynamic risk factors. These could then be used to generate theories and hypotheses relating to relationships between certain risk factors or domains and recidivism (Haig, 2005). It would also require a greater emphasis on validating and replicating the findings of other research in order to ensure that we are identifying true phenomena rather than idiosyncrasies of particular datasets (Beech, 1998; Cumming, 2012). It is hoped that through changing how we identify dynamic risk factors, we might be able to develop a deeper and more meaningful understanding of how these factors contribute to the generation and maintenance of offending, as well as how these factors combine to determine the overall level of risk of an offender.

The use of dynamic risk measures in practice contexts

Most studies of the reliability and validity of dynamic risk assessment measures have been conducted in research rather than applied settings, in that the measures are generally used by researchers or developers rather than by professionals in a correctional context (e.g. parole officers, forensic psychologists, and custodial officers). This raises questions about whether the reliability and validity of these measures will be maintained when they are no longer being scored by trained researchers or research assistants, but instead by staff who may have many other responsibilities.

Reasons why we might expect differences in the scoring of these measures by correctional compared to research staff are the lack of specialised, standardised training; high levels of work-related stress (National Institute of Justice, 2007); and large workloads and time pressures leading to a greater reliance on clinical or professional judgment rather than a strict adherence to scoring guidelines (Jones, Brown, & Zamble, 2010; Public Safety Canada, 2008). This would be particularly salient for measures that use a largely unstructured scoring format, allowing for a greater influence of personal heuristics and cognitive biases (Payne, Bettman, & Johnson, 1993). It has also been suggested by some researchers that this reliance on clinical judgement rather than the structured scoring criteria might result from a reluctance of professionals to accept the idea that their judgements might be less accurate than purely quantitative methods of assessing risk (Schlager, 2009; Schneider, Ervin, & Snyder-Joy, 1996). There is also some evidence to suggest that the fear of political and professional implications of having rated someone as low risk who later goes on to reoffend (even if the rating was correct) leads correctional staff to manipulate dynamic scores in a way that over-estimates risk, with large resource and financial implications for the corrections service as a whole (Lanterman, Boyle, & Ragusa-Salerno, 2014; Schlager, 2009; Schneider et al., 1996).

A further threat posed to the validity of risk assessment in applied settings is the quality of training provision for these measures. Previous research has indicated that there is a positive association between the quality of training provided to scorers and the predictive validity of risk assessment (Lowenkamp, Latessa, & Holsinger, 2004). For example, formal instruction on the use of the measures led by trained practitioners is superior to 'bootstrap' training led by inexperienced or untrained colleagues, and the provision for hands-on practice improves quality (Lowenkamp et al., 2004; U.S. Department of Justice, 2007). The importance of training with risk assessment tools was highlighted by Andrews et al. (2011), who reported a series of meta-analyses using a total of 101 validation studies on the LSI risk assessment tool. The studies were assessed on a number of factors that might moderate the predictive validity of the LSI, including length of follow-up, sample characteristics (such as gender and nationality), and LSI 'allegiance' (defined as the level of involvement of the LSI developers in data collection for the study). Andrews et al. found that LSI allegiance was a significant moderator of the predictive validity of the LSI, with the stronger the allegiance, the higher the predictive validity. They suggested that LSI allegiance might be best understood as a proxy for the quality of the implementation and integrity in research methods (such as the selection of appropriate outcome measures). Andrews et al.'s (2011) results highlight the importance of a close adherence to scoring and implementation guidelines that are developed during quality training, in order to ensure maximal utility of the risk assessment tool in question.

Because performance in applied settings is essential for the utility of a risk assessment measure, it is important that we understand fully how reliability and validity of a given measure are affected by extending use from a research to an applied setting. Jones et al. (2010) investigated the extent to which the predictive ability of risk as assessed by parole officers differed from the predictive ability of risk scored by researchers. They used a prospective design where risk was measured at multiple time points in order to best emulate real-world use of the measures. In order to further emulate real-world circumstances, parole officers provided crude proxy ratings of each area of dynamic risk based on their perceptions of offender circumstances and were not subject to quality assurance processes. Researchers, on the other hand, provided detailed and structured assessments of risk based on multi-dimensional case review (including semi-structured interviews and file reviews) and were subjected to routine quality assurance (such as inter-rater reliability checks). Contrary to expectation, researchers found that the predictive ability of the ratings of the parole officers and researchers were not significantly different, with AUCs of .76 and .79, respectively, indicating medium-high levels of predictive validity. In addition, ratings of external acute risk factors (such as employment) were highly correlated between the two groups, although those for internal acute risk factors (such as stress) were not significantly correlated. Thus, the ability of parole officers to predict recidivism based on crude proxies of risk was equal to that of highly structured and multi-dimensional assessments of risk. Jones et al. suggested that perhaps the extensive level of interaction between parole officers and offenders enabled them to gain a better picture of important collateral information about the offender, such as family, education, and interaction with other health providers.

Although Jones et al. (2010) results are encouraging in that they suggest that risk assessment can be valid in an applied setting, it is important to note that the parole officers in this study were not expected to strictly adhere to scoring guidelines for each measure, but instead rated their perceptions of how a risk factor related to a given individual, in a similar way to the procedure used for structured clinical judgement tools. In other words, while it appears as though risk assessment can be accurate and valid in applied contexts, it is not so clear that the validity of actuarial tools can be transferred as successfully between research and practical contexts. It is important to note that as actuarial measures of dynamic risk continue to improve in their level of predictive validity and in the provision of estimated base rates of offending for different risk bands (e.g. for the VRS-SO; Olver, Beggs Christofferson, Grace, & Wong, 2014), it will become increasingly important that professionals are able to utilise structured risk assessment tools accurately. The ability of professionals to provide estimates of recidivism rates by risk level becomes even more significant as the possible sentencing options for high-risk offenders become increasingly restrictive and intrusive in the lives of offenders (e.g. preventive detention and extended supervision orders in New Zealand; Ryan, Wilson, Kilgour, & Reynolds, 2013). Thus, given that the extant literature largely supports the notion that the validity of risk assessment can change substantially depending on implementation and adherence to guidelines, more effort is warranted to ensure protocols are in place for effective training and ongoing quality assessment for those responsible for risk assessment in a professional context.

Measuring change in dynamic risk

In addition to identifying those most at risk of reoffending, another vital task for professionals in applied settings is determining whether and to what extent individuals' levels of risk have changed. The link between this function and the concept of dynamic risk is clear – after all, a crucial component of the concept of dynamic risk is that it is just that – dynamic, or in other words, changeable. Although we acknowledge the criticism made by some authors that the measurement of change in dynamic risk is not meaningful in terms of addressing the causes of offending (e.g. see Ward, 2015), nonetheless it may have practical importance in terms of predicting future risk. However, this changeability has seemed to be more readily accepted in theory than actually tested in research. For some oft-cited dynamic risk factors, although an empirical link with recidivism has been established, and there may be face validity in terms of being changeable, studies have often only examined them at one point in time (e.g. Beech et al., 2002; Dempster & Hart, 2002).

Where more recent studies have begun to explore change, findings have been mixed. For example, a negligible amount of change was found in one study on psychometric test scores intending to tap into dynamic risk factors for violence, across a 20-month treatment programme for inpatient forensic mental health patients (Hildebrand & de Ruiter, 2012). This raises a problem evident in the psychometric assessment of dynamic risk: the difficulty in determining whether null results regarding change across treatment are the result of true lack of change (i.e. a poor treatment effect due to programme ineffectiveness or participant factors such as poor motivation), insensitive measurement relating to the tests chosen, or, that the 'dynamic' factors under investigation are not really dynamic. In contrast, other studies have reported significant improvements between pre-treatment and post-treatment psychometric test scores relating to dynamic risk areas such as pro-criminal attitudes, family/marital relationships, and education/employment (Brooks Holliday, Heilbrun, & Fretz, 2012). Likewise, substantial apparent changes from pre- to post-treatment have tended to be found when dynamic factors have been measured psychometrically among sex offenders (e.g. Hudson, Wales, Bakker, & Ward, 2002; Marques, Wiederanders, Day, Nelson, & Van

Ommeren, 2005). However, it is possible that such findings reflect a social desirability response bias, which we consider below.

In many studies in which dynamic risk changes have been explored, recidivism outcomes were not included in the investigations. Arguably, as well as needing to be empirically linked to recidivism, and changeable, it is also inherent in the definition of dynamic risk factors that any changes should be *meaningful* (i.e. linked to changes in actual reoffending risk). In fact, this is a central tenet of the needs principle of offender rehabilitation as described by Andrews and Bonta (2010). However, as noted by Serin, Lloyd, Helmus, Derkzen, and Luong (2013), the question of whether changes (i.e. in dynamic risk factors) are reliably associated with recidivism likelihood is relatively unexplored. Research has only more recently begun to test the assumption empirically.

In one test of the link between treatment change and outcome, Beggs and Grace (2011) demonstrated that specific within-treatment changes in dynamic risk factors in the desired direction, measured psychometrically, can be linked with reduced recidivism at follow-up. In doing so, they reported on the problematic nature of analysing raw change scores: on any given test, individuals with pre-treatment scores towards the more problematic end of the scale (indicating higher levels of dynamic risk) have the opportunity to show greater levels of change across treatment, as they have more 'room to move'. This is also relevant to the issue of SDR in self-report testing, which we discuss in greater detail, with reference to the Beggs and Grace study, below. However a further problem is also clear: given that both riskier scores and lower change should theoretically be linked with higher recidivism, yet those with riskier scores have the opportunity to attain higher change scores, use of raw change scores is inherently flawed. To manage this issue, Beggs and Grace employed a method of regression in which pre-treatment scores were partialled out of the prediction equation. This allowed a more meaningful pattern of results to emerge, in which positive treatment change was associated with reduced sexual recidivism overall, and for three out of four dynamic risk domains (employing the Allan et al.'s (2007) framework: social inadequacy, sexual interests, and anger/hostility; the fourth domain, pro-offending attitudes, approached significance). This technique has subsequently been applied by Olver, Nicholaichuk, Kingston, and Wong (2014) in their exploration of therapeutic change and recidivism using a psychometric risk prediction instrument (the Violence Risk Scale-Sexual Offender Version; VRS-SO).

Other studies have employed a different method known as clinically significant change methodology to explore the link between within-treatment changes in dynamic risk and recidivism (e.g. Barnett, Wakeling, Mandeville-Norden, & Rakestrow, 2013; Olver, Beggs Christofferson, & Wong, 2015). This method avoids the problems associated with raw change scores, as in addition to considering change magnitude, post-treatment scores are evaluated against non-deviant norms to determine whether the individual has qualitatively 'improved', 'recovered', is 'already ok' (i.e. never scored outside the normative range), or remained 'unchanged'. While this method offers a user-friendly and readily interpretable classification system for individuals based on what their dynamic risk test scores say about their treatment outcome, Olver and colleagues (2015) and others (e.g. Barnett et al., 2013) have overviewed the limitations of the method and noted mixed findings, in particular that the usefulness of the output is dependent on the quality of the measures used. In general, Olver et al. (2015) suggested that the use of a single, purpose-designed risk tool containing multiple dynamic factors, such as the VRS-SO or the STABLE 2007 (see Hanson, Harris, Scott, & Helmus, 2007), may offer advantages over the psychometric battery approach for the consistent and meaningful applied measurement of dynamic risk factors, and change in these across treatment.

One common factor in the change studies discussed above is that the assessment of dynamic risk occurred at only two points in time – prior to, and then following, treatment. Whilst studies employing this design have been very useful in terms of establishing empirical relationships between specific changes in dynamic risk and decreased recidivism, and exploring the clinical measurement of within-treatment changes, they have focused exclusively on the period of treatment engagement as the change mechanism for risk. However, theoretically speaking, other factors could influence the presence or expression of dynamic risk (resulting in change), such as maturation (Hirschi & Gottfredson, 1983), social context and influences (Sampson & Laub, 1995), or in the case of sex offenders, age-related decline in sexual response (Blanchard & Barbaree, 2005). It has also been suggested that including at least three waves of assessment increases the probability of detecting change (Brown, Amand, & Zamble, 2009). A recent multi-wave study by Greiner, Law, and Brown (2014) illustrated the tracking of seven major theorised dynamic risk factors (employment, personal/emotional factors, substance use, criminal attitudes, criminal associates, family functioning, and community functioning) among female offenders following their release from prison, across four assessment waves at six-monthly intervals. They found that all seven factors were significantly related to survival time without reoffending in the community, and that prediction was improved by their use of multiple assessments of dynamic risk across time. On the other hand, change across multiple waves using a well-validated dynamic risk tool for sex offenders, the STABLE 2007, has been found to not be associated with recidivism (Hanson et al., 2007). As such, although assessing dynamic risk factors at multiple time points both during and after treatment appears to be a promising technique in terms of improving the assessment of change, it is apparent that there are other factors that contribute to the mixed results of studies on change. It is possible that part of the problem lies with our current conceptualisation of what constitutes a dynamic risk factor, as discussed in previous sections.

Clearly, more research is needed on the assessment of changes in dynamic risk, with numerous challenges having been identified for applied settings. As discussed above, dynamic risk evaluations in applied settings typically have a great impact on individuals' progress through the criminal justice system, and assessments of change (across treatment or with continued repeat assessments) are certainly no different. For clinicians this carries a great responsibility, and the need to ensure that the methods we select to assess the changes made by our clients are both capable of detecting change that has occurred, and meaningful in terms of being predictive of actual reductions in the likelihood of recidivism. Although a number of the factors that affect the accuracy of risk assessment (including the issue of generalisability discussed above) can be mitigated by the selection of appropriate methods on the part of the clinician, there are a number threats to predictive validity that are not so easily avoided when using current assessment tools. We now turn to a discussion of one of the more prominent of these threats: SDR.

Threats to validity of dynamic risk measures: SDR

One important threat to the validity of dynamic risk assessments, particularly those in which offender self-reports play a role, is impression management or SDR (see Tan & Grace, 2008, for review). SDR refers to the tendency of some individuals to respond in ways that are likely to elicit approval from others, and to refrain from responding in ways that would be met with disapproval (Crowne & Marlowe, 1964). In terms of self-report measures, this tendency means that individuals may be influenced to respond to individual items not only based on their beliefs relating to the item content, but also what they believe to be a socially appropriate response. Such patterns of responding pose a unique challenge within an offender population, where an idiosyncratic desire to appear 'overly positive' (Paulhus, 2002) is further augmented by a penal system that creates clear incentives for individuals to present in a positive way for parole boards, judges, probation officers, and other individuals making decisions affecting the length and type of custodial sentences (Davis, Thake, & Weekes, 2012).

To the extent that offender self-reports are considered in classification and parole decisions, assessing the credibility of those reports is obviously important. The inaccuracies in measurement that could potentially result from SDR threaten not only the classification and parole decisions, but also affect the ability to assess accurately the level of dynamic risk or need of an individual offender. Some psychometric measures used to assess dynamic risk factors have highly transparent items, so that it is fairly obvious to the responder as to what the test is measuring and therefore what the socially acceptable responses might be. For example, the Abel–Becker Cognitions Scale (Abel et al., 1989), which is commonly used to assess offence-supportive beliefs and attitudes with sexual offenders against children, includes items such as 'I show my love and affection to a child by having sex with her (him)' and 'A child who doesn't physically resist an adult's sexual advances really wants to have sex with the adult'. Using transparent measures makes it relatively easy for offenders to minimise or deny problematic attitudes, and to exaggerate any positive or pro-social traits.

Because of these potential problems with offender self-reports, researchers have often used measures of SDR as part of psychometric batteries to assess dynamic risk (e.g. Beech, 1998). Variance associated with SDR is then partialled out prior to making a dynamic risk classification (cf. Saunders, 1991). Although this is a common practice, there is little evidence that correcting for SDR in this manner improves the accuracy of decision making in applied settings in general (McGrath, Mitchell, Kim, & Hough, 2010). Results with forensic samples are similar. Mills and Kroner (2006) found that using the impression management subscale of the Balanced Inventory of Desirable Responding (BIDR; Paulhus & John, 1998) to correct the self-reports of incarcerated offenders on a measure of dynamic risk decreased, not increased, the predictive validity for recidivism (although note that the decrease was not statistically significant). Recently, Stevens et al. (2015) showed that correcting sexual offenders' self-reported dynamic risk scores for SDR (measured by the Marlowe–Crowne Social Desirability Scale; Crowne & Marlowe, 1964) had virtually no effect on predictive validity for sexual recidivism.

Because removal of SDR variance does not improve the correlation of self-report dynamic risk measures with recidivism, researchers have suggested that SDR scales like the BIDR or MCSDS may actually be measuring a personality trait or enduring disposition related to need for social approval. According to this view, SDR may be correlated with dynamic risk factors (indeed, SDR was negatively correlated with dynamic risk in Mills and Kroner (2006) and Stevens et al. (2015); see also Mathie and Wakeling (2010), but is not related to recidivism risk directly). This view is consistent with a recent reinterpretation of SDR by Uziel (2010), who suggested that instead of response bias, measures of SDR should be regarded as 'interpersonally oriented self-control', that is, SDR reflects the individual's ability to adjust to social situations and seek approval from others.

Thus, more research is needed on the nature of SDR in forensic settings, but there appears to be little justification for using SDR measures to adjust for response bias. However, this does not imply that response bias is not a problem, or that the transparent nature of many self-report measures is not a cause for concern when assessing dynamic risk. Indeed, there is strong evidence that impression management has a major impact on offender's self-reports. As discussed above, Beggs and Grace (2011) compared responses of sexual offenders to a psychometric battery both before and after treatment and found that medium-to-large gains (in terms of effect size) were reported by men across all variables in the battery. Pre-treatment scores were strongly correlated with change scores (average $R^2 = .33$). Interestingly, Beggs and Grace found that the predictive validity of change scores for recidivism increased when variance associated with pre-treatment scores was partialled out, exemplifying suppressor effects (with some correlations actually reversing direction). That is, measures of treatment gain based on self-reports were more valid predictors of recidivism when the initial level of risk was taken into account. They interpreted this as evidence that offenders with higher pre-treatment risk scores had more potential to show greater change, given the fixed range of possible scores in the battery. Thus, their results showed that self-reported change scores should not be taken at face value and were likely biased by impression management, but when the pre-treatment levels of risk were controlled for, provided a potentially valid measure of treatment change. Similar results were reported subsequently by Olver, Beggs Christofferson, et al. (2014).

Although further research is needed in order to more fully understand what SDR actually is, how it is structured, and how it affects risk assessment in different offender populations, overall research suggests that SDR may not be the large challenge that many assume it to be, and that its impact on the ability to measure dynamic risk with self-reports may be less severe than originally thought.

Conclusion

In terms of the overall accuracy and utility of risk assessment tools, the move towards a greater consideration of dynamic risk factors when assessing risk has been a promising step forward. Not only has the inclusion of dynamic factors shown to improve the predictive validity of actuarial tools (Craissati & Beech, 2003; Gendreau et al., 1996; Hanson & Harris, 2000), but these measures are also theoretically able to inform treatment targets, allow for the assessment of change in risk over time, and incorporate more meaningful risk factors that can be connected to the aetiology and maintenance of antisocial behaviour, all of which are important considerations for a rehabilitative approach to criminal justice. However, it is important to note that the way in which these tools are developed and utilised will moderate the relationship between these theoretical benefits of incorporating dynamic risk factors and how these tools function in reality.

As discussed above, the current research methods used to identify dynamic risk factors, and the ways in which we combine and apply these factors to the measurement of risk, is possibly creating a disconnect between the theoretical conceptualisation of dynamic risk and what these tools are measuring in practice. While dynamic risk assessment tools may be reasonably accurate in their predictions of reoffending, it is important that we recognise that this does not necessarily mean that the risk factors used in these measures are psychologically meaningful, or that they contribute to our understanding of the aetiology of, or indeed to the desistance from, antisocial behaviour (Heffernan & Ward, 2015). As such, it is vital that we consider the methodology utilised when identifying important predictors of risk and remember that the development of meaningful knowledge about risk necessarily includes knowledge of aetiology and causal networks (Borsboom et al., 2004; Haig, 2005, 2012).

It is also important to recognise that the predictive validity of quantitative risk measures is in a large part dependent on the sample used in the validation; for this reason, we highlight the necessity of validating measures in different countries or jurisdictions, and with different types of offenders. In addition to the type and demographics of offenders, the predictive validity of risk assessment tools is also highly impacted on by the way in which the measure is applied, both in terms of the quality of training provided on a given measure, and in the adherence to scoring guidelines demonstrated by the clinician or researcher (Lowenkamp et al., 2004; Schlager, 2009). Assessments of risk that incorporate self-report measures also have the added threat of validity of responses, which might be affected by offender biases, both conscious and sub-conscious; although the literature largely suggests that the concern about the erosion of prediction accuracy as a result of offenders 'faking good' is not empirically founded (Beggs & Grace, 2011; Olver, Nicholaichuk, et al., 2014; Stevens et al. (2015)) one still must consider the impact of biased responding on the ability of clinicians to gauge the specific level and types of needs that should form the focus of treatment.

Addressing these applied and theoretical challenges related to the assessment of dynamic risk highlights requires a change in the methodologies and analytical techniques used in dynamic risk research (e.g. increased use of causal modelling and confirmatory factor analysis), as well as a move towards a more theoretically driven identification of relevant dynamic risk factors. However, a significant first step in this process will be widely acknowledging these areas of difficulty, and generating discussion both about the extent of these issues and other ways in which these challenges can be resolved. It is hoped that a careful consideration of these topics can lead to the development of other ways in which these challenges can be faced, and the true potential of dynamic risk factors in their application to risk assessment can be realised.

Disclosure statement

No potential conflict of interest was reported by the authors.

References

Abel, G. G., Gore, D. K., Holland, C. L., Camp, N., Becker, J. V., & Rather, J. (1989). The measurement of the cognitive distortions in child molesters. *Annals of Sex Research*, *2*, 135–152.

Allan, M., Grace, R. C., Rutherford, B., & Hudson, S. M. (2007). Psychometric assessment of dynamic risk factors for child molesters. *Sexual Abuse: A Journal of Research and Treatment, 19*(4), 347–367. doi:10.1177/107906320701900402

Andrews, D. A., & Bonta, J. (1995). *LSI-R: The Level Of Service Inventory-Revised user's manual*. Toronto: Multi-Health Systems.

Andrews, D. A., & Bonta, J. (2010). *The psychology of criminal conduct* (5th ed.). Boston: Anderson Publishing Ltd.

Andrews, D. A., Bonta, J., & Wormith, J. S. (2006). The recent past and near future of risk and/or need assessment. *Crime & Delinquency, 52*(1), 7–27. doi:10.1177/0011128705281756

Andrews, D. A., Bonta, J., Wormith, J. S., Guzzo, L., Brews, A., Rettinger, J., & Rowe, R. (2011). Sources of variability in estimates of predictive validity: A specification with Level of Service general risk and need. *Criminal Justice and Behavior, 38*(5), 413–432. doi:10.1177/0093854811401990

Andrews, D. A., Guzzo, L., Raynor, P., Rowe, R. C., Rettinger, L. J., Brews, A., & Wormith, J. S. (2012). Are the major risk/need factors predictive of both female and male reoffending?: A test with the eight domains of the level of service/case management inventory. *International Journal of Offender Therapy and Comparative Criminology, 56*(1), 113–133. doi:10.1177/0306624x10395716

Barnett, G. D., Wakeling, H., Mandeville-Norden, R., & Rakestrow, J. (2013). Does change in psychometric test scores tell us anything about risk of reconviction in sexual offenders? *Psychology, Crime & Law, 19*(1), 85–110.

Beech, A. R. (1998). A psychometric typology of child abusers. *International Journal of Offender Therapy and Comparative Criminology, 42*(4), 319–339.

Beech, A. R., Friendship, C., Erikson, M., & Hanson, R. K. (2002). The relationship between static and dynamic risk factors and reconviction in a sample of U.K. child abusers. *Sexual Abuse: A Journal of Research and Treatment, 14*(2), 155–167. doi:10.1177/107906320201400206

Beggs, S. M., & Grace, R. C. (2010). Assessment of dynamic risk factors: An independent validation study of the Violence Risk Scale: Sexual Offender version. *Sexual Abuse: A Journal of Research and Treatment, 22*(2), 234–251. doi:10.1177/1079063210369014

Beggs, S. M., & Grace, R. C. (2011). Treatment gain for sexual offenders against children predicts reduced recidivism: A comparative validity study. *Journal of Consulting and Clinical Psychology, 79*(2), 182–192. doi:10.1037/a0022900

Belknap, J. (2014). *The invisible woman: Gender, crime, and justice* (4th ed.). Belmont, CA: Thomson Wadsworth Publishing Company.

Blanchard, R., & Barbaree, H. E. (2005). The strength of sexual arousal as a function of the age of the sex offender: Comparisons among pedophiles, hebephiles, and teleiophiles. *Sexual Abuse: A Journal of Research and Treatment, 17*(4), 441–456.

Bonta, J. (1996). Risk-needs assessment and treatment. In A. T. Harland (Ed.), *Choosing correctional options that work: Defining the demand and evaluating the supply* (pp. 18–32). Thousand Oaks, CA: Sage.

Borsboom, D. (2005). *Measuring the mind: Conceptual issues in contemporary psychometrics*. Cambridge: Cambridge University Press.

Borsboom, D., Mellenbergh, G. J., & van Heerden, J. (2004). The concept of validity. *Psychological Review, 111*(4), 1061–1071. doi:10.1037/0033-295X.111.4.1061

Brooks Holliday, S., Heilbrun, K., & Fretz, R. (2012). Examining improvements in criminogenic needs: The risk reduction potential of a structured re-entry program. *Behavioral Sciences & The Law, 30*(4), 431–447.

Brown, S. L., Amand, M. D. S., & Zamble, E. (2009). The dynamic prediction of criminal recidivism: A three-wave prospective study. *Law and Human Behavior, 33*(1), 25–45.

Campbell, M. A., French, S., & Gendreau, P. (2009). The prediction of violence in adult offenders: A meta-analytic comparison of instruments and methods of assessment. *Criminal Justice and Behavior, 36*(6), 567–590.

Chenane, J. L., Brennan, P. K., Steiner, B., & Ellison, J. M. (2015). Racial and ethnic differences in the predictive validity of the Level Of Service Inventory–Revised among prison inmates. *Criminal Justice and Behavior, 42*(3), 286–303. doi:10.1177/0093854814548195

Cohen, J. (1994). The earth is round (p <.05). *American Psychologist, 49*(12), 997–1003. doi:10.1037/0003-066X.49.12.997

Colliver, J. A., Conlee, M. J., & Verhulst, S. J. (2012). From test validity to construct validity … and back? *Medical Education, 46*(4), 366–371. doi:10.1111/j.1365-2923.2011.04194.x

Craissati, J., & Beech, A. (2003). A review of dynamic variables and their relationship to risk prediction in sex offenders. *Journal of Sexual Aggression, 9*(1), 41–55.

Crowne, D. P., & Marlowe, D. (1964). *The approval motive: Studies in evaluative dependence.* New York, NY: Wiley.

Cumming, G. (2012). *Understanding the new statistics: Effect sizes, confidence intervals, and meta-analysis.* New York, NY: Routledge.

Davis, C. G., Thake, J., & Weekes, J. R. (2012). Impression managers: Nice guys or serious criminals? *Journal of Research in Personality, 46*(1), 26–31. doi:10.1016/j.jrp.2011.11.001

Dempster, R. J., & Hart, S. D. (2002). The relative utility of fixed and variable risk factors in discriminating sexual recidivists and nonrecidivists. *Sexual Abuse: A Journal of Research and Treatment, 14*(2), 121–138.

Falk, R., & Greenbaum, C. W. (1995). Significance tests die hard: The amazing persistence of a probabilistic misconception. *Theory & Psychology, 5*(1), 75–98.

Fisher, D., Beech, A. R., & Browne, K. (1999). Comparison of sex offenders to nonoffenders on selected psychological measures. *International Journal of Offender Therapy and Comparative Criminology, 43* (4), 473–491.

Gannon, T. A., Ward, T., & Collie, R. (2007). Cognitive distortions in child molesters: Theoretical and research developments over the past two decades. *Aggression and Violent Behavior, 12*(4), 402–416. doi:10.1016/j.avb.2006.09.005

Gendreau, P., Goggin, C., & Smith, P. (2002). Is the PCL-R really the "unparalleled" measure of offender risk? A lesson in knowledge cumulation. *Criminal Justice and Behavior, 29*(4), 397–426. doi:10.1177/0093854802029004004

Gendreau, P., Little, T., & Goggin, C. (1996). A meta-analysis of the predictors of adult offender recidivism: What works. *Criminology, 34*(4), 575–608.

Greiner, L. E., Law, M. A., & Brown, S. L. (2014). Using dynamic factors to predict recidivism among women: A four-wave prospective study. *Criminal Justice and Behavior, 42*(5), 457–480. doi:10.1177/0093854814553222

Haig, B. D. (2005). An abductive theory of scientific method. *Psychological Methods, 10*(4), 371–388. doi:10.1037/1082-989X.10.4.371

Haig, B. D. (2009). Inference to the best explanation: A neglected approach to theory appraisal in psychology. *The American Journal of Psychology, 122*(2), 219–234.

Haig, B. D. (2012). From construct validity to theory validation. *Measurement: Interdisciplinary Research and Perspectives, 10*(1–2), 59–62. doi:10.1080/15366367.2012.681975

Haig, B. D. (2013). Detecting psychological phenomena: Taking bottom-up research seriously. *The American Journal of Psychology, 126*(2), 135–153. doi:10.5406/amerjpsyc.126.2.0135

Haig, B. D. (2014). The philosophy of quantitative methods. In *The Oxford handbook of quantitative methods in psychology: Foundations* (pp. 7–31). Oxford: Oxford University Press.

Hanson, R. K., Harris, A., Scott, T., & Helmus, L. (2007). *Assessing the risk of sexual offenders on community supervision: The Dynamic Supervision Project.* (Report no. 2007–05). Ottawa, ON: Public Safety and Emergency Prepardness Canada.

Hanson, R. K., & Harris, A. J. R. (2000). Where should we intervene? Dynamic predictors of sexual offense recidivism. *Criminal Justice and Behavior, 27*(1), 6–35. doi:10.1177/0093854800027001002

Hanson, R. K., & Morton-Bourgon, K. E. (2009). The accuracy of recidivism risk assessments for sexual offenders: A meta-analysis of 118 prediction studies. *Psychological Assessment, 21*(1), 1–21. doi:10.1037/a0014421

Heffernan, R., & Ward, T. (2015). The conceptualization of dynamic risk factors in child sex offenders: An agency model. *Aggression and Violent Behavior, 24*, 250–260. doi:10.1016/j.avb.2015.07.001

Hildebrand, M., & de Ruiter, C. (2012). Psychopathic traits and change on indicators of dynamic risk factors during inpatient forensic psychiatric treatment. *International Journal of Law and Psychiatry, 35*, 276–288. doi:10.1016/j.ijlp.2012.04.001

Hirschi, T., & Gottfredson, M. (1983). Age and the explanation of crime. *American Journal of Sociology, 89*(3), 552–584.

Holtfreter, K., & Cupp, R. (2007). Gender and risk assessment: The empirical status of the LSI-R for women. *Journal of Contemporary Criminal Justice, 23*(4), 363–382. doi:10.1177/1043986207309436

Hudson, S. M., Wales, D. S., Bakker, L., & Ward, T. (2002). Dynamic risk factors: The Kia Marama evaluation. *Sexual Abuse: A Journal of Research and Treatment, 14*(2), 103–119.

Jones, N. J., Brown, S. L., & Zamble, E. (2010). Predicting criminal recidivism in adult male offenders: Researcher versus parole officer assessment of dynamic risk. *Criminal Justice and Behavior, 37*(8), 860–882. doi:10.1177/0093854810368924

Lanterman, J. L., Boyle, D. J., & Ragusa-Salerno, L. M. (2014). Sex offender risk assessment, sources of variation, and the implications of misuse. *Criminal Justice and Behavior, 41*(7), 822–843. doi:10.1177/0093854813515237

Lowenkamp, C. T., Latessa, E. J., & Holsinger, A. M. (2004). Empirical evidence on the importance of training and experience in using the Level Of Service Inventory-Revised. *Topics in Community Corrections*, 49–53.

Loza, W. (2005). *Self-Appraisal Questionnaire*. Toronto, ON: Multi-Health Systems.

Loza, W., Dhaliwal, G., Kroner, D. G., & Loza-Fanous, A. (2000). Reliability, construct, and concurrent validities of the Self-Appraisal Questionnaire: A tool for assessing violent and nonviolent recidivism. *Criminal Justice and Behavior, 27*(3), 356–374. doi:10.1177/0093854800027003005

Mann, R. E., Hanson, R. K., & Thornton, D. (2010). Assessing risk for sexual recidivism: Some proposals on the nature of psychologically meaningful risk factors. *Sexual Abuse: A Journal of Research and Treatment, 22*(2), 191–217. doi:10.1177/1079063210366039

Marques, J. K., Wiederanders, M., Day, D. M., Nelson, C., & Van Ommeren, A. (2005). Effects of a relapse prevention program on sexual recidivism: Final results from California's Sex Offender Treatment and Evaluation Project (SOTEP). *Sexual Abuse: A Journal of Research and Treatment, 17*(1), 79–107.

Marshall, W., Hamilton, K., & Fernandez, Y. (2001). Empathy deficits and cognitive distortions in child molesters. *Sexual Abuse: A Journal of Research and Treatment, 13*(2), 123–130.

Mathie, N. L., & Wakeling, H. C. (2010). Assessing socially desirable responding and its impact on self-report measures among sexual offenders. *Psychology, Crime & Law, 17*(3), 215–237.

McGrath, R. E., Mitchell, M., Kim, B. H., & Hough, L. (2010). Evidence for response bias as a source of error variance in applied assessment. *Psychological Bulletin, 136*(3), 450–470. doi:10.1037/a0019216

Mills, J. F., & Kroner, D. G. (2006). Impression management and self-report among violent offenders. *Journal of Interpersonal Violence, 21*(2), 178–192. doi:10.1177/0886260505282288

National Institute of Justice. (2007). *Helping probation and parole officers cope with stress*. Retrieved from https://www.ncjrs.gov/pdffiles1/nij/220107.pdf

Neidigh, L., & Krop, H. (1992). Cognitive distortions among child sexual offenders. *Journal of Sex Education and Therapy, 18*(3), 208–215.

Nunes, K. L., & Babchishin, K. M. (2012). Construct validity of Stable-2000 and Stable-2007 scores. *Sexual Abuse: A Journal of Research and Treatment, 24*(1), 29–45. doi:10.1177/1079063211404921

Ó Ciardha, C., & Gannon, T. A. (2011). The cognitive distortions of child molesters are in need of treatment. *Journal of Sexual Aggression, 17*(2), 130–141. doi:10.1080/13552600.2011.580573

Odgers, C. L., Moretti, M. M., & Reppucci, N. D. (2005). Examining the science and practice of violence risk assessment with female adolescents. *Law and Human Behavior, 29*(1), 7–27. doi:10.1007/s10979-005-1397-z

Olver, M. E., Beggs Christofferson, S. M., Grace, R. C., & Wong, S. C. P. (2014). Incorporating change information into sexual offender risk assessments using the Violence Risk Scale–Sexual Offender version. *Sexual Abuse: A Journal of Research and Treatment, 26*(5), 472–499. doi:10.1177/1079063213502679

Olver, M. E., Beggs Christofferson, S. M., & Wong, S. C. P. (2015). Evaluation and applications of the clinically significant change method with the Violence Risk Scale-Sexual Offender version: Implications for risk-change communication. *Behavioral Sciences & the Law, 33*(1), 92–110. doi:10.1002/bsl.2159

Olver, M. E., Nicholaichuk, T. P., Kingston, D. A., & Wong, S. C. P. (2014). A multisite examination of sexual violence risk and therapeutic change. *Journal of Consulting and Clinical Psychology, 82*(2), 312–324. doi:10.1037/a0035340

Olver, M. E., Nicholaichuk, T. P., & Wong, S. C. P. (2014). The predictive and convergent validity of a psychometric battery used to assess sexual offenders in a treatment programme: An 18-year follow-up. *Journal of Sexual Aggression, 20*(2), 216–239. doi:10.1080/13552600.2013.816791

Paulhus, D. L. (2002). Socially desirable responding: The evolution of a construct. In H. I. Braun, D. N. Jackson, & D. E. Wiley (Eds.), *The role of constructs in psychological and educational measurement* (pp. 49–69). Mahwah, NJ: Lawrence Erlbaum.

Paulhus, D. L., & John, O. P. (1998). Egoistic and moralistic biases in self-perception: The interplay of self-deceptive styles with basic traits and motives. *Journal of Personality, 66*(6), 1025–1060.

Payne, J. W., Bettman, J. R., & Johnson, E. J. (1993). *The adaptive decision maker.* Cambridge: Cambridge University Press.

Public Safety Canada. (2008). *Outside the walls.* Ottawa, Canada. Retrieved from http://www.publicsafety.gc.ca/cnt/cntrng-crm/csc-scc-rvw-pnl/report-rapport/otsd-wll-eng.aspx

Reisig, M. D., Holtfreter, K., & Morash, M. (2006). Assessing recidivism risk across female pathways to crime. *Justice Quarterly, 23*, 384–405.

Rogers, R., & Dickey, R. (1991). Denial and minimization among sex offenders. *Annals of Sex Research, 4*(1), 49–63.

Rozeboom, W. W. (1960). The fallacy of the null-hypothesis significance test. *Psychological Bulletin, 57* (5), 416–428.

Rozeboom, W. W. (1997). Good science is abductive, not hypothetico-deductive. In L. L. Harlow, S. A. Mulaik & J. H. Steiger (Eds.), *What if there were no significance tests?* (pp. 335–392). Mahwah, NJ: Lawrence Erlbaum Associates Publishers.

Ryan, J., Wilson, N., Kilgour, G., & Reynolds, N. (2013). Balancing efficiency and accuracy: Guidelines for the psychological assessment of extended supervision orders for child sex offenders in New Zealand. *Psychiatry, Psychology and Law, 21*(1), 139–157. doi:10.1080/13218719.2013.793154

Sampson, R. J., & Laub, J. H. (1995). *Crime in the making: Pathways and turning points through life.* Cambridge, MA: Harvard University Press.

Saunders, D. G. (1991). Procedures for adjusting self-reports of violence for social desirability bias. *Journal of Interpersonal Violence, 6*(3), 336–344. doi:10.1177/088626091006003006

Schlager, M. D. (2009). The organizational politics of implementing risk assessment instruments in community corrections. *Journal of Contemporary Criminal Justice, 25*(4), 412–423. doi:10.1177/1043986209344555

Schneider, A. L., Ervin, L., & Snyder-Joy, Z. (1996). Further exploration of the flight from discretion: The role of risk/need instruments in probation supervision decisions. *Journal of Criminal Justice, 24*(2), 109–121. doi:10.1016/0047-2352(95)00059-3

Schwalbe, C. S. (2008). A meta-analysis of juvenile justice risk assessment instruments: Predictive validity by gender. *Criminal Justice and Behavior, 35*(11), 1367–1381. doi:10.1177/0093854808324377

Serin, R. C., Lloyd, C. D., Helmus, L., Derkzen, D. M., & Luong, D. (2013). Does intra-individual change predict offender recidivism? Searching for the Holy Grail in assessing offender change. *Aggression and Violent Behavior, 18*(1), 32–53.

Serin, R. C., Mailloux, D. L., & Wilson, N. J. (2012). *The Dynamic Risk Assessment of Offender Re-entry (DRAOR).* Unpublished user manual.

Shepherd, S. M., Luebbers, S., & Dolan, M. (2013). Gender and ethnicity in juvenile risk assessment. *Criminal Justice and Behavior, 40*(4), 388–408. doi:10.1177/0093854812456776

Stevens, C. D. J., Tan, L., & Grace, R. C. (2015). Socially-desirable responding and psychometric assessment of dynamic risk in sexual offenders against children. Under revision for *Psychology, Crime & Law.*

Tan, L., & Grace, R. C. (2008). Social desirability and sexual offenders: A review. *Sexual Abuse: A Journal of Research and Treatment, 20*(1), 61–87. Retrieved from http://sax.sagepub.com/content/20/1/61.abstract

U.S. Department of Justice. (2007). *The importance of assessment in sex offender management: An overview of key principles and practices*. Silver Spring. Retrieved from http://www.csom.org/pubs/assessment_brief.pdf

Uziel, L. (2010). Rethinking social desirability scales: From impression management to interpersonally oriented self-control. *Perspectives on Psychological Science, 5*(3), 243–262.

Veysey, B. M., & Hamilton, Z. (2007). Girls will be girls: Gender differences in predictors of success for diverted youth with mental health and substance abuse disorders. *Journal of Contemporary Criminal Justice, 23*(4), 341–362. doi:10.1177/1043986207309435

Ward, T. (2015). Dynamic risk factors: Scientific kinds or predictive constructs. *Psychology, Crime & Law*, 22(01-02), 2–16.

Ward, T., & Beech, A. R. (2014). Dynamic risk factors: A theoretical dead-end? *Psychology, Crime & Law, 21*(2), 100–113. doi:10.1080/1068316X.2014.917854

Ward, T., & Casey, A. (2010). Extending the mind into the world: A new theory of cognitive distortions in sex offenders. *Aggression and Violent Behavior, 15*(1), 49–58. Retrieved from http://www.sciencedirect.com/science/article/pii/S1359178909001001

Ward, T., Hudson, S. M., Johnston, L., & Marshall, W. L. (1997). Cognitive distortions in sex offenders: An integrative review. *Clinical Psychology Review, 17*(5), 479–507.

Wong, S., & Gordon, A. E. (1999–2003). *The Violence Risk Scale*. Unpublished manuscript. University of Saskatchewan, Saskatoon, Saskatchewan, Canada.

Wong, S., Olver, M. E., Nicholaichuk, T. P., & Gordon, A. (2003). *The Violence Risk Scale-Sexual Offender version (VRS-SO)*. Saskatoon: Regional Psychiatric Centre and University of Saskatchewan.

Yesberg, J. A., Scanlan, J. M., Hanby, L. J., Serin, R. C., & Polaschek, D. L. L. (2015). Predicting women's recidivism: Validating a dynamic community-based 'gender-neutral' tool. *Probation Journal, 62*(1), 33–48. doi:10.1177/0264550514562851

Dynamic risk and sexual offending: the conundrum of assessment

Sharon Casey

School of Psychology, Faculty of Health, Deakin University, Melbourne, VIC, Australia

ABSTRACT

The potential to reduce sexual victimisation, promote community safety, and decrease incarceration costs has resulted in considerable progress in terms of how we understand and predict sexual recidivism. And yet, the past decade has seen a degree of fragmentation emerge as research attention has shifted away from relative risk prediction (with its focus on static risk factors) to the identification of factors capable of reducing risk through intervention (i.e. dynamic risk). Although static and dynamic risk are often treated as orthogonal constructs [Beech, A. R., & Craig, L. A. (2012). The current status of static and dynamic factors in sexual offender risk assessment. *Journal of Aggression, Conflict and Peace Research*, *4*(4), 169–185. doi:10.1108/17596591211270671], there are arguments to support a claim that the two are in fact functionally related [see Ward, T. (2015). Dynamic risk factors: Scientific kinds or predictive constructs. *Psychology, Crime & Law* (in 22(01–02), 2–16); Ward, T., & Beech, A. R. (2015). Dynamic risk factors: A theoretical dead-end? *Psychology, Crime & Law*, *21*(2), 100–113. This discussion clearly affects how we assess dynamic risk. This review considered several commonly used methods of assessment and the evidence offered for their predictive accuracy. Of note were differences in the predictive accuracy of single psychometric measures versus composite scores of dynamic risk domains and the conventions used for establishing effect sizes for risk assessment tools.

The conundrum of dynamic risk assessment and sexual offending

Few crimes command public attention and evoke a level of outrage as strong as that associated with sexual offences. Frequently perceived as dangerous, resistant to rehabilitation, and highly likely to reoffend (Farkas & Stichman, 2002; Harris & Socia, 2014), sexual offenders in many jurisdictions have become subject to unique legislative responses including mandatory registration, community notification, residency restrictions, and civil commitment for sexually violent predators. Given the potential to reduce sexual victimisation, promote community safety, and decrease incarceration costs, considerable research attention has led to progress in terms of understanding and predicting sexual recidivism (Craissati, Bierer, & South, 2011; Olver, Beggs Christofferson, Grace, & Wong, 2014). However, a degree of fragmentation has also emerged over the past decade or so as research attention has shifted away from relative risk prediction (with its focus on static risk factors) to the identification of factors capable of reducing risk through intervention (i.e. dynamic risk).

The breadth of work undertaken in the area of dynamic risk has been summarised in several influential meta-analyses, namely Hanson and Bussière (1998), Hanson and Morton-Bourgon (2004, 2005), and Mann, Hanson, and Thornton (2010). These studies highlighted that no single risk factor is sufficiently strongly correlated with sexual recidivism to be a sole predictor, thus making it necessary to combine risk factors to produce an overall evaluation of risk. It also emerged that the strongest predictors for sexual offending differ from those for general offending. Thus outcomes from these meta-analyses have informed which dynamic risk factors are typically assessed (via structured ratings and psychometric testing) and targeted in treatment. According to Mann et al., the greatest empirical support for a relationship between dynamic risk and the prediction of recidivism applies to the following factors: sexual preoccupation, any deviant sexual interest (e.g. sexual preference for children, sexualised violence, multiple paraphilias), offense-supportive attitudes, emotional congruence with children, lack of emotionally intimate relationships with adults, lifestyle impulsivity, general self-regulation problems, poor cognitive problem solving, resistance to rules and supervision, grievance/hostility, and negative social influences. Although the authors offered no explanation regarding the causal nature of these risk factors, they nonetheless proposed they should serve as treatment targets.

Mann et al.'s (2010) approach is, of course, consistent with the central tenet of Andrews and Bonta's (2010) Risk-Need-Responsivity (RNR) model which stipulates that dynamic risks (i.e. criminogenic needs) are changeable and that bringing about positive change will lead to a reduction in recidivism. However, despite Hanson, Morton-Bourgon, Helmus, and Hodgson's (2009) meta-analysis demonstrating the RNR's applicability to sexual offending, evidence for a definite link between changes in dynamic risk and reduced recidivism remains limited (Hanson & Morton-Bourgon, 2005; Langton, 2003; Olver & Wong, 2011; Quinsey, Khanna, & Malcolm, 1998; but *cf.* Olver, Beggs Christofferson, et al., 2014; Olver, Wong, Nicholaichuk, & Gordon, 2007). This clearly raises questions about the RNR paradigm and, as a corollary, the assessments based on its framework and how these assessments are interpreted. While that discussion is beyond the scope of this paper, the importance of construct and predictive validity with regard to sexual offender assessment tools based on both static and dynamic factors cannot be underplayed. These tools inform legal (e.g. civil commitment, preventative detention, parole, probation, length of community supervision) and clinical (i.e. treatment intensity) decision-making processes for sexual offenders who seek treatment and/or enter the criminal justice system (Singh, Grann, & Fazel, 2011). In view of the gravity of such decisions, it is critical that risk assessment tools are based on a strong empirical base and display high levels of predictive validity (Tully, Chou, & Browne, 2013).

Dynamic risk factors for sexual offending include (deviant) sexual interests and sexual preoccupation; distorted cognitions supportive of sexual offending; problematic socio-affective functioning; and self-regulatory problems (see Craig, Browne, Stringer, & Hogue, 2008). While this *should* clarify assessment (i.e. in terms of its constituent elements) it has not. In fact, a lack of clarity remains about how we understand the very notion of dynamic risk (see Ward & Beech, 2015). The focus of this review will therefore be on the assessment of dynamic risk; the different types of measures available for assessment and what has been gleaned by way of accuracy regarding those tools. But before turning to these issues, it is first useful to briefly revisit static risk measures. While this may seem at odds with purpose of the review, the rationale for doing so has been previously raised by Beech and Craig (2012) who noted that static and dynamic risk are generally treated separately by researchers and practitioners who assume the relationship between the two is orthogonal. Several static factors have repeatedly been demonstrated to predict sexual recidivism. Further adding to the confusion is ambiguity regarding an operational definition of dynamic risk (Taxman, Caudy, & Pattavina, 2013). Arguments put forward by Ward (2015; Ward & Beech, 2015) serve to undermine any notion of orthogonality. If one follows the line of Ward's suppositions, it is much more likely that static and dynamic risk factors *are* functionally linked (Beech & Craig, 2012) and, for this reason, that which applies to dynamic risk factors – particularly the interpretation of accuracy indices – may also be of relevance to assessments using static risk factors when these tools are administered contemporaneously.

Actuarial risk assessment

Since being introduced, actuarial assessment risk assessment instruments (ARAIs) have dominated the offender risk prediction and management landscape, particularly in the domains of violent and sexual offending (Beech & Craig, 2012). Also commonly referred to as second generation (2G) assessments (Andrews, Bonta, & Wormith, 2006), ARAIs share a number of characteristics. Each adopts an explicit coding scheme with factors shown to be empirically related to the prediction of an event (typically recidivism) scored as present or absent. Total scores are then summed and converted (via experience tables) to probabilistic estimates of that event occurring (Mossman, 2013), which are transformed to categorical risk groups (e.g. low, medium, and high). Category membership is linked to the relative frequency of the event over specified follow-up periods (Dawes, Faust, & Meehl, 1989; Hanson & Morton-Bourgon, 2009; Mossman, 2013). To maintain validity, many ARAIs are regularly updated with empirically based revisions and the expansion of normative samples (Harris & Hanson, 2010). There are, however, several problems with ARAIs, one of the most notable of which is perhaps the derivation of ARAIs from base rates. Mossman (2015) has noted the underlying assumption that the normative data used to translate ARAI scores to probabilities of recidivism are constant across offender groups. However, risk prediction has been shown to be more accurate for White offenders than for those from other ethnic groups, a finding which has been attributed to differences in offending base rates between ethnicities (Singh et al., 2011). Consequently, while an ARAI may be effective in terms of ranking individuals from different populations, there will be differences in the probabilities associated with each score due to differences in population base rates (Mossman, 2006; Singh, 2013). Additional problems include that ARAIs emerge from a largely atheoretical approach and scale construction is based on correlative associations with a predicted event (Craig & Beech, 2010; Rossegger et al., 2013). Despite these limitations and some recent criticism (e.g. Cooke & Michie, 2010, 2011; Craig, Browne, & Stringer, 2003; Hart, Michie, & Cooke, 2007), simplicity, ease of administration and scoring, and relative accuracy (e.g. Campbell, French, & Gendreau, 2009; Hanson & Morton-Bourgon, 2009; Singh et al., 2011) has served to maintain their popularity. That said, Craig and Beech (2010) have pointed out this apparent simplicity comes with the potential for ARAI data to be misused, resulting in the misinterpretation and incorrect presentation of results.

In the assessment of sexual offenders, ARAIs are comprised, predominantly, of static risk factors. Static risk factors for sexual offending have been found to include age at first conviction, victim characteristics (e.g. male, unrelated, and stranger), developmental (e.g. juvenile offender), offence history (e.g. prior sexual and criminal offences, history of violence, non-contact offences), and clinical factors (e.g. evidence of psychopathy) (see Craig, Browne, Stringer, & Beech, 2005). Although commonly used ARAIs do not include every known predictor or, for that matter, are ARAIs always consistent in terms of which predictors are included, they nevertheless remain the primary method of risk assessment for sexual offenders. Among the most frequently used of the 2G instruments are the Rapid Risk Assessment for Sexual Offense Recidivism (RRASOR; Hanson, 1997), Static-99 (Hanson & Thornton, 2000) and Static 99-R (Phenix, Helmus, & Hanson, 2012), and the Risk Matrix 2000/S (RM2000/S; Thornton et al., 2003), and Sex Offender Risk Appraisal Guide (SORAG; Quinsey, Harris, Rice, & Cormier, 1998). The Minnesota Sex Offender Screening Tool–Revised (MnSOST-R; Epperson, Kaul, & Hesselton, 1998) is an example of a 2G ARAI that includes four dynamic risk factors (e.g. treatment while incarcerated). Despite some variation in item content, validation studies have consistently demonstrated the predictive validity of these measures across samples and jurisdictions (e.g. Allan, Dawson, & Allan, 2006; Craig, Beech, & Browne, 2006; Ducro & Pham, 2006; Kingston, Yates, Firestone, Babchishin, & Bradford, 2008; Skelton, Riley, Wales, & Vess, 2006) and while there is some variation across single studies this is likely a function of differences in sexual offender subgroups (e.g. recidivism base rates, victim type, and offender characteristics).

Why is the predictive accuracy of ARAIs relevant to assessments of dynamic risk? Two reasons: Potential non-orthogonality and the impact this has on predictive accuracy (i.e. the extent to which they are non-orthogonal will impact on how correlated the items are and hence the incremental validity). By way of support for a claim of non-orthogonality, consider the aetiological model of risk proposed by Beech and Ward (2004) in which they argue that historical risk factors function as markers for psychological vulnerabilities or traits (i.e. sexual self-regulation; general self-regulation/self-management; offence-supportive cognitions; level of interpersonal functioning). To test this proposition, the authors used four well-known risk tools (Static 99; Hanson & Thornton, 2000; SORAG, Quinsey, Harris, et al., 1998; MnSOST-R, Epperson et al., 1998; SVR-20, Boer, Wilson, Gauthier, & Hart, 1997) and mapped items by the apparent markers being tapped at a dispositional level. The majority of items mapped onto two vulnerability domains: sexual self-regulation (60% Static 99; 50% MnSOST; 25% SVR-20; 21% SORAG) and general self-regulation/self-management (50% SORAG; 40% SVR-20; 31% MnSOST-R; 30% Static-99). Ward and Beech would argue that the former is a marker for deviant sexual interest (Thornton, 2002) and the latter (which incorporates impulsivity) for sexual violence (see Prentky, Knight, Lee, & Cerce, 1995). It is this capacity to mark 'offence-related proclivities in certain individuals' (Ward, 2015, p. 102) which makes ARIAs good predictors of risk. Moreover, Ward and Beech's aetiological model clearly illustrates non-orthogonality, at least on the domains of sexual self-regulation and general self-relation, both of which have been identified by Mann et al. (2010) as empirically supported dynamic risk factors. The assessment of dynamic risk can be undertaken using specifically designed structured rating tools (e.g. STABLE; Hanson, Harris, Scott, & Helmus, 2007; Beech Deviancy Classification, Beech, 1998; Beech & Fisher, 2004; Beech, Friendship, Erikson, & Hanson, 2002) or pre/post-test psychometric testing, although the goal is usually the same: to determine the incremental contribution of the dynamic risk factors (Craig, Thornton, Beech, & Browne, 2007; Olver et al., 2007; Thornton, 2002).

Dynamic risk assessment

The dominant RNR paradigm (Andrews & Bonta, 2010) conceptualises dynamic risk as enduring psychological or behavioural features shown not only to correlate with recidivism but, due to their variability, amenable to change following intervention (Bonta, 1996; Hanson & Bussière, 1998; Hanson & Harris, 2001; Harris & Hanson, 2010; Proulx, Perreault, & Ouimet, 1999; Thornton, 2002). Dynamic factors are further delineated as either stable or acute. *Stable* dynamic risk factors are those with a tendency to be persistent characteristics (i.e. stable over time) that change over an extended period (e.g. cognitive distortions, deviant sexual arousal). *Acute* dynamic risk factors, on the other hand, are more fluctuating or rapidly changing (e.g. negative emotional state, substance abuse, and victim acquisition behaviours) and can daily, even hourly. Consequently, acute dynamic risk is said to have the potential to signal the time at which offending is at greatest risk of occurring.

As noted, Beech and Ward (2004; Ward & Beech, 2015) have challenged the RNR framework and proposed an aetiological model of risk. According to their model, stable dynamic risk factors reflect *psychological vulnerability* factors (e.g. self-regulation, offence-supportive cognitions) or *traits* that increase an individual's propensity to engage in sexually abusive behaviour. Stable dynamic risk factors serve as markers for these vulnerabilities, while the final element in their model, *states*, are similar to acute risk factors and have been framed as triggering events or contextual risk factors (e.g. deviant sexual arousal, deviant thoughts, and fantasies). The likelihood of sexual offending is said to be increased when an interaction occurs between state and trait factors. By way of example, offence-supportive cognitions (trait) can be activated and thereby produce deviant thoughts and fantasies (state), which is a known precursor of sexual offending (see Mann et al., 2010). Another reconceptualisation of the stable/acute classification is Mann et al.'s (2010) concept of *psychologically meaningful* risk factors. In this model, risk factors are individual *propensities* which, like traits, involve enduring characteristics (i.e. feelings, thoughts, and behaviours), the expression of which is predictable although the timeframe in which that expression occurs is not. As characteristics of the individual, propensities are also an expression of the individual's interaction with both the environment and its inhabitants. Consequently, an offender may contribute to their recidivism risk in particular ways through consistency in self (i.e. via their propensities) and consistencies in their environment (e.g. gravitating towards high-crime neighbourhoods, criminal associates). In this sense, Mann et al. are drawing attention to the role of environmental interaction and the interpretation that interaction plays in the aetiology of problematic behaviour.

A recent review of the theoretical issues related to risk and its conceptualisation by Ward and Beech (2015) argued that neither Beech and Ward (2004) nor Mann et al. (2010) provide a theoretical explanation for the causal properties ascribed to risk, irrespective of whether it is defined as psychological vulnerabilities or psychologically meaningful risk factors. In their view, the failure by the researchers to consider the structure and function of dynamic risk factors has resulted in a lack of advancement in terms of understanding the hypothesised causal processes involved (see Ward, 2015). One might also add that in both cases, this hinders further advancement in terms of modifying current approaches to dynamic risk assessment. What follows is a discussion of structured risk assessments and commentary on the findings with respect to predictive and incremental validity.

Structured risk assessments

The most well-known structured dynamic risk assessment frameworks for adults include the STABLE-2007/ACUTE-2007 (Hanson et al., 2007), Structured Risk Assessment and its close derivative the Structured Assessment of Risk and Need (SRA; Thornton, 2002), Beech Deviancy Classification (Beech, 1998; Beech et al., 2002), and the Violence Risk Assessment Scale-Sexual Offender version (VRS-SO; Wong, Olver, Nicholaichuk, & Gordon, 2003). The Juvenile Sex Offender Assessment Protocol–II (J-SOAP-II) is a widely used dynamic risk assessment tool for juvenile sexual offenders. Unlike ARAIs which, in most instances, can be completed by file review and collateral information, assessment using these tools require consideration of evidence from a range of sources in order to make a judgment about the presence, absence, and/or strength of each dynamic factor. With the exception of the VRS-SO, assessment incorporates the administration of an ARAI (e.g. Static-99; Hanson & Thornton, 2000; RM2000; Thornton et al., 2003) together with a range of psychometric tools which constitute the dynamic risk element of the assessment.

Beech deviancy scale

The Beech Deviancy Scale (Beech, 1998; Beech & Fisher, 2004) is a psychological typology that distinguishes between high and low deviancy offenders based on the presence of stable dynamic risk factors (i.e. pro-offending attitudes, socio-affective functioning). Developed using a battery of psychometric tests purportedly tapping the relevant domains, cluster analysis techniques were used to divide child molesters into the final two groupings. Based on a scoring protocol, High Deviance men display: high levels of cognitive distortions about children, highly distorted attitudes about their victims, sexual obsessions, and self-reported sexual deviance patterns (Beech, 1998). They also report problems forming adult intimate attachments, showing a preference for having their emotional needs met by children, while experiencing other socio-affective difficulties (e.g. low self-esteem, loneliness; Beech, 1998; Beech & Ford, 2006). In contrast, there is an absence of generalised cognitive distortions with Low Deviance men, no evidence of emotional identification with children (in fact, it has been shown to be lower than non-offender groups; see Fisher, Beech, & Browne, 1999). Although Low Deviance men exhibit social inadequacy problems, it is not as marked as that found in High Deviance men.

In its current format assessment is comprised of eight scales, three which measure pro-offending attitudes (i.e. the *Emotional Identification with Children Subscale* of the Children & Sex Questionnaire, Beckett, 1987; *Victim Empathy Distortions*, Beckett & Fisher, 1994; *Short Self-Esteem Scale*, Thornton, 1989) and five measures of socio-affective functioning (*UCLA Emotional Loneliness Scale*, Russell, Peplau, & Cutrona, 1980; *Under-assertiveness/Over-*

assertiveness Subscales, Social Response Inventory, Keltner, Marshall, & Marshall, 1981; *Personal Distress Scale*, Interpersonal Reactivity Index, Davis, 1983; *Nowicki-Strickland Locus of Control Scale*, Nowicki, 1976; Nowicki & Duke, 1983). Beech and Fisher (2004) simplified the original scoring system by introducing weighted scores on each of the measures whereby the most discriminating (canonical correlations exceeding .40) were assigned three points (e.g. Sexual Interest in Children scale), the next (canonical correlations exceeding 0.20) were assigned two points (e.g. UCLA Emotional Loneliness scale), and the least discriminating measures (canonical correlations below 0.20) assigned one point (e.g. Personal Distress scale). The maximum weighted score when summated is 17, with a High Deviance cut-off of eight or above.

Early investigations indicated support for the additional assessment of dynamic risk. For example, Beech et al. (2002) found that psychometrically assessed deviancy in a small sample of child abusers (6-year follow-up) provided incremental predictive validity to that derived from the Static 99 (Hanson & Thornton, 2000). Similar findings were reported by Beech and Ford (2006), again a small sample of 51 sexual offenders with static risk was assessed using the Risk Matrix 2000 (RM2000; Thornton et al., 2003). Only High/Very High risk RM2000 scorers were reconvicted at 2- and 5-year follow-up. On dynamic risk, there was a greater likelihood for High Deviance men to be reconvicted for a sexual offence at 2-year and 5-year follow-up (13%, 44%, respectively) than Low Deviance men (4%, 10%), although given the sample size this represented two cases for each period for the higher deviancy group and one case each for the lower deviancy offenders.

Structured assessment of risk and need (structured risk assessment)

The Structured Assessment of Risk and Need (also known as the Structured Risk Assessment [SRA], Thornton, 2002) is a research-guided, multistep framework that integrates a Static Risk Assessment (RM2000/S; Thornton et al., 2003; or Static 99), an assessment of treatment needs (Initial Deviancy Assessment [IDA] in the SRA) and an evaluation of progress based on treatment response to determine treatment change (see Craig et al., 2007; Tully, Browne, & Craig, 2015). Once an offender's risk has been determined and risk band identified, the next step is to assess for the presence or absence of 16 (15 in Tully et al.) dynamic risk factors. These are grouped across four domains: sexual interests, distorted/offence-supportive attitudes, relationships (social and emotional functioning), and self-management. On the basis of psychometric data, personal history information, interviews, and file reviews, each factor is rated on a 3-point scale (0 = not present; 1 = present but not a central characteristic; 2 = a central characteristic). The rating occurs twice: once for proximal factors ('offence chain') and a second time with respect to the offender's life in general ('generality'). Any item that scores 2 in both contexts is designated a treatment need. Within the UK prison and parole system, low deviance is defined as the presence of no or few dynamic risk factors (i.e. 0 or 1 domain with scores of 2 in generality and offense chain); moderate deviance is two domains with risk with scores of 2 in both generality and offense chain; high deviance offenders score 2 across 3 or 4 domains 2 for both generality and offense chain.

Evidence for incremental validity is primarily based on studies investigating the SRA (e.g. Craig et al., 2007; Wakeling, Beech, & Freemantle, 2013; Wakeling, Freemantle, Beech, & Elliott, 2011) although a recent study by Tully et al. (2015) has considered recidivism outcomes from the SARN. In their examination of whether the integration of statistical and psychological risk predicts sexual reconviction, Craig et al. (2007) used an updated test battery to measure the four domains (i.e. sexual interests, distorted attitude, socio-affective functioning, self-management) of the SRA. These were combined to provide a Psychological Deviance Index (PDI) based on the number of dysfunctional domains. In terms of predicting recidivism from dynamic risk domains and the PDI, the largest effects over 2- and 5-year follow-up was found for the sexual interests domain (AUC $= .86$, $p < .001$ and AUC $= .72$, $p < .001$ respectively). The effect size for the PDI, while smaller, was nonetheless significant for both follow-up periods (AUC $= .75$, $p = .02$ and AUC $= .69$, $p = .02$). On this basis, the authors argued for a linear relationship between sexual reconviction and the PDI although recidivism was only assessed over a 5-year period and resulted in a reduction in effect size of .06. One might argue there is a need for a longer follow-up period with a larger sample size (despite the base rate for reconviction at 5 years being 12%) to add weight to this claim. Interestingly, the Static 99 did not predict recidivism at either 2- or 5-year follow-up (AUC $= .66$, $p = .14$ and AUC $= .60$, $p = .20$) and, as with the dynamic risk factors, the effect size showed a decrease over the 3-year period. Given the preceding findings, not surprisingly, the only evidence of incremental validity was on the sexual interests domain (at both 2- and 5-year follow-up) when the full-scale Static 99 and Static subscales were entered into the equation. When this latter analysis was conducted, the influence of the self-management domain appears to increase marginally and come within range of significance (Wald $= 3.417$, $p = .065$, Exp(B) $= .484$ to Wald $= 4.035$, $p = .045$, Exp(B) $= .438$). A major issue with the study is the decreasing effect sizes as this occurs with both the static and dynamic risk factors. The largest discrepancy over a 3-year period is .10 sexual interests deviancy, with only one increased noted (.02) on the distorted attitudes. While one can question the impact of environmental or individual factors on psychometric test results, it also raises questions about the efficacy of the test battery.

Wakeling et al.'s (2011) study, which attempted to find the best predictors of violence and sexual recidivism based on static (RM2000; Thornton et al., 2003) and dynamic assessment risk assessment (a psychometric test battery), found that three static variables consistently emerged as the strongest predictors of recidivism (age at release from prison; number of sexual appearances; number of criminal appearances). Initial attempts to include single measure pre- and post-treatment dynamic variables failed to add to the predictive power of these static variables although when these were combined as psychometric risk domains, pre-treatment scores measuring socio-affective problems was found to be a significant predictor of recidivism (albeit in a model which only included dynamic variables; i.e. static variables were removed). When domain scores were combined to produce a Psychological Deviancy Index (PDI), the pre-treatment PDI remained significant in the prediction model (HR $= 1.16$, $\chi^2 = 5.37$, $p = .02$). Thus the psychometric scores added to the predictive power in terms of predicting recidivism although the contribution was much smaller than the static variables of younger age at release (HR $= 0.94$, $\chi^2 = 82.49$, $p < .001$), number of sexual offences (HR $= 1.62$, $\chi^2 = 16.42$, $p < .001$), number of criminal offences (HR $=$ 2.06, $\chi^2 = 90.36$, $p < .001$), but almost on par with evidence of ever having had a non-contact offence (HR $= 1.43$, $\chi^2 = 4.04$, $p = .045$).

A follow-up study by Wakeling et al. (2013) differed in that it included measures of sexual interest domain (absent from the earlier study), considered clinically significant change on treatment outcome measures, and examined whether treatment change was related to recidivism. Treatment change, based on the categories outlined by Jacobson, Roberts, Berns, and McGlinchey (1999[1]), showed that on the majority of measures the largest proportion of offenders were in the unchanged group (15.9–63.3%) and the smallest in the deteriorated (2.1–10.4%) group. Recidivism (reconviction) by SARN domain showed significant associations on three of the four, namely: Sexual Interests ($\chi^2 = 4.60$, $p < .05$), Socio-affective problems ($\chi^2 = 5.67$, $p < 0.05$), and self-regulation problems ($\chi^2 = 12.90$, $p < .001$). As one might expect, significantly lower levels of recidivism was found across all domains in those designated as not requiring change as compared to those still requiring change. When examined by offence type, none of the significant associations between domain status and reconviction rate held for rapists while for child molesters, socio-affective problems and self-regulation problems remained significant. The particular relevance of this study is that it supports claims by other researchers regarding the importance of individual change versus the use of group statistics (e.g. Mandeville-Norden, Beech, & Hayes, 2008; Nunes, Babchishin, & Cortoni, 2011). Yet despite these promising findings, overall change status failed to add significantly to the predictive power of a modified version of the RM2000/S. Thus while the earlier study by Wakeling et al. (2011) showed that a composite score of pre-treatment deviancy (based on psychometric assessment) was associated with recidivism, change status on the constructs incorporated in that measure were not.

In the most recent analysis of the SARN (the Treatment Needs Analysis version or SARN-TNA), Tully et al. (2015) utilised AUC statistic to examine its capacity to predict relative risk. Neither the static or dynamic risk tools was found to significantly predict sexual reconviction at 2- or 4-year follow-up (SARN: AUC = .59, $p = .194$ and AUC = .57, p = .242 respective; RM2000/S: AUC = .53, $p = .639$ and AUC = .53, $p = .592$ respectively). In other words, the performance of both measures was no better than chance. Of the four SARN domains, the sexual interests showed moderate predictive validity at both 2- and 4-year follow-up (AUC = .65, $p = .035$ and AUC = .68, $p = .004$) and was shown to predict recidivism via logistic regression. One major difference between the usual assessment strategies adopted in the SARN (and a point acknowledged by Tully et al.) was the use of assessor clinical judgment. They note that findings based on the psychometric analysis of SARN domains appear to have more successfully predicted reconviction (e.g. Craig et al., 2007; Thornton, 2002; Wakeling et al., 2011).

STABLE 2007/ACUTE 2007

The STABLE-2007/ACUTE-2007 (and preceding versions) are the most widely used sexual offender dynamic risk assessment tools Canada and the US (McGrath, Cumming, Burchard, Zeoli, & Ellerby, 2010). An interview- and file-based tool, the STABLE-2007 is comprised of 13 relatively enduring but changeable factors that reflect five stable dynamic dimensions: (i) significant social influences; (ii) intimacy deficits; (iii) sexual self-regulation problems; (iv) general self-regulation problems; (v) (non)co-operation with supervision (Hanson et al., 2007). Factors are assessed using three-point ratings scales (0 = no problem; 1 = some concern/slight problem; 2 = present/definite concern) with total scores ranging from 0 to 26. Total scores are assigned to one of three empirically derived need categories (Low 0–3; Moderate, 4–11; and High, 12–26). The ACUTE-2007 is comprised of seven rapidly changeable risk factors, which form two discrete factors: sexual preoccupations, victim access, rejection of supervision, and hostility; emotional collapse, collapse of social supports, and substance abuse (Hanson et al., 2007). Recommended cut-off scores on the 4-item factor are: none = low, one (maybe/possible problem) = moderate, and two or more = high. Where all acute factors are used, cut-scores are as follows: none = low, one–two = moderate, and three or more = high.

The first examination of predictive and incremental validity of the STABLE-2007 was undertaken as part of the Dynamic Supervision Project (DSP; Hanson et al., 2007), which also demonstrated the utility in combining static, stable, and acute risk factors to assist in the supervision of community-based sexual offenders. Turning first to predictive validity, the STABLE-2007 showed a significant association with recidivism (AUC = .76), with the figure marginally lower when breaches were included in the analysis (AUC = .73). Incremental validity, examined via Cox regression analysis (controlling for Static 99 scores), revealed the contribution of the STABLE-2007 was significant to both types of sexual recidivism (sexual: $ß = .059$, $p = .049$; sexual + breaches: $ß = .099$, $p < .001$). Predictive accuracy of the acute variables were examined using a series of different analyses (most recent rating within 45 days of recidivism; average rating within 45 days; average rating within 90 days; average rating within 183 days/6 months). The significant predictors for sexual recidivism were victim access, sexual preoccupations, rejection of supervision, and hostility (for 90 and 183 days); averaging acute ratings over longer time periods serves to increase predictive accuracy. Despite important modifications made to the tools as part of the DSP, a major limitation of the research was the low rate of absolute recidivism, particularly for sexual offenders (< 10%).

Recently, Helmus, Hanson, Babchishin, and Thornton (2015) examined whether the STABLE-2007 added incremental predictive accuracy to the Risk Matrix 2000. Analysis was based on data drawn from the DSP study with a follow-up period ranging from 1 to 10 years. Relative predictive accuracy (i.e. discrimination) on the RM2000 was strongest for sexual offending (AUC = .695) and sexual offending including breaches (AUC = .685). Subsequent analyses showed the STABLE-2007 was moderately related to all three Risk Matrix scales: RM2000/S, $r = .425$, $p < .001$; RM2000/V, $r = .309$, $p < .001$; and RM2000/C, $r = .417$, $p < .001$. The STABLE's incremental validity for sexual offences when used in conjunction with the RM2000/S approached significance (Wald = 3.66, $p = .056$) and was significant when sexual offences included breaches (Wald = 8.91, $p = .003$); it also predicted all other offence types with the RM2000/S, RM2000/V, and RM2000/C. An examination of the magnitude of the incremental validity shows these are not large. This is evident when looking at the AUCs for the combined STABLE-2007/Risk Matrix scales. For example, whereas the combination of the Risk Matrix 2000/S and the STABLE-2007 revealed effect sizes predicting sexual and any sexual recidivism of AUC = .69 and .71, respectively, only the latter prediction increased on the combined measure (i.e. from .685 to .71). Such an improvement is modest at best. Moreover, it says little in terms of how one might use the information from the assessment. How much weight would a clinician, for example, give to the each of the domains that constitute the STABLE when addressing the offender's criminogenic needs?

Sex offender treatment intervention and progress scale (SOTIPS)

A more recently developed measure, the SOTIPS (McGrath, Lasher, & Cumming, 2011) is derived from the Sex Offender Treatment Needs and Progress Scale (SOTNPS; McGrath & Cumming, 2001, 2003) which is used extensively across the US (McGrath et al., 2010). The revised instrument differs from other assessments discussed in that it is designed for multiple administrations (i.e. 6 monthly intervals) and is designed to be used to examine change in dynamic risk following participation in treatment. Its purpose, therefore, is to aid in the identification and monitoring of supervision and treatment needs for adult male sex offenders. Comprised of 16 items, the measure has three subscales: Sexual Deviance (i.e. sexual attitudes, sexual interest, offence responsibility, sexual risk management, sexual behaviour, stage of change), Criminality (i.e. antisocial behaviour, supervision co-operation, antisocial attitudes, impulsivity, treatment co-operation), and Social Stability and Supports (residence stability, employment stability, problem solving, emotion management, social influences). Items are initially scored at intake and then every 6 months using a 4-point scale: minimal to no need for improvement, some need for improvement, considerable need for improvement, and very considerable need for improvement. Total scores can range from 0 to 48 and are organised into three risk/need groups: low (0–10), moderate (11–20), and high (21–48). The instrument is used in conjunction with the Static-99R (Helmus, Thornton, Hanson, & Babchishin, 2012) to assess both static and dynamic risk.

Predictive validity was examined by McGrath et al. (2011) over 1 and 3 years, providing for six assessment points on each of the SOTIPS risk categories. This revealed that at Time 1, the SOTIPS prediction was low (1-year follow-up: AUC = .60, $p > .05$; 3-year follow-up: AUC = .61, $p < .05$), although it improved markedly with moderate prediction at Time 2 (1-year follow-up: AUC = .81, $p < .001$; 3-year follow-up: AUC = .61, $p < .001$) and Time 3 (1-year follow-up: AUC = .77, $p < .01$; 3-year follow-up: AUC = .72, $p < .01$).[2] Separate analyses considered the predictive validity of offenders with adult-only victims (20.4%) versus those with child-only victims (75.8%) across the six assessments. SOTIPS scores for child-only victim offenders were found to predict all types of recidivism investigated (i.e. sexual, violent, any criminal, and return to prison) at 1 and 3-year follow-up; for adult-only victims, scores were only significant predictors of return to prison with the exception of Time 2 scores which also predicted any criminal and violent recidivism.

Looking next at incremental validity, the Static 99-R was generally a better predictor at Time 1 (1-year sexual recidivism, for example, AUC = .81, $p < .001$ versus AUC = .66, $p < .05$), with similar rates of prediction noted at Time 2 (1-year sexual recidivism, for example, AUC = .81, $p < .001$ versus AUC = .85, $p < .001$), whereas the dynamic measure was the stronger predictor at Time 3 (1-year sexual recidivism, for example, AUC = .57, $p > .05$ versus AUC = .78, $p < .05$). Interestingly, the results were inconsistent for the subscale scores across Time 1, but statistically significant for all conditions at Times 2 and 3 (AUCs = .61 to .82). Using binomial logistic generalised estimating equations (GEE) to create risk band categories (i.e. Static-99R × SOTIPS combinations), 3-year sexual recidivism rates for offenders in each band were calculated. This revealed that in combining the two measures there were significant improvements in the predictive power across the four risk categories than was found when simply using the Static-99R for the 1- and 3-year follow-up periods (i.e. between 20% and 43% at 1-year; 10% and 30% at 3-year follow-up). What the findings suggest, then is that whereas the Static-99R appeared a better predictor at Time 1, the two tools were equivalent at Time 2 and the SOTIPS was the better predictor at Time 3. While these results suggest the measure is promising, the follow-up period of 3 years is short, particularly for sexual offenders. That prediction peaks at Time 2 would suggest that perhaps the static factors are, to use the vernacular of Beech and Ward (2004), serving as risk markers for underlying traits (dynamic risk). As with measures described above, the strength of the effect size appears to diminish over a short time interval, highlighting the need for longitudinal studies.

Violence risk scale: sexual offender version

Of the structured dynamic risk measures described herein, the format of the Violence Risk Scale-Sexual Offender Version (VRS-SO; Olver et al., 2007) is perhaps the most familiar. Comprised of 24 items it includes 7 static (i.e. criminal history, victim and offender demographics) and 17 dynamic items which, according to developers, are empirically, theoretically, or conceptually related to an increased risk for sexual recidivism (e.g. cognitive distortions, deviant sexual preference, intimacy deficits). Items are rated on a 4-point (0, 1, 2, 3) scale with higher scores indicative of an increased risk for sexual recidivism. Dynamic risk rated as 2 or 3 are designated as criminogenic need and therefore targeted for treatment. Items are grouped into three areas: Sexual Deviance, Criminality, and Treatment Responsivity. Treatment targets are given a stages-of-change baseline/pre-treatment rating to assess motivation and readiness for change. Treatment change involves reassessment at post-treatment with stage progression based shifts in stages (as evidence by incremental reductions of 0.5 per stage). The procedure is applied to each dynamic item to produce post-treatment scores on each, with the sum of all dynamic items plus total static items providing a post-treatment risk rating.

Olver and Wong's (2011) evaluation of predictive validity compared VRS-SO and Static 99 (Hanson & Thornton, 1999) scores in a sample of treated sex offenders over a 10-year follow-up period. It revealed, first, that those in the high-risk/low-change group reoffended at a rate that was significantly higher (36%) than their high-risk counterparts who achieved greater levels of treatment change (24%). Next, an examination of predictive accuracy revealed the Static 99 showed moderate levels (AUCs .64–.67) for conviction on the three lower levels of change whereas the relationship with high change was close to negligible (AUC = .56). Although the AUCs were marginally larger, a similar pattern emerged for VRS-SO dynamic variables across the four change groups. Pre- (AUCs .64–.70) and post-treatment (AUCs .65–.70) scores significantly predicted conviction and, although larger than the Static 99, did not predict conviction at the highest level of change (AUCs of .63 and .65 for pre- and post-treatment respectively). In a subsequent study, Olver, Kingston, Nicholaichuk, and Wong (2014) included a psychometric self-report test battery (e.g. cognitive distortions, aggression/hostility, empathy, loneliness, social intimacy, acceptance of responsibility) in their predictive validity analysis. Pre- and post-treatment scores on the psychometric measures demonstrated weak or non-significant relationships to sexual recidivism (pre-treatment AUCs .36–.61; post-treatment AUCs .39–.66). However, the authors noted that some of the psychometric measures (e.g. Rape and Molest scales, Bumby, 1996; Sex Offender Assessment of Responsibility, Peacock, 2000) were not designed to appraise recidivism risk while others (e.g. loneliness, social intimacy) are not offender population constructs. Of note is that the measures not designed for offender populations have been used, for example, in the SARN (Thornton, 2002) and show greater predictive validity when used in conjunction with others measures (rather than single items) to assess deviancy domains. In addition to prediction of sexual offences, the study also included violent and general recidivism. However, the only significant relationships in the test battery involved that between post-treatment scores of aggression and predictions of violence (AUC = .67) and both pre- and post-treatment on the same measure and general recidivism. Finally, the incremental contribution of change to reduced recidivism involved controlling of pre-treatment scores and actuarial risk (Static-99R) with the calculation of standardised residual change scores (RCZs). No change was significantly associated with reduced sexual recidivism but positive changes in aggression scores were associated with reduced violent and general recidivism.

Conclusions

What does the preceding summary of structured dynamic risk tools tell us about their usefulness in the context of assessing sexual offenders? The most telling point is that the majority of risk prediction variance is explained by the static component of the assessment and that the incremental validity of dynamic risk factors is limited. Does this mean that dynamic risk factors fail to tell us anything about the individual? That will depend largely on what position is taken regarding the relationship between static and dynamic risk. If one adopts the aetiological model described by Beech and Ward (2004; Ward & Beech, 2015), clearly the two will be related, although it remains unclear how this model can be used to inform the assessment process. Adapting the principles into a formal assessment tool would help elucidate some elements of the model. Olver et al. (2007) take a different stance, arguing that attempts to demonstrate incremental validity are unnecessary; that the utility, and thus function, of dynamic risk is treatment planning and risk reduction. Assessment plays a necessary role here and there are some who would argue that items included on the VRS-SO are inconsistent with what Douglas and Skeem (2005) suggest are the components that make a risk factor dynamic, (i) being antecedent to, and increasing the propensity for, a behaviour; (ii) the capacity to change spontaneously or in response to treatment; and (iii) predicting change in recidivism following intervention. Finally, there is the perspective that 'real' dynamic predictors should demonstrate incremental validity to static risk factors and that change on that variable should effect an appreciable change in risk (Harris et al., 2003). However, to demonstrate incremental validity one must first have a clearly operationalised construct and that clearly is not the case. More work is needed in this regard.

A second issue to consider is that some of the measures described above – excluding the VRS-SO (Olver et al., 2007) and STABLE-2007/ACUTE-2007 (Hanson et al., 2007) – rely heavily on psychometric test batteries (e.g. Beech Deviancy Scale, Beech, 1998; SARN, Thornton, 2002). These can differ between studies even when the same assessment tool is involved. For example, while Wakeling et al. (2011, 2013) replicated Thornton's (2002) original test battery, Craig et al. (2007) opted for different measures despite all ostensibly using the SRA or SARN. Of course as there were different aims, so too different methodologies were adopted by the researchers. Nonetheless, the strength of the relationship between the dynamic risk factors and recidivism was low even when one takes into account such factors as sample sizes, base rates for reoffending, and variations in population. One notable difference between outcomes related to the predictive value of individual psychometric test scores versus psychometric domain composite scores. In most studies the effect sizes, when evident, were small to moderate but, irrespective of the analysis used it was typically stronger when domains or total scores were used. This is, of course, consistent with meta-analytic findings that show single risk factors are not strongly enough correlated with sexual recidivism to be sole predictors (Hanson & Bussière, 1998; Hanson & Morton-Bourgon, 2004, 2005; Mann et al., 2010). The stronger approach certainly appears to be domain and/or total scores.

One last point that needs to be made both with respect to overall effect size and incremental validity is how these are interpreted. The most commonly used statistical method for establishing predictive accuracy is receiver operating characteristic (ROC) area under the curve (AUC) analysis (Mossman, 1994; Swets, Dawes, & Monahan, 2000). While ROC analysis provides several ways of summarising prediction accuracy, here we are concerned with two commonly used indices. The first index, the area under the curve (AUC), is a simple summary of overall accuracy which involves a comparison of sensitivity or 'hit rate' (i.e. percentage of reoffenders correctly identified as high risk on assessment) with specificity (i.e. percentage of non-reoffenders correctly identified as low risk). False positives (false alarm rate) is reciprocal to sensitivity (true positives); false negatives (miss rate) is reciprocal to specificity. Calculating the effect size of the prediction method is another way that the overall accuracy of prediction can be summarised. ROC curves and standardised mean differences (Cohen's *d*) are based on similar statistical models and the convention has become to convert AUC values to Cohen's *d* using the values of .20, .50, and .80 as small, medium, and large, respectively (Cohen, 1988). In the broad field of behavioural research this has come to represent AUC values of .56, .64, and .71 (Rice & Harris, 2005). By way of comparison, other discipline areas have suggested: .50–.70 rather low accuracy, .70–.90 useful for some purposes, and .90–1.0 rather high accuracy (Swets, 1988); or 0.50 no discrimination, .70–.80 acceptable discrimination, .80–.90 excellent discrimination (Hosmer & Lemeshow, 2000).

While clearly there is a difference between what is acceptable in the medical sciences in terms of true positives and false negatives, criticism has been levelled at adopting the small, medium, large classification without heeding Cohen's (1988) sentiments when assigning those labels as a rule of thumb (in the estimation of effect sizes). In fact, Cohen pointed out that such arbitrary labels would be problematic (see Mossman, 2013). He stated that '… qualitative concepts as "large" are sometimes understood as absolute, sometimes as relative; and thus they run a risk of being misunderstood' (Cohen, 1988, p. 12). Rather than being the 'geusstimate' he had proposed, they have become standards by which accuracy is judged. It is worth noting that Rice and Harris (2005) acknowledged that the categories were provided as a tentative rule of thumb. Perhaps researchers have become complacent with seemingly 'strong' effect sizes found on the current battery of assessment tools and willing to accept incremental validity in the range of .02–.04 as sufficient evidence that the assessment tool is meeting the criteria of evidence-based assessment.

In conclusion, the way forward in dynamic risk assessment, it seems, is by taking a step back. A step back in terms of theory development, from which can emerge the constructs that might define and explain risk. This should, in turn, inform the development of assessment tools which can be validated according to best practice and evidence-based assessment guidelines. Of course, this is perhaps a little Utopian given the reality of the situation. Perhaps it requires two streams of enquiry that share knowledge: one that undertakes the basic research and disseminates the findings and the other that continues with current practice and uses new information to bring about change and publishes the outcomes of those new endeavours.

Notes

1. Deteriorated: demonstrates reliable change but in the undesired direction; Unchanged: no reliable change; Improved: demonstrates reliable change but not within the range of normal functioning post-treatment; Recovered: demonstrates reliable change and clinical significance; Already okay: individuals whose scores were in the desirable range both pre- and post-treatment.
2. Note: Time 1 = SOTIPS score at 0–3 months after client started treatment; Time 2 = 4–9 months; and Time 3 = 10–15 months.

Disclosure statement

No potential conflict of interest was reported by the author.

References

Allan, A., Dawson, D., & Allan, M. M. (2006). Prediction of the risk of male sexual reoffending in Australia. *Australian Psychologist*, *41*, 60–68. doi:10.1080/00050060500391886

Andrews, D. A., & Bonta, J. (2010). *The psychology of criminal conduct* (5th ed.). New Providence, NJ: LexisNexis.

Andrews, D. A., Bonta, J., & Wormith, S. J. (2006). The recent past and near future of risk and/or need assessment. *Crime & Delinquency*, *52*, 7–27. doi:10.1177/0011128705281756

Beckett, R. C. (1987). *The children and sex questionnaire*. Unpublished manuscript.

Beckett, R. C., & Fisher, D. (1994). *Assessing victim empathy: A new measure*. Paper presented at the 13th Annual Conference of ATSA (the Association for the Treatment of Sexual Abusers). San Francisco, CA.

Beech, A. R. (1998). A psychometric typology of child abusers. *International Journal of Offender Therapy and Comparative Criminology*, *42*, 319–339. doi:10.1177/0306624X9804200405

Beech, A. R., & Craig, L. A. (2012). The current status of static and dynamic factors in sexual offender risk assessment. *Journal of Aggression, Conflict and Peace Research*, *4*(4), 169–185. doi:10.1108/17596591211270671

Beech, A. R., & Fisher, D. D. (2004). Treatment of sexual offenders in prison and probation settings. In H. Kemshall & G. McIvor (Eds.), *Research highlights in social work: Sex offenders: Managing the risk* (pp. 137–164). London: Jessica Kingsley.

Beech, A. R., & Ford, H. (2006). The relationship between risk, deviance, treatment outcome and sexual reconviction in a sample of child sexual abusers completing residential treatment for their offending. *Psychology, Crime & Law*, *12*, 685–701.

Beech, A. R., Friendship, C., Erikson, M., & Hanson, R. K. (2002). The relationship between static and dynamic risk factors and reconviction in a sample of UK child abusers. *Sexual Abuse: A Journal of Research and Treatment*, *14*, 155–167. doi:10.1177/107906320201400206

Beech, A. R., & Ward, T. (2004). The integration of etiology and risk in sexual offenders: A theoretical framework. *Aggression and Violent Behavior*, *10*, 31–63. doi:10.1016/j.avb.2003.08.002

Boer, D. P., Wilson, R. J., Gauthier, C. M., & Hart, S. D. (1997). *Manual for the Sexual Violence Risk-20*. Vancouver, BC: The Mental Health, Law and Policy Institute and the Simon Fraser University.

Bonta, J. (1996). Risk-needs assessment and treatment. In A. T. Harland (Ed.), *Choosing correctional options that work* (pp. 18–32). Thousand Oaks, CA: Sage.

Bumby, K. M. (1996). Assessing the cognitive distortions of child molesters and rapists: Development and validation of the MOLEST and RAPE scales. *Sexual Abuse: A Journal of Research and Treatment, 8*, 37–54. doi:10.1177/107906329600800105

Campbell, M., French, S., & Gendreau, P. (2009). The prediction of violence in adult offenders: A meta-analytic comparison of instruments and methods of assessment. *Criminal Justice and Behavior, 36*, 567–590. doi:10.1177/0093854809333610

Cohen, J. (1988). *Statistical power analysis for the behavioral sciences* (2nd ed.). Hillsdale, NJ: Erlbaum.

Cooke, D., & Michie, C. (2010). Limitations of diagnostic precision and predictive utility in the individual case: A challenge for forensic practice. *Law and Human Behavior, 34*, 259–274. doi:10.1007/s10979-009-9176-x

Cooke, D., & Michie, C. (2011). Violence risk assessment: Challenging the illusion of certainty. In B. McSherry & P. Keyzer (Eds.), *Dangerous people: Policy, prediction, and practice* (pp. 147–161). New York, NY: Routledge.

Craig, L. A., & Beech, A. R. (2010). Towards a guide to best practice in conducting actuarial risk assessments with sex offenders. *Aggression and Violent Behavior, 15*, 278–293. doi:10.1016/j.avb.2010.01.007

Craig, L. A., Beech, A. R., & Browne, K. D. (2006). Cross validation of the Risk Matrix 2000 sexual and violent scales. *Journal of Interpersonal Violence, 21*, 612–633. doi:10.1177/0886260506286876

Craig, L. A., Browne, K. D., & Stringer, I. (2003). Risk scales and factors predictive of sexual offence recidivism. *Trauma, Violence, & Abuse, 4*, 45–68. doi:10.1177/1524838002238945

Craig, L. A., Browne, K. D., Stringer, I., & Beech, A. (2005). Sexual recidivism: A review of static, dynamic and actuarial predictors. *Journal of Sexual Aggression, 11*, 65–84. doi:10.1080/13552600410001667733

Craig, L. A., Browne, K. D., Stringer, I., & Hogue, T. E. (2008). Sexual reconviction rates in the United Kingdom and actuarial risk estimates. *Child Abuse & Neglect, 32*, 121–138. doi:10.1016/j.chiabu.2007.09.002

Craig, L. A., Thornton, D., Beech, A., & Browne, K. D. (2007). The relationship of statistical and psychological risk markers to sexual reconviction in child molesters. *Criminal Justice and Behavior, 34*, 314–329. doi:10.1177/0093854806291416

Craissati, J., Bierer, K., & South, R. (2011). Risk, reconviction and "sexually risky behavior" in sex offenders. *Journal of Sexual Aggression, 17*, 153–165. doi:10.1080/13552600.2010.490306

Davis, M. H. (1983). Measuring individual differences in empathy: Evidence for a multiple dimensional approach. *Journal of Personality and Social Psychology, 44*, 113–126. doi:10.1037/0022-3514.44.1.113

Dawes, R. M., Faust, D., & Meehl, P. E. (1989). Clinical versus actuarial judgment. *Science, 243*, 1668–1674. doi:10.1126/science.2648573

Douglas, K. S., & Skeem, J. L. (2005). Violence risk assessment: Getting specific about being dynamic. *Psychology, Public Policy, and Law, 11*, 347–383. doi:10.1037/1076-8971.11.3.347

Ducro, C., & Pham, T. (2006). Evaluation of the SORAG and the Static-99 in Belgian sex offenders committed to a forensic facility. *Sexual Abuse: A Journal of Research and Treatment, 18*, 15–26. doi:10.1177/107906320601800102

Epperson, D. L., Kaul, J. D., & Hesselton, D. (1998). *Minnesota sex offender screening tool-revised (MnSOST-R) technical paper: Development, validation, and recommended risk level cut scores.* Retrieved from https://rsoresearch.files.wordpress.com/2012/01/ia-state-study.pdf

Farkas, M. A., & Stichman, A. (2002). Sex offender laws: Can treatment, punishment, incapacitation, and public safety to be reconciled? *Criminal Justice Review, 27*, 256–283. doi:10.1177/073401680202700204

Fisher, D., Beech, A., & Browne, K. (1999). Comparison of sex offenders to non-sex offenders on selected psychological measures. *International Journal of Offender Therapy and Comparative Criminology, 43*, 473–491. doi:10.1177/0306624X99434006

Hanson, R. K. (1997). *The development of a brief actuarial risk scale for sexual offense recidivism.* (User Report No. 1997–04). Ottawa: Department of the Solicitor General of Canada. Retrieved from http://www.defenseforsvp.com/Resources/Hanson_Static-99/RRASOR.pdf

Hanson, R. K., & Bussière, M. T. (1998). Predicting relapse: A meta-analysis of sexual offender recidivism studies. *Journal of Consulting and Clinical Psychology, 66*, 348–362. doi:10.1037/0022-006X.66.2.348

Hanson, R. K., & Harris, A. J. R. (2001). A structured approach to evaluating change in sexual offenders. *Sexual Abuse: A Journal of Research and Treatment, 13*, 105–122. doi:10.1177/107906320101300204

Hanson, R. K., Harris, A. J. R., Scott, T. L., & Helmus, L. (2007). *Assessing the risk of sexual offenders on community supervision: The Dynamic Supervision Project* (Corrections Research User Report No. 2007–05). Ottawa, ON: Public Safety Canada. Retrieved from http://www.publicsafety.gc.ca/cnt/rsrcs/pblctns/ssssng-rsk-sxl-ffndrs/ssssng-rsk-sxl-ffndrs-eng.pdf

Hanson, R. K., Morton-Bourgon, G., Helmus, L., & Hodgson, S. (2009). The principles of effective correctional treatment also apply to sexual offenders: A meta-analysis. *Criminal Justice and Behavior, 36*, 865–891. doi:10.1177/0093854809338545

Hanson, R. K., & Morton-Bourgon, K. E. (2004). *Predictors of sexual recidivism: An updated meta-analysis* (Corrections User Report No. 2004–02). Ottawa, ON: Public Safety Canada. Retrieved from http://www.static99.org/pdfdocs/hansonandmortonbourgon2004.pdf

Hanson, R. K., & Morton-Bourgon, K. E. (2005). The characteristics of persistent sexual offenders: A meta-analysis of recidivism studies. *Journal of Consulting and Clinical Psychology, 73*, 1154–1163. doi:10.1037/0022-006X.73.6.1154

Hanson, R. K., & Morton-Bourgon, K. E. (2009). The accuracy of recidivism risk assessments for sexual offenders: A meta-analysis of 118 prediction studies. *Psychological Assessment, 21*, 1–21. doi:10.1037/a0014421

Hanson, R. K., & Thornton, D. (1999). *Static 99: Improving actuarial risk assessments for sex offenders* (User Report 99-02). Ottawa, ON: Department of the Solicitor General of Canada. Retrieved from http://www.static99.org/pdfdocs/static-99-coding-rules_e.pdf

Hanson, R. K., & Thornton, D. (2000). Improving risk assessment for sex offenders: A comparison of three actuarial scales. *Law and Human Behavior, 24*(1), 119–136. doi:10.1023/A:1005482921333

Harris, A. J., & Socia, K. M. (2014). What's in a name? Evaluating the effects of the "Sex Offender" label on public opinions and beliefs. *Sexual Abuse: A Journal of Research and Treatment*. Advance online publication retrieved from http://sax.sagepub.com.ezproxy-b.deakin.edu.au/content/early/2014/12/24/1079063214564391.full.pdf+html doi:10.1177/1079063214564391

Harris, A. J. R., & Hanson, R. K. (2010). Clinical, actuarial and dynamic risk assessment of sexual offenders: Why do things keep changing? *Journal of Sexual Aggression, 16*, 296–310. doi:10.1080/13552600.2010.494772

Harris, G. T., Rice, M. E., Quinsey, V. L., Lalumiere, M. L., Boer, D., & Lang, C. (2003). A multisite comparison of actuarial risk instruments for sex offenders. *Psychological Assessment, 15*, 413–425. doi:10.1037/1040-3590.15.3.413

Hart, S. D., Michie, C., & Cooke, D. J. (2007). Precision of actuarial risk assessment instruments: Evaluating the 'margins of error' of group v. individual predictions of violence. *The British Journal of Psychiatry, 190*, s60–s65. doi:10.1192/bjp.190.5.s60

Helmus, L., Hanson, R. K., Babchishin, K. M., & Thornton, D. (2015). Sex offender risk assessment with the Risk Matrix 2000: Validation and guidelines for combining with the STABLE-2007. *Journal of Sexual Aggression, 21*, 136–157. doi:10.1080/13552600.2013.870241

Helmus, L., Thornton, D., Hanson, R. K., & Babchishin, K. M. (2012). Improving the predictive accuracy of Static-99 and Static-2002 with older sex offenders: Revised age weights. *Sexual Abuse: A Journal of Research and Treatment, 24*, 64–101. doi:10.1177/1079063211409951

Hosmer, D. W., & Lemeshow, S. (2000). *Applied logistic regression* (2nd ed.). New York, NY: John Wiley & Sons.

Jacobson, N. S., Roberts, L. J., Berns, S. B., & McGlinchey, J. B. (1999). Methods for determining the clinical significance of treatment effects: Description, application and alternatives. *Journal of Consulting and Clinical Psychology, 67*, 300–307.

Keltner, A. A., Marshall, P. G., & Marshall, W. L. (1981). Measurement and correlation of assertiveness and social fear in a prison population. *Corrective and Social Psychiatry, 27*, 41–47.

Kingston, D. A., Yates, P. M., Firestone, P., Babchishin, K., & Bradford, J. (2008). Long term predictive validity of the Risk Matrix 2000: A comparison with the Static-99 and the Sex offender risk appraisal guide. *Sexual Abuse: A Journal of Research and Treatment, 20,* 466–484. doi:10.1177/1079063208325206

Langton, C. M. (2003). Contrasting approaches to risk assessment with adult male sexual offenders: An evaluation of recidivism prediction schemes and the utility of supplementary clinical information for enhancing predictive accuracy. *Dissertation Abstracts International, 64*(04), 1907B. (UMI No. NQ78052).

Mandeville-Norden, R., Beech, A., & Hayes, E. (2008). Examining the effectiveness of a UK community-based sexual offender treatment programme for child abusers. *Psychology, Crime & Law, 14*(6), 493–512.

Mann, R. E., Hanson, R. K., & Thornton, D. (2010). Assessing risk for sexual recidivism: Some proposals on the nature of psychologically meaningful risk factors. *Sexual Abuse: A Journal of Research and Treatment, 22*(2), 191–217. doi:10.1177/1079063210366039

McGrath, R. J., & Cumming, G. F. (2001, 2003). *The sex offender treatment needs and progress scale–version 2001, 2003.* Middlebury, VT: Author.

McGrath, R. J., Cumming, G. F., Burchard, B. L., Zeoli, S., & Ellerby, L. (2010). *Current practices and emerging trends in sexual abuser management: The safer society 2009 North American survey.* Brandon, VT: Safer Society Press. Retrieved from http://www.safersociety.org/uploads/WP141-Current_Practices_Emerging_Trends.pdf

McGrath, R. J., Lasher, M. J., & Cumming, P. F. (2011). The sex offender treatment intervention and progress (SOTIP) scale: Psychometric properties and incremental validity with the Static 99. *Sexual Abuse: A Journal of Research and Treatment, 24,* 431–458. doi:10.1177/1079063211432475

Mossman, D. (1994). Assessing predictions of violence: Being accurate about accuracy. *Journal of Consulting and Clinical Psychology, 62,* 783–792. doi:10.1037/0022-006X.62.4.783

Mossman, D. (2006). Another look at interpreting risk categories. *Sexual Abuse: A Journal of Research and Treatment, 18,* 41–63. doi:10.1177/107906320601800104

Mossman, D. (2013). Evaluating risk assessments using receiver operating characteristic (ROC) analysis: Rationale, advantages, insights, and limitations. *Behavioral Sciences and the Law, 31,* 23–39. doi:10.1002/bsl.2050

Mossman, D. (2015). From group data to useful probabilities: The relevance of actuarial risk assessment in individual instances. *The Journal of the American Academy of Psychiatry and the Law, 43,* 93–102. Retrieved from http://www.jaapl.org/content/43/1/93.full.pdf

Nowicki, S. (1976). *Adult Nowicki-Strickland Internal-External locus of control scale. Test manual.* Department of Psychology, Emory University, Atlanta, GA.

Nowicki, S., & Duke, M. P. (1983). The Nowicki-Strickland life-span locus of control scales: Construct validation. In H. M. Lefcourt (Ed.), *Research with the locus of control construct: Vol. 2. Developments and social problems* (pp. 9–49). New York, NY: Academic Press.

Nunes, K. L., Babchishin, K. M., & Cortoni, F. (2011). Measuring treatment change in sex offenders: Clinical and statistical significance. *Criminal Justice and Behaviour, 38*(2), 157–173. doi:10.1177/0093854810391054

Olver, M. E., Beggs Christofferson, S. M., Grace, R. C., & Wong, S. C. P. (2014). Incorporating change information into sexual offender risk assessments using the violence risk scale-sexual offender version. *Sexual Abuse: A Journal of Research and Treatment, 26,* 472–499. doi:10.1177/1079063213502679

Olver, M. E., Kingston, D. A., Nicholaichuk, T., & Wong, S. C. P. (2014). A psychometric examination of treatment change in a multisite sample of treated Canadian federal sexual offenders. *Law and Human Behavior, 38,* 544–559. doi:10.1037/lhb0000086

Olver, M. E., & Wong, S. C. P. (2011). A comparison of static and dynamic assessment of sexual offender risk and need in a treatment context. *Criminal Justice and Behavior, 38,* 113–126. doi:10.1177/0093854810389534

Olver, M. E., Wong, S. C. P., Nicholaichuk, T., & Gordon, A. (2007). The validity and reliability of the violence risk scale-sexual offender version: Assessing sex offender risk and evaluating therapeutic change. *Psychological Assessment, 19,* 318–329. doi:10.1037/1040-3590.19.3.318

Peacock, E. J. (2000). *Sex offender acceptance of responsibility scales.* Warkworth, ON: Warkworth Institution, Correctional Service of Canada.

Phenix, A., Helmus, L., & Hanson, R. K. (2012). *Static-99R & Static-2002R: Evaluators' handbook*. Retrieved from http://www.static99.org/

Prentky, R. A., Knight, R. A., Lee, A. F., & Cerce, D. D. (1995). Predictive validity of lifestyle impulsivity for rapists. *Criminal Justice and Behavior, 22*, 106–128. doi:10.1177/0093854895022002002

Proulx, J., Perreault, C., & Ouimet, M. (1999). Pathways in the offending process of extrafamilial sexual child molesters. *Sexual Abuse: A Journal of Research and Treatment, 11*, 117–129. doi:1079-0632/99/0400-011

Quinsey, V. L., Harris, G. T., Rice, M. E., & Cormier, C. A. (1998). *Violent offenders: Appraising and managing risk*. Washington, DC: American Psychology Association.

Quinsey, V. L., Khanna, A., & Malcolm, P. B. (1998). A retrospective evaluation of the regional treatment centre sex offender treatment program. *Journal of Interpersonal Violence, 13*, 621–644. doi:10.1177/088626098013005005

Rice, M. E., & Harris, G. T. (2005). Comparing effect sizes in follow-up studies: ROC area, Cohen's *d*, and *r*. *Law and Human Behavior, 29*, 615–620. doi:10.1007/s10979-005-6832-7

Rossegger, A., Gerth, J., Seewald, K., Urbaniok, F., Singh, J. P., & Endrass, J. (2013). Current obstacles in replicating risk assessment findings: A systematic review of commonly used actuarial instruments. *Behavioral Sciences and the Law, 31*, 154–164. doi:10.1002/bsl.2044

Russell, D., Peplau, L. A., & Cutrona, C. A. (1980). The revised UCLA loneliness scale: Concurrent and discriminant validity evidence. *Journal of Personality and Social Psychology, 39*, 472–480. doi:10.1037/0022-3514.39.3.472

Singh, J. (2013). Predictive validity performance indicators in violence risk assessment: A methodological primer. *Behavioral Sciences & The Law, 31*, 8–22. doi:10.1002/bsl.2052

Singh, J. P., Grann, M., & Fazel, S. (2011). A comparative study of violence risk assessment tools: A systematic review and meta-regression analysis of 68 studies involving 25,980 participants. *Clinical Psychology Review, 31*, 499–513. doi:10.1016/j.cpr.2010.11.009

Skelton, A., Riley, D., Wales, D., & Vess, J. (2006). Assessing risk for sexual offenders in New Zealand: Development and validation of a computer-scored risk measure. *Journal of Sexual Aggression, 12*, 277–286. doi:10.1080/13552600601100326

Swets, J. A. (1988). Measuring the accuracy of diagnostic systems. *Science, 240*, 1285–1293. doi:10.1126/science.3287615

Swets, J. A., Dawes, R. M., & Monahan, J. (2000). Psychological science can improve diagnostic decisions. *Psychological Science in the Public Interest, 1*, 1–26. doi:10.1111/1529-1006.001

Taxman, F. S., Caudy, M. S., & Pattavina, A. (2013). Risk-need-responsivity (RNR): Leading towards another generation of the model. In F. S. Taxman & A. Pattavina (Eds.), *Simulation strategies to reduce recidivism: Risk need responsivity (RNR) modeling in the criminal justice system* (pp. 285–307). New York, NY: Springer.

Thornton, D. (1989). Self-Esteem scale. Unpublished manuscript (Available from David Thornton, P.O. Box 700, Sand Ridge Secure Treatment Center, 1111 North Road, Mauston, Wisconsin 53948).

Thornton, D. (2002). Constructing and testing a framework for dynamic risk assessment. *Sexual Abuse: A Journal of Research and Treatment, 14*, 139–153. doi:10.1177/107906320201400205

Thornton, D., Mann, R., Webster, S., Blud, L., Travers, R., Friendship, C., & Erikson, M. (2003). Distinguishing and combining risks for sexual and violent recidivism. *Annals of the New York Academy of Sciences, 989*, 225–235. doi:10.1111/j.1749-6632.2003.tb07308.x

Tully, R. J., Browne, K. D., & Craig, L. A. (2015). An examination of the predictive validity of the Structured Assessment of Risk and Need-Treatment Needs Analysis (SARN-TA) in England and Wales. *Criminal Justice and Behavior, 42*, 509–528. doi:10.1177/0093854814553096

Tully, R. J., Chou, S., & Browne, K. D. (2013). A systematic review on the effectiveness of sex offender risk assessment tools in predicting sexual recidivism of adult male sex offenders. *Clinical Psychology Review, 33*, 287–316. doi:10.1016/j.cpr.2012.12.002

Wakeling, H., Beech, A. R., Freemantle, N. (2013). Investigating treatment change and its relationship to recidivism in a sample of 3773 sex offenders in the UK. *Psychology, Crime & Law, 19*, 233–252.

Wakeling, H., Freemantle, N., Beech, A. R., & Elliott, I. A. (2011). Identifying predictors of recidivism in a large sample of United Kingdom sexual offenders: A prognostic model. *Psychological Services, 8*, 307–318. doi:10.1037/a0025516

Ward, T. (2015). Dynamic risk factors: Scientific kinds or predictive constructs. *Psychology, Crime & Law, 22*(1–2), 2–16.

Ward, T., & Beech, A. R. (2015). Dynamic risk factors: a theoretical dead-end? *Psychology, Crime & Law, 21*(2), 100–113.

Wong, S., Olver, M. E., Nicholaichuk, T. P., & Gordon, A. (2003). *The violence risk scale: Sexual offender version (VRS-SO)*. Saskatchewan: Regional Psychiatric Centre and University of Saskatchewan, Saskatoon.

Understanding dynamic risk factors for violence

Gabrielle Klepfisz[a], Michael Daffern[a,b] and Andrew Day[c]

[a]Centre for Forensic Behavioural Science, Swinburne University of Technology, Melbourne, Australia; [b]Victorian Institute of Forensic Mental Health, Melbourne, Australia; [c]School of Psychology, Faculty of Health, Deakin University, Melbourne, Australia

ABSTRACT

Recent years have seen a consensus emerge regarding the dynamic risk factors that are associated with future violence. These risk factors are now routinely assessed in structured violence risk assessment instruments. They provide a focus for treatment in structured group programmes. However, relatively little attention has been paid to risk-related theoretical issues, whether these dynamic risk factors are causally related or simply correlates of violent offending, or the extent to which they change as a consequence of treatment. More challenging is the lack of evidence to suggest that changes in these dynamic risk factors actually result in reductions in violent offending. In this paper we consider the meaning of the term dynamic risk, arguing that only those factors that, when changed, reduce the likelihood of violent recidivism, can be considered to be truly dynamic. We conclude that few of the violence risk factors commonly regarded as dynamic fulfil this requirement. There is a need to think more critically about assessment findings and treatment recommendations relating to dynamic risk, and conduct research that establishes, rather than assumes, that certain dynamic risk factors are directly related to violence. Some suggestions for advancing knowledge and practice are provided.

Assessing the potential for future violence is an everyday activity for many forensic mental health professionals. Although this may appear to involve the simple identification of those factors that are associated with violent behaviour, the multifaceted, multiply determined, and multifunctional nature of violence (Anderson & Bushman, 2002; Daffern, Howells, & Ogloff, 2007; Douglas & Skeem, 2005) presents many challenges. The aim of this paper is to critique current knowledge about a key area of violence risk assessment, the identification of what are commonly known as *dynamic risk factors*. We provide a critical overview of how dynamic risk factors are defined, and the evidence that exists to demonstrate their utility in both predicting violent behaviour and informing treatment. We then discuss some of the limitations of current knowledge and offer suggestions for advancing practice in this area.

What are dynamic risk factors?

Modern conceptualisations of dynamic risk factors can be traced back to Andrews' (1989) suggestion that practitioners and researchers should seek to identify the characteristics of prisoners and their circumstances that might be subject to change during a sentence, considering which of these might reasonably be expected to increase or reduce recidivism. Andrews referred to these changeable, active, and dynamic factors as *criminogenic needs* and, over 25 years later, our core understanding of dynamic risk remains essentially unchanged, although increasingly subject to critique and reformulation (Douglas & Skeem, 2005; Ward, 2015a). Andrews' suggestion was notable in a historical context in which assessments of risk were often based on unstructured clinical judgement or restricted to the appraisal of a small number of static historical factors, such as an offender's age or number of previous offences. Although these factors statistically predict future violent offending, they are, by definition, immutable (Jones, Brown, & Zamble, 2010) and, as such, they are likely to be of limited value in guiding treatment or assessing change in risk over time. As McNaughton Nicholls and Webster (2014) have subsequently observed, the identification of dynamic risk factors can help to establish reasonable targets for interventions that reduce the likelihood of violent re-offending, establish whether meaningful progress is being made against set treatment targets, and inform the choice of appropriate risk management strategies. Indeed, one of the main reasons to consider dynamic risk is in relation to the suggestion that interventions are most effective when they change those factors that are most closely related to violence (Andrews & Bonta, 2010). Implicit in this idea is that risk is imminent and greatest when dynamic risk factors are active (e.g. for an individual whose alcohol use increases their violence propensity, violence risk would be imminent and heightened when the individual is intoxicated).

How are dynamic risk factors conceptualised?

Inherent in most conceptualisations of dynamic risk is a distinction between risk status and risk state. *Risk status* refers to inter-individual differences in risk level, which are largely based on static factors that are invariant over time (Blanchard, 2013). An individual's risk status tells us about both his or her level of baseline risk and the required intensity of intervention. Conversely, *risk state* refers to the risk level of a particular individual at a particular time, taking into account biological, psychological, social, and situational variables (Douglas & Skeem, 2005). It has been suggested that risk state factors can be meaningfully grouped into two categories based on the extent to which they are changeable: *stable* dynamic risk state factors (e.g. normative beliefs supportive of violence) are learned behaviours and personal skills, deficits, or self-management styles that are not expected to change over months or years; *acute* dynamic risk state factors (e.g. angry mood) can change rapidly, within minutes, hours, or days (Hanson & Harris, 2001; Hanson, Harris, Scott, & Helmus, 2007; Hendry, 2013).

Douglas and Skeem (2005) suggest that for a risk factor to be considered 'dynamic' it must possess three components: it must be an antecedent to, and increase the propensity for, violence; it must be able to change spontaneously or as a result of treatment efforts; and it must predict changes in violent recidivism as a result of intervention. However, it is common practice to simply record whether commonly occurring dynamic risk factors are 'present' or 'absent' for a given individual and whether they are associated with violence propensity, rather than to determine whether they meet each of these criteria for the particular individual being assessed. An improvement would be to consider whether the risk factor, if present, is relevant for the individual. *Relevant* risk factors are those that are functionally related to the commission of violence (Hart & Logan, 2011) and thus represent those needs that should be targeted both in treatment and risk management plans (Douglas, Hart, Webster, & Belfrage, 2013). For example, the dynamic risk factor of substance use may be assessed as 'present' for an individual who has a history of substance use, but if there is no history of violence occurring under the influence of, or withdrawing from, drugs or alcohol, then substance use is unlikely to be 'relevant' to any judgement about the potential for future harm (Logan, 2014). Changes in relevant risk factors should, theoretically, result in changes in violent recidivism.

This distinction highlights the need to also differentiate between dynamic risk factors on the basis of the degree or type of association with violence (see Blanchard, 2013). According to Kraemer and colleagues (Kraemer et al., 1997), a *correlate* is a variable that is associated with violence, but where no temporal or directional association is known, that is, whether the risk factor either precedes or follows violence and whether the risk factor is a proximate trigger for violence or distal predisposing factor; a *risk factor* is a correlate that precedes violence and is associated with an increased likelihood of violence; and a *causal risk factor* is a variable that precedes, and increases, the likelihood of violence, fluctuates over time, and when changes in this risk factor occur, concomitant change in the likelihood of violence also occurs. The definition of a *causal risk factor* is consistent with that of a *dynamic risk state factor* and places emphasis on the need to establish, rather than assume, that a risk factor is, in a meaningful way, causative of violence. In short, it requires that a logical connection is established and that alternate explanations are excluded (Haynes, 1992).

According to Ward and Beech (2015), a significant problem with current practice in this area is that many risk factors currently referred to as 'dynamic' are not causal in any straightforward sense. Ward (2015a) argues that once a risk factor is conceptualised as causal, one is obligated to articulate the nature of the underlying causes or processes that lead to violence. However, even if one can demonstrate that violence follows the presence of a particular risk factor, this neither establishes causality nor how different risk factors interact and combine to explain why an individual offends violently. Ward's suggestion is that current descriptions of dynamic risk factors refer to vague and composite constructs that include both trait and state components and which do not adequately explain offending. Problems with self-regulation, for example, are often described in terms of dynamic risk, but include both angry mood (a mental state) and poor problem-solving (an enduring trait). Ostensibly, both angry mood and poor problem-solving may influence self-regulation via different causal pathways, and these components of self-regulation problems may be more or less dynamic. Although angry mood is highly changeable, difficulties with problem-solving tend to be more stable over time and context.

An additional issue that requires consideration is the mechanism by which a dynamic risk factor causes violence. For instance, it can act as a *driver* (motivator) by increasing the perceived rewards or attractiveness of violence as a behavioural option; it can act as a *destabiliser* which impairs the individual's ability to monitor and control decision-making; or it can act as a *disinhibitor* which decreases the perceived costs or negative consequences of violence (Douglas et al., 2013; Hart & Logan, 2011). Each risk factor will have to be considered for every individual being assessed to determine whether the risk factor acts as a driver, destabiliser or disinhibitor. If it does none of these things then it cannot be considered relevant to the risk for violence.

Dynamic risk factors for violent re-offending

Notwithstanding these conceptual issues, Douglas and Skeem (2005) have identified what they consider to be the most promising dynamic risk factors for violence. These include impulsiveness, negative affectivity, psychosis, antisocial attitudes, substance use and related problems, interpersonal relationships, and treatment alliance and adherence. Other commonly cited dynamic risk factors for violence include a lack of insight, negative distrustful attitudes, and egocentricity/narcissism (Hildebrand & de Ruiter, 2012). A number of contemporary violence risk tools require these items to be rated in their assessment protocols. For example, completion of the Violence Risk Scale (VRS; Wong & Gordon, 2003) requires consideration of 20 different dynamic risk factors (violent lifestyle, criminal personality, criminal attitudes, work ethic, criminal peer association, interpersonal aggression, emotional control, violence during institutionalisation, weapon use, insight into violence, mental disorder, substance abuse, relationship stability, community support, release back to high-risk situations, violence cycle, impulsivity, cognitive distortions, adherence with community supervision, and security level of anticipated release institution). Another widely used tool to assess violence risk, the Historical-Clinical-Risk Management-20 version 3 (HCR-20^{v3}; Douglas et al., 2013), includes *recent problems with* insight, violent ideation or intent, symptoms of major mental disorder, instability, and treatment/supervision response, and predicted *future problems with* professional services and plans, living situation, personal support, treatment/supervision response, and stress/coping. Critically, the HCR-20^{v3} also assesses the relevance of each dynamic risk factor.

Many dynamic risk factors are common to both instruments (e.g. adherence with supervision/supervision response; mental disorder and symptoms of major mental disorder; see Table 1, below) and this likely explains why the dynamic scales on these different risk assessment instruments have broadly similar levels of predictive validity when they are used actuarially (see Yang, Wong, & Coid, 2010; note, this analysis was based on the earlier version of the HCR-20, which bears considerable similarity with the latest version, but does assess some different dynamic variables).

Are dynamic risk factors for violence truly dynamic?

The dynamic risk factors identified in the VRS and the HCR-20^{v3} were selected on the basis of their empirical and theoretical relationships with violent behaviour. Guy et al. (2013), for example, describe the evidence that supports the inclusion of HCR-20^{v3} items (evidence for HCR-20^{v2} items is discussed by Guy & Wilson, 2006); evidence for the inclusion of the VRS items is presented in the VRS manual. Accordingly, we examine the grounds for whether certain risk factors should be considered to be dynamic using the criteria proposed by Douglas and Skeem (2005): that the factor is an antecedent to, and increases

Table 1. Dynamic risk factors for violence as assessed by the VRS and HCR-20^{v3}.

VRS and HCR-20^{v3} Dynamic Items					
	Attitudinal and cognitive factors	Impulsivity and self-regulation deficits	Affective dyscontrol	Lifestyle needs associated with criminality	Items that don't fit into a domain
VRS	D3. Criminal attitudes	D17. Impulsivity	D6. Interpersonal aggression	D1. Work ethic	D1. Violent lifestyle
	D10. Insight into violence		D7. Emotional control	D5. Criminal peers	D2. Criminal personality
	D11. Mental disorder		D11. Mental disorder	D14. Community support	D8 Violence during institutionalisation
	D18. Cognitive distortion			D15. Released to high-risk situations	D9. Weapon use
				D19. Compliance with community supervision	D10. Violence cycle
				D20. Security level of release institution	
HCR-20	C1. Recent problems with insight	C4. Recent problems with instability (e.g. impulsive)	C3. Recent problems with major mental disorder (e.g. mania, irritability, labile mood)	R2. Future problems with living situation	C5. Recent problems with treatment or supervision response
	C2. Recent problems with violent ideation or intent (e.g. hostile attribution bias)	R5. Future problems with stress/coping	C4. Recent problems with instability (e.g. distress, irritability, anger, and volatility)	R3. Future problems with personal support	R1. Future problems with professional services or plans
	C3. Recent problems with major mental disorder (e.g. hallucinations, disorganisation)				R4. Future problems with treatment or supervision response
	C4. Recent problems with instability (e.g. cognitive distortions)				

the propensity for, violence; that it is able to change spontaneously or as a result of treatment efforts; and that it can predict change in violent recidivism as a result of intervention.

As mentioned, a risk factor is a variable that *precedes* violence and is associated with an increased likelihood of violence (Kraemer et al., 1997). Notably, establishing whether a dynamic risk factor is an antecedent to violence is difficult in the absence of robust longitudinal studies to show that it precedes violence. Although many prospective studies have explored associations between dynamic risk factors and subsequent violence, temporality cannot be established when participants have a history of violence, given that violence may, of course, have led to the establishment of the dynamic risk factor. For example, attitudes that support violence may have arisen from or developed as a consequence of engaging in prior acts of violence. Nevertheless, multiple individual risk factors for violence have been identified. For example, procriminal attitudes (that is, attitudes supportive of crime, seeing little need to maintain law, and having little respect for law/authority) have been identified as one of the strongest predictors of criminal offending (whether sexual, violent, or general) in a series of studies (Gendreau, Little, & Goggin, 1996; Helmus, Hanson, Babchishin, & Mann, 2013) and a body of research has established that psychosis is significantly associated with an increase in the odds of future violent behaviour (e.g. Douglas, Guy, & Hart, 2009). However, the evidence for other factors is inconsistent. Harris and Rice (2015), for example, recently reported data on the association between violent recidivism and a range of variables reflecting offenders' attitudes and circumstances, usually during their first post-index offence admission. Even in a study with considerable statistical power, some of the most commonly assessed dynamic risk factors (e.g. denial) bore no predictive relationship with violence, while others (e.g. criminal attitudes, unsatisfactory accommodation) were considerably more influential. The absence of 'insight' and 'wanted or interested in treatment', for example, bore no relationship with violent recidivism, despite comparable items being included in the HCR-20^{V3} (Recent problems with insight) and VRS (insight into violence). Furthermore, some factors included in these prominent risk assessment instruments, such as 'violence during institutionalisation' and 'recent problems with treatment and/or supervision response' do not appear to represent truly dynamic risk factors based on Douglas and Skeem's (2005) criteria. Violence during institutionalisation, for example, is a manifestation of other dynamic risk factors; this variable may best be considered to be a proxy variable – or a *risk marker* – for pervasive criminal attitudes, and established tendencies, or involvement with an antisocial peer group, that actually underlie and contribute to an individual's violent behaviour. Although it is clearly important to manage violence during institutionalisation, and this is clearly a correlate of violence following release (see Mooney & Daffern, 2011), violence during institutionalisation is not a true dynamic risk factor in the sense in which we are using the term here. Another way of thinking about this difference between 'proxy' and 'truly dynamic' variables is by considering the treatment that would be required to reduce these areas of risk; we would think more here about treating the variables that contribute to violence during institutionalisation rather that treating violence during institutionalisation per se. Finally, it is incumbent on clinicians to determine whether particular risk factors are *functionally* related to violence propensity for the individual being assessed, and to thus differentiate those variables that have a causal relationship with violence and differentiate these from risk markers. Critically, the relevance ratings included in the HCR-20^{V3} require assessors to consider whether each risk factor is important for the individual being assessed and this may overcome some of the limitations in drawing from nomothetic analyses and applying these findings to individuals.

The second criterion for dynamic risk is that relevant risk factors can change, either spontaneously (over time) or as a result of intervention. Less attention is given to this criterion than the former, which focuses on establishing predictive accuracy. A good example of a risk factor that meets this second criterion is angry arousal. Although anger is neither necessary, nor sufficient, for the perpetration of violence, angry arousal has been shown to be associated with both aggressive and violent behaviour (Howells, 2004; Novaco, 2011). In addition, both the intensity and the experience of anger and its expression can fluctuate over time, and can decrease as a result of anger management or similar intervention strategies (Deffenbacher, Oetting, & DiGiuseppe, 2002). The extensive literature on persuasion and attitude change (e.g. Petty, Wheeler, & Tormala, 2003), and evidence that violent offenders who complete medium- and high-intensity violence intervention programmes can show significant reductions in criminal attitudes over the course of treatment (Klepfisz, O'Brien, & Daffern, 2014), provide further support for suggestions that criminal thinking styles also fulfil this criterion. Another example is substance use, given that intoxication and the use of substances wax and wane, even among heavy users, and evidence suggests that substance use can change following treatment (Messina, Grella, Cartier, & Torres,

2010). These are only a few examples; for a more complete review the reader is referred to Douglas and Skeem (2005).

Douglas and Skeem's (2005) third criterion for dynamic risk is that changes in the risk factor must predict changes in violent recidivism as a result of intervention. Inherent in the logic of many treatment programmes is the idea that changes in dynamic risk will reduce violence propensity (Beggs, 2010). There is, however, only limited evidence to suggest that completion of violent offender treatment will lead to a reduction in violent recidivism (Polaschek & Collie, 2004), and even less evidence that reduced re-offending results from change in identified areas of dynamic risk. A review by Serin, Lloyd, Helmus, Derkzen, and Luong (2013), for example, examined the relationship between intra-individual change in risk factors and recidivism. They concluded that although decreases in pro-criminal attitudes, criminal peers, family dissention, anger, and negative affect were all associated with decreased recidivism, only three out of the 53 studies reviewed examined violent re-offending and there were a number of methodological limitations in many of the studies included.

Several studies have examined change across time using repeat administration of structured risk assessment tools. Lewis, Olver, and Wong (2013), for example, reported that VRS change scores were significantly negatively correlated ($r = -.21$, $p = .01$) with violent recidivism, and maintained at 3-year follow-up ($r = -.23$, $p = .02$), even after controlling for pre-treatment levels of risk. In a sample 662 male offenders (both violent and non-violent) under community supervision following release from prison, Kroner and Yessine (2013) examined whether a cognitive-behavioural intervention targeting criminal and antisocial attitudes would lead to reductions in recidivism. At the group level, the treatment group was 53% less likely to be convicted of a new offence than the control group. At the individual-level, however, only the variable measuring attitudes towards associates, which was not a central focus of the treatment programme, was associated with decreased recidivism.

Although useful, dual-time point studies are limited in so far as one can only infer linear change (i.e. increasing or decreasing). For this reason, multiple time-point studies should be considered, as they allow for the measurement of different patterns and trajectories of change (Hendry, 2013). Furthermore, these typically provide a more robust method of examining the dynamic nature of risk as the systematic assessment and re-assessment of dynamic risk can help establish whether meaningful progress is being made against set treatment targets. There are only a few published studies that have used this method. In one, Douglas, Strand, and Belfrage (2011) used repeated measures ANOVA to show that change on the HCR-20 Clinical scale was significantly associated with reduced violence in a sample of 174 forensic psychiatric inpatients. They reported a linear decrease in total Clinical scale scores over four assessments, each six months apart, although it was change from the first assessment to the second assessment that predicted subsequent violence.

One limitation of this study (and others that have reported data on the association between change scores on the HCR-20^{V3} Clinical and Risk Management Scales and subsequent violence) is that it relies on aggregated data and does not report the association between individual items and violence. Such analyses may also attenuate or mask significant effects among those who do, or do not, benefit from treatment (Beggs, 2010), highlighting the importance of also measuring change in dynamic risk at the individual-level

(Fazel, Singh, Doll, & Grann, 2012). In one of the few studies of violent offender treatment that has attempted this, Klepfisz et al. (2014) reported that raw change, reliable change, and clinically significant change for scores on measures of three dynamic risk factors did not predict either re-offending or the time taken to re-offend (violently) in a sample ($n = 42$) of violent offenders. Only one participant achieved reliable change on all three variables and only four achieved reliable change on at least two measures. In another, this time involving a sample of sexual offenders, Beech and Ford (2006) reported that all 51 offenders who obtained clinically significant change did not re-offend, whereas 14% of those who did not change, did. However, in a much larger sample of 3402 sexual offenders receiving community-based treatment, Barnett, Wakeling, Mandeville-Norden, and Rakestrow (2013) found no relationship between clinically significant change and recidivism once risk level was taken into account. Finally, Olver, Kingston, Nicholaichuk, and Wong (2014) reported very small to moderate pre-treatment and post-treatment change on measures of cognitive distortions, aggression/hostility, empathy, loneliness, social intimacy, and sex offender acceptance of responsibility, with scores on these measures being only weakly and inconsistently related to sexual, violent, and general recidivism.

Discussion

Ostensibly the identification of dynamic risk factors is important for three reasons: (1) to assess risk for future violence; (2) to establish targets that can guide treatment; and (3) to measure treatment progress or change that leads to reductions in recidivism. It seems clear from this review, however, that more rigour is needed in the identification of dynamic risk factors that, when changed, will be followed by reductions in recidivism. A list of broad treatment targets cannot substitute for an adequate understanding of how change processes work and of the relevance of dynamic risk factors for any individual in treatment (Polaschek, 2012). It is important then to understand how and when individual influences operate and which factors are directly related to behaviour change. In order to accomplish this, we make several proposals.

First, clinicians and researchers need to determine not only whether particular risk factors are present, but also the relevance of each risk factor to the person in light of Blanchard and Douglas (2011) finding that 'relevance' ratings are stronger than 'presence' ratings for the prediction of violence. By determining which risk factors are relevant, we can begin to develop hypotheses about what caused an individual to perpetrate violence and how best to prevent future violence. It thus moves the assessment process from descriptive accounts of dynamic risk to more causal models and provides a bridge between nomothetic and idiographic levels of analysis (Douglas et al., 2013). Relevance ratings also allow practitioners to more fully consider whether the offender has achieved intra-individual treatment change on those variables that are functionally related to their offending. As both Polaschek (2012) and Ward (2015b) have argued, a priority for future development is to bridge the conceptual gap that exists between an identified list of high priority dynamic risk factors, or targets for change, and the theoretical resources needed to translate these factors into intervention design, individual clinical formulations, treatment plans, and methods to assess change. Second, it is critical that a treatment outcome literature builds so that evidence relating to change in dynamic risk factors and its association with subsequent violent offending can be acquired.

Finally, much more work is needed to integrate theoretical and empirical research into applied violence risk assessment. A pressing concern here is the lack of coherence between theoretical explanations of violent behaviour and the prediction and management of violence risk (Ward, 2014). Currently, the theoretical foundations of contemporary violence risk assessment tools are not clear, and dynamic risk factors identified as important to the assessment task are not always selected in ways that are consistent with all three criteria identified by Douglas and Skeem (2005).

More attention needs to be paid to the underlying explanatory (etiological) processes that culminate in violence given that it is currently unclear how dynamic risk factors and psychological mechanisms interact (Heffernan & Ward, 2015). Nonetheless, when considering violent offending, it is easy to see how existing theories can accommodate a conceptualisation of dynamic risk. The General Aggression Model (GAM; Anderson & Bushman, 2002), for example, draws heavily on the development and use of knowledge structures for perception, interpretation, decision-making and action, highlighting the role of the person in the situation. Static and stable dynamic factors (features of the person), which together may be thought of as the person's preparedness to be aggressive, interact reciprocally with situational factors to influence aggression propensity by affecting cognition (e.g. activating aggressive thoughts/procriminal attitudes), affect (e.g. stimulating anger) and arousal (e.g. increasing physiological arousal). Both person and situational factors may exacerbate or exaggerate the likelihood of violence. The knowledge structures that increase violence propensity include perceptual schemata (used to identify phenomena, including social events and personal insults); person schemata (such as beliefs about a particular person or group of people); and behavioural scripts (which contain information about how people behave under certain circumstances). Although the GAM is not immersed in the language of 'dynamic risk', it views violence as multiply determined and transactional in nature, and illustrates how static and dynamic risk factors might be broken down into their causal elements. These include psychological and social processes associated with goals, plans, and actions that reduce an individual's capacity to function in an adaptive and prosocial way, both internally and in the context of wider social, cultural, and environmental networks (see Ward, 2015b).

What is clear is that the causes of aggression and violence comprise a number of interacting processes, none of which are necessary or sufficient for violence to occur. Accordingly, even if a specific dynamic risk factor exhibits a causal relationship with violence, it is unrealistic to expect change in any single dynamic risk factor to predict recidivism; violence is related to an array of risk factors and we would need to see change in various areas for there to be meaningful reductions in the risk for violence. The MacArthur Violence Risk Assessment Study noted this many years ago (Monahan et al., 2001):

> Of the scores of variables whose relationship with violence we studied in this project, many (indeed most) had some significant association with future violence. None of these relationships was sufficiently strong, however, for it to be fairly said that a given variable constituted the cause of violence, even for a subgroup of patients .... Our data are most consistent with the view that the propensity for violence is the result of the accumulation of risk factors, no one of which is either necessary or sufficient for a person to behave aggressively toward

others. People will be violent by virtue of the presence of different sets of risk factors. There is no single path in a person's life that leads to an act of violence. (p. 142)

Accordingly, when measuring treatment-related changes, it seems prudent to employ multi-item risk assessment instruments that capture numerous risk factors for violence, rather than measuring single constructs. This approach is supported by research that has shown that change in total dynamic scores (on the VRS and the HCR-20^{V3}) is significantly related to change in violent recidivism (Douglas et al., 2011; Lewis et al., 2013). Similarly, recent research on change in protective factors has shown that an increase in these factors may also be associated with reductions in violent behaviour (de Vries Robbé, de Vogel, Douglas, & Nijman, 2014). It is important to note however that very little research on the nature and operation of protective factors for violence has been conducted, and attempts to identify protective factors should be subject to scrutiny such as using equivalent criteria to those established by Douglas and Skeem (2005).

Another possible way to bridge the gap in evidence that exists between the influence of single causal dynamic risk factors and aggregated scores is to conceptualise dynamic risk in terms of broad levels, or domains, that subsume a number of more specific risk factors. In the sexual offending field, for example, Thornton (2002, 2013) has proposed that the dynamic risk factors that are thought to underlie sexual offending can be grouped into four risk-relevant domains, which then draws attention to 'a wider range of dynamic risk factors than is assumed in much clinical practice' (2002, p. 140).

Polaschek (2006) identifies four risk factor domains commonly targeted in violent offender rehabilitation: (i) attitudinal factors (e.g. procriminal attitudes and cognitive or information-processing biases); (ii) impulsivity and self-regulation deficits; (iii) affective dyscontrol (e.g. anger, hostility, and poor coping skills); and (iv) lifestyle related needs that also predict general criminality (e.g. substance abuse, criminal peers, poor interpersonal skills, and family relationships). Notably, existing theories, such as the General Aggression Model, provide one way to conceptualise risk that also accommodates these broader categorisations or domains. For example, static and stable dynamic factors (features of the person), interact with lifestyle factors associated with criminality, such as being released back to high-risk situations with criminal associates, which then influence the person's affect (emotional control and aggression), attitudes/cognition (criminal attitudes, beliefs that violence is acceptable), and arousal (impulsivity, ability to cope with stress). Ostensibly these composite constructs interact to determine an appraisal of the situation and whether violence/aggression is an appropriate behavioural outcome. Table 1 (above) shows how the VRS and HCR-20^{V3} dynamic items map onto these proposed domains, illustrating how some dynamic items do not fit within the broad domains identified by Polaschek (2006), possibly indicating that more domains are required. Additionally, more of the VRS items consider lifestyle factors. Both measures provide little assessment of impulsivity and self-regulation deficits, although multiple items from both tests explore the other domains.

Future research might investigate whether change at the domain/s level in the VRS and HCR-20^{V3} is helpful for assessing change following treatment, and whether such change significantly predicts violence propensity beyond global assessment of change in all dynamic risk factors. The ability to detect change will, of course, depend largely on the ability to operationalise the constructs (Blanchard, 2013), and there is an opportunity to explore and improve approaches to the measurement of both domains of dynamic risk and for individual risk factors. For example, there are very few methods that permit the reliable and valid assessment of some risk factors, such as violent ideation and intent, including aggressive behavioural script rehearsal (Gilbert & Daffern, submitted for publication).

An additional problem associated with assessment tools that neglect aggression theory is the danger of selectivity. Whilst comprehensive, contemporary risk assessment measures such as the VRS and HCR-20^{V3} do not claim to provide an exhaustive list of dynamic risk factors, and they may fail to adequately consider some important dynamic risk factors that are implicated in theories of aggression and violence. For example, in their Comprehensive Assessment of Psychopathic Personality (CAPP), Cooke, Hart, Logan, and Michie (2012) recommend specific assessment of the interpersonal drivers (captured by the CAPP's *attachment*[1] and *dominance*[2] domains) of violence. There is evidence that interpersonal style, particularly hostility and dominance, is associated with violent offending and as well as indications that reductions in interpersonal hostile-dominance are meaningfully associated with reductions in violent offending (Daffern et al., 2013). This may provide grounds for inclusion in new iterations of multi-component risk assessment tools.

In summary, to be classified as a dynamic risk factor it is important to consider whether the factor is an antecedent to, and increases the propensity for, violence; the extent to which it is able to change spontaneously or as a result of treatment efforts; and whether change is associated with reduced violent re-offending. Dynamic risk factors are clearly relevant to assessment and treatment; the way they are conceptualised in risk assessment instruments provides a framework for comprehensive assessments and risk management and intervention. However, there is clearly much work to be done to ensure that those factors often considered to be 'dynamic' do, indeed, meet these criteria and are relevant to the needs of the individual being assessed. Although many dynamic risk factors have predictive validity, they have limited explanatory power and some are simply proxies, and thus cannot be directly targeted in treatment. Problems with the identification of single dynamic risk factors, as well as with the measurement of composite categories of risk, also require attention, as well as the lack of evidence to suggest that changes in dynamic risk as a result of treatment are closely and directly related to behaviour change. Although, theoretically, we need to be more precise about the causal mechanisms underpinning violence, practically we need to look broader, and consider how reductions in multiple dynamic risk factors or risk domains, might independently and cumulatively be related to reduced violence.

Notes

1. Which refers to difficulties with interpersonal affiliation, such as the failure to form close, stable emotional bonds with others.
2. Which refers to difficulties with interpersonal agency, such as excessive status-seeking and assertiveness.

Disclosure statement

No potential conflict of interest was reported by the authors.

References

Anderson, C. A., & Bushman, B. J. (2002). Human aggression. *Annual Review of Psychology, 53*, 27–51. doi:10.1146/annurev.psych.53.100901.135231

Andrews, D. A. (1989). Recidivism is predictable and can be influenced: Using risk assessments to reduce recidivism. *Forum on Corrections Research, Risk Assessment and Prediction, 1*(2), 11–17. Retrieved from http://www.csc-scc.gc.ca/text/pblct/forum/special/a1e.pdf

Andrews, D. A., & Bonta, J. (2010). *The psychology of criminal conduct* (5th ed.). New Providence, NJ: Matthew Bender.

Barnett, G. D., Wakeling, H., Mandeville-Norden, R., & Rakestrow, J. (2013). Does change in psychometric test scores tell us anything about risk of reconviction in sexual offenders? *Psychology, Crime & Law, 19*(1), 85–110.

Beech, A. R., & Ford, H. (2006). The relationship between risk, deviance, treatment outcome and sexual reconviction in a sample of child sexual abusers completing residential treatment for their offending. *Psychology, Crime & Law, 12*(6), 685–701.

Beggs, S. (2010). Within-treatment outcome among sexual offenders: A review. *Aggression and Violent Behavior, 15*(5), 369–379. doi:10.1016/j.avb.2010.06.005

Blanchard, A. J. E. (2013). Dynamic risk factors in violence risk assessment: A multiple time-point evaluation of the HCR-20 and START. (Master of Arts), Simon Fraser University, Canada.

Blanchard, A. J. E., & Douglas, K. S. (2011). APLS Undergraduate Paper Award (First Place): The Historical-Clinical-Risk Management-Version 3: The inclusion of idiographic relevance ratings in violence risk assessment. Invited poster presented at the annual convention of the American-Psychology Law Society, Miami, FL.

Cooke, D. J., Hart, S. D., Logan, C., & Michie, C. (2012). Explicating the construct of psychopathy: Development and validation of a conceptual model, the Comprehensive Assessment of Psychopathic Personality (CAPP). *International Journal of Forensic Mental Health, 11*, 242–252. doi:10.1080/14999013.2012.746759

Daffern, M., Howells, K., & Ogloff, J. R. P. (2007). What's the point? Towards a methodology for assessing the function of psychiatric inpatient aggression. *Behaviour Research and Therapy, 45*, 101–111. doi:10.1080/14789949.2013.834069

Daffern, M., Thomas, S., Lee, S., Huband, N., McCarthy, L., Simpson, K., & Duggan, C. (2013). The impact of treatment on hostile-dominance in forensic psychiatric inpatients: Relationsihps between change in hostile-dominance and recidivism following release from custody. *The Journal of Forensic Psychiatry & Psychology, 24*(6), 675–687. doi:10.1080/14789949.2013.834069

Deffenbacher, J. L., Oetting, E. R., & DiGiuseppe, R. A. (2002). Principles of empirically supported interventions applied to anger management. *Counseling Psychologist, 30*, 262–280. doi:10.1177/0011000002302004

Douglas, K. S., Guy, L. S., & Hart, S. D. (2009). Psychosis as a risk factor for violence to others: A meta-analysis. *Psychological Bulletin, 135*(5), 679–706. doi:10.1037/a0016311

Douglas, K. S., Hart, S. D., Webster, C. D., & Belfrage, H. (2013). *HCR-20 ^{V3} Historical, Clinical, Risk Management (Version 3): Professional guidelines for evaluating risk of violence*. Burnaby: Mental Health, Law, and Policy Institute, Simon Fraser University.

Douglas, K. S., & Skeem, J. L. (2005). Violence risk assessment: Getting specific about being dynamic. *Psychology, Public Policy, and Law, 11*(3), 347–383. doi:10.1037/1076–8971.11.3.347

Douglas, K. S., Strand, S., & Belfrage, H. (June, 2011). *Dynamic risk: Evaluating the nature and predictive validity of change on the Clinical and Risk Management scales of the HCR-20*. Paper presented at the 11th Annual Conference of the International Association of Forensic Mental Health Services, Barcelona, Spain.

Fazel, S., Singh, J. P., Doll, H., & Grann, M. (2012). Use of risk assessment instruments to predict violence and antisocial behaviour in 73 samples involving 24 827 people: Systematic review and meta-analysis. *British Medical Journal, 345*, e4692. doi:10.1136/bmj.e4692

Gendreau, P., Little, T., & Goggin, C. (1996). A meta-analysis of the predictors of adult offender recidivism: What works! *Criminology, 34*, 575–608. doi:10.1111/j.1745-9125.1996.tb01220.x

Gilbert, F., & Daffern, M. (submitted for publication). Aggressive scripts and violent behaviour: A conceptual framework.

Guy, L. S., & Wilson, C. M. (2006). *Empirical support for the HCR-20: An annotated bibliography of the 20 items (1997–2005)*. Burnaby: Mental Health, Law, and Policy Institute, Simon Fraser University.

Guy, L. S., Wilson, C. M., Douglas, K. S., Hart, S. D., Webster, C. D., & Belfrage, H. (2013). *HCR-20 Version 3: Item-by-item summary of violence literature*. HCR-20 Violence Risk Assessment White Paper Series, #3. Burnaby: Mental Health, Law, and Policy Institute, Simon Fraser University.

Hanson, R. K., & Harris, A. J. R. (2001). A structured approach to evaluating change among sexual offenders. *Sexual Abuse: A Journal of Research and Treatment, 13*(2), 105–122. doi:10.1177/107906320101300204

Hanson, R. K., Harris, A. J. R., Scott, T., & Helmus, L. (2007). *Assessing the risk of sexual offenders on community supervision: The dynamic supervision project*. (Cat. No.: PS3-1/2007-5), Canada: Public Safety Canada. Retrieved from http://www.publicsafety.gc.ca/cnt/rsrcs/pblctns/ssssng-rsk-sxl-ffndrs/index-eng.aspx

Harris, G. T., & Rice, M. E. (2015). Progress in violence risk assessment and communication: Hypothesis versus evidence. *Behavioral Sciences and the Law, 33*(1), 128–145. doi:10.1002/bsl.2157

Hart, S. D., & Logan, C. (2011). Formulation of violence risk using evidence-based assessments: The structured professional judgment approach. In P. Sturmey & M. McMurran (Eds.), *Forensic case formulation* (pp. 83–106). Chichester: Wiley-Blackwell.

Haynes, S. N. (1992). *Models of causality in psychopathology*. New York, NY: Macmillan.

Heffernan, R. & Ward, T. (2015). The conceptualization of dynamic risk factors in child sex offenders: An agency model. (Unpublished chapter).

Helmus, L., Hanson, R. K., Babchishin, K. M., & Mann, R. E. (2013). Attitudes supportive of sexual offending predict recidivism: A meta-analysis. *Trauma, Violence, & Abuse, 14*(1), 34–53. doi:10.1177/1524838012462244

Hendry, M. C. (2013). Hostile attribution bias as a dynamic risk factor in civil psychiatric patients and criminal offenders: Change over time and relationship to violence and recidivism. (Doctor of Philosophy), Simon Fraser University, Canada.

Hildebrand, M., & de Ruiter, C. (2012). Psychopathic traits and change on indicators of dynamic risk factors during inpatient forensic psychiatric treatment. *International Journal of Law and Psychiatry, 35*(4), 276–288. doi:10.1016/j.ijlp.2012.04.001

Howells, K. (2004). Anger and its links to violent offending. *Psychiatry, Psychology and Law, 11*(2), 189–196. doi:10.1375/1321871042707278

Jones, N. J., Brown, S. L., & Zamble, E. (2010). Predicting criminal recidivism in adult male offenders: Researcher versus parole officer assessment of dynamic risk. *Criminal Justice and Behavior, 37*(8), 860–882. doi:10.1177/0093854810368924

Klepfisz, G., O'Brien, K., & Daffern, M. (2014). Violent offenders' within-treatment change in anger, criminal attitudes, and violence risk: Associations with violent recidivism. *International Journal of Forensic Mental Health, 13*(4), 348–362. doi:10.1080/14999013.2014.951107

Kraemer, H., Kazdin, A., Offord, D., Kessler, R., Jensen, P., & Kupfer, D. (1997). Coming to terms with the terms of risk. *Archives of General Psychiatry, 54*, 337–343. doi:10.1001/archpsyc.1997.01830160065009

Kroner, D. G., & Yessine, A. K. (2013). Changing risk factors that impact recidivism: In search of mechanisms of change. *Law and Human Behavior, 37*(5), 321–336. doi:10.1037/lhb0000022

Lewis, K., Olver, M. E., & Wong, S. C. P. (2013). The violence risk scale: Predictive validity and linking changes in risk with violent recidivism in a sample of high-risk offenders with psychopathic traits. *Assessment, 20*(2), 150–164. doi:10.1177/1073191112441242

Logan, C. (2014). The HCR-20 version 3: A case study in risk formulation. *International Journal of Forensic Mental Health, 13*(2), 172–180. doi:10.1080/14999013.2014.906516

McNaughton Nicholls, C., & Webster, S. (2014). *Sex offender management and dynamic risk: Pilot evaluation of the Active Risk Management System*. UK: Retrieved from https://www.gov.uk/government/publications

Messina, N., Grella, C. E., Cartier, J., & Torres, S. (2010). A randomized experimental study of gender-responsive substance abuse treatment for women in prison. *Journal of Substance Abuse Treatment, 38*, 97–107. doi:10.1016/j.jsat.2009.09.004

Monahan, J., Steadman, H. J., Silver, E., Appelbaum, P. S., Clark Robbins, P., Mulvey, E. P., … Banks, S. (2001). *Rethinking risk assessment: The MacArthur study of mental disorder and violence*. New York, NY: Oxford University Press.

Mooney, J. L., & Daffern, M. (2011). Institutional aggression as a predictor of violent recidivism: Implications for parole decision making. *International Journal of Forensic Mental Health, 10*(1), 52–63. doi:10.1080/14999013.2010.550984

Novaco, R. W. (2011). Anger dysregulation: Driver of violent offending. *Journal of Forensic Psychiatry & Psychology, 22*, 650–668. doi:10.1177/0093854810391054

Olver, M. E., Kingston, D. A., Nicholaichuk, T. P., & Wong, S. C. (2014). A psychometric examination of treatment change in a multisite sample of treated Canadian federal sexual offenders. *Law and Human Behavior, 38*(6), 544–559. doi:10.1037/lhb0000086

Petty, R. E., Wheeler, S. C., & Tormala, Z. L. (2003). Persuasion and attitude change. In T. Millon & M. J. Lerner (Eds.), *Handbook of psychology: Personality and social psychology* (Vol. *5*, pp. 353–382). New York, NY: Wiley.

Polaschek, D. L. L. (2006). Violent offender programmes: Concept, theory, and practice. In C. R. Hollin & E. J. Palmer (Eds.), *Offending behaviour programmes: Development, application and controversies*. Chichester: Wiley.

Polaschek, D. L. L. (2012). An appraisal of the risk-need-responsivity (RNR) model of offender rehabilitation and its application in correctional treatment. *Legal and Criminological Psychology, 17*(1), 1–17. doi:10.1111/j.2044-8333.2011.02038.x

Polaschek, D. L. L., & Collie, R. M. (2004). Rehabilitating serious violent adult offenders: An empirical and theoretical stocktake. *Psychology, Crime & Law, 10*(3), 321–334.

Serin, R. C., Lloyd, C. D., Helmus, L., Derkzen, D. M., & Luong, D. (2013). Does intra-individual change predict offender recidivism? Searching for the Holy Grail in assessing offender change. *Aggression and Violent Behavior, 18*(1), 32–53. doi:10.1016/j.avb.2012.09.002

Thornton, D. (2002). Constructing and testing a framework for dynamic risk assessment. *Sexual Abuse: A Journal of Research and Treatment, 14*(2), 139–153. doi:10.1177/107906320201400205

Thornton, D. (2013). Implications of our developing understanding of risk and protective factors in the treatment of adult male sexual offenders. *International Journal of Behavioral Consultation and Therapy, 8*(3–4), 62–65. doi:10.1037/h0100985

de Vries Robbé, M., de Vogel, V., Douglas, K. S., & Nijman, H. L. (2014). Changes in dynamic risk and protective factors for violence during inpatient forensic psychiatric treatment: Predicting reductions in post-discharge community recidivism. *Law and Human Behavior, 39*(1), 53–61. doi:10.1037/lhb0000089

Ward, T. (2014). The explanation of sexual offending: From single factor theories to integrative pluralism. *Journal of Sexual Aggression, 20*, 130–141. doi:10.1080/13552600.2013.870242

Ward, T. (2015a). Dynamic risk factors and offender rehabilitation: A comparison of the Good Lives Model and the Risk-Need Responsivity Model. (Unpublished chapter).

Ward, T. (2015b). Detection of dynamic risk factors and correctional practice. *Criminology & Public Policy, 14*(1), 105–111. doi:10.1111/1745-9133.12115

Ward, T., & Beech, A. R. (2015). Dynamic risk factors: A theoretical dead-end? *Psychology, Crime & Law, 21*(2), 100–113.

Wong, S. C., & Gordon, A. (2003). *Violence risk scale manual*. Canada: Department of Psychology, University of Saskatchewen.

Yang, M., Wong, S. C., & Coid, J. (2010). The efficacy of violence prediction: A meta-analytic comparison of nine risk assessment tools. *Psychological Bulletin, 136*(5), 740–767. doi:10.1037/a0020473

Developing a theory of dynamic risk

David Thornton

Research Unit, Sand Ridge Secure Treatment Center, Madison, WI, USA

ABSTRACT

The Propensities Model is now the dominant applied conceptualization of dynamic risk factors for sexual offending. In this paper five important limitations of this model are identified: it asserts causality but does not explain it; it does not represent human agency; it offers no account of what is involved in the development of propensities; it does not explain stable change in risk; and its account of the operation of static factors is a theoretical leap not supported by the evidence. A more elaborate theoretical framework is developed by integrating ideas from Ward's Good Lives model, Beck's account of schema modes, and Fishbein and Ajzen's Theory of Reasoned Action. This more elaborate framework incorporates the Propensities Model in a way that mitigates its limitations. Implications for research, assessment, and rehabilitation are explored.

Introduction

Professionals working with sexual offenders are commonly asked to characterize their risk and treatment needs. In the general field of correctional psychology the dominant, empirically informed model is the Risk-Need-Responsivity framework developed by Andrews and Bonta (2006). Within this framework social or psychological factors that are empirically and theoretically linked to offending are postulated to be appropriate targets for effective correctional services. These factors are called Criminogenic Needs, and sometimes also described as dynamic risk factors. A popular application of this framework to sexual offenders has been developed by Hanson and Harris (2000), Hanson, Bourgon, Helmus, and Hodgson (2009) and Hanson, Harris, Scott, and Helmus (2007). This distinguishes static, stable and acute risk factors with the former being statistical predictors that cannot be targeted in treatment, while the latter two are dynamic risk factors with different temporal properties so that stable factors might be targeted by treatment programs seeking to produce enduring changes in risk while acute factors might be attended to by those responsible for day-to-day community risk management.

Empirical attempts to assess stable and acute risk factors have called this distinction into question since in Hanson et al. (2007) it appeared to be the average of successive assessments of 'acute' risk factors that was more predictive rather than the most recent assessment. In response to this kind of finding, later writing (Mann, Hanson, & Thornton, 2010) has reconceptualized dynamic risk factors as enduring propensities. Whether or not propensities are manifested is assumed to depend on an interaction between the ongoing environment and the strength of the propensity. This notion seems consistent with Ward and Beech (2006)'s suggestion that stable dynamic factors should be understood as traits while acute risk factors would be the state expression of these traits released by triggering/ contextual factors.

Similar ideas have been articulated by Knight and Thornton (2007), Thornton, (2002) and Thornton and Knight (2013). In these writings enduring propensities are conceptualized as long-term vulnerabilities (LTVs) which may activate in response to environmental triggers. Absence of expressions of an LTV in a particular setting may simply reflect that the relevant environmental triggers were not present or that the environment affords little opportunity for the external expression of the vulnerability. Hence, when the individual returns to a setting that provides the relevant triggers and allows related behavior to be displayed, a quiescent LTV may re-activate and drive behavior.

Ward and Beech (2006) also made the interesting proposal that static risk factors gain their predictive value because they mark the past operation of enduring psychological risk factors. This idea was endorsed and elaborated by Mann et al's (2010) suggestion that the static/dynamic distinction should be abandoned. They propose that we should instead think simply in terms of psychologically meaningful risk factors that may be manifested (and measured) in a variety of ways.

Taken together, these writings suggest that what might be called the Propensities Model is now the dominant applied conceptualization of dynamic risk factors for sexual offending. Stated simply the Propensities Model is composed of three central ideas: dynamic risk factors are best understood as enduring propensities; events and settings affect the likelihood that a propensity will be activated; and, the short-term likelihood of offending will depend on the extent to which relevant propensities are currently active and the environment affords the opportunity for them to influence offending behavior.

Limitations of the propensities model

In its current state of development, the Propensities Model is subject to five important limitations: it asserts causality but does not explain it; it does not represent human agency; it offers no account of what is involved in the development of propensities; it does not explain stable change in risk; and its account of the operation of static factors is a theoretical leap not supported by the evidence. Each of these limitations will be explored below.

In the Propensities Model the assertion of causality amounts to little more than the drawing of an arrow on a flow chart. No account is given of how a propensity causes a change in risk. In this sense the Propensities Model is theoretically shallow.

The Propensities Model is mechanistic. Nothing in its structure allows for the fact that humans are purposive and that much behavior is goal-directed. It insufficiently represents goals, purposes, and motivation, and it contains no model describing how choices are made.

The Propensities Model contains no theoretical account of how sustained change in risk might take place. The model allows that risk might change in an enduring way if risk-related propensities themselves change but it contains no representation of how that might take place. If risk-related propensities do not change, then the model implies that risk will vary between settings, but otherwise should not change. Of course this could be true. However, Hanson, Harris, Helmus, and Thornton (2014) found that, for each five years that sex offenders are in the community without being known to reoffend sexually, their risk of future sexual offending approximately halves. This effect is particularly striking for 'high-risk' offenders who have a history of persistent offending. These individuals show progressive, and very marked, declines in risk as they spend time in the community without offending. These results could be explained away by supposing that substantial initial misclassification of the 'high-risk' group took place but its most straightforward interpretation is that risk can sometimes change in a substantial and sustained way. Accordingly, a theoretical model of risk should provide a coherent account of how this can happen.

The Propensities Model asserts that static risk indicators gain their predictive power by indirectly reflecting risk-related propensities. If this is correct, then when the relationship between these propensities and recidivism is statistically controlled, the relationship of static risk factors to recidivism should vanish. However, studies which examine the joint predictiveness of static instruments and more direct measures of risk-related propensities typically find that static factors continue to make a robust contribution to prediction even when our measures of propensities are controlled (e.g. Craig, Thornton, Beech, & Browne, 2007; Olver, Wong, Nicholaichuk, & Gordon, 2007; Thornton & Knight, 2013). Of course this finding might be explained away by postulating that static factors are much better measured than risk-related propensities, or reflect propensities that we do not yet know how to measure, but clearly this result hardly supports this aspect of the Propensities Model. Rather it suggests that static factors capture something qualitatively different from the factors that have been identified as propensities.

Steps toward a more helpful model

This paper seeks to articulate a useful, theoretically meaningful, model of dynamic risk. More specifically the intention is for the model to incorporate some central elements of the Propensities Model while mitigating the limitations described in the previous section. A (hopefully) more helpful model will be built up by addressing these limitations by drawing on theoretical and empirical developments drawn from the Good Lives Model (Ward & Gannon, 2006; Ward & Stewart, 2003), the Theory of Reasoned Action (TRA; Fishbein & Ajzen, 2010), and Beck's (1996) account of schema modes.

Causality and human agency

The first two limitations listed can usefully be addressed together. The theoretically shallow representation of the causal role of propensities can be addressed by incorporating a more explicit representation of human agency. This requires two elements to be represented: sources of motivation (what do people want) and the goal-directed decision-making (how do people guide their behavior to seek what they want).

An attractive framework for describing sources of motivation has been developed by Ward and Gannon (2006) and Ward and Stewart (2003) under the rubric of the Good Lives Model. Relevant contributions from this model for the present purposes are (a) a typology of potential sources of motivation (called 'primary goods') (b) understanding offending as strategy for attaining primary goods that is adopted when legal ways of attaining them are blocked by personal limitations or environmental disadvantages. This model includes a sense of agency as one of the primary goods but more importantly from the present perspective is that it represents offending as arising from goal-seeking behavior (seeking personally relevant primary goods). Primary goods are identified as life, knowledge, excellence in play, excellence in work, agency (autonomy and self-directedness), inner peace, friendship (including intimate, romantic and family relationships), community (connection to wider social groups), spirituality, happiness (feeling good in the here and now), and creativity (Purvis, 2010; Ward & Gannon, 2006).

It is worth noting that although there is some empirical support for the particular primary goods identified in the Good Lives model (Purvis, 2010; Ward & Gannon, 2006) this is clearly not the only possible model of motivation. Indeed, one might argue that dynamic risk factors relevant to sexual offending predominantly relate to distortions in how sex, social connection, and self-determination are sought. However, the primary goods identified by the Good Lives model subsume these specific motivations and there is some merit in the Good Lives model's greater comprehensiveness. Another concern is that describing something as a universal primary good suggests that it ought to have an evolutionarily based biological substrata but substantive foundational investigations of this kind seem not to have been attempted in elaborating the Good Lives model. Despite these concerns, the Good Lives typology of primary goods, perhaps with a few tweaks, is a good enough model of motivation for the present purposes.

Incorporating the Good Lives typology of primary goods provides a basis for understanding the goals people pursue but it does not provide an explicit representation of how motives lead to goal-directed behavior. At the other end of the mechanisms underlying goal-directed behavior are the proximate determinants of the attractiveness of a specific behavior. These can be usefully represented using concepts from the TRA (Fishbein & Ajzen, 2010), a slightly modified version of which is adopted here. Attraction toward a behavioral option can be understood as resulting from a weighted combination of three processes. These are: (1) outcome expectancies (called attitudes toward the behavior in the TRA and related to the attractiveness of the outcomes that come to mind when thinking of engaging in the behavior); (2) social pressure (called subjective norms in the TRA and related to beliefs about how likely valued others are to engage in or approve of this kind of behavior); and (3) self-efficacy (called perceived behavior control in the TRA and related to the person's belief that they can successfully enact the behavior). The TRA is not the only empirically supported model of decision-making. Nevertheless, it has been very successful in empirically modeling a wide range of actions (Fishbein & Ajzen, 2010) and is good enough for the present purposes.

Simplifying for the purposes of theoretical analysis, a person with a history of sexual offending can be thought of as repeatedly having to select between different psychologically available ways of attaining the primary goods that they currently care about. Some of these ways of attaining primary goods take them toward engaging in further sexual offending (antisocial options) while others will take them away from sexual offending (prosocial options). Each option will subjectively and (largely implicitly) be evaluated as having a combination of outcome-expectations, social pressure, and self-efficacy that determines its attraction. The probability of an option becoming a goal will depend on the balance between the attractions of the different options that occur to the individual.

Situated between personally relevant primary human goods and the proximate determinants of the attractiveness of different behaviors is the intermediate zone of schemas, scripts, and strategies. Over time individuals pursuing particular primary human goods will develop representations of recurrent features of their environment that facilitate or impede this pursuit, scripts for behavioral sequences that have been useful as well as more general strategies. These can be understood as organized in terms of schema with (i) triggering components that scan the world to activate the schema when it is relevant, (ii) a model of key features of the world into which the individual's current situation will be mapped when the schema is active, (iii) motivational urges related to achieving particular primary human goods when the world is represented this way, and (iv) associated scripts and strategies. This way of using the schema construct corresponds approximately to what Beck (1996) called schema modes. It would be possible to conceptualize what are here called schema as composed of cognitive schema, motivational schema, behavioral schema, etc., but as Beck (1996) described, in practice, all these elements tend to activate together and function as an integrated unit.

Schema normally develop because they are (at least in the short-term) functional at the time. Schema regulation is required for a number of reasons: the current situation may activate conflicting schema; increased experience may indicate that different schema are helpful in different settings; a schema that yields short-term benefits may lead to longer term costs; or schema that worked well as a child may no longer be helpful as an adult. Normal schema operation will, therefore, include flexible regulation of schema activation and deactivation in response to what is currently functional. Schema may be described as maladaptive when this flexible regulation is ineffective so that the schema misrepresents the nature of the current environment or generates urges, scripts, and strategies that are harmful to the individual or to others affected by the individual's behavior.

A number of factors may contribute to the development of overly rigid maladaptive schema. Genetic vulnerabilities, probably in interaction with adverse childhood events, may lead to deficiencies in the biological substrata for self-regulation processes (see, e.g. Coyne & Wright, 2014) or to excessive intensity of biological responses (see, e.g. Caspi et al., 2002) making regulation harder. Sometimes schema will generate behavior that elicits responses from others that tend to confirm the core beliefs that are central to the schema. Finally, if schema that were functional earlier in life are a very poor fit to the adult environment it may simply be hard for the individual to develop the kind of interaction with their adult environment that would let them develop more functional schema.

Schema activation plays a central role in determining which scripts or strategies are psychologically available to the individual. By 'psychologically available' scripts or strategies is meant the range of actions that come to mind to pursue goals. At least three factors interact to limit what is psychologically available. These are the opportunities that the immediate situation and the larger setting afford the fit between these opportunities and the individual's repertoire, and the degree to which the situation and setting trigger particular schema and so render schema-related scripts and strategies cognitively accessible while not calling other options to mind. When these processes are working effectively the situation and setting, in conjunction with activated schema, prime a limited number of relevant behaviors so that only these are psychologically available.

Within this framework, risk-related propensities are largely situated in this intermediate zone of schema operation. There they have their effect by increasing the psychological availability and attractiveness of antisocial behavioral options relative to the psychological availability and attractiveness of prosocial possibilities. This expansion of the Propensities Model both incorporates an account of human agency and provides richer ways of understanding how risk-related propensities influence criminal behavior.

Understanding change in risk

The Propensity Model can already account for two kinds of change in risk. It predicts that risk will fluctuate according to whether recent events have activated relevant propensities and according to whether the immediate situation affords prosocial or antisocial opportunities. It also predicts that risk will differ between settings when these settings differ in the frequency and intensity of triggering events and in the kinds of opportunities afforded. What the Propensity Model less easily explains is sustained change in risk occurring over extended periods of time within the same setting.

Two additional concepts provide useful ways of understanding this kind of change. One of these is the self-regulation of propensities. The other is the development of resources.

Self-regulation of a propensity may develop if the individual perceives the propensity as having led him into trouble. Its effectiveness depends on the individual developing a motivation to regulate the propensity, developing the skills to do so, and reliably applying those skills even when the propensity has been activated. Olver et al. (2007), in a series of studies with the Violence Risk Scale – Sex Offender Version (VRS-SO:), have demonstrated that changes in self-regulation of propensities are associated with corresponding changes in recidivism rates (Olver, Beggs-Christofferson, Grace, & Wong, 2014; Olver, Beggs-Christofferson, & Wong, 2015; Olver & Wong, 2011). This effect is now established as incremental to both static risk factors and pretreatment assessment of risk-related propensities. So, for example, according to the logistic regression equation published by Olver et al. (2015), people with relatively high-static and pretreatment dynamic risk could have a five-year sexual recidivism rate of 23% if they developed no self-regulation in response to treatment, or as low as 12% if they showed twice the amount of change that was usually produced by the treatment programs studied.

These treatment-related changes in schema regulation can be understood as an artificial augmentation of normal schema regulation processes. They can be seen as compensating for developmental failures in normal schema regulation.

Enduring change can also occur without artificial intervention through the development of resources. It is proposed that when someone decides to pursue a particular kind of antisocial option they engage in problem-solving in the service of that option and as they do this repeatedly will build up schema that support and automate the activity. For example, they may build up schema representing vulnerable victims or opportunities of offending and incorporate a widening repertoire of offense-tactics into these schema. They will also experience recurrent internal challenges to offending including qualms, feelings of guilt, and fears about consequences. These will elicit further problem-solving designed to allay this negative affect and this in turn will be incorporated into schema so that neutralization of these challenges is automated. Finally, individuals who offend repeatedly will tend to seek out persons who support (or at least, do not condemn) their activities, or who may be helpful in identifying opportunities to offend. Thus, their social networks will change in character so they become increasingly supportive of their antisocial behavior. In effect then, repeatedly problem-solving in the service of antisocial behavior leads to the development of internal and external resources supportive of that behavior. Similarly, when someone pursues a prosocial option they will build internal and external resources supportive of that course of action. These resources may change all three proximate determinants of decision-making. They may change outcome-expectations, they may change beliefs about what others will support, and they may change confidence that the behavior can be successfully enacted.

The development of supportive resources can explain enduring change that occurs without a change in the underlying propensities. Thus, when someone repeatedly makes prosocial choices over a period of years this can be expected to make a substantial difference to the prosocial resources available to them and consequently their risk would be expected to fall in response. Of course, the experience of life that resulted from those prosocial choices and developed prosocial resources might also lead to a change in the underlying propensities, the two possibilities are not mutually exclusive, but a change in underlying propensities is not necessary to explain a substantial change in risk. This theoretical idea is consistent with developing work on protective factors. Instruments like the SAPROF (de Vogel, de Ruiter, Bouman, & de Vries Robbé, 2012) operationalize the concept of prosocial resources and research with it has indicated that more developed protective factors moderate the effect of risk on reoffending (de Vries Robbé, de Vogel, Koster, & Bogaerts, 2015).

Static versus dynamic risk factors

Considering the role of resources also explains why static risk factors seem to have a predictive value beyond that explained by their overlap with propensities. Static actuarial assessments designed to assess risk of sexual offending typically have many items reflecting the frequency and range of past sexual offending. These items may, therefore, also reflect the accumulation of antisocial resources that occurred as a side effect of repeated offending. As already noted, this would include such things as skills in detecting vulnerable victims, skills in grooming potential victims or those who might protect them, knowing which parts of the offense experience they enjoy and so how to maximize that, skills in regulating anxiety about getting caught, etc. Additionally, they may have lost or distanced themselves from prosocial friends, while making friendships with others who are more tolerant of offending. While the balance of prosocial versus antisocial associates is incorporated in some instruments for assessing propensities, most aspects of developing expertize in offending are not. Thus, the concept of resources provides a good theoretical way to understand why static instruments have predictive power that is incremental to measures of propensities.

Ways propensities may operate

Within this elaborated model there are a number of ways that risk-related propensities may operate. This will be illustrated by examining three of the empirically supported propensities identified by Mann et al. (2010), Sexual Preoccupation, Lack of Emotionally

Intimate Relationships with Adults, and Lifestyle Impulsivity. The three were chosen because empirical support for their relationship with sexual recidivism is strong and because they are diverse.

Sexual preoccupation

According to Mann et al. (2010) this risk factor refers to 'an abnormally intense interest in sex that dominates psychological functioning' (p. 8). Within the present framework it can be understood in terms of the role sex plays in serving multiple primary goods. Sexual activity most directly serves the Primary Good of Happiness (pleasure in the moment) but it can also serve multiple other primary goods: furthering emotional intimacy in the context of romantic relationships; furthering inner peace (when sexual behavior or fantasy is used to cope with distressing affect); supporting a sense of agency (when sex is an arena within which the individual feels powerful); excellence in play (when individuals feel sexually appreciated by their lovers); and even, in some circumstances, excellence in work. For the individual with a strong propensity to sexual preoccupation experiencing a need for any of a wide range of primary human goods will activate a schema in which the world is represented in terms of sexual opportunities, strong sexual urges are felt, and scripts and strategies for sexual behavior are primed. Sex is then experienced as the central route to satisfying multiple primary goods, such that other ways to satisfy these goals are either much less psychologically available or seen as less effective. Difficulty accessing any kind of sexual outlet would create a kind of desperation as many primary goods would be threatened. The individual will, therefore, often seek sexual activity and be less easily deterred from specific sexual behaviors by potential costs associated with their illegality.

Lack of emotionally intimate relationships with adults

According to Mann et al. (2010) this factor applies where the individual is unable to form sustained marital-type relationships or where such relationships are marred by repeated conflict and/or infidelity. Emotionally intimate marital-type relationships most directly satisfy the primary good that is labeled Friendship in the Good Lives Model but which is better understood as a biologically prepared need for emotional closeness, mutual support, and mutual nurturance. Other primary goods served can include inner peace, happiness in the moment (including that provided by sexual activity), and agency.

Schema relevant to this factor will include those representing the self in relationship to others (the familiar adult attachment styles: Bartholomew & Horowitz, 1991) and a developing schema representing the specific relationship the individual is now in. The various insecure attachment styles (anxious; dismissive or fearful) will make it harder to achieve or sustain an emotionally intimate marital-type relationship and will also be reinforced by the experience of non-intimate relationships. Emotionally intimate marital-type relationships may relate to risk through a number of mechanisms.

An emotionally intimate marital relationship may provide legitimate and easily accessible opportunities for sexual activity as well as satisfying needs for emotional closeness, mutual support, and mutual nurturance. Further, one of the effects of being in an emotionally intimate marital relationship can be to provide increased structure and self-regulation as these functions may be scaffolded by a partner. Additionally, a partner (depending on their attitudes) may exert social pressure against sexual offending. The collective effect of these three potential mechanisms may be for this kind of relationship to function as a protective factor.

Being unable to form marital-type relationships or only being able to sustain them briefly, by contrast, may leave the individual with the pains of loneliness, and set them up to seek emotional intimacy through dysfunctional routes. For example, some rapists believe they achieve a kind of emotional intimacy with someone by raping them. More commonly, men who have difficulty achieving emotional intimacy with adults may try to satisfy this need by forming pseudo-romantic relationships with children. The longer someone lives without this relational protective factor, the more opportunity there is for them to develop dysfunctional ways of meeting needs for sex and emotional intimacy. The more often dysfunctional strategies are used, the more skilled and psychologically available they will become and hence the more likely they will be to be used.

Lifestyle impulsiveness

According to Mann et al. (2010) this risk-related propensity refers to 'low self-control, chronic instability in housing and employment, lack of meaningful daily routines, irresponsible decisions, and limited or unrealistic long-term goals' (p. 12). These features can be understood as reflecting two interacting failures: difficulties in regulating schema that deliver short-term gratifications and failing to develop schema that depict an orderly lifestyle as a route to multiple primary human goods. The operation of the factor is liable to be self-reinforcing in the sense that repeated failures of this type will create a chaotic lifestyle in which short-term consequences are much more predictable than long-term consequences. This factor can be understood as resulting from the interplay of vulnerabilities in genetic and brain systems supporting self-control (e.g. Aharoni et al., 2014; Coyne & Wright, 2014), the failure to learn self-control skills during childhood, and an absence of external supports for self-control.

This factor can be expected to push toward sexual recidivism through at least two routes, impacting outcome expectancies and social pressure. Most sexual offending, like many other kinds of crime, involves a short-term benefit to the individual with potential wider and longer term negative consequences. Since this propensity involves failures to either value, or represent in the moment, longer term negative consequences, its presence means that outcome expectancies for sexual crimes are likely to be more positive. Additionally, lifestyle impulsiveness is liable to lead to the person's social network including a higher proportion of individuals who are tolerant of criminal behavior so that social pressure against it is reduced.

Implications for research, assessment, and rehabilitation

Implications for research

The Propensity Model invites research that examines the statistical association between factors claimed to be risk-related propensities and recidivism outcomes. Propensities are normally inferred from patterns of past behavior but they are not understood more deeply. The theoretical elaboration developed here invites researchers to explore the relationship between risk-related propensities and more fundamental factors on which the propensity depends. It also invites researchers to explore how a propensity (or the factors underlying it) impacts the proximate determinants of behavior (outcome expectancies; social pressure; and self-efficacy).

Another potential range of studies has to do with exploring how different kinds of intervention affect the factors underlying propensities. Traditional recidivism studies are not easily able to ask this kind of question since they take too long and strong experimental designs are hard to implement. Evaluations of the effect of treatment components on specific factors that underlie propensities may be more fruitful. They can provide more specific feedback (what impacts what) in a much faster timescale and can use waiting list control group designs.

These promising possibilities depend on the development of methodologies to measure factors underlying propensities. This, in turn, will require its own program of research. For example, how does one assess the psychological availability of different behaviors? Fortunately, the wider research literature now has well-developed paradigms for assessing priming effects and some (e.g. the Implicit Association Task) have been used with sexual offenders (e.g. Nunes, Hermann, & Ratcliffe, 2013).

Implications for assessment

The theoretical developments articulated here would encourage at least four foci in assessment. These are the risk-related propensities applicable to the individual, the factors that underlie these propensities, the internal and external resources supportive of antisocial behavior, and the internal and external resources supportive of prosocial behavior. Internal resources supporting prosocial behavior can be subdivided into skills and motivation to regulate risk-related propensities versus skills and motivation supportive of prosocial ways of achieving personally relevant primary goods. In either case motivation can be understood in terms of how the proximate determinants of the attractiveness of behavior are affected by the schema liable to be activated in different environments.

These considerations will allow more in depth case formulations. Potential treatment targets will be more richly identified. A more balanced emphasis on the protective effects of resources supporting prosocial behavior versus resources supporting antisocial behavior will be possible. Risk will be understood as an emergent property deriving from dynamic interactions of internal and external variables rather than as a property of the individual expressed in terms of the rate of recidivism associated with a risk factor score. Among other things this will make it easier to understand the three-way interaction between mental illness, dynamic risk factors, and external protective factors that is critical in assessing sexual offenders with major mental illness (Kelley & Thornton, 2015).

Implications for rehabilitation

From the present perspective treatment can be seen as augmenting the natural process of schema regulation. Schema regulation is designed to allow sufficient adaptation to a changing environment to allow the person to develop and sustain a satisfying connection to personally relevant primary goods.

Effective treatment depends on creating a therapeutic environment that heightens motivation to connect to primary goods in a prosocial way and assists in the development of internal and external resources to support this. As individuals bond with therapists and their treatment group social pressure to connect to primary goods in a prosocial way is heightened. In the therapeutic process itself skilled therapists lead individuals to discover and attend to personally relevant factors that shift outcome expectancies in a way that further heightens the attractiveness of prosocial behavior. And finally, both their own initial successes in self-management and the sight of others succeeding heightens the individual's belief that they too can live differently. In these ways the therapeutic process cumulatively renders seeking to connect to primary goods in a prosocial way more attractive. As individuals persist in acting on this attraction they will develop sufficient internal and external resources to stabilize a healthier way of functioning.

For some individuals with a history of sexual offending the above will be a sufficient process. In contrast, where multiple risk-related propensities reflect strong and poorly regulated schema, treatment will also need to target these schema processes. Here the treatment environment will need to initially minimize the degree to which maladaptive schema are triggered while also avoiding over-reactions to inevitable lapses when these schema are triggered. How this proceeds will depend on whether the primary issue is the strength and content of maladaptive schema or whether it is impairment of regulatory capacities by such things as major mental illness, cognitive deficits, or biological weaknesses in the brain systems underlying self-regulation.

In the former case, as prosocial resources are strengthened, the therapeutic process will need to focus on sensitive material in a way that at least partially trigger schema activity so that the individual can learn to regulate this. Here the therapeutic art is to keep the process within the window where schema are activated but the individual's resources are sufficient to manage their response. In the latter case, the question will be whether it is possible to strengthen regulatory resources sufficiently or whether long-term supportive management is required. This should not be taken to imply indefinite confinement in secure institutions. Rather the issue is how to provide sufficient support while increasing the individual's autonomy and enabling them to connect to primary goods without needing to engage in problematic behavior.

Disclosure statement

No potential conflict of interest was reported by the author.

References

Aharoni, E., Mallett, J., Vincetn, G. M., Harenski, C. L., Calhoun, V. D., Sinnott-Armstrong, W., Gazzaniga, M. S., & Kiehl, K. (2014). Predictive accuracy in the neuroprediction of arrest. *Social Neuroscience 9*(4). doi:10.1080/17470919.2014.907201

Andrews, D. A., & Bonta, J. (2006). *The psychology of criminal conduct* (4th ed.). Newark, NJ: LexisNexis/Anderson.

Bartholomew, K., & Horowitz, L. M. (1991). Attachment styles among young adults: A test of the four category model. *Journal of Personality and Social Psychology 61*(2), 226–244. doi:10.1037/0022-3514.61.2.226

Beck, A. T. (1996). Beyond belief: A theory of modes, personality, and psychopathology. In P. Salkovskis (Ed.), *Frontiers of cognitive therapy* (pp. 1–25). New York, NY: Guilford.

Caspi, A., McClay, J., Moffit, T. E., Mill, J., Martin, J., Criag, I. W., … Poulton, R. (2002). Role of genotype in the cycle of violence in maltreated children. *Science, 297*, 851–854.

Craig, L. A., Thornton, D., Beech, A., & Browne, K. D. (2007). The relationship of statistical and psychological risk marker to sexual reconviction in child molesters. *Criminal Justice and Behavior, 34*, 314–329.

Coyne, M. A., & Wright, J. P. (2014). The stability of self-control across childhood. *Personality and Individual Differences, 69*, 144–149.

Fishbein, M., & Ajzen, I. (2010). *Predicting and changing behavior: The reasoned action approach.* New York, NY: Psychology Press (Taylor & Francis).

Hanson, R. K., Bourgon, G., Helmus, L., & Hodgson, S. (2009). The principles of effective correctional treatment also apply to sexual offenders: A meta-analysis. *Criminal Justice and Behavior, 36*, 865–891.

Hanson, R. K., & Harris, A. J. R. (2000). Where should we intervene? Dynamic predictors of sex offense recidivism. *Criminal Justice and Behavior, 27*, 6–35.

Hanson, R. K., Harris, A. J. R., Helmus, L., & Thornton, D. (2014). High risk sex offenders may not be high risk forever. *Journal of Interpersonal Violence, 29*, 2792–2813. doi:10.1177/0886260514526062

Hanson, R. K., Harris, A. J. R., Scott, T., & Helmus, L. (2007). *Assessing the risk of sexual offenders on community supervision: The Dynamic Supervision Project.* Corrections Research User Report 2007-05. Ottawa: Public Safety Canada.

Kelley, S. M., & Thornton, D. (2015). Assessing risk of sex offenders with major mental illness: Integrating research into best practices. *Journal of Aggression, Conflict, and Peace Research, 7*, 258–274. doi:10.1108/JACPR-02–2015–0162

Knight, R. A., & Thornton, D. (2007). *Evaluating and improving risk assessment schemes for sexual recidivism: A long term follow up of convicted sexual offenders.* Final Report: US Department of Justice, Award Number 2003-WG-BX-1002. Retrieved from http://www.ncjrs.gov/pdffiles1/nij/grants/217618.pdf

Mann, R. E., Hanson, R. K., & Thornton, D. (2010). Assessing risk for sexual recidivism: Some proposals on the nature of psychologically meaningful risk factors. *Sexual Abuse: A Journal of Research and Treatment, 22*, 191–217. doi:10.1177/1079063210366039

Nunes, K. L., Hermann, C. A., & Ratcliffe, K. (2013, June 12). Implicit and explicit attitudes towards rape are associated with sexual aggression. *Journal of Interpersonal Violence, 28*(13), 2657–2675. Advance online publication. doi:10.1177/0886260513487995

Olver, M. E., Beggs-Christofferson, S. M., Grace, R. C., & Wong, S. C. P. (2014). Incorporating change information into sexual offender risk assessments using the Violence Risk Scale – Sexual Offender version. *Sexual Abuse: A Journal of Research and Treatment, 26*, 472–499. doi:10.1177/1079063213502679

Olver, M. E., Beggs-Christofferson, S. M., & Wong, S. C. P. (2015). Evaluation and applications of the clinically significant change method with the Violence Risk Scale – Sexual Offender Version: Implications for risk-change communication. *Behavioral Sciences & the Law, 33*, 92–110. doi:10.1002/bsl.2159

Olver, M. E., & Wong, S. C. P. (2011). A comparison of static and dynamic assessment of sexual offender risk and need in a treatment context. *Criminal Justice and Behavior, 38*, 113–126. doi:10.1177/0093854810389534

Olver, M. E., Wong, S. C. P., Nicholaichuk, T., & Gordon, A. (2007). The validity and reliability of the Violence Risk Scale – Sex Offender version: Assessing sex offender risk and evaluating therapeutic change. *Psychological Assessment, 19*, 318–329. doi:10.1037/1040–3590.19.3.318

Purvis, M. (2010). *Seeking a good life: Human goods and sexual offending.* Saarbrucken: Lambert Academic Press.

Thornton, D. (2002). Constructing and testing a framework for dynamic risk assessment. *Sexual Abuse: A Journal of Research and Treatment, 14*, 139–153. doi:10.1023/A:1014620214905

Thornton, D., & Knight, R. A. (2013, December 30). Construction and validation of SRA-FV Need Assessment. *Sex Abuse, A Journal of Research and Treatment*. doi: 10.1177/1079063213511120

de Vogel, V., de Ruiter, C., Bouman, Y., & de Vries Robbé, M. (2012). *SAPROF: Guidelines for the assessment of protective factors for violence risk.* The Netherlands: Van der Hoeven Stichting.

de Vries Robbé, M., de Vogel, V., Koster, K., & Bogaerts, S. (2015). Assessing protective factors for sexually violent offending with the SAPROF. *Sexual Abuse: A Journal of Research and Treatment*, *27*, 51–70. doi:10.1177/1079063214550168

Ward, T., & Beech, A. R. (2006). An integrated theory of sexual offending. *Aggression and Violent Behavior*, *11*, 44–63. doi:10.1016/j.avb.2005.05.002

Ward, T., & Gannon, T. A. (2006). Rehabilitation, etiology, and self-regulation: The comprehensive Good Lives Model of treatment for sexual offenders. *Aggression and Violent Behavior*, *11*, 77–94.

Ward, T., & Stewart, C. A. (2003). The treatment of sex offenders: Risk management and good lives. *Professional Psychology, Research and Practice*, *34*, 353–360.

Dynamic risk and protective factors

Ralph C. Serin[a], Nick Chadwick[a] and Caleb D. Lloyd[b]

[a]Department of Psychology, Carleton University, Ottawa, ON, Canada; [b]Department of Psychology, University of Texas at El Paso, El Paso, TX, USA

ABSTRACT

This paper reviews the literature regarding the identification and measurement of risk factors considered imminent precipitants of subsequent criminal conduct (i.e. dynamic risk factors). This paper also frames these risk factors against the so-called protective factors that are presumed to mitigate risk. Commonality among recent dynamic risk and protective measures reflects general agreement regarding viable candidate variables. Empirical studies suggest such factors yield incremental predictive validity and should inform case-formulaic understanding of criminal conduct and pathways to desistance, although this is not common practice. As well, definitional and measurement considerations are not well advanced and speak to the need for further conceptual clarity.

Beginning in the 1980s, correctional and forensic psychology has been either blessed or cursed, depending on one's viewpoint, with an abundant proliferation of risk assessment instruments. Despite decades of risk assessment research, the field is limited in its understanding of the immediate features (whether situational or intrapersonal) that influence an individual to take criminal action (Farrington, 2011; Yang & Mulvey, 2012) or forego criminal action when presented with an opportunity for crime (i.e. crime desistance; Maruna, 2010). Accordingly, after conducting a meta-analytic review of risk instruments, Yang, Wong, and Coid (2010) advocated for research that identifies situational contingencies that precipitate violence (i.e. dynamic risks). As such, the purpose of this paper is to review the current state of literature on the factors that may be relatively proximal triggers of criminal behaviour and the features that may simultaneously serve to inhibit criminal behaviour (i.e. protective factors).

By the early 1980s, opposition to measures with exclusively static risk factors was beginning to develop, primarily because these scales could not identify intervention targets, and if scores could change, the range of potential change was greatly restricted, and unidirectional (i.e. clients could only be rated worse; Bonta, 1996; Wong & Gordon, 2006). Importantly, involvement in treatment could not improve scores, leading to the improbable and nonviable practice of treatment completion having no impact on an individual's predicted outcome. At the same time, there was some concern regarding how nomothetic findings (i.e. group aggregate data) might apply to the individual.

Andrews and Bonta (2010) presented a hierarchy of risk factors intended to identify appropriate targets for rehabilitation programmes; their choice of variables was consistent with a conceptualisation of dynamic risk factors as relatively slow-evolving features. Their description of these targets as *criminogenic needs* came to be considered synonymous with the concept of dynamic risk. However, change scores on risk and need measures such as the Level of Service Inventory-Revised (LSI-R; Andrews & Bonta, 1995) purported to measure criminogenic needs have demonstrated only minimal effect sizes (e.g. Vose, Smith, & Cullen, 2013). This suggests that these criminogenic needs may have utility for risk prediction and general case planning, but appreciably less utility for examining intra-individual change, at least when these constructs are measured using the initial approaches to need assessment.

Importantly, the absence of criminogenic needs was implicitly considered to indicate the presence of a strength, but this distinction was rarely explicitly formalised in the operational application of the risk and need (RNR) model (Polaschek, 2012), which led to criticisms that the risk and need model is a deficit-based framework. As such, by the early 2000s, there was a movement for current practice to be replaced with a more strengths-based approach to offender assessment (Rogers, 2000; Ward & Brown, 2004). The emerging concern towards assessing prosocial features represents a profound shift in the contemporary risk assessment lexicon, by introducing the concept of protective factors as variables that may mitigate offender risk. We review the importance of protective factors in a later section of this paper.

Defining dynamic risk factors

Within the literature, there remains ambiguity surrounding how to exactly define and conceptualise a dynamic risk factor in the context of both prediction and rehabilitation (Ward, 2015). In essence, the term criminogenic need has become equivalent to dynamic risk, but this viewpoint is arguably incomplete both conceptually and empirically. As noted by Yang et al. (2010), a second key feature that should emerge from a set of theoretically dynamic risk variables is the ability to identify precipitants of offender outcome; this represents a different task compared to assessing whether risk scores change over time due to intervention. In essence, this refers to the *timing* of the dynamic risk assessment, such that there should be a closely proximal association between observed change on a dynamic risk factor and an imminent recidivism outcome. This suggests the conceptualisation of dynamic risk factors could vary depending on either a prison or community setting, with definitions in the former setting emphasising treatment targets that change, while definitions in the latter setting emphasise immediate antecedents that trigger criminal actions.

Ultimately, dynamic risk factors, by definition, must demonstrate change, and reductions in these risk factors must lead to simultaneous reductions in level of risk for future recidivism (Brown, St. Amand, & Zamble, 2009; Caudy, Durso, & Taxman, 2013; Hanson & Harris, 2000; Howard & Dixon, 2013; Jones, Brown, & Zamble, 2009; Lewis, Olver, & Wong, 2012). Since dynamic factors can purportedly change, it would also be logically reasonable for community supervision officers (CSOs) to regularly incorporate new information about dynamic risk variables into case plans and modify risk management strategies accordingly.

However, most prior studies have not focused explicitly on these defining features, but have rather been occupied with whether dynamic risk variables significantly predict recidivism (with mixed results, especially when researchers first control for static predictors). By contrast, less research has focused on establishing that dynamic variables or scales exhibit the features that are core to the field's conceptualisation of dynamic risk variables. For example, the majority of research has examined theoretically dynamic risk factors at one specified point of time. This amounts to treating a dynamic variable as static, and provides no information regarding whether the variable shows change over time, or whether more proximal assessments may serve as better indicators of imminent risk. To investigate change processes, at least two assessments of risk are necessary to observe differences; to effectively model a change process, experts point out that at least three distinct assessments of dynamic risk are required, since only multiple time points allow researchers to partition measurement error from true change (Brown et al., 2009; Singer & Willett, 2003). Most clearly, a single measurement of a dynamic item (e.g. substance use severity) does not provide the assessor with dynamic information, nor does it allow researchers to argue that the variable exhibits truly dynamic features.

Thus, by definition, research should show that dynamic risk factors exhibit change, are associated with outcomes, and, in particular, that proximal changes are related to imminent risk to re-offend. In a similar way, Kraemer and colleagues (1997) present useful criteria for defining dynamic risk factors. First, research must show that the theoretically dynamic factor can be changed through intervention or the passage of time (e.g. aging). Second, the presence of the risk factor must be associated with an increase in the offender's probability of recidivism. Last, research must demonstrate that any changes in risk preceded the outcome. Despite using the language of causality, Kraemer and colleagues' (1997) framework is not truly experimental (i.e. most risk variables can neither be ethically nor logically assigned to individuals), and thus cannot eliminate the possibility that unobserved causal variables explain the observed association. As such, researchers should avoid using causal language when describing results from longitudinal, non-experimental research, and instead emphasise the *association* between the psychosocial variables and behavioural outcomes. Furthermore, although rehabilitation research offers the potential that risk variables may be experimentally manipulated in a way that can suggest causal impact (when random assignment is utilised, and intra-individual changes are confirmed to result from the intervention), there is currently scant evidence that within-programme changes can be measured precisely enough to provide the necessary experimental evidence to support causal statements about dynamic risk (Banse, Koppehele-Gossel, Kistemaker, Werner, & Schmidt, 2013; Beggs, 2010; Helmond, Overbeek, Brugman, & Gibbs, 2014; Scott, 2004; Serin, Lloyd, Helmus, Derkzen, & Luong, 2013).

Finally, Douglas and Skeem (2005) have contributed to discussion about the temporal relationship between dynamic risk factors and outcomes by differentiating between *risk status* and *risk state*; the former referring to a group risk estimate and the latter referring to fluctuating change in offender risk. Further, these risk state variables could change rapidly (e.g. level of anger) or gradually (e.g. antisocial attitudes). Perhaps somewhat simplistically, we have mused that static factors indicate *who* is at risk while dynamic factors indicate *when* they are at risk.

We conceptualise dynamic risk and protective factors as situated at different points along the age–crime curve (Serin, Lloyd, & Hanby, 2010); dynamic risk factors relate to crime acquisition and expression while protective factors reflect crime desistance. These desistance factors are agentic, reflecting human and social capital that mitigate risk, which will be discussed later in the paper.

Measures of dynamic risk

The field is now witnessing the emergence of new dynamic risk measures intended to assess idiographic (acute) changes in risk, and simultaneously inform imminent case planning and risk management. This new wave of dynamic risk measures represents a common interest in identifying acute factors that are sensitive to change over the short term and for which such change is related to client/offender outcome. Hence, changes on these acute factors should inform both case planning and risk management in *real time*.

One example in the forensic mental health field is the Short-Term Assessment of Risk and Treatability (START; Desmarais, Nicholls, Wilson, & Brink, 2012; Nicholls, Brink, Desmarais, Webster, & Martin, 2006). The START is a structured professional judgment (SPJ) approach that provides a framework for structuring the assessment of dynamic risk and protective factors. This measure incorporates 20 items that can be scored as either a vulnerability or an asset. To date, the measure has demonstrated good interrater agreement in initial research with a sample of 137 forensic psychiatric patients ($ICC_2 = .87$, $p < .001$; Nicholls et al., 2006), as well as good predictive accuracy using strength total score and vulnerability total score for any aggression. The START violence risk estimate ($n = 119$) yielded good predictive validity for aggression in the 3 months following the START assessment, including any aggression (AUC = .80), verbal aggression (AUC = .78), physical aggression towards objects (AUC = .84), and physical aggression towards others (AUC = .85; Desmarais et al., 2012). On the strength of such findings, the START has been swiftly implemented and it is currently used in at least 10 countries. It appears to have become the preferred dynamic risk measure for use in forensic mental health settings.

In the corrections field, examples include the Inventory of Offender Risk, Needs, and Strengths (IORNS; Miller, 2006), the Service Planning Instrument (SPIn; Orbis, 2003), and the Dynamic Risk Assessment of Offender Reentry (DRAOR; Serin, 2007). The IORNS is a self-report questionnaire and these others are SPJ approaches. The IORNS demonstrated acceptable internal consistency (α ranging from .51 to .91; Miller, 2006) and concurrent validity ($r = .45$, $p < .01$ with LSI-R total score). In addition, mean scores differentiated offender outcome over a 15-month follow-up ($n = 162$).

The DRAOR (Serin, 2007) is a SPJ instrument that considers Stable and Acute dynamic risk and Protective factors. The DRAOR was developed to assist CSOs in the assessment, and reassessment, of their clients' circumstances throughout the supervision process. For research purposes, a total score is calculated by summing the Acute and Stable scales and subtracting the Protective scale; however, in practice, a total score for the DRAOR is not calculated. Rather, items in each subscale are totalled to provide a summary of potential problem areas for CSOs to address. In the original implementation study in New Zealand among a sample of parolees ($n = 3{,}498$; total assessments $\sim 97{,}000$), AUCs ranged from .67 to .72 when prospectively predicting violation behaviour (Hanby, 2013). Importantly, Cox regression survival analysis indicated the DRAOR. Total score predicted incrementally over a valid static risk measure (RoC*RoI, Bakker, Riley, & O'Malley, 1999) (Hanby 2013). Last, DRAOR appears to also have utility irrespective of client gender (Yesberg, Scanlan, Hanby, Serin, & Polaschek, 2015).

Table 1 presents dynamic risk items from each of these measures for comparison. The IORNS scales are presented, but items are either extrapolated or amalgamated where appropriate to focus on comparable constructs, even if the item definitions differ between authors. The DRAOR distinguishes between stable and acute dynamic factors; both are reflected in Table 1. In Table 1, items that are included in three or four measures are shaded, to highlight where there is reasonable commonality across the measures.

With 23 variables across these 4 measures, it appears there is no shortage of candidate dynamic risk factors. As a result, we speculate it would be productive for future research to examine the ways these factors are defined, and how they are measured, rather than searching for additional items. It may be useful to attempt to conceptualise this class of new dynamic risk factors according to their influence on risk. From Table 1, the majority appear to be internal factors presumably within the control of the individual (e.g. self-regulation, accepts responsibility, criminal orientation). Fewer appear to be situational or external to the individual (e.g. employment, gang involvement), which is curious given the presumed importance of these variables in predicting imminence of criminal conduct. Nonetheless, *if* these represent a reasonable inventory of treatment needs, it is important to consider how these relate to a theory of criminal conduct (Ward, 2015) and the extent to which extant programming can address these areas.

Table 1. Comparison of acute dynamic risk factors included in risk assessments.

Dynamic risk items	SPIn	START	IORNS (scales)	DRAOR
Impulsivity	x	x		x
Rule/treatment adherence/treatability	x	x		x
Sensitivity to provocation	x			x
Easily angered/emotional state/irritability	x	x	x	x
Negative attitudes/criminal orientation	x	x	x	x
Psychopathy			x	
Interpersonal problems		x	x	x
Substance abuse		x	x	x
Hostility	x		x	x
Negative social influences		x	x	x
Insight/awareness/sense of entitlement		x		x
Plans/goal setting		x		
Coping/problem-solving		x		x
Mental state/negative mood		x		x
Conduct/accepts responsibility	x	x		x
Self-care/personal resources/living situation/environmental resources/material resources		x	x	x
Attachment with others				x
Employment history	x			x
Employment motivation	x			
Gangs	x			
Homicidal/suicidal ideation	x	x		
History of sexual aggression	x			
Marital – perpetrator of domestic violence, partner with antisocial history/access to victims	x			x

Note: x indicates the presence of the item within the risk assessment.

Defining protective factors

Research investigating the relationship between protective factors and recidivism among general offenders is scarce, and protective factors have been theorised more than they have been investigated. The recent increased interest in the utility of protective factors in risk assessment reflects, in part, dissatisfaction with a risk assessment model that solely focuses on deficits or needs. Our understanding of candidate protective factors comes from three areas: current research regarding the application of protective factors in risk assessment (de Vogel, de Ruiter, Bouman, & de Vries Robbé, 2009); positive psychology as it is applied to offender supervision (Woldgabreal, Day, & Ward, 2014); and the desistance literature (Maruna, 2010). As well, but to a lesser extent, given the empirical evidence regarding reductions in criminal behaviour for correctional programme completers, we suggest it is productive to examine current correctional programming to find factors that contribute to offender success, such as through changes in knowledge, skills, and attributes.

Drawing upon research with juvenile offenders, there are two frameworks that propose different mechanisms underlying how protective factors may relate to recidivism (Rutter, 2000). According to a compensatory model, risk and protective factors are cumulative, with each risk factor increasing the odds of recidivism and each protective factor decreasing the odds of recidivism. Under this model, multiple risk factors are additive, whereas protective factors subtract from the cumulative risk; thus, the number of total factors that are present is more important than which specific factors are present. Thus, the model fails to distinguish how protective factors might differ in salience. Recognising that personal salience is unique to the individual, consider how one critically powerful protective factor (such as a high-quality relationship) might be more strongly related to an individual's choice to discontinue criminal action, compared to the presence of numerous but weakly salient factors (such as reluctance to return to prison and procriminal role models).

The second proposed model is an interactive model that asserts that protective factors are relevant only in the presence of risk factors. Within this model, the impact of protective factors on criminal outcomes varies depending on the level of risk, such that risk is reduced when both risk factors and protective factors are highly present, whereas protective factors have little or no impact on likelihood of recidivism when risk is already low.

Relatedly, the presence of a strength factor should not necessarily be considered to have a protective effect. For any strength factor to be protective, the individual must exercise some agency, meaning in the face of an opportunity for crime, the individual actively chooses an adaptive, functional, and non-criminal response. We consider risk (i.e. financial hardship, access to illicit substances, opportunity for quick and easy money) to be unavoidable, yet criminal action arises when a person *chooses* to engage in criminal conduct when faced with at-risk situations. If one accepts this conceptualisation, then protective factors moderate risk but do not reduce risk. Accordingly, intervention should assist offenders to choose adaptive and functional responses to criminal opportunities, rather than simply adopt a risk avoidance perspective (Mann, Webster, Schofield, & Marshall, 2004).

Results with youth (Fitzpatrick, 1997) supported a buffering model, suggesting that risk factors appear to become more salient when protective factors are non-existent or minimal. These findings reinforce the definition proposed by Rutter (1985, 1987) which emphasised the ability of protective factors to modify or improve an individual's response to some hazard known to increase the probability of a negative outcome.

Elsewhere, we have argued that an understanding of criminal behaviour must include both risk and desistance factors (Serin et al., 2010). These desistance factors (i.e. events and attributions that lead to cessation from crime) encompass what the field refers to as protective factors. Seminal work by Sampson and Laub (1992, 2005) identified key events (e.g. employment, marriage, and military service) that precede or lead to crime desistance. Maruna (2010) nicely summarised the broader desistance literature, identifying numerous desistance factors that reflect a blend of personal and social capital. Salient desistance factors include: getting older and maturing (van Mastrigt & Farrington, 2009); family and relationships (Laub, Nagin, & Sampson, 1998; Maruna, LeBel, & Lanier, 2003); sobriety (Walters, 1998); employment (Uggen, 2000); hope and motivation (LeBel, Burnett, Maruna, & Bushway, 2008); having a place in a social group (Farrall, 2004); not having a criminal identity (Chiricos, Barrick, Bales, & Bontrager, 2007); and being believed in (Rex, 1999). The assumption is that these factors buffer or mitigate risk, thereby leading to cessation from criminal conduct.

The various terms used to reflect a protective factor (i.e. protective, promotive, stabilisers, and desistance) underscore the field's current confusion regarding how these factors may influence client outcome, and how these factors may be conceptually distinct from known risk factors. Specifically, it is unclear if most view protective factors as buffers that mitigate risk, factors that decrease risk, or truly protective factors that function independent of risk. As well, it is equally unclear if scholars and clinicians share similar definitions of protective factors. Yet, overall, the field has generally embraced the importance of client strengths, and the lack of clear definitions should not obscure this consensus. We also note the general consensus is not unanimous, since key scholars in the area of risk assessment (Baird, 2009; Harris & Rice, 2015) strongly assert that protective factors are simply the obverse of risk factors (and, thus, do not need to be independently assessed) and that strident supporters of the construct have given it mythical properties, far beyond what has been empirically demonstrated.

Clearly, then, within the literature, there exists a lack of clarity and some confusion regarding how to conceptualise the idea of strengths. Lösel and Farrington's (2012) work in this area has been perhaps most instructive. They define a buffering protective factor as 'a variable that predicts a low probability of offending among persons at risk or interacts with a risk factor to nullify its effect' (p. S9). Specifically, a protective factor is one that interacts with risk, reducing the impact of a negative event (e.g. recidivism), such that the addition of each protective factor further moderates the effect of risk exposure (Fougere & Daffern, 2011; Jessor, Van Den Bos, Vanderryn, Costa, & Turbin, 1995; Lodewijks, de Ruiter, & Doreleijers, 2010). For example, poor parental supervision predicts offending in low income families; however, high income protects youth in families characterised by poor parental supervision, such that offending likelihood is reduced even in the presence of this risk factor (Lösel & Farrington, 2012). The key distinction for the definition of a protective factor, then, is the interaction between the protective factor and risk.

In contrast, strengths-based factors have also been referred to as promotive factors, which are conceptually and operationally different than protective factors (Jones, Brown, Robinson, & Frey, 2015). Promotive factors are best defined as variables that are negatively correlated with recidivism, such that as a promotive factor increases, the risk of recidivism decreases (Harris, 2013). Unlike protective factors, promotive factors directly reduce re-offending, but are not independent of risk (Loeber, Pardini, Stouthamer-Loeber, & Raine, 2007; Van der Put et al., 2011). Examples of promotive factors can include good social skills, good academic achievement, high motivation at school, consistent discipline, and higher family income (Loeber, Slot, & Stouthamer-Loeber, 2008). A promotive factor such as academic achievement is simply the inverse of a risk factor (i.e. difficulties attaining educational achievement).

Jones and colleagues (2015) proposed to amalgamate different definitions of protective factors and broadly consider them as strength factors; this is consistent with earlier views by Laub and colleagues (1998; Sampson & Laub, 2005). This suggests that a protective factor can co-exist with risk factors, and account for variability in outcome in an otherwise high-risk group of offenders. In an effort to quantify meaning of strengths in relation to risk, they propose defining these as any positive or prosocial facet that would intuitively buffer the risk of a criminal outcome. Once relevant strength factors are quantifiably linked to criminal outcomes and recidivism, refining these constructs based on their contributions to the assessment of risk (i.e. as a protective or promotive factor) could be a logical next step.

In an effort to evaluate potential relationships between protective factors and recidivism, Ullrich and Coid (2011) examined 15 proposed protective factors among a large sample of offenders who were followed for an average of 5 years. Of the 15 factors examined, results indicated that items assessing social support, emotional support, spare time spent with prosocial family and friends, involvement in religious activities, and closeness with others demonstrated promotive effects for violence after release from incarceration. After controlling for risk, spare time spent with family or friends demonstrated a significant independent effect on recidivism. In other words, individuals with this strength factor experienced lower rates of recidivism during the follow-up periods, regardless of the level of risk. A key finding of this research was that the relationship between strength factors and recidivism changed over time; factors that were promotive in year 1 may not have been in year 2 or 3 (Ullrich & Coid, 2011). Brown and colleagues (2009) reported similar findings for the potential temporal effect of dynamic risk factors, suggesting the field needs to consider follow-up time frame in order to incorporate temporal context into assessments, case planning, and risk management. Finally, of particular note, Jones and colleagues (2015) provided a rare finding that risk and strength scores significantly interacted, illustrating that high strength scores were particularly effective for attenuating recidivism among higher risk cases (i.e. fulfilling the strictest definition of protective factor).

Attention towards protective factors is expected to not only assist in the comprehensive assessment of an offender's risk and rehabilitation potential, but help foster a therapeutic alliance, promote recovery, and possibly motivate the offender towards desistance. Specifically, when offenders become aware that their prosocial progress will be recognised by their supervising officer, offenders are likely to attend more to building and pursuing strengths (Ullrich & Coid, 2011). Further, research on desistance from crime (i.e. crime cessation) suggests that protective factors may represent some of the internal and external mechanisms that underlie the process of exiting crime (Serin & Lloyd, 2009). For example, qualitative interviews with high risk offenders revealed that offenders who successfully remained crime-free for a period of 5 years indicated that positive support from family and recognising the costs associated with crime were critical to their success in the community (HaggÅrd, Gumpert, & Grann, 2001).

Embedded within this research are factors that reflect a positive psychology perspective (i.e. human goods) that are important for offender success. Woldgabreal and colleagues (2014) nicely summarise the shifts in criminal justice philosophy that have set the stage for a new perspective regarding offender supervision. An initial rehabilitation theme moved to a brokerage model following the pessimism spawned by Martinson's (1974) work, with rehabilitation giving way to retribution (Cromwell & Killinger, 1994). Ward and Salmon (2009) note the intent shifted to imposing an appropriate punitive sanction to balance the social harm resulting from the offence. While there was, and remains, a political expedience to this model, it should be highlighted that an individual is sent to prison to be rehabilitated not to be punished. Spiralling costs of crime and prisons and recent evidence that certain correctional practices can reduce re-offending (Chadwick, DeWolf, & Serin, 2015; Robinson et al., 2012; Smith, Gendreau, & Swartz, 2009) have led to a more empirical than ideological approach in many jurisdictions.

With that has come an interest in understanding how staff might contribute to offender success. This has set the stage for CSOs to become agents of change (Bourgon, Gutierrez, & Ashton, 2011) as reflected in recent core correctional practice curricula (e.g. Strategic Training Initiative in Community Supervision, Bonta et al., 2011; Staff Trained at Reducing Re-arrest, Lowenkamp, Holsinger, Robinson, & Alexander, 2014; Proactive Community Supervision, Sachwald, Eley, & Taxman, 2006). Essentially, CSOs are being asked to contribute to offender success, not simply monitor risk, by actively engaging clients and teaching skills. The expectation appears to be to improve client skills (i.e. problem-solving, self-control) and reduce criminal thinking. While these recent advances in supervision models and practices have been welcomed by many jurisdictions, it is especially important to focus on intra-individual changes in client identity and attributions. This is where positive psychology is poised to make an important contribution.

Positive psychology focuses on human strengths to enhance optimal client functioning and to balance the current emphasis on deficits (Duckworth, Steen, & Seligman, 2005). However, this is not intended to be a naïve approach, such that one that ignores problem-focused approaches such as risk assessment and management (Seligman & Csikszentmihalyi, 2000). Within the criminal justice context, this means that client outcomes should be enhanced when needs are identified and managed, and strengths are developed and supported. The end goal of this approach is not only to reduce re-offending but also to have clients become functioning, purposeful, and contributing members of society.

Woldgabreal and colleagues (2014) carefully reviewed the positive psychology literature and highlighted four specific constructs that should enhance client outcome in the context of community supervision (although the constructs should also be transferable and relevant for in-prison programming). These authors propose psychological flexibility, self-efficacy, optimism, and hope as key constructs that have conceptual and practical benefits to complement existing offender risk management approaches. Psychological flexibility is a core element of human functioning (Bond, Hayes, & Barnes-Holmes, 2006). It has been described as 'the extent to which an offender's internal resources (strengths) can be utilised to facilitate pro-social pursuits' (Woldgabreal, et al., 2014, p. 35) and an 'ability to flexibly utilise their cognitive repertoire to pursue goals in pro-social ways' (Woldgabreal et al., 2014, p. 35). The suggestion appears to be that cognitive flexibility yields resiliency in the face of pervasive or acute risk situations.

Self-efficacy, another construct from positive psychology, is a judgement (by self and others) that one has the required abilities to organise and execute specific tasks (Bandura, 1989), such as remaining crime-free. Competence can come from both internal and external influences. Hence, experience of mastery or failure in attempting to desist from crime will impact an offender's perception of self-efficacy and influence their future willingness to desist. The success of others in the offender's immediate social group can similarly influence their perception of self-efficacy. Seeing others succeed can enhance success. For example, the offender who sees someone in their group treatment succeed or someone on community supervision reach a milestone is relevant. Celebrations of offender success would augment this influence, as would the nature of reinforcement they receive from peers and corrections officials. Finally, Bandura (1989) notes that an excessive level of physiological and emotional stress can impede beliefs about one's competence.

Scheier and Carver (1985) present optimism as an inherent and stable human characteristic that helps individuals faced with challenging situations by creating the expectation that desired goals are attainable. Optimism therefore incorporates both expectancy and explanatory styles. Compared to desisting ex-offenders, for active offenders, negative internal attributions are associated with persisting in criminal behaviour (Maruna & Farrall, 2004). Examining offender narratives, Maruna and Farrall were able to discern differences between active and desisting offenders in terms of positive and negative scripts in explaining their course of action. However, it is unclear to what extent other researchers might consider any external attributions by active offenders to be rationalisations or neutralisations.

Hope, a related construct, is best defined by Snyder et al. (1991) as 'a cognitive set that is based on a reciprocally derived sense of successful agency (goal directed determination) and pathways (planning of ways to meet goals)' (p. 571). There is an agentic component to this definition, whereby the offender engages in affirmative self-talk (i.e. 'I can do this'). The pathways component relates to an ability to conceive alternative options if the original approach is thwarted. Interestingly, hope has been found to be independent of self-efficacy (Magaletta & Oliver, 1999) and optimism (Scheier & Carver, 1985) in predicting general well-being. It would seem that hope relates to an internal cognitive set while optimism refers to outcome expectancies (Woldgabreal et al., 2014).

These positive constructs do not exist in isolation and LeBel and colleagues (2008) observed that desistance from crime is the outcome of a complex and dynamic interaction between subjective/agency factors and social/environmental factors. As such, both motivation and opportunities are required, and it is likely impossible to disentangle their priority or sequencing, since this may logically differ between individuals. LeBel and colleagues alluded to these subjective/agency factors and social/environmental factors as being protective, but it is also possible that they could be iatrogenic. Nonetheless, they conclude that with an adequate sense of hope, a person may both select into and take advantage of positive social opportunities, such as employment or prosocial relationships. In essence, these events are expected to feed back into the offender's motivation, further encouraging more adaptive ways to manage potentially adverse situations.

The application of positive psychology constructs to corrections may be challenging and certainly requires a clearer conceptual model and unambiguous operational definitions. With this review in mind, it is of interest to determine to what extent current risk assessment measures that include protective factors reflect internal and external states indicative of positive psychology and crime desistance.

Assessment of protective factors

Despite the lack of conceptual clarity surrounding protective factors, numerous researchers have developed measures that blend strength assessment into a risk measurement paradigm (Structured Assessment of Protective Factors (SAPROF), SPIn, START, & DRAOR). As mentioned previously, the START incorporates strengths; a recent study found that mean strength scores were higher for patients who did not display any aggressive tendencies throughout the follow-up (Desmarais et al., 2012).

Similarly, the SPIn (Orbis Partners, 2003) is a stand-alone comprehensive measure of risk, needs, and strengths. Strengths are scored using Likert-type scales that can be summed to produce both domain totals and an overall strength score. Recent research ($N = 3656$) demonstrated good predictive accuracy for male ($n = 2{,}962$; AUC = .77), female ($n = 694$; AUC = .77), aboriginal ($n = 635$; AUC = .75), and non-aboriginal offenders ($n = 3{,}021$; AUC = .76; Jones et al., 2015).

The SAPROF (de Vogel et al., 2009) was developed as a dynamic addition to the Historical Clinical Risk management-20 (HCR-20; Webster, Douglas, Eaves, & Hart, 1997). The instrument consists of 17 items, including 2 static factors and 15 protective factors that are assessed to identify potential goals or targets for intervention. The SAPROF is designed to prospectively prevent recidivism by informing treatment rather than be used as a prediction tool. In a retrospective validation, de Vries Robbé, de Vogel, and de Spa (2011) found that SAPROF total scores were able to significantly predict non-recidivism (defined as lack of violent offence) with stability over three follow-up periods ($r_{pb} = -.35$ at 1 year, $r_{pb} = -.38$ at 2 years, and $r_{pb} = -.35$ at 3 years). Overall psychometric properties of the SAPROF appear sufficient (de Vries Robbé et al., 2011). Further, results have suggested that, when combined with a dynamic measure of risk, the inclusion of protective factors from the SAPROF improved the overall prediction of recidivism at both a 3-year follow-up and a long-term follow-up (de Vries Robbé, de Vogel, & Douglas, 2013). The SAPROF shows promise as a structured assessment, but has only been utilised among forensic samples to date and is preferably used to augment the risk assessment by the HCR-20 V3 (Douglas, Hart, Webster, & Belfrage, 2013).

Finally, as noted earlier, one of the subscales of the DRAOR includes protective items. In a sample of 3372 offenders on community supervision (base rate 49% for any violation), the protective domain demonstrated a moderate level of predictive accuracy (AUC = .67; Hanby, 2013).

Table 2 presents the candidate items for protective factors gleaned from these three measures (START, SAPROF, & DRAOR) and Ullrich and Coid's (2011) research. It is worth noting that these independent programmes of research generated similar items at the same time. As in Table 1, items are extrapolated where appropriate and items are amalgamated where the authors' descriptions appear to be reflecting comparable constructs. Several SAPROF items were reflected in the dynamic risk list as well.

As with the dynamic risk items listed above in Table 1, there are adequate candidate protective factors and substantial overlap among the contemporary new generation of risk and

Table 2. Comparison of protective factors.

Item	SAPROF	START	DRAOR	SPIn
Social support/social network	x	x	x	x
Emotional support/intimate relationship	x	x		x
Structured leisure	x			x
Employment/training/own income	x	x		x
Stable accommodation/living circumstance	x	x		x
Intelligence	x			
Secure attachment/attachment to children/satisfaction in current intimate relationship	x	x	x	x
Empathy	x			
Coping	x	x		
Self-control	x	x		x
Motivation for treatment	x	x	x	x
Positive attitudes towards authority/prosocial identity	x	x	x	x
Life goals/plans	x		x	
Professional care/self-care	x	x		
External control	x		x	
Attachment to children	x			x
Non-hostile attributions				x

Note: x indicates the presence of the item within the assessment.

protective risk assessment measures. It is perhaps instructive to re-conceptualise these proposed candidate factors as reflecting human (internal) versus social (external) capital, aspects of change within the crime desistance literature. Compared to the list of dynamic risk factors reflected in Table 1, slightly more social capital factors appear to be considered protective.

Events versus attributes

Many identified desistance factors are events in one's life that positively influence behaviour, specifically the avoidance of previously rewarding criminal conduct. These events are then opportunities that can potentially act as signals to supervision officers that a client's life is changing. However, when a potential desistance-related event occurs, it is important to consider and affirm whether the event is having the necessary salutary influence. Take the example of employment. If a client attributes his or her job to be personally unimportant, then it is unlikely to have a protective effect when that client is faced with a high-risk situation. That is, the opportunity to gain income from crime might be offset by the presence of a meaningful job only, not simply any possible employment. This is why employment, like other events, has a subjective component. A job in which the client is invested will be more protective than simply having a job.

Given the importance of identity and agency in understanding crime desistance (Lloyd & Serin, 2012), we speculate that potential strengths are always filtered through client attributions. Essentially, attitudes towards crime and attitudes towards desistance become filters through which the client views the world around them. Potential strengths must be evaluated, at the case level, by accessing client perspectives, prior to these factors being affirmed as viable protective/promotive factors.

Case formulation

One benefit to advancing research that identifies dynamic risk and protective factors is the opportunity for CSOs to engage in a more case-formulaic approach to case planning and risk management. The assessment of dynamic risks according to similarity to offence antecedents and patterns (Daffern, Jones, & Shrine, 2010) allows the CSO to better identify imminent risk and sequencing of risk factors. The greater the number of dynamic risks or the more acute the dynamic risks, the more directive should the CSO's response be. Moreover, it is reasonable that higher static risk cases warrant greater attention and resource allocation regarding frequency of contact and dosage of intervention. By definition, the dynamic needs will be case-specific, regardless of static risk. This means varying patterns of internal states and situations can be identified and addressed in a case plan, consistent with the dynamic risk assessment.

For protective factors a similar opportunity exists. CSOs can review earlier periods of primary desistance (Maruna & Farrall, 2004) and use this to motivate the offender. Systematic assessments of human and social capital protective factors can also be used to determine where a particular client may be along the desistance pathway. Again, the present assumption is that a greater number of protective factors (especially internal) reflect closer proximity to becoming a secondary desister (Maruna & Farrall, 2004) although this requires empirical confirmation. Certainly, a CSO can meaningfully comment on changes in internal states (e.g. criminal identity, agency) and the presence of protective factors (e.g. attachment to employment and supportive prosocial relationships) when describing differences between cases with similar static risk scores and resultant differences in how the cases are managed.

Case study

Imagine you have two similarly aged male clients on your caseload. Both are serving the same sentence for the same crime and both have the same score on a validated static risk measure, indicating they are moderate risk (35% likelihood) to re-offend within the next 12 months. Both clients are now on supervision following a 6-month period of incarceration. Following an initial meeting to discuss the conditions of supervision and role clarification, you make arrangements to see them again, as court ordered, in a month. Client A has secured work, passed his drug screen, and has stable accommodation. During the first session, he expressed amenability towards treatment and a commitment to set his life in order so that he might see his young son, now living with his ex-wife. During your first session with Client B, he expressed resistance towards supervision, saying it was a waste of time. Within that first month he had not only failed to secure work but indicated that he felt jobs you had arranged for him to check out were beneath him. Moreover, he missed his drug screen, saying he could not find transportation at the time.

Evidently, these two individuals are exhibiting differing trajectories. The point of these dynamic risk measures is to standardise assessments so that staff can be apprised of relevant changes. In some cases this may lead to increased sanctions and monitoring, as well as intervention. For others, it may provide a timely opportunity to engage with the client, recognise their challenges and to support their efforts. Regardless, it allows everyone to both take note of and record that clients A and B are clearly dissimilar in meaningful ways that will likely influence their outcome.

Model – protective factors and risk management

Using static risk assessment as a benchmark or baseline, we conceptualise dynamic and protective factors functioning in a competing manner where dynamic risk is offset by protective factors, as reflected in the connecting opposing arrows in Figure 1. While there is some conceptual appeal in using the desistance nomenclature of human and social capital, this potentially minimises the importance that situations and appraisals have on dynamic risk (LeBel et al., 2008). Similarly, protective factors seem to be a combination of specific events, but also the explanatory attributions ascribed to these events (Maruna & Farrall, 2004).

Discussion

It appears that there is reasonable agreement among researchers regarding the merits and utility of incorporating dynamic and protective factors in assessment with a view towards enhancing offender case management. The description and measurement of these items varies across measures, suggesting more research is required. Nonetheless, three of the measures highlighted (SPIn, START, DRAOR) demonstrate change scores over time which are meaningfully related to client outcome. Importantly, research on these measures also demonstrates that risk prediction is increased by the inclusion of protective factors. Clinically, inclusion of strengths changes the conversation between CSO and client from one of risk avoidance and monitoring to one of challenging and supporting change and growth. This implies that in order to be meaningful, CSO/client contacts must be of sufficient duration (Lowenkamp, Alexander, & Robinson, 2013).

Certainly, there is a need for conceptual clarity in this area. For instance, can measures truly be considered dynamic if there is no re-assessment? This paper has focused on dynamic risk measures that purport to assess imminent risk, but what is a preferred time for such re-assessments? Regarding protective factors, for many CSOs comfortable with a strict monitor and supervise model, the consideration of protective factors might seem foreign. Psychology has an important role to play regarding knowledge translation in this area. For instance, little is known regarding how to instil protective factors in our

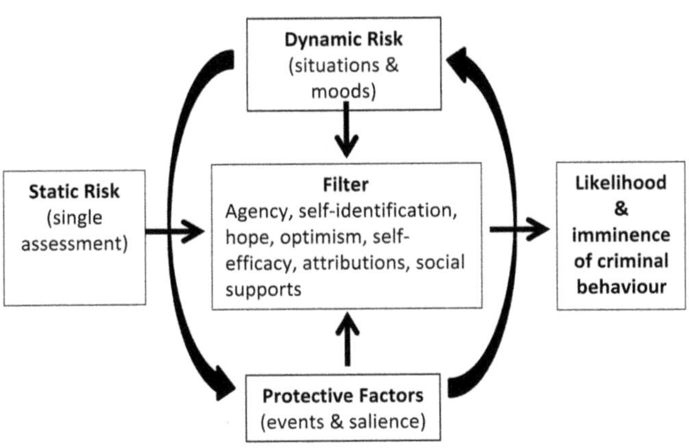

Figure 1. Model of dynamic risk and protective factors impacting criminal behaviour.

clients. Moreover, we presume a focus on strengths will enhance the working relationship, an important component of client success (Kennealy, Skeem, Eno Louden, & Manchak, 2012; Skeem, Eno Louden, Polaschek, & Camp, 2007), but this has not been empirically confirmed.

Informing risk assessment with the systematic use of standardised protocols should advance our understanding regarding key risk and protective constructs. However, too great an emphasis on broad constructs may obscure our ability to make gains at the client level. Hopefully, focusing on the individual will ensure case-specific refinements in both dynamic risk assessment and an understanding of client strengths which should lead to improved case management. Nonetheless, despite the promise of more expansive assessment instruments, several issues merit comment. The first has to do with potential lack of clarity among protective factors and potential collinearity if used for prediction rather than explanation. The second relates to the need for attention towards both dynamic risk and protective factors regarding definitional and measurement refinement, in order to yield more operationally viable items and instruments. At this stage in theory and measurement development, protective factors reflect a philosophy more than an assessment methodology. How protective factors function and how they might be incorporated into case planning and risk management also warrants additional consideration. What is clear, however, is that the field is embracing their usage and that there is commonality among measures that have incorporated protective factors or strengths. Several studies have now demonstrated that protective factors augment risk prediction; their presence indicates a reduction in rates of re-offending. From the perspective of a CSO, one wonders how much it matters if proposed protective factors are simply promotive or truly protective. However, it seems to matter greatly that CSOs and other corrections staff recognise the importance of offender evaluations and appraisals regarding risk situations and desistance events as these seem related to subsequent client outcome.

In the past, various metaphors have been used to reflect and describe the offender change process. Maruna, Lebel, Mitchell, and Naples (2004) eloquently describe the Pygmalion process and the impact of labelling as a lens through which social reactions and agentic experiences are evaluated. Previously, Serin and Lloyd (2009) used the transformation from the caterpillar to the butterfly to describe the somewhat mysterious journey from being an active offender to desisting ex-offender. Given that desistance must arise from an interaction between and individual's internal motivation and opportunities the community provides, we wonder if a preferred analogy would emphasise collaboration and shared commitment to finding pathways to success. While desistance requires offenders to clear the way for a foundation, design a blueprint, and commit to putting in effort to build the home they envision, correctional staff must care to permit, validate, and oversee these efforts, and the broader community must provide the raw materials required to erect the walls and roofs. We look forward to the time when offenders, corrections staff, and community partners build these homes together.

Disclosure statement

No potential conflict of interest was reported by the authors.

References

Andrews, D., & Bonta, J. (1995). *Level of Service Inventory–Revised.* North Tonawanda, NY: Multi-Health Systems.

Andrews, D. A., & Bonta, J. (2010). *The psychology of criminal conduct* (5th ed.). New Providence, NJ: LexisNexis Matthew Bender.

Baird, C. (2009). A question of evidence: A critique of risk assessment models used in the justice system. *A special report prepared for the National Council on Crime and Delinquency.*

Bakker, L., Riley, D., & O'Malley, J. (1999). *Risk of reconviction: Statistical models predicting four types of re-offending*. Wellington: Department of Corrections Psychological Service.

Bandura, A. (1989). Regulation of cognitive processes through perceived self-efficacy. *Developmental Psychology, 25*(5), 729–735. doi:10.1037/0012-1649.25.5.729

Banse, R., Koppehele-Gossel, J., Kistemaker, L. M., Werner, V. A., & Schmidt, A. F. (2013). Pro-criminal attitudes, intervention, and recidivism. *Aggression and Violent Behavior, 18*, 673–685. doi:10.1016/j.avb.2013.07.024

Beggs, S. (2010). Within-treatment outcome among sexual offenders: A review. *Aggression and Violent Behavior, 15*, 369–379. doi:10.1016/j.avb.2010.06.005

Bond, F. W., Hayes, S. C., & Barnes-Holmes, D. (2006). Psychological flexibility, ACT, and organizational behavior. *Journal of Organizational Behavior Management, 26*(1–2), 25–54. doi:10.1300/J075v2 10.1300/J075v26n01_02 6n01_02

Bonta, J. (1996). Risk-needs assessment and treatment. In A. T. Harland (Ed.), *Choosing correctional options that work: Defining the demand and evaluating the supply* (pp. 18–32). Thousand Oaks, CA: Sage.

Bonta, J., Bourgon, G., Rugge, T., Scott, T. L., Yessine, A. K., Gutierrez, L., & Li, J. (2011). An experimental demonstration of training probation officers in evidence-based community supervision. *Criminal Justice and Behavior, 38*, 1127–1148. doi:10.1177/0093854811420678

Bourgon, G., Gutierrez, L., & Ashton, J. (2011). The evolution of community supervision practice: The transformation from case manager to change agent. *Irish Probation Journal, 8*, 28–48.

Brown, S. L., St. Amand, M. D., & Zamble, E. (2009). The dynamic prediction of criminal recidivism: A three-wave prospective study. *Journal of Law and Human Behavior, 33*, 25–45. doi:10.1007/s10979-008-9139-7

Caudy, M. S., Durso, J. M., & Taxman, F. S. (2013). How well do dynamic needs predict recidivism? Implications for risk assessment and risk reduction. *Journal of Criminal Justice, 41*, 458–466. doi:10.1016/j.jcrimjus.2013.08.004

Chadwick, N., DeWolf, A. H., & Serin, R. C. (2015). Effectively training community supervision officers: A meta-analytic review of the impact on offender outcome. *Criminal Justice and Behavior, 42*(10), 977–989. doi:10.1177/0-093854815595661

Chiricos, T., Barrick, K., Bales, W., & Bontrager, S. (2007). The labelling of convicted felons and its consequences for recidivism. *Criminology, 45*(3), 547–581. doi:10.1111/j.1745-9125.2007.00089.x

Cromwell, P. F., & Killinger, G. G. (1994). *Community-based corrections: Probation, parole, and intermediate sanctions* (3rd ed.). New York: West.

Daffern, M., Jones, L., & Shrine, J. (2010). *Offence paralleling behaviour: A case formulation approach to offender assessment and intervention*. Chichester: Wiley-Blackwell.

Desmarais, S. L., Nicholls, T. L., Wilson, C. M., & Brink, J. (2012). Using dynamic and protective factors to predict inpatient aggression: Reliability and validity of START assessments. *Psychological Assessment, 24*(3), 685–700. doi:10.1037/a0026668

Douglas, K. S., Hart, S. D., Webster, C. D., & Belfrage, H. (2013). *HCR-20v3: Assessing risk for violence: User guide*. Burnaby: Mental Health, Law, and Policy Institute, Simon Fraser University.

Douglas, S. K., & Skeem, J. L. (2005). Violence risk assessment: Getting specific about being dynamic. *Psychology, Public Policy, and Law, 11*(3), 347–383. doi:10.1037/1076-8971.11.3.347

Duckworth, A. L., Steen, T. A., & Seligman, M. E. (2005). Positive psychology in clinical practice. *Annual Review of Clinical Psychology, 1*, 629–651. doi:10.1146/-annurev.clinpsy.1.102803.144154

Farrall, S. (2004). Social capital and offender reintegration: Making probation desistance focussed. In S. Maruna & R. Immarigeon (Eds.), *After crime and punishment: Pathways to offender reintegration* (pp. 57–84). Cullompton: Willan.

Farrington, D. P. (2011). The integrated cognitive antisocial potential (ICAP) theory. In D. P. Farrington (Ed.), *Integrated developmental and life-course theories of offending* (pp. 73–92). New Brunswick, NJ: Transaction.

Fitzpatrick, K. M. (1997). Fighting among America's youth: A risk and protective factors approach. *Journal of Health and Social Behavior, 38*(2), 131–148. doi:10.2307/2955421

Fougere, A., & Daffern, M. (2011). Resilience in young offenders. *International Journal of Forensic Mental Health, 10*, 244–253. doi:10.1080/14999013.2011.598602

HaggÅrd, U., Gumpert, C. H., & Grann, M. (2001). Against all odds: A qualitative follow-up of high-risk violent offenders who were not reconvicted. *Journal of Interpersonal Violence, 16*, 1048–1065. doi:10.1177/088626001016010005

Hanby, L. (2013). *A longitudinal study of dynamic risk, protective factors, and criminal recidivism: Change over time and the impact of assessment timing* (Doctoral dissertation). Carleton University, Ottawa, ON, Canada.

Hanson, K. R., & Harris, A. J. (2000). Where should we intervene? Dynamic predictors of sexual offense recidivism. *Criminal Justice and Behavior, 27*(1), 6–35. doi:10.1177-0093854800027001002

Harris, M. (2013). *An exploration of strengths, promotive, and protective factors among justice involved youth* (Master's thesis). Retrieved from Library and Archives Canada. (Amicus No. 42348768)

Harris, G. T., & Rice, M. E. (2015). Progress in violence risk assessment and communication: Hypothesis versus evidence. *Behavioral Sciences and the Law, 33*, 128–145. doi:10.1002/bsl.2157

Helmond, P., Overbeek, G., Brugman, D., & Gibbs, J. C. (2014). A meta-analysis on cognitive distortions and externalizing problem behavior: Associations, moderators, and treatment effectiveness. *Criminal Justice, and Behavior, 42*, 245–262. doi:10.1177/00938548145-52842

Howard, P. D., & Dixon, L. (2013). Identifying change in the likelihood of violent recidivism: Causal dynamic risk factors in the OASys violence predictor. *Journal of Law and Human Behavior, 37*(3), 163–174. doi:10.1037/lhb0000012

Jessor, R., Van Den Bos, J., Vanderryn, J., Costa, F. M., & Turbin, M. S. (1995). Protective factors in adolescent problem behavior: Moderator effects and developmental change. *Developmental Psychology, 31*(6), 923–933. doi:10.1037/0012-1649.31.6.923

Jones, N. J., Brown, S. L., Robinson, D., & Frey, D. (2015). Incorporating strengths into quantitative assessments of criminal risk for adult offenders: The Service Planning Instrument. *Criminal Justice and Behavior, 42*, 321–338. doi:10.1177/009385-4814547041

Jones, N. J., Brown, S. L., & Zamble, E. (2009). Predicting criminal recidivism in adult male offenders: Researcher versus parole officer assessment of dynamic risk. *Criminal Justice and Behavior, 37*(8), 860–882. doi:10.1177/0093854810368924

Kennealy, P. J., Skeem, J. L., Eno Louden, J., & Manchak, S. M. (2012). Firm, fair, and caring officer-offender relationships protect against supervision failure. *Law and Human Behavior, 36*(6), 496–505. doi:10.1037/h0093935

Kraemer, H. C., Kazdin, A. E., Offord, D. R., Kessler, R. C., Jensen, P. S., & Kupfer, D. J. (1997). Coming to terms with the terms of risk. *Archives of General Psychiatry, 54*(4), 337–343. doi:10.1001/archpsyc.1997.01830160065009

Laub, J. H., Nagin, D. S., & Sampson, R. J. (1998). Trajectories of change in criminal offending: Good marriages and the desistance process. *American Sociological Review, 63*, 225–238.

LeBel, T. P., Burnett, R., Maruna, S. & Bushway, S. (2008). The 'chicken and egg' of subjective and social factors in desistance from crime. *European Journal of Criminology, 5*(2), 131–159. doi:10.1177/1477370807087640

Lewis, K., Olver, M. E., & Wong, S. C. (2012). The Violence Risk Scale: Predictive validity and linking changes in risk with violent recidivism in a sample of high-risk offenders with psychopathic traits. *Assessment, 20*(2), 150–164. doi:10.1177/1073191112441242

Lloyd, C. D., & Serin, R. C. (2012). Agency and outcome expectancies for crime desistance: Measuring offenders' personal beliefs about change. *Psychology, Crime and Law, 18*(6), 543–565. doi:10.1080/1068316X.2010.511221

Lodewijks, H. P., de Ruiter, C., & Doreleijers, T. A. (2010). The impact of protective factors in desistance from violent reoffending: A study in three samples of adolescent offenders. *Journal of Interpersonal Violence, 25*(3), 568–587. doi:10.177/0886260509334403

Loeber, R. Pardini, D. A., Stouthamer-Loeber, M., & Raine, A. (2007). Do cognitive, physiological, and psychosocial risk and promotive factors predict desistance from delinquency in males? *Development and Psychopathology, 19*, 867–887. doi:10.1017/S09545-79407000429

Loeber, R., Slot, N. W., & Stouthamer-Loeber, M. (2008). A cumulative developmental model of risk and promotive factors. In R. Loeber, N. W. Slot, P. H. Van der Laan, & M. Hoeve (Eds.), *Tomorrow's criminals. The development of child delinquency and effective interventions* (pp. 133–161). Farnham: Ashgate.

Lösel, F., & Farrington, D. P. (2012). Direct protective and buffering protective factors in the development of youth violence. *American Journal of Preventative Medicine, 43*(2S1), S8–S23. doi:10.1016/j.amepre.2012.04.029

Lowenkamp, C. T., Alexander, M., & Robinson, C. R. (2013). Using 20 minutes wisely: Community supervision officers as agents of change. In J. Smykla & M. Crow (Eds.), *Offender reentry: 21st Century issues*. Burlington, MA: Jones & Bartlett.

Lowenkamp, C. T., Holsinger, A. M., Robinson, C. R., & Alexander, M. (2014). Diminishing or durable treatment effects of STARR? A research note on 24 month re-arrest rates. *Journal of Crime and Justice, 37*(2), 275–283. doi:10.1080/0735648X.2012.753849

Magaletta, P. R., & Oliver, J. M. (1999). The hope construct, will, and ways: Their relations with self-efficacy, optimism, and general well-being. *Journal of Clinical Psychology, 55*(5), 539–551. doi:10.1002/(SICI)1097-4679(199905)

Mann, R. E., Webster, S. D., Schofield, C., & Marshall, W. L. (2004). Approach versus avoidance goals in relapse prevention with sexual offenders. *Sexual Abuse: A Journal of Research and Treatment, 16*, 65–75.

Martinson, R. (1974). What works? Questions and answers about prison reform. *The Public Interest, 35* (2), 22–54.

Maruna, S. (2010). *Understanding desistance from crime*. A report for the Ministry of Justice and National Offender Management Services. Retrieved from www.safeground.org.uk/wp-content/uploads/desistance-fact-sheet.pdf

Maruna, S., & Farrall, S. (2004). Desistance from crime: A theoretical reformulation. *Kölner Zeitschrift für Soziologie und Sozialpsychologie, 43*, 171–194.

Maruna, S., LeBel, T. P., & Lanier, C. (2003). Generativity behind bars: Some 'redemptive truth' about prison society. In E. de St. Aubin, D. McAdams, & T. Kim (Eds.), *The generative society: Caring for future generations* (pp. 131–151). Washington, DC: American Psychological Association.

Maruna, S., Lebel, T. P., Mitchell, N., & Naples, M. (2004). Pygmalion in the reintegration process: Desistance from crime through the looking glass. *Psychology, Crime & Law, 10*(3), 271–281.

van Mastrigt, S. B., & Farrington, D. P. (2009). Co-offending, age, gender and crime type: Implications for criminal justice policy. *British Journal of Criminology, 49*(4), 552–573. doi:10.1093/bjc/azp021

Miller, H. A. (2006). A dynamic assessment of offender risk, needs, and strengths in a sample of general offenders. *Behavioural Sciences and the Law, 24*, 767–782. doi:10.1002/bsl.728

Nicholls, T. L., Brink, J., Desmarais, S. L., Webster, C. D., & Martin, M. L. (2006). The Short-Term Assessment OF Risk and Treatability (START): A prospective validation study in a forensic psychiatric sample. *Assessment, 13*, 313–327. doi:10.1177/1073191106290559

Orbis Partners (2003). *Service Planning Instrument (SPIn)*. Ottawa, ON: Author.

Polaschek, D. L. L. (2012). An appraisal of the risk-need-responsivity (RNR) model of offender rehabilitation and its application in correctional treatment. *Legal and Criminological Psychology, 17*, 1–17. doi:10.111/j.2044A8333.2011.02038.x

Rex, S. (1999). Desistance from offending: Experiences of probation. *Howard Journal of Criminal Justice, 38*(4), 366–383. doi:10.1111/1468-2311.00141

Robinson, C. R., Lowenkamp, C. T., Holsinger, A. M., VanBenschoten, S., Alexander, M., & Oleson, J. C. (2012). A random study of Staff Trained at Reducing Re-arrest (STARR): Using core correctional practices in probation interactions. *Journal of Crime and Justice, 35*(2), 167–188. doi:10.1080/0735648X.2012.674823

Rogers, R. (2000). The uncritical acceptance of risk assessment in forensic practice. *Law and Human Behavior, 24*(5), 595–605. doi:10.1023/A:1005575113507

Rutter, M. (1985). Resilience in the face of adversity: Protective factors and resistance to psychiatric disorder. *British Journal of Psychiatry, 147*, 598–611. doi:10.1192/bjp.147.6.598

Rutter, M. (1987). Psychosocial resilience and protective mechanisms. *American Journal of Orthopsychiatry, 57*(3), 316–331. doi:10.1111/j.1939-0025.1987.tb03541.x

Rutter, M. (2000). Resilience reconsidered: Conceptual considerations, empirical findings, and policy implications. In J. P. Shonkoff & S. J. Meisels (Eds.), *Handbook of early childhood intervention* (pp. 651–682). New York, NY: Cambridge University Press.

Sachwald, J., Eley, E., & Taxman, F. (2006). *An ounce of prevention: Proactive supervision reduces violation behavior*. Retrieved October 4, 2015 from http://www.scsenate.gov/archives/citizensinterestpage/SentencingReformCommission/RetreatPresentations/AnOunceofPreventionNIC2006.pdf

Sampson, R. J., & Laub, J. H. (1992). Crime and deviance in the life course. *Annual Review of Sociology, 18*, 63–84. doi:10.1146/annurev.so.18.080192.000431

Sampson, R. J., & Laub, J. H. (2005). A life-course view of the development of crime. *The Annals of the American Academy of Political and Social Science, 602*(1), 12–45. doi:10.1177/0002716205280075

Seligman, M. E., & Csikszentmihalyi, M. (2000). Positive psychology: An introduction. *American Psychological Association, 55*(1), 5–14. doi:10.1037//0003-066X.55.1.5

Scheier, M. F., & Carver, C. S. (1985). Optimism, coping, and health: Assessment and implications of generalized outcome expectancies. *Health Psychology, 4*, 219–247. doi:10.1037/0278-6133.4.3.219

Scott, K. L. (2004). Predictors of change among male batterers: Application of theories and review of empirical findings. *Trauma, Violence, & Abuse, 5*, 260–284. doi:10.1177/1524838003264339

Serin, R. (2007). *The Dynamic Risk Assessment Scale for Offender Re-Entry (DRAOR)* (Unpublished scale). Carleton University, Ottawa, ON, Canada.

Serin, R. C., & Lloyd, C. D. (2009). Examining the process of offender change: The transition to crime desistance. *Psychology, Crime, and Law, 15*(4), 347–364. doi:10.180/1068316080-2261078

Serin, R. C., Lloyd, C. D., & Hanby, L. J. (2010). Enhancing offender re-entry: An integrated model for enhancing offender re-entry. *European Journal of Probation, 2*(2), 53–75.

Serin, R. C., Lloyd, C. D., Helmus, L., Derkzen, D. M., & Luong, D. (2013). Does intra-individual change predict offender recidivism? Searching for the Holy Grail in assessing offender change. *Aggression and Violent Behavior, 18*, 32–53. doi:10.1016/j.avb.20-12.09.002

Singer, J. D., & Willett, J. B. (2003). *Applied longitudinal data analysis: Modelling change and event occurrence*. New York, NY: Oxford University Press.

Skeem, J., Eno Louden, J., Polaschek, D., & Camp, J. (2007). Relationship quality in mandated treatment: Blending care with control. *Psychological Assessment, 19*(4), 397–410. doi:10.1037/1040-3590.19.4.397

Smith, P., Gendreau, P., & Swartz, K. (2009). Validating the principles of effective intervention: A systematic review of the contributions of meta-analysis in the field of corrections. *Victims & Offenders, 4*(2), 148–169. doi:10.1080/15564880802612581

Snyder, C. R., Harris, C., Anderson, J. R., Holleran, S. A., Irving, L. M., Sigmon, S. T., … Harney, P. (1991). The will and the ways: Development and validation of an individual-differences measure of hope. *Journal of Personality and Social Psychology, 60*(4), 570–585. doi:http://dx.doi.org.proxy.library.carleton.ca/10.1037/0022-3514.60.4.570

Uggen, C. (2000). Work as a turning point in the life course of criminals: A duration model of age, employment, and recidivism. *American Sociological Review, 65*(4), 529–546.

Ullrich, S., & Coid, J. (2011). Protective factors for violence among released prisoners-effects over time and interactions with static risk. *Journal of Consulting and Clinical Psychology, 79*(3), 381–390. doi:10.1037/a0023613

Van der Put, C. E., Deković, M., Stams, G. J. J., Van der Laan, P. H., Hoeve, M., & Van Amelsfort, L. (2011). Changes in risk factors during adolescence implications for risk assessment. *Criminal Justice and Behavior, 38*(3), 248–262.

de Vogel, V., de Ruiter, C., Bouman, Y., & de Vries Robbé, M. (2009). *SAPROF: Guidelines for the assessment of protective factors for violence risk*. Utrecht: Forum Educatief.

Vose, B., Smith, P., & Cullen, F. T. (2013). Predictive validity and the impact of change in total LSI-R score on recidivism. *Criminal Justice and Behavior, 40*, 1383–1396. doi:10.1177/009-3854813508916

de Vries Robbé, M., de Vogel, V., & Douglas, K. S. (2013). Risk factors and protective factors: A two-sided dynamic approach to violence risk assessment. *Journal of Forensic Psychiatry & Psychology, 24*(4), 440–457. doi:10.1080/14789949.2013.818162

de Vries Robbé, M., de Vogel, V., & de Spa, E. (2011). Protective factors for violence risk in forensic psychiatric patients: A retrospective validation of the SAPROF. *International Journal of Forensic Mental Health, 10*, 178–186. doi:10.1080/14999013.2011.600232

Walters, G. D. (1998). *Changing lives of crime and drugs: Intervening with substance-abusing offenders*. New York, NY: Wiley.

Ward, T. (2015). Dynamic risk factors: Scientific kinds or predictive constructs. Special edition of *Psychology, Crime and Law, 22*(1–2), 2–16.

Ward, T., & Brown, M. (2004). The good lives model and conceptual issues in offender rehabilitation. *Psychology, Crime and Law, 10*(3), 243–257. doi:10.1080/10683-160410001662744

Ward, T., & Salmon, K. (2009). The ethics of punishment: Implications for correctional practice. *Aggression and Violent Behavior, 14*(4), 239–247. doi:10.1016/j.avb.2009.03.009

Webster, C. D., Douglas, K. S., Eaves, D., & Hart, S. D. (1997). *HCR-20. Assessing the risk of violence. Version 2*. Burnaby: Simon Fraser University and Forensic Psychiatric Services Commission of British Columbia.

Woldgabreal, Y., Day, A., & Ward, T. (2014). The community-based supervision of offenders from a positive psychology perspective. *Aggression and Violent Behavior, 19*(1), 32–41. doi:10.1016/j.avb.2013.12.001

Wong, S. C. P., & Gordon, A. E. (2006). The validity and reliability of the violence risk scale: A treatment-friendly violence risk assessment tool. *Psychology, Public Policy, and Law, 12*, 279–309. doi:10.1037/1076-8971.12.3.279

Yang, M., Wong, S. C. P., & Coid, J. (2010). The efficacy of violence prediction: A meta-analytic comparison of nine risk assessment tools. *Psychological Bulletin, 136*(5), 740–767. doi:10.1037/a0020473

Yang, S., & Mulvey, E. P. (2012). Violence risk: Re-defining variables from the first-person perspective. *Aggression and Violent Behavior, 17*, 198–207. doi:10.1016/j.avb.2-012.02.001

Yesberg, J. A., Scanlan, J., Hanby, L. J., Serin, R. C., & Polaschek, D. L. L. (2015). Predicting women's recidivism: Validating a dynamic community-based 'gender-neutral' tool. *Probation Journal, 62*(1), 33–48. doi:10.1177/02645505145628510264550514562851

Desistance and dynamic risk factors belong together

Devon L. L. Polaschek

School of Psychology, Victoria University of Wellington, Wellington, New Zealand

ABSTRACT

Depending on definitions, dynamic risk factors and desistance are either highly intertwined or aligned with distinctly separate paradigms. This paper describes and critiques each concept, and then reviews research on how they may be linked, including some preliminary findings from a longitudinal study of the early phases of desistance in high-risk offenders. I argue that seeking to understand how reductions in dynamic risk work together with the development of the psychological components of desistance will shed the most light on how offenders move from persistence to the maintenance of desistance.

Depending on the definition of desistance, dynamic risk factors (DRFs) and desistance are either inextricably intertwined or do not appear to belong together in the same sentence. This paper considers the basis for these two views, and presents some preliminary findings from a longitudinal study (the New Zealand Parole Project (NZPP)), in order to argue that that the first position offers potentially the more fruitful approach.

DRFs have been subject to serious scrutiny in the last few years on both conceptual and empirical grounds. Empirically, the quality of research on whether DRFs perform as defined is limited and methodologically poor in quality, with a preponderance of non-significant findings (Kroner & Yessine, 2013). Conceptually, DRFs are vaguely and diversely defined: requiring further development to be translated into detailed theories of mechanism, and to inform individual formulations (Ward, 2015). Desistance has become a popular term in criminal psychology in the last decade, but is also variously and confusingly defined, Many claims have been made about how it can be achieved, but there has been little research on the processes that links active criminality to eventual cessation.

This paper initially defines and critiques both DRFs and desistance, before examines the relationship between the two, focusing mainly on higher risk offenders (i.e. those who are prioritised for intervention according to the Risk principle; Andrews & Bonta, 2010). These offenders' DRFs are an embarrassment of riches, and desistance often comes only with considerable difficulty.

Dynamic risk factors

Definitions

DRFs can be traced back to Andrews and Bonta's work in the early 1980s. They defined them as 'dynamic attributes of offenders and their circumstances that, when changed, are associated with changes in the chances of recidivism' (Andrews, Bonta, & Hoge, 1990, p. 31). This definition recognises both individuals' trait-like factors (e.g. negative emotionality and poor problem-solving skills) and environmental circumstances that can be similarly enduring and stable (e.g. exposure to others who are abusing alcohol and drugs, lack of employment opportunities).

A little later, DRFs were divided into acute and stable (e.g. Hanson & Harris, 2000). This distinction has been considered useful in separating out trait-like factors from those that might be regarded as triggering states (e.g. being drunk, recent conflict; Beech & Ward, 2004; Ward, Polaschek, & Beech, 2006) or transient environmental factors (Wortley, 2008).

Finally, even more recently, and with the revival of interest in positive psychology, strength-based approaches and desistance-related issues, DRFs have been distinguished from protective factors. The latter have been variously defined as 'influences that modify, ameliorate or alter a person's response to some environmental hazard that predisposes a maladaptive outcome' (Rutter, 1985, p. 600) or 'those factors that can compensate for a person's risk factors and thus play an important part in the overall risk judgment' (Vries Robbé & Vogel, 2013, p. 293).

This compensating effect has sometimes been described as *buffering,* because the factor is relevant only in the presence of a high level of the risk factor it buffers (statistical moderation; Lösel & Farrington, 2012). However, Vries Robbé and colleagues also suggest that protective factors mediate risk factors: directly reducing the impact of risk factors on outcomes. As an example, social connectedness may be a buffer: being socially isolated may not enhance offending propensity in people with low levels of criminal attitudes, but prosocial support may weaken the risk of offending in those whose propensity is fuelled by other risk factors (e.g. criminal attitudes, poor problem-solving skills). A mediating relationship may be seen in the way in which the development of social support enhances emotional regulation, for example, which in turn reduces propensity for crime.

Critique

As is typical of Andrews and Bonta's work, theirs is a pragmatic rather than theoretically deep or epistemically satisfactory definition (Polaschek, 2012: Ward, Melser, & Yates, 2007). Quite simple research designs can verify it empirically, although they surprisingly rarely have (Serin, Lloyd, Helmus, Derkzen, & Luong, 2013), probably mainly for methodological reasons. It is useful for guiding prospectively the design, and retrospectively the identification of interventions and services that are most likely to lead to reductions in recidivism. Work at this operationally concrete level is important because of its utility in guiding decisions when interventions are to be provided on a large scale (e.g. across an entire correctional system). Using this definition, Andrews and Bonta (2010) have been able to demonstrate that diverse programmes that share only a focus on changing some common dynamic attributes in higher risk offenders and with some attention to responsivity have prevented myriad crimes. This is no small achievement given the lack of theory underlying DRFs, the otherwise limited evidence of the soundness of intervention designs, and the operational obstacles.

Within correctional psychology as elsewhere, it is important alongside empirical validation, to develop more complete and satisfying conceptual understandings of the key ideas, such as DRFs, based on recognition that without such theory building, we may truncate our ability to explain criminal behaviour and to change it through intervention (Heffernan & Ward, in press). Ward and colleagues have done much to draw attention to the poor quality of theory development, especially in the sex-offender area, and in some cases have sought to rebuild existing theory (2007). They have argued for recognition that DRFS are observable phenomena: the 'front end' for complex constructs that contain actual causal elements (Ward & Beech, 2015), not the elements themselves. It is an easy argument to accept.

However, the task that then confronts us is formidable. What appears to be needed is at least one Level II (i.e. single factor) theory that unpacks each relevant DRF. Although some researchers may remain hopeful that for each DRF there is an 'exact mechanism' (Vries Robbé & Vogel, 2013, p. 294), multiple mechanisms are more likely. Therefore multiple theories may be required for factors such as 'antisocial cognitions' or 'criminogenic beliefs' given that they may conceal multiple more homogeneous constructs (Nunes, Hermann, Maimone, & Woods, 2014). Further, it is likely that as important as individual causal factors may be, understanding how they interact with each other may be just as, or even more important. It may be some time before the inherent complexity is sufficiently unpacked to feed into intervention in a manner that can actually make a difference to our clients and the people who live around them.

Relationship to protective factors

Confusion about DRFs extends to other terms such as protective factors. For example, in the developmental literature, protective factors are separated from risk factors because the latter are conceptualised as pre-existing vulnerabilities (Rutter, 1985; Lösel & Farrington, 2012). However, no such distinctions are evident in the tertiary prevention arena. In fact one of the causes of confusion around aetiology, DRFs and dynamic protective factors (DPFs) arises from the failure to distinguish between causal factors in the onset of an offending career, and the key factors that maintain current propensity to offend (i.e. current causal factors; see discussion of asymmetrical causation, below). In high risk criminally active offenders in their 30s it is reasonable to suppose that some of these current causal risk factors may be similar to those that caused the onset of criminality, but others will more likely be the result of human development and secondary consequences of the criminal justice system coming in to play as the persisting criminal ages (see Moffitt, 1993).

But what then is the relationship between DRFs and DPFs? In theory, current (i.e. dynamic) protective factors can have at least three distinct definitions: (a) as the relative absence of a DRF (i.e. its reverse); (b) as an independent factor such as a desistance-promoting actor that has a non-linear relationship to reoffending (e.g. high involvement in religious activities; Ullrich & Coid, 2011). As the strength of the factor declines it no longer discriminates between recidivists and desisters; (c) as a buffer: a factor that may not in itself predict crime but when present alters the relationship between one or more risk factors that are present, and crime commission (Farrington, 2007).

Almost all tertiary crime prevention research on DPFs and reconviction or its absence – presumably highly relevant to desistance – shows them to be reverse versions of risk factors (Harris & Rice, 2015; Webster, Nicholls, Martin, Desmarais, & Brink, 2006). There are often obvious conceptual overlaps between DPFs and DRFs (e.g. emotional volatility vs. emotional regulation skills; absence of stable marital relationship vs. stable marital relationship, etc.). But statistical claims may be made that when DPFs are uniquely contributing to risk prediction, they represent a unique class of variables. However, usually protective factor instruments and scales – for example, the SAPROF (Vogel, Ruiter, Bouman, & Vries Robbé, 2012) and the DRAOR (Serin, 2007; Serin, Mailloux, & Wilson, 2012) – also correlate statistically significantly with predominantly DRF instruments and scales (e.g. Vries Robbé & Vogel, 2011, 2013; Yesberg & Polaschek, 2015). Together these two points suggest that when found to be incrementally predictive over the initial list of risk factors in regressions, their unique contribution might still be partially or entirely explained as the contribution of risk factors not in the original list but now being called 'protective factors'. Research on potentially protective factors that are not inverted risk factors has been rare (see Woldgabreal, Day, & Ward, in press; for an example), and is an important area of future enquiry.

Protective factors that act as buffers (i.e. interact with risk factors only when the risk factor is high, but have no direct effect themselves) are a distinct phenomenon that is not considered further here. But the remainder of this paper considers protective factors that can be understood as inverse risk factors interchangeably with the corresponding DRF. In other words, given the shortcomings of current theory and research distinguishing dynamic risk and DPFs, the working definition of a DRF I adopt here embraces both.

Person vs. environment based

Confusion in current definitions of DRFs also encompasses whether they are located in the person or the environment. Broadly speaking, criminological theory tends to locate them more often in the environment, while the types of psychology most often applied to criminal behaviour (e.g. clinical) place more emphasis on within-person variables. So a preference for criminal peers would be a person variable, and an environment riddled with such peers is the environmental equivalent.

For the purposes of this paper – and until enough theory develops to reduce the chaos appreciably – it may be helpful to think about DRFs using the heuristic of associative networks and spreading activation theory appropriated from cognitive psychology: as a complex network of nodes with links between them (Collins & Loftus, 1975). The nodes here are putative current risk/protective factors for reoffending and the links between nodes reflect the complex ways that changes in a factor – whatever its exact nature and location in the person or environment – can influence others. The heuristic embraces the possibility that factors that are not present at levels of 'clinical significance' or high environmental threat per se may nevertheless become influential when activated by related nodes that are. The model is four dimensional because alongside the three-dimensional current relationships between these environmental and person factors, they also influence each other longitudinally, over time, in complex sequences of interaction that may unfold over seconds, or be days, weeks, even years apart. Envisioning the problem this way – which is certainly consistent with the complexity evident when working with individual offenders – again makes it easy to see why theoretical progress has been slow. We turn now to the concept of desistance, again outlining definitions and then critiquing it using current theory and research.

Desistance

Definitions

Just as between every cigarette, a smoker is in a state of abstinence, so offenders are desisting between each criminal act. At its simplest, desistance in the criminological literature is simply the absence of reoffending, or, often in research, technically the absence of reconvictions. But actually both the process of desisting and the outcome have been referred to as desistance. So, desistance has been defined both as the appearance of somewhat arbitrary periods of conviction-free activity (e.g. 10 years), and as the psychological processes associated with staying crime-free.

For example, Serin and Lloyd (2009) describe desistance as an outcome that includes having already achieved some psychological change: 'desistance is not obtained in the early stages of transition even as an offender begins to be crime-free. Desistance has not occurred until prosocial habits, legitimate employment and self-regulation have taken hold … ' (Serin & Lloyd, 2009, p. 359). Maruna and Farrall (2004) defined primary desistance as any respite from criminal activity without any self-awareness or intent being required, but for secondary desistance, a (usually longer) period of non-offending went hand-in-hand with self-awareness, and even identity change in the offender. Recognising how far apart these two types or stages may be for some offenders, Maruna and Farrall (2004) proposed a third intermediate stage. 'Proto-secondary desistance' refers to a conscious cessation of criminal activity for several years that is followed by resumption of criminal behaviour.

Desistance definitions also need to deal with the complex issues of offending career length and the volume and pattern of activity that characterises each offender's behaviour. So for offenders who offend infrequently a longer period might be required to define more advanced stages of desistance transitions. Intermittency must also be taken into account. Stopping and restarting offending are common phenomena, but limited research on offending over the entire life-course, but most especially the later stages, also makes it difficult to predict what type or phase of desistance an offender is in when crime-free (Piquero, 2004).

For some offenders, desistance may not mean complete cessation of legal transgressions; many 'law-abiding' people also do not live by that standard. Some offenders regard themselves as having desisted when they have given up all but the most trivial forms of crime (Leibrich, 1993). Some may calibrate the severity of their ongoing offending so as to maintain valued prosocial aspects of their lives such as employment, a relationship and parenting (King, 2014). Others therefore have suggested that rather than requiring absolutely no offending, achieving a 'stable rate empirically indistinguishable from zero' might be more realistic criterion for data analysis at least (Bushway, Piquero, Mazerolle, Broidy, & Cauffman, 2001, p. 500). Still, we do not know whether the psychological processes and milestones are the same for these 'mostly desisters' as for those who embrace 'straight' life with something approaching religious zeal (Maruna, 2001).

Critique

In parallel with DRFs, desistance theory also is grappling with the relative roles of person and environmental factors. However, the dimension of time is more important in understanding desistance, leading to complex challenges relating to reciprocal causation, and to the importance of recognising the putative stages in the process different theories and research address.

Person vs. environment based

The extreme environmental position on the process of desistance comes from Sampson and Laub's (1993) social structural theory, and their long-term follow-up with the Gluecks' sample of men who entered adulthood in the 1950s.They deemphasised psychological processes in favour of 'turning points': social environmental milestones (e.g. marriage or entering the military) for the persisting offender. Their research did find evidence of cognitive transformations (i.e. internal subjective processes running in parallel with social events), but they downplayed the importance of these (Laws & Ward, 2011). Interestingly, they noted that some offenders did not report in retrospect any conscious awareness of their own desistance process (Laub & Sampson, 2003), raising the possibility that awareness is not needed to define desistance, and that narrative identity accounts which emphasise awareness (e.g. Maruna, 2001) are a function of later cohorts of more psychologically aware of desisters.

Maruna's work is often suggested to offer a critique of desistance from the extreme person-variable perspective; his innovative thinking on desistance derives in large part from his Liverpool desistance study, which was a retrospective examination of two samples chosen to 'maximize the likelihood of identifying individuals at the two extremes of a long process of change' (Maruna, 2001, p. 45). His persisters indicated that their offending was ongoing and they felt powerless to 'go straight' (Maruna, 2001), even though some at least were thoroughly tired of the consequences of crime. In fact the passivity and defeatism of his persisters is striking; bearing little resemblance to other samples described in the desistance literature.

The desisters, while certainly not complacent with their status, were people who thought their last offence had occurred two to three years previously: a substantial achievement in a career criminal. Desisters gave coherent narrative accounts of current state that emphasised their 'true self' and displayed a distorted sense of both their current purpose in life, and their control over their futures, referred to as 'making good' (Maruna, 2001, p. 9).

Maruna has argued that his desisters' accounts of how they achieved their current position are not retrospective in the sense that the interviewees were still active in pursuing desistance (2001). But of course in psychological terms the accounts are retrospective: the desisters are looking back on how they got to where they are, and developing a narrative to explain it. So it cannot be argued from the results that factors to which desisters attributed their success in hindsight (e.g. identity change) actually caused the success they reported. Instead the currently reported factors are seen to be agentically involved in maintaining crime-free status.

Most people who are pursuing desistance at any one time are probably on the 'middle ground': people Maruna's narrative research explicitly sought to exclude. Maruna's focus on desistance as a maintenance process is also seen in his later definitions. His definition of secondary desistance (Maruna & Farrall, 2004), outlined in the previous section, is as an outcome rather than a process (King, 2014): an outcome that turns out not to have been achieved if an aware offender who is intentionally desisting and making some changes in identity then is reconvicted. Missing from Maruna and Farrell's definitions appears to be a transitional period of indeterminate length (i.e. varying from days to years) in which the offender is indeed not offending and is consciously seeking to be a non-offender. Perhaps this phase should be termed 'active desistance': a term that would recognise that both agency and some form of crime abstinence are both present – which is distinct from their 'proto-desistance', but the elapsed crime-free time is still relatively short compared to the previous offending career. This transitional state is not recognised as desistance in Maruna's outcome-based conceptualisation, and it was not an aim of his research to examine it.

The key contributions of Maruna's study to defining desistance lie in the sharp contrasts of the persistence and desistance samples, and especially in the recognition that once achieved, maintaining desistance is still an agentic process.

Giordano's cognitive transformation theory is also a more person-based account of desistance than Sampson and Laub's: thus addressing the theoretical puzzle of why social structural factors can be present but gain little traction (Giordano, Cernkovich, & Rudolph, 2002). Based on research with young women and men from a much later cohort of Americans Giordano identified four steps in cognitive transformations associated with desistance:

1. Openness to change, a necessary but not sufficient preliminary step.
2. Reacting positively to the presence of hooks. Recognising an opportunity to engage in some form of bond or activity that will deter offending or cut the offender off from risk factors in the environment (and potentially in himself).
3. Self-reflection, the ability to imagine or conceive of oneself as a different person.
4. Transformation of the (former) offender's views of his previous lifestyle and activities; they are no longer attractive or relevant.

Giordano's research with the sample as adults was also retrospective. But because she used a continuous measure of adult criminal involvement, it covers the continuum from complete desistance to unreformed persistence, and the qualitative components portray the process over time, just as Maruna's work does. Whereas Maruna's findings suggest little role for environmental challenges she suggests that cognitive factors are most relevant between extremes on the advantage–disadvantage continuum.

As others have suggested, this middle ground is the psychological home of ambivalence: of wavering and zigzagging between persistence and desistance (Burnett, 2004; Healy, 2010; Leibrich, 1993). Burnett also suggested that categorising people as persisters and desisters 'misrepresents the switching, vacillating nature of desistance from offending'. She found that although critical events did result in turning points for some offenders, for most '(i)nstead of crossroads and junctions, a more apt analogy is that of a multi-lane motorway, the middle lane representing the individual's ambivalence and the lanes either side representing persistence and desistence' (Burnett, 2000, p. 6).

What do we know about people in this transition to secondary desistance: those who may be continuing to reoffend from time to time but periodically wanting and trying to desist? Re-entry research offers one model for examining this issue.

What can re-entry tell us about desistance?

Inevitably because all of the major studies and resulting theories rest significantly on retrospection, it is difficult to be confident about the relative roles of environment and person. Just as with the DRF literature, a fuller understanding of the interactions between social structural and subjective or internal psychological factor requires prospective research.

The available studies that come closest to a prospective design are limited to relatively short follow-up periods, typically after participants have been recruited during a period in prison. That means that desistance is confounded with re-entry, which may be a special case of desistance transition.

Of these studies, Burnett's research – known as the Oxford Recidivism Study (1992) – is the most revealing about the early stages of desistance (or not). She followed 130 men with histories of property offending through 3 interviews conducted just prior to release from prison, 4–6 months after release ($n = 99$) and 7–20 months after release ($n = 67$ men including 10 not interviewed during the first period following release). She found that while 80% of participants wanted to 'go straight' prior to release, 60% had new offences in the follow-up period. Of the 80% about half (41% of the whole sample) said before release that they probably or definitely would be able to achieve desistance. Fitting with Giordano's research, a key finding was that a crime-free life was regarded as a 'best-case scenario', requiring that certain social and personal conditions be in place (e.g. sufficient income, avoiding alcohol or drug use). Without these requirements, the men hoped otherwise, but recognised they might well return to crime (Burnett, 2000). In other words they lacked confidence or self-efficacy with regard to desistance, potentially because of practical obstacles associated with re-entry.

The size of Burnett's sample limited the statistical analyses. But persisters anticipated they would find life more difficult in the community, and in turn reported more social difficulties on follow-up (employment, accommodation, relationships, drug abuse, etc.).

Although focused more on reconviction than desitance, LeBel, Burnett, Maruna, and Bushway (2008) explicitly tackled the chicken vs. egg problem with Burnette's earlier sample. They used a range of 'subjective/agency' variables measured prior to release to examine influence on social and environmental variables measured months later, and reconviction histories 10 years later. Analyses suggested that greater hope and less internalised stigma just prior to release each predicted desistance, but ratings of regret ($p = .06$), shame and identity as a family man did not. Ratings of re-entry problems 4–6 months after release were also predictive. For reimprisonment, only re-entry problems was significant ($p < .05$), with hope, identity as a family man, and low stigma all close to significance ($.05 < ps \leq .10$). But when combined with re-entry problems, none of the subjective variables except internalised stigma were independently predictive of recidivism. This study then was a glimpse into the world of potential interactions between subjective and social factors in desistance, but showed just how important practical re-entry issues can be. However, sample size precluded analyses examining whether pre-release subjective factors were mediated by social factors in the community.

In short, theory suggests the importance both of psychological factors and life circumstances in desistance, whether as a process or outcome. We have only a patchy picture of the transition from offender to non-offender. In all but the lowest risk offenders, desistance appears to be a zigzagging process, and longitudinal research documenting the waxing and waning of criminal involvement that includes measurement of relevant social and psychological variables (including DRFs) is understandably rare. Maruna's Liverpool desistance study stands out for its documentation of a small sample of people who were achieving a relatively long period of desistance. At the other end of the process are studies of repeat criminals who have just been released from prison or been on supervision for very short periods (Healy, 2010). That there may be fundamentally different phases to desistance over time, and that processes may be different for those who have more or fewer internal and external obstacles to overcome are key questions waiting to be answered.

What links DRFs to the process of desistance?

Having laid out some of the key issues in definitions of dynamic risk, and describing and critiquing theory and research on desistance, I now examine whether they can or should be considered together: first in relation to the Risk-Need-Responsivity (RNR) model, and second, through the lens of asymmetrical causation. The paper wraps up with some empirical data from the NZPP as an example of how DRFs and desistance may be linked, early in the transition to desistance.

Definitions of both DRFs and of desistance determine one's views on whether and how these two constructs are related. Much of the older criminological research into desistance has dealt with offenders at a distance. Large datasets have been statistically analysed, with desistance defined as an absence of convictions. Little attention has been given to the more difficult-to-measure DRFs in this endeavour. DRFs, by definition should have strong statistical relationships to this narrow conceptualisation of desistance, since it is the definition that is the basis for DRF-based scales' predictive validity; people with few or no DRFs will have an overall lower level of risk, which means more of them will be successful in avoiding reconviction than those who have many.

The RNR model and desistance

But observations like this about statistical relationships miss the more interesting critiques of the premier model of the role of DRFs in desistance. In the offender rehabilitation field the adoption of the RNR model drives the focus on changes in DRFs as the principal approach to promoting desistance. However, more recently theorists and commentators have hypothetically bifurcated tertiary crime prevention into 'risk-management'[1]-oriented treatment vs. positive interventions that support the development of desistance processes; most notably those associated with the GLM[2] (McNeill, 2012). According to this way of thinking, a focus on DRFs is perhaps incompatible with, or at least weakly equipped for, the promotion of desistance (Laws & Ward, 2011; McNeill, Farrall, Lightowler, & Maruna, 2012). To somewhat simplify the argument for brevity: offenders who undertake interventions within the RNR umbrella are subject to an approach to desistance that is indirect, and excessively focused on relapse prevention/risk management strategies which translate during and after treatment into the pursuit of avoidance goals ('don't do X'). Taken together these negatively focused elements smother or hinder the enhancement of the processes that actually drive desistance (McNeill, 2012). To optimally assist offenders in achieving desistance, human services instead need to support offenders in developing or freeing their sense of personal agency, and in aspiring towards and setting goals that embrace a more positive lifestyle based on the authentic pursuit of primary goods (e.g. relatedness, excellence in work; Ward & Gannon, 2006). Engaged in this pursuit, their DRFs will automatically drop away, or become irrelevant (Laws & Ward, 2011), and the person will consequently be much more successful in desistance.

The RNR model is – on the face of it – may appear not to be attuned to psychological desistance processes (Laws & Ward, 2011) given that it is based on research that emphasises which interventions with offenders – from employment to education to psychological treatment, to any form of human service endeavour – increase the number of people who do not reoffend. The most outstanding contribution of Andrews and Bonta lay in identifying which features of programmes should be quantified in order to distil what the effective ingredients were for identification of other effective interventions, and the design of new ones. One of those ingredients was the content: time spent on changing DRFs through any plausible means to hand. A focus on how that happens – especially the psychological factors by which interventions lead to behavioural change and transitions into desistance – was not 'front and centre' in RNR research and actually, remains an important priority for the whole field (Polaschek, 2012). Likewise, the main focus of the background aetiological model for RNR is risk-oriented, and is therefore likely to be rather limited in its ability to explain the psychological factors involved in desistance (Serin & Lloyd, 2009).

But is psychological desistance really only a by-product of a focus on reducing DRFs? Is it true that RNR-consistent treatment approaches have no direct role in desistance through the development of positive, protective factors. They have sometimes been portrayed that way, in descriptions that gloss over *how* RNR-consistent programmes actually deal with DRFs (Polaschek, 2012). For example:

> The principal difference between [GLM and RNR] perspectives rests in risk management [RNR] approaches having a primary focus on the detection and modification of criminogenic needs (i.e., dynamic risk factors), while strengths-based perspectives converge on creating or increasing competencies and skills for offenders while indirectly reducing risk. (Fortune & Ward, 2013, p. 148)

Note here the absence of detail about the methods by which RNR approaches modify criminogenic needs. The only effective human services approach to working with offenders to reduce DRFs is to assist offenders in developing protective capabilities and skills that will ameliorate those very factors. Part of this work includes inspiring the offender to use these capabilities and skills to desist and otherwise improve their lives. RNR approaches can and do reduce DRFs through the development of strengths at the same time as promoting 'non-offending' though presumably not as comprehensively or explicitly as 'strength-based' approaches.

If RNR-consistent programmes do seek to promote desistance, then the important and largely unanswered question becomes whether they have an impact on other key psychological and environmental mechanisms involved in the transition to desistance. For example, do they have an impact on Giordano et al.'s suggestion that ex-offenders can imagine "for themselves a different kind of self" (2002, p. 1040)? Do they increase hooks for change as they have suggested? And if so how? The only theoretical account to date of the relationship between psychological treatment and desistance centres on a GLM-based view of sex-offender treatment (Göbbels, Ward, & Willis, 2012). We need both theory and research exploring how RNR approaches to ameliorating DRFs influence the psychological drivers of desistance, whether particular variants of intervention approach are more effective than others, and whether the main influences directly or indirectly alter dynamic risk vs. protective factors. However, the NZPP data below support the contention that DRFs are highly relevant to desistance, especially following treatment, and especially in the case of re-entry.

Asymmetrical causality: aetiological and contemporaneous influences on desistance

An intriguing assertion pertinent to the relationship between risk factors and desistance is that of *asymmetrical causality.* In 1998 Uggen and Piliaven sought to draw together people from two schools of criminological research: aetiological theorists and desistance researchers. They noted that interventions with offenders based on factors that contributed to the onset of a criminal career appeared to be ineffective once that career was underway. They argued that aetiological factors for crime therefore became increasingly irrelevant to desistance. Their observation should be no surprise to anyone with a background in behavioural psychology; that the factors that initiate and maintain behaviour diverge, especially over a long learning history. With criminal offenders, maturation changes priorities, needs and expertise (e.g. young men's interest in proving themselves by fighting with their peers becomes partner violence as they settle into longer term sexual relationships; see Klooster, 2011).

Although Uggen and Piliavin (1998) were talking about much older, essentially static aetiological factors when they suggested that risk factors poorly accounted for desistance, could their conclusion be applied to DRFs as well? It seems unlikely. No matter then how causally opaque, or to what extent dynamic risk and protective factors are proxies of some kind, they have the advantage over static, largely historical factors; they are both more up to date because of their changeability, and relatedly, draw from psychologically meaningful information based on the offender being assessed. Thus they are measures of *current* factors – factors that could precipitate new offences or provide resilience against them – not factors that were only influential in the onset of a criminal career, which for high-risk violent offenders in New Zealand who are entering intensive prison-based treatment programmes, is often at least two decades earlier. Asymmetric causation implies that current DRFs are central to desistance.

Serin and Lloyd's (2009) psychological model of the transition from persistence to desistance notes the causal asymmetry argument, but like Uggen and Piliaven, limits it to more historic aetiological factors, noting that desistance will ... 'involve the reversal of dynamic risk factors' (p. 354). They also suggest that the same psychological mechanisms that explain changes in criminal behaviour also will explain desistance, and that we have yet to show convincingly that there are psychological characteristics associated with desistance that are independent of risk factors, though that does not mean they do not exist (Serin & Lloyd, 2009).

An alternative approach to asymmetrical causation that may have implications for desistance processes comes from applying Moffitt's (1993) concepts of *cumulative continuity, contemporary continuity* and *snares. Contemporary continuity* in this context is the idea that aetiological risk factors *may* continue to influence persistence and desistance in adulthood. For example, temperamental factors such as impulsivity and lack of persistence in childhood may carry forward into adulthood and continue to disrupt desistance directly (Moffitt, 1993; see Moffitt et al., 2011 for evidence). These factors may be changeable, but not easily. They may be one category of current stable DRFs.

Cumulative continuity refers to the processes by which early aetiological factors set off a chain of consequences through time that themselves make desistance difficult. For example, youthful lack of persistence and impulsivity lead to failure in education which leads to boring, ill-paid jobs which are often temporary in nature; this poor work history narrows future work options, which in turn affects financial circumstances and so on. A number of DRFs and obstacles to desistance can be understood with reference to cumulative continuity.

Snares are consequences of crime that can be sizeable obstacles to desistance, but perhaps should not be thought of as stable DRFs, but rather as triggers to desistance failure. For example, having a criminal record limits employment opportunities, just as time in prison prevents one from paying off earlier debts that make for crippling financial circumstances on release, or being in prison may lead a first offender to acquire a drug habit that makes later life success difficult. The concept of snares can be difficult to distinguish in some cases from cumulative continuity for those with an early career onset. But it is particularly useful in accounting for those offenders with a later onset of criminality (e.g. in adolescence rather than childhood) who nevertheless end up with adult conviction trajectories that resemble those of life-course persistent offenders: the latter is the type Moffitt described as demonstrating both early neuro-temperamental and social disadvantage, and as accounting for most crime (Moffitt, Caspi, Harrington, & Milne, 2002).

Applying these mechanisms here, contemporary DRFs can come both from longstanding aetiological factors that still have a direct influence on contemporary levels of dynamic risk and protection, and from their cumulative consequences. Combined with snares – mainly in the form of obstacles to desistance – these conceptually distinct classes of DRFS may independently undermine agency for desistance and the development of a pro-social identity.

DRFs and early or proto-desistance

Arguments for asymmetrical causation and the existence of distinct classes of DRFs are important to tying DRFs to desistance, but still do little to clarify their roles in different phases of desistance. For those who work rehabilitatively with offenders, the most important phase of desistance is certainly the early stages of transition 'off-sentence', particularly following a period of psychological treatment in prison and re-entry into the community. Offenders achieving more sustained desistance such as those in Maruna's (2001) research seem to speak little of DRFs; perhaps they are most prominent early on.

Much of this paper has argued conceptually for relationships between DRFs and desistance. However, there has been little research to date to assist with such arguments. The final section describes some recent empirical findings that are germane to understanding relationships between DRFs and psychological components of desistance early in the process. One purpose of this example is to encourage more research that investigates psychological desistance, rather than simply linking DRFs to reconviction.

The NZPP: an example of contemporary research on DRFs and short-term desistance

The NZPP is a longitudinal study of about 300 high risk violent male prisoners recruited just prior to parole, and then reinterviewed at 2 months, 6 months, and if possible 12 months after release. Half had recently completed intensive treatment in a special unit for high-risk prisoners that have previously been shown to reduce reconviction risk (HRSTUs; see Polaschek & Kilgour, 2013, for more information).

The other half, the comparison sample, had undertaken no or quite minimal rehabilitation programming during the same sentence. The two samples were otherwise similar on characteristics present prior to treatment but at release treated men had significantly lower dynamic risk scores and significantly higher quality and more feasible release plans. They were also already more engaged in change on DRFs at release than the comparison men, and showed a host of other positive post-treatment differences.

The NZPP measured DRFs in prison using the Violence Risk Scale (VRS; Wong & Gordon, 2000). It includes 20 dynamic items with diverse relationships to putative psychological and social causes of reoffending. A recent factor analysis suggested that VRS is actually a mix of protective and risk factors (Polaschek, 2015b).

Once the men were out of prison, their probation officers measured DRFs and DPFs using the New Zealand adaptation of the Dynamic Risk Assessment for Offender Reentry (DRAOR; Serin et al., 2012; see Serin, 2007 for original). The DRAOR is completed by probation officers at every reporting session. The findings discussed here will examine the interactions between DRFs and the offender's psychological engagement in desistance across the first year.

Pre-release desistance engagement, DRFs and 12-month desistance

Prior to release, most NZPP prisoners wanted to desist from crime, and many said they had already been desisting for some time in prison, and furthermore had been trying to desist in the period prior to their most recent offences (i.e. usually those that brought them into prison for this sentence; Polaschek & Yesberg, 2015). Most also thought they had changed for the better in prison, and reported new, more prosocial and desistance-oriented identities (Polaschek, Bell, Casey, Dickson, & Yesberg, 2014).

However, this is a high-risk sample, and reconviction can occur very rapidly. A quarter of these men will be reimprisoned for an offence committed within 3 months of release (Nadesu, 2007; Polaschek, 2015a). So what is the role of DRFs in this early post-release period? And how do they relate to desistance-related concepts?

Desistance engagement in these studies is the combination of ratings of wanting to, confidence in, and planning for desistance. We recently showed that prisoners' ratings of these three concepts were all significantly higher just prior to release in those who were completely free of offences – even parole violations – in the first 12 months afterwards (Polaschek & Yesberg, 2015).

Prior to release, VRS total scores for DRFs, and total stage of change scores – indicators of the extent to which the man was working to change risk factors – were each significantly related to the extent to which the offender was planning to desist, their desire to desist and confidence about their ability to desist. Dynamic risk, and engagement in desistance each independently predicted who was reconvicted in the first year after release. But when current dynamic risk was replaced by current engagement in change on DRFs, desistance engagement was no longer predictive: suggesting that current engagement in reducing DRFs is more related to desistance engagement than dynamic risk scores themselves.

Mechanisms for desistance 3 months after release

But desistance transitions in prisoners re-entering the community are about more than just not getting reconvicted. I examined a series of structural equation models that related pre-release ratings to ratings 3 months after release, and then to official desistance after the first year. Pre-release, DRF scores and engagement in desistance both independently predicted *both* dynamic risk *and* quality of life in the community at 3 months and each of these in turn independently predicted official desistance maintained at 12 months. The quality of life variable was made up of the Probation Officer's ratings in the domains of prosocial support, employment, physical and mental health, use of leisure time, financial status and management of drugs, alcohol and contacts with criminal peers. Desistance engagement was composed of strength of identity as a desister, commitment to, and confidence in continuing with desistance. Dynamic risk and protective factors were measured using the DRAOR (Serin et al., 2012). The results were the same when PRFs were substituted for DRFs at 3 months. We might expect this continuity from DRFS at release through DRFs at 3 months to desistance, and from desistance engagement at release through quality of life at 3 months to desistance. But the cross-over – the independent prediction, when all of the above is taken into account – by the opposite paths (pre-release DRFs to 3-month quality of life, and pre-release desistance engagement to 3-month DRFs) would not be expected. It reveals that dynamic risk, psychological components of desistance and quality of life are working together longitudinally to influence official desistance at a later point.

However, in a second model, when quality of life was replaced with engagement in desistance at 3 months, the results were simpler. As before, both pre-release dynamic risk and engagement in desistance independently contributed to dynamic risk or protective scores 3 months into life in the community, which in turn predicted reconviction at 12 months. But engagement in desistance at 3 months did not mediate between pre-release variables and reconviction status at 12 months.

These results are based on two empirically validated measures of DRFs, and suggest that DRFs have a crucial role in predicting who survives the first 12 months after release. The findings also show DRFs and psychological desistance engagement prior to release are intertwined in predicting desistance. Lower DRFs contributed to official desistance through improving the quality of a parolee's overall lifestyle soon after release, which itself protects against recidivism. Taken together these models suggest that there is no clear demarcation between DRFs and more positive factors (e.g. identification with desistance, a more positive lifestyle in the community).

One additional point about the NZPP data is worthy of attention. As I noted earlier, half of the sample had completed an intensive psychological treatment programme of 8–12 months duration prior to parole. The pattern of relationships between desistance and dynamic risk variables was found to be equivalent in treated and comparison participants. But the treatment sample had significantly more positive scores on all variables (i.e. lower risk and higher protective factors, greater engagement with desistance processes and better quality of life in the community) than those who did not attend the programme, and, in turn significantly lower rates of reconviction. They also independently rated themselves as having greater agency for desistance and were rated by therapists and researchers as being significantly more engaged in behaviour changes consistent with desistance. These results come from a series of routinely delivered programmes that identify themselves as being consistent with RNR principles; demonstrating that programmes with the policy goal of reducing reoffending by tackling dynamic risk, in turn build protective skills and life circumstances, and support agency and identity changes during the highest risk phase of transition into the community.

Conclusions and future directions

Making connections between DRFs and desistance is a challenging task. Both concepts are confusing to define, and definitions are crucial to determining how they are related. Both concepts are multifarious, and expose just how little we know empirically, and how much progress there is to make theoretically in this important domain. That said, if we look back over two decades, we have made progress in accepting that DRFs can change, and that desistance is a complex process with significant psychological components. Jointly these two assertions indicate that psychology has an important future role in better understanding desistance.

Most research on psychological aspects of desistance, and on DRFs, is correlational, or qualitative, retrospective, with small samples and other methodological limitations. There is a significant need for larger longitudinal studies, enabling more complex statistical examinations of relationships between key constructs, including efforts to unpack more homogeneous mechanisms from among the wide array of variables currently implicated. Empirical work on dynamic risk, strength and protective factors and how they relate both to offenders' internal desistance processes and to actual behaviour is crucial to constraining theory building, which itself has a formidable task in front of it. Knowing more about how offenders themselves define desistance and their progress towards it would also be illuminating, especially for offenders whose conviction history slowly declines rather than suddenly stopping.

I have only touched on intervention in this paper, but this is also an important area for attention. Intervention resources are always going to be fewer than is needed, so how can they be best used to support desistance? New Zealand's HRSTUs added release planning some time ago to their psychological treatment programme, with the result that their graduates have much better plans than comparison high-risk offenders, which in turn predict community outcomes (Polaschek, Yesberg, & Chauhan, in press). But these are primarily 'survival' plans. Are there other low-intensity positive interventions that might support the desistance process, or that should be included among the brief interventions

New Zealand probation officers now work through with parolees? And are different interventions more suited to different phases or stages of desistance?

With regard to DRFs, I share the concern of other authors in this issue that they need much more careful definition, suggesting that they can be distinguished by, among other things, their location in the environment or person, and whether they have been aetiological or are 'downstream' consequences of other aetiological processes. It is not clear whether they are equally important in all phases of desistance. The NZPP findings suggest DRFs may be a primary mechanism in short-term desistance transitions but perhaps they recede into insignificance over longer periods.

The NZPP research also examined the roles of DPFs and found them to be similar to DRFs. However, these were not buffering protective factors, but those that may be mediators of outcomes; supporting the view that current claims about distinctions between dynamic risk and protective factors may be somewhat illusory. More elucidation of *how* a particular factor is thought to be protective might make the case more compelling. Protective buffering factors particularly warrant sustained investigation in the desistance field: requiring more moderation-type analyses.

Desistance and DRFs share definitional problems, and confusion about the relative roles of person-based and environmental factors. I have argued in this paper that they should not be separated, paradigmatically or in research or practice. Given the current state of our field, it is time that more investment was placed in understanding how they work together.

Notes

1. The authors of the GLM use the term 'risk management' to refer to the RNR model. But this term is confusing because the focus first and foremost of RNR-conforming interventions is on risk *reduction,* with the teaching of strategies to manage risk post-intervention a relatively small or non-existent part of these programmes. By contrast, sex-offender programmes, which did not adopt the RNR framework to the same extent as the mainstream correctional programmes, were instead for a time heavily invested in Relapse Prevention, a framework in which every aspect of treatment may be subsumed within a focus on risk management (e.g. Laws, 1989).
2. Although the GLM was not initially designed with desistance in mind, it was later adapted for a desistance focus (Laws & Ward, 2011).

Acknowledgements

The NZPP data set is the result of many hours of hard work from the original research team: Drs Rebecca Bell, Allanah Casey, Sophie Dickson and Julia Yesberg, and thanks also to Tadhg Daly for his invaluable assistance. The research was supported financially and practically by the New Zealand Department of Corrections, Victoria University of Wellington, and by Fulbright New Zealand.

Disclosure statement

No potential conflict of interest was reported by the author.

References

Andrews, D. A., & Bonta, J. (2010). *The psychology of criminal conduct* (5th ed.). Newark, NJ: Matthew Bender.

Andrews, D. A., Bonta, J., & Hoge, R. D. (1990). Classification for effective rehabilitation: Rediscovering psychology. *Criminal Justice and Behavior, 17*, 19–52.

Beech, A. R., & Ward, T. (2004). The integration of etiology and risk in sexual offenders: A theoretical framework. *Aggression and Violent Behavior, 10*, 31–63.

Burnett, R. (1992). *The dynamics of recidivism*. Oxford: University of Oxford Centre for Criminological Research.

Burnett, R. (2000). Understanding criminal careers through a series of in-depth interviews. *Offender Program Report, 4*(1), 1–15.

Burnett, R. (2004). To reoffend or not to reoffend? The ambivalence of convicted property offenders. In S. Maruna, & R. Immarigeon (Eds.), *After crime and punishment: Pathways to offender reintegration* (pp. 152–180). Cullumpton: Willan.

Bushway, S., Piquero, A. R., Mazerolle, P., Broidy, L., & Cauffman, E. (2001). An empirical framework for studying desistance as a process*. *Criminology, 39*, 491–516.

Collins, A. M., & Loftus, E. F. (1975). A spreading-activation theory of semantic processing. *Psychological Review, 82*, 407–428.

Farrington, D. P. (2007). Origins of violent behavior over the life span. In D. J. Flannery, A. T. Vazsonyi, & I. D. Waldman (Eds.), *The Cambridge handbook of violent behavior and aggression* (pp. 19–48). Cambridge: Cambridge University Press.

Fortune, C. A., & Ward, T. (2013). The rehabilitation of offenders: Striving for good lives, desistance, and risk reduction. I. In J. Helfgott (Ed.), *Criminal psychology volume 4* (Vol. *19*, pp. 147–173). New York, NY: Springer.

Giordano, P. C., Cernkovich, S. A., & Rudolph, J. L. (2002). Gender, crime and desistance: Toward a theory of cognitive transformation. *American Journal of Sociology, 107*, 990–1064.

Göbbels, S., Ward, T., & Willis, G. M. (2012). An integrative theory of desistance from sex offending. *Aggression and Violent Behavior, 17*, 453–462.

Hanson, R. K., & Harris, A. J. R. (2000). Where should we intervene? Dynamic predictors of sexual offence recidivism. *Criminal Justice and Behavior, 27*, 6–35.

Harris, G. T., & Rice, M. E. (2015). Progress in violence risk assessment and communication: Hypothesis versus evidence. *Behavioral Sciences and the Law, 33*, 128–145.

Healy, D. (2010). *The dynamics of desistance: Charting pathways through change*. Abingdon: Routledge.

Heffernan, R., & Ward, T. (in press). The conceptualization of dynamic risk factors in child sex offenders: An agency model. *Aggression & Violent Behavior, 24*, 250–260.

King, S. (2014). *Desistance transitions and the impact of probation*. Abingdon: Routledge.

Klooster, J. van't. (2011). *Development of violence across the lifespan: A preliminary model* (Master's thesis). Victoria University of Wellington, New Zealand. Retrieved from http://hdl.handle.net/10063/1996

Kroner, D. G., & Yessine, A. K. (2013). Changing risk factors that impact recidivism: In search of mechanisms of change. *Law and Human Behavior, 37*, 321–336.

Laub, J. H., & Sampson, R. J. (2003). *Shared beginnings, divergent lives: Delinquent boys to age 70*. Cambridge, MA: Harvard University Press.

Laws, D. R. (Ed.). (1989). *Relapse prevention with sex offenders*. New York, NY: Guilford.

Laws, D. R., & Ward, T. (2011). *Desistance from sex offending: Alternatives to throwing away the keys*. New York, NY: Guilford.

LeBel, Thomas P., Burnett, Ros, Maruna, Shadd, & Bushway, Shawn. (2008). The 'chicken and egg' of subjective and social factors in desistance from crime. *European Journal of Criminology, 5*, 131–159.

Leibrich, J. (1993). *Straight to the point: Angles on giving up crime*. Dunedin: University of Otago/Department of Justice.

Lösel, F., & Farrington, D. P. (2012). Direct protective and buffering protective factors in the development of youth violence. *American Journal of Preventive Medicine, 43*(2S1), S8–S23.

Maruna, S. (2001). *Making good: How ex-convicts reform and rebuild their lives*. Washington, DC: American Psychological Association.

Maruna, S., & Farrall, S. (2004). Desistance from crime: A theoretical reformulation. *Kölner Zeitschrift für Soziologie und Sozial Psychologie, 42*, 1–24.

McNeill, F. (2012). Four forms of "offender" rehabilitation: Towards an interdisciplinary perspective. *Legal & Criminological Psychology, 17*, 18–36.

McNeill, F., Farrall, S., Lightowler, C., & Maruna, S. (2012). Reexamining evidence-based practice in community corrections: Beyond "a confined view" of what works. *Justice Research and Policy, 14*, 35–60.

Moffitt, T. E. (1993). Adolescence-limited and life-course-persistent antisocial behavior: A developmental taxonomy. *Psychological Review, 100*, 674–701.

Moffitt, T. E., Arseneault, L., Belsky, D., Dickson, N., Hancox, R. J., Harrington, H., ... Caspi, A. (2011). A gradient of childhood self-control predicts health, wealth and public safety. *Proceedings of the National Academy of Sciences, 108*, 2693–2698.

Moffitt, T. E., Caspi, A., Harrington, H., & Milne, B. J. (2002). Males on the life-course-persistent and adolescence-limited antisocial pathways: Follow-up at age 26 years. *Development and Psychopathology, 14*, 179–207.

Nadesu, A. (2007). *Reconviction patterns of released prisoners: A 36-months follow-up analysis*. Wellington: Department of Corrections Policy Development (unpublished report).

Nunes, K. L., Hermann, C. A., Maimone, S., & Woods, M. (2014). Thinking clearly about violent cognitions: Attitudes may be distinct from other cognitions. *Journal of Interpersonal Violence, 38*, 1322–1347.

Piquero, A. R. (2004). Somewhere between persistence and desistance: The intermittency of criminal careers. In S. Maruna, & R. Immarigeon (Eds.), *After crime and punishment: Pathways to offender reintegration* (pp. 102–125). Cullompton: Willan.

Polaschek, D. L. L. (2012). An appraisal of the risk-need-responsivity model of offender rehabilitation and its application in correctional treatment. *Legal and Criminological Psychology, 17*, 1–17.

Polaschek, D. L. L. (2015a, June). *Reintegration, rehabilitation, or both? Unpacking factors that contribute to community outcomes for high risk violent offenders.* Paper presented at the Keynote address at the Third North American Corrections and Criminal Justice Psychology Conference, June 5 2015, Ottawa, Canada.

Polaschek, D. L. L. (2015b). *Violence risk scale validation project: Summary report*. Wellington, NZ: Unpublished report for the Office of the Chief Psychologist, Department of Corrections.

Polaschek, D. L. L., Bell, R. K., Casey, A. R., Dickson, S. R., & Yesberg, J. A. (2014). *New Zealand Parole Project*. Unpublished raw data, Victoria University of Wellington.

Polaschek, D. L. L., & Kilgour, T. G. (2013). New Zealand's special treatment units: The development and implementation of intensive treatment for high-risk male prisoners. *Psychology, Crime & Law, 19*, 511–526.

Polaschek, D. L. L., & Yesberg, J. A. (2015). Desistance in high-risk prisoners: Pre-release self-reported desistance commitment and perceptions of change predict 12-month survival. *Practice: The New Zealand Corrections Journal, 3*(1), 24–29.

Polaschek, D. L. L., Yesberg, J. A., & Chauhan, P. (in press). *Surviving the first year: An integrated examination of potential mechanisms for successful re-entry in high-risk treated and comparison prisoners on parole* (Manuscript under review).

Rutter, M. (1985). Resilience in the face of adversity: Protective factors and resistance to psychiatric disorder. *British Journal of Psychiatry, 147*, 598–611.

Sampson, R. J., & Laub, J. H. (1993). *Crime in the making: Pathways and turning points through life*. Cambridge, MA: Harvard University Press.

Serin, R. C. (2007). *The dynamic risk assessment for offender re-entry (DRAOR)*. Ontario: Carleton University (Unpublished User Manual).

Serin, R. C., & Lloyd, C. D. (2009). Examining the process of offender change: The transition to crime desistance. *Psychology, Crime & Law, 15*(4), 347–364.

Serin, R. C., Lloyd, C. D., Helmus, L., Derkzen, D. M., & Luong, D. (2013). Does intra-individual change predict offender recidivism? Searching for the holy grail in assessing offender change. *Aggression & Violent Behavior, 18*, 32–53.

Serin, R. C., Mailloux, D. L., & Wilson, N. J. (2012). *The dynamic risk assessment for offender re-entry (DRAOR), New Zealand adaptation* (Unpublished user manual). Ottawa: Carleton University.

Uggen, C., & Piliavin, I. (1998). Asymmetrical causation and criminal desistance. *Journal of Criminal Law and Criminology*, *88*, 1399–1422.

Ullrich, S., & Coid, J. W. (2011). Protective factors for violence among released prisoners – effects over time and interactions with static risk. *Journal Consulting and Clinical Psychology*, *79*, 381–390.

Vogel, V. de, Ruiter, C. de, Bouman, Y., & Vries Robbé, M. de. (2012). *Structured assessment of protective factors for violence risk*. Utrecht: Van Der Hoeven Stichting.

Vries Robbé, M. de, & Vogel, V. de. (2011). Protective factors for violence risk in forensic psychiatric patients: A retrospective validation study of the SAPROF. *International Journal of Forensic Mental Health*, *10*, 178–186.

Vries Robbé, M. de, & Vogel, V. de. (2013). Protective factors for violence risk: Bringing balance to risk assessment and management. In C. Logan, & L. Johnstone (Eds.), *Managing clinical risk: A guide to effective practice* (pp. 293–310). Abingdon: Routledge.

Ward, T. (2015). Dynamic risk factors: Scientific kinds or predictive constructs. *Psychology, Crime, and Law*, *22*(1–2), 2–16.

Ward, T., & Beech, A. R. (2015). Dynamic risk factors: A theoretical dead-end? *Psychology, Crime & Law*, *21*(2), 100–113.

Ward, T., & Gannon, T. A. (2006). Rehabilitation, etiology, and self-regulation: The comprehensive good lives model of treatment for sexual offenders. *Aggression and Violent Behavior*, *11*, 77–94.

Ward, T., Melser, J., & Yates, P. M. (2007). Reconstructing the risk, need, responsivity model: A theoretical elaboration and evaluation. *Aggression and Violent Behavior*, *12*, 208–228.

Ward, T., Polaschek, D. L. L., & Beech, A. R. (2006). *Theories of sexual offending*. Chichester: Wiley.

Webster, C. D., Nicholls, T. L., Martin, M., Desmarais, S. L., & Brink, X. (2006). Short-term assessment of risk and treatability (START): The case for a new structured professional judgment scheme. *Behavioral Sciences and the Law*, *24*, 747–766.

Woldgabreal, Y., Day, A., & Ward, T. (in press). Linking positive psychology to offender supervision outcomes: The mediating role of psychological flexibility, general self-efficacy, optimism, and hope. *Criminal Justice and Behavior*, (Manuscript under review).

Wong, S., & Gordon, A. (2000). *Violence Risk Scale*. Saskatoon: University of Saskatchewan.

Wortley, R. K. (2008). Situational precipitators of crime. In R. K. Wortley, & L. Mazerolle (Eds.), *Environmental criminology and crime analysis* (pp. 48–69). Cullompton: Willan.

Yesberg, J. A., & Polaschek, D. L. L. (2015). Assessing dynamic risk and protective factors in the community: Examining the validity of the dynamic risk assessment for offender Re-entry. *Psychology, Crime & Law*, *21*, 80–99.

From dynamic risk factors to causal processes: a methodological framework

Tony Ward and Clare-Ann Fortune

Psychology Department, Victoria University of Wellington, Wellington, New Zealand

ABSTRACT

It is becoming increasingly apparent that dynamic risk factors are unable to function as explanations of offending because they are composite constructs, which contain a mixture of putative causes, states of affairs, and problematic cognitive, affective, behavioural and social states associated with crime. In this paper we draw from psychopathology research and theory on the conception and classification of mental disorders to develop the Dynamic Risk Research Framework (DRRF). In our opinion, the assumptions and methodological tool associated with this framework can better focus research into the causes of offending by making use of the information provided by dynamic risk factors. A conceptual framework such as the DRRF can arguably translate this valuable information into deep, coherent explanations, and ultimately, more streamlined and precise intervention strategies.

What are the major themes emerging from this special issue concerning the role of dynamic risk factors in the explanation of offending, and in the assessment and treatment of individuals who have committed serious crimes? A number of authors have highlighted conceptual problems such as definitional vagueness and narrowness, a conflation of the domains of explanation and prediction, and doubts over the construct validity of dynamic risk factors (Durrant, 2015; Hannah-Moffat, 2016; Thornton, 2015; Vernham & Nee, 2015; Ward, 2015). While appreciating the potential value of dynamic risk factors as *markers* of etiological and causal processes in different types of offenders, doubts were expressed about the coherency of this construct. From a psychometric perspective, Cording, Beggs-Christofferson, and Grace (2015) and Wakeling, Beech, Szumski, and Fremantle (2015), identified a number of troubling psychometric 'soft spots' in measurement that have not been adequately addressed by researchers and practitioners. In terms of assessment and treatment, Casey (2015) and Klepfisz, Daffern, and Day (2015) worry about the capacity of dynamic risk factors to direct treatment and whether or not changes in these risk indicators actually measure changes in the causes of offending. Finally, Polaschek (2015) and Serin and Chadwick (2015) examined the conceptual and practice relationships between dynamic risk factors, and desistance processes, arguing that there are some important associations that could be translated into practice initiatives. Despite acknowledging these positive contributions, both sets of authors were uneasy about the ongoing definitional problems and expressed uncertainty over the theoretical status of dynamic risk factors.

So where does that leave us? On the one hand the concept of dynamic risk factors has been used in forensic and correctional research and practice domains for over 20 years. They are well entrenched and to many have satisfactorily established their epistemic and programme credentials. The Risk–Need–Responsivity Model is built around the concept of dynamic risk factors and their ability to classify offenders into high, medium, and low risk groups for intervention purposes (Andrews & Bonta, 2010). It is obvious that the concept of dynamic risk factors and the classification principles relating to it are a foundation stone of contemporary correctional practice. However, on the other hand, a combination of theoretical and empirical reviews have revealed deep conceptual problems and concerns about the ability of dynamic risk factors to adequately inform correctional policy, research and practice (see the papers in this special issue). It is important to stress that we are not referring to the *predictive* utility of dynamic risk factors, but rather their capacity to identify the *causal mechanisms* generating crime and its associated psychological and social problems. It is their capacity to explain offending that is in doubt. This is a serious shortcoming given their increasing use in guiding the assessment and rehabilitation of offenders (Andrews & Bonta, 2010; Mann, Hanson, & Thornton, 2010; Ward & Beech, 2015).

Drawing from the papers in this special issue, we argue that dynamic risk factors are unable to function as explanations of offending because: (a) they are *composite constructs* comprised of multiple, sometimes conflicting causal elements; (b) they contain a *mixture* of putative causes, states of affairs, and problematic cognitive, affective, behavioural and social states associated with crime; and (c) they are partly *normative* and therefore are as much social and cultural concepts as scientific ones. Given these problems, how can the forensic and correctional fields progress and avoid becoming trapped in theoretical and practice dead ends? We think there is a way out of the impasse.

Transdiagnostic mechanisms, research domain criteria, and causal systems

Intense debate has occurred in the area of psychopathology for the last 30 years or so, concerning the nature of mental disorders and their classification (e.g. Borsboom, Epskamp, Kievit, Cramer, & Schmittmann, 2011; Cuthbert & Kozak, 2013; Kincaid & Sullivan, 2014; Lilienfeld, 2014). An important part of this debate has focused on the relationship between signs and symptoms of mental disorders and their underlying causes (Borsboom, 2008). In an ideal world, basing psychiatric diagnosis on psychopathology signs and symptoms would enable clinicians to infer the existence of underlying causal processes, thereby providing a strong theoretical rationale for treatment. In such a scenario, each disorder would have its own distinct set of symptoms and signs, generated by a unique set of causes, or even a single cause. In essence, it is useful to view the unique cluster of symptoms comprising mental disorders as their causal signatures. Unfortunately, there has been virtually no progress in locating the causes of mental disorders such as depression, schizophrenia, or anxiety and instead clinicians have been forced to rely on diagnostic systems entirely founded on the *manifestations* of hypothesised causes. The worry is that trying to diagnosis mental disorders entirely upon the basis of symptoms such as low mood, insomnia, delusions, or panic attacks is a bit like attempting to identify physical diseases using overlapping and common symptoms like fever, muscle aches, or fatigue. There are multiple diseases capable of causing these symptoms, each with its own underlying set of disease processes. Without the ability to detect these processes, diagnosis will lack validity and therefore be unable to effectively guide treatment.

Because they are not underpinned by knowledge of the relevant causes of mental disorders, psychiatric classification manuals such as the *Diagnostic and Statistical Manual-5* (DSM; American Psychiatric Association, 2013) suffer from problems of disorder heterogeneity and overlapping diagnostic criteria. There are numerous ways symptoms can co-vary and present within a particular category such as major depression, and different disorders may share a number of symptoms. The upshot of this lack of specificity is that clients with the same diagnosis can present in markedly different ways, and similar symptom patterns may have different causes. The lack of coherency and the existence of porous boundaries between disorders make it extremely difficult to develop effective treatments and valid assessment protocols.

Research domain criteria project

Frustrated by the lack of progress in psychopathology research, in part due to a lack of knowledge of the causal processes generating symptoms, the US National Institute of Mental Health (NIMH) has initiated the Research Domain Criteria project (RDoC; see Cuthbert & Kozak, 2013). According to Morris and Cuthbert (2012) the aim of the RDoC project is to develop new ways of classifying mental disorders based initially on five domains of psychological processes and their instantiation in neurobiology. In their recent paper on the RDoC Morris and Cuthbert (2012, p. 30) stated that:

> The long-term goals of the project are to validate tasks for use in clinical trials, identify new targets for treatment development, define meaningful clinical subgroups for the purpose of treatment selection, and provide a pathway by which research findings can be translated into changes in clinical decision making. In the near term, efforts under the RDoC initiative will focus on identifying broad domains of functioning and their constituent dimensional constructs, developing reliable and valid measures across a range of units of analysis for each construct, and supporting studies to determine the full range of variation present in clinical and nonclinical populations with respect to the various domains.

The initial five domains were selected because psychological and neuroscience research evidence supported their existence, although they were seen as provisional and were expected to be refined, and even added to, as new research evidence became available. The five functional systems are: *negative valance systems* (systems that function to detect current, sustained, and potential threats, and loss), *positive valance systems* (systems involving approach motivation, reward responsiveness, and habit formation), *cognitive systems* (systems involved with attention, perception, memory, language, and effortful control), *systems for social processes* (systems such as theory of mind, social dominance, attachment, self-representation, and facial expression identification), and *arousal and regulatory systems* (systems involved in arousal and resting state activity). To facilitate research into the causes of mental disorders based on this model, the NIMH created a matrix with the five domain constructs and their associated systems (labelled 'dimensions') on a vertical axis and what is referred to as units of analysis on the horizontal axis. These units of analysis are as follows: genes, molecules, cells circuits, physiology, behaviour, and self-report. The role of the units of analysis is to discover the components and mechanisms that constitute the core psychological systems using data gathered at the different levels. The aim is to work out how normal psychological systems function and what occurs if they are faulty in some way. Thus the intention is to build a comprehensive picture of a normally functioning mind and to develop hypotheses about mental disorders based on this understanding. In addition, according to RDoC theorists, research into the psychological processes should be undertaken within a developmental context and needs to take into account the relevant social and physical environments. While there is particular interest in researching the neurobiological processes instantiating the five psychological systems, the RDoC project is not considered by its proponents to be reductionist in orientation. Their argument is that while the brain mediates all psychological processes and resulting first person experiences, the social and developmental contexts bearing on individuals play important roles in the development of normal and abnormal functioning.

Transdiagnostic approaches

Around the same time the RDoC project was gathering momentum psychotherapy theorists argued that adopting *a transdiagnostic* approach (i.e. searching for shared mechanisms causing different disorders and their symptoms) to mental health interventions could overcome the conceptual and practical problems of treatment created by classification manuals such as DSM-5 (Garland & Howard, 2013; Mansell, Harvey, Watkins, & Shafran, 2009). Problems that had their origin in the well-documented issues of symptom overlap, within category variability in clinical presentation, and high levels of comorbidity (i.e. co occurrence of disorders within the same, and between diagnostic categories). Researchers noticed how frequently different mental disorders responded to the same types of interventions and speculated that they might have some causal processes in common. For example, metacognitive interventions seemed to reduce symptoms in individuals diagnosed with a variety of emotional disorders (Mansell et al., 2009). Barlow et al. (2011 unified protocol for the treatment of emotional disorders produced promising preliminary results. However, the fact that the same interventions reduced symptoms in different types of disorders was hard to explain from the standard psychopathology perspective. From the standard viewpoint, each mental disorder had its own set of causal processes, and therefore required unique treatment strategies to alter these causes.

Mansell et al. (2009, p. 7) described the transdiagnostic approach to Cognitive Behaviour Therapy (CBT) treatment of mental disorders in the following way:

> Thus, in contrast to the disorder-specific approach, the "transdiagnostic" approach to CBT hypothesizes that there is a range of cognitive and /or behavioral maintenance processes shared across psychological disorders, that is, processes that are elevated in a wide range of psychological disorders relative to nonpsychiatric controls and
> that causally contribute to the development and/or maintenance of symptoms. ... The transdiagnostic approach thus proposes that there is added value for understanding and treating psychological disorders by focusing on common and unified factors across disorders.

Psychological mechanisms identified by researchers as 'transdiagnostic' include: (1) attentional bias to emotionally significant stimuli (e.g. a tendency to overly focus on shape and weight related cues in eating disorders); (2) memory bias for events that are congruent with individuals' current emotional states (e.g. a bias towards recalling 'failure' experiences when depressed); (3) thought suppression (e.g. suppressing contamination fears in obsessive-compulsive disorder); (4) repetitive negative thinking (e.g. constant self depreciating thoughts in depression); (5) attentional or behavioural avoidance of internal states or external situations (e.g. avoidance of feared objects in phobia); and (6) overly general memories for self related events and experiences (e.g. lack of concrete autobiographical memories in depression). A number of different inquiry strategies have been developed by transdiagnostic researchers to aid their search for common causal processes, depending on the particular problems in question. For example, a symptom-based approach sought to identify the mechanisms causing single symptoms, such as elevated mood, irrespective of the specific diagnosis. By way of contrast, a universal, multiple process strategy was employed to discover the various causal processes generating symptoms in a number of mental disorders (Mansell et al., 2009).

Implications

RDoC and transdiagnostic theorists started from different investigation points, with the former hoping to identify the causal processes constituting core psychological systems while the latter were more interested in the development of unified treatment protocols. Despite these separate initial foci of inquiry, both groups were extremely interested in conceptualising and classifying mental disorders in terms of a core set of psychological processes, and to discover what happens when they either malfunction or perform in a suboptimal way. At the risk of overly simplifying matters, there are a number of basic assumptions both projects share that we would like to outline. This is mainly because they will form the conceptual basis for the development of a methodological framework to translate dynamic risk factors into causal processes that will be discussed later in the paper. The shared assumptions are:

- The symptoms (and signs) of psychopathology are proximally caused by psychological processes instantiated in brain circuits and reflected in behaviour and first person experiences within certain contexts;
- The integrity of the functioning of these psychological processes is best construed in dimensional terms, and therefore the differences between abnormal and normal functioning is one of degree;
- Psychopathology, while proximally mediated by brain circuitry, is best explained by reference to the development of the organism and its interaction with social, physical, and cultural environments;
- Ideally, aetiological factors (e.g. developmental adversity, head injury, learning history), psychological and neurobiological causal mechanisms, and their development and interaction over time within certain contexts should all figure in comprehensive explanations of symptoms;
- The classification and treatment of mental disorders should be based on our best theories of core psychological processes and their causal interactions;

- Therefore, the optimal explanatory strategy for the conceptualisation, and explanation of psychopathology is that of integrative pluralism – building theories at different levels, each level containing emergent properties that are not reducible to the others, and which collectively provide a rich account of the onset, development, and maintenance of mental disorders.

The RDoC matrix is intended to provide researchers with a methodological framework for organising theory directed research into psychopathology. Researchers are encouraged to concentrate on clusters of symptoms, irrespective of DSM-5 diagnoses, and by utilising the different units of analysis gradually collect data to uncover the nature of the psychological mechanisms listed on the vertical axis, for example, cognitive processes. In essence, the units of analysis provide evidence for the clinical phenomena and the psychological and neurobiological mechanisms that generate them. The RDoC matrix and accompanying research guidelines are not intended to be a algorithm for discovering causal mechanisms, but rather simply a way of systematically concentrating research on causal processes, making sure that each of the systems constituting, and affecting, the casual mechanism are investigated. In a sense, it provides a blueprint for inquiry and arguably does not beg any questions about the validity of DSM-5 or other classification systems. However, on our reading of the literature on the RDoC, it is reasonable to assume that conceptions of mental disorders arrived at by the use of the RDoC methodology will not fit into the DSM-5 categories, and subsequent classification systems are more likely to be structured along causal lines.

Turning dynamic risk factors into causes: A preliminary framework

In our view, there are useful lessons for correctional and forensic researchers to learn from the above theoretical and methodological developments in the domain of psychopathology. In brief, we propose that a dynamic risk causal framework, building on the RDoC project and transdiagnostic theory, can provide researchers with a methodological structure for translating dynamic risk factors into their causal and 'symptom' components. In some respects, this suggestion continues the work on the aetiology of risk by researchers such as Beech and Ward (2004), Mann et al. (2010), and Ward and Beech (2015). The latter in particular, argued that dynamic risk factors can be broken down into causal, contextual, and state factors in the form of exemplars (i.e. prototypical types of offenders with the causal processes and their generation of problems/symptoms outlined).

However, it is important to stress that our intention in this paper is simply to sketch a *possible* methodological framework with a number of related assumptions to guide its application to dynamic risk factors. The causal processes we identify, and the levels of analysis listed, are *not* to be taken as definitive but are merely suggestive. They are based on causal processes evident in the RDoC, transdiagnostic theory, and research in the correctional domain, and in this respect are at least plausible candidates.

Drawing the analogy

Most offenders are not diagnosed with a major mental disorder and therefore at first glance it is hard to see the relevance of research on the nature and classification of mental disorders for this group. Despite the apparent differences, in our view there are important similarities between symptoms of psychopathology and dynamic risk factors, and the standard ways of accounting for them.

First, if you adopt the view that symptoms and the causal processes that generate them are best construed in dimensional terms rather than categorical ones, then the relevance of ideas arising from the RDoC and transdiagnostic projects is easier to see. Offenders often struggle with mood regulation (e.g. anger, fear, guilt) and the self-regulation of behaviour (e.g. impulsivity, maladaptive goals). In addition, some individuals convicted of crimes experience significant social difficulties and exhibit dysfunctional ways of thinking about other people and their own relationships. For example, they might believe that adults are likely to reject or punish them if they disclose their feelings, and subsequently turn to children to meet their intimacy and sexual needs. Thus, it is reasonable to conclude that many offenders exhibit significant levels of clinical symptoms without ever reaching the required threshold for a DSM-5 diagnosis.

Second, the explanation of offending and subsequent rehabilitation programmes should be directed at the clusters of problems ('symptoms') exhibited by offenders rather than offending behaviour. This is because what constitutes an offence is legally (normatively) defined, however, what is of interest from an intervention perspective is the reasons why individuals' offend. And the search for reasons typically starts with a description of the cognitive, emotional, behavioural, and environmental difficulties experienced by offenders at the time they commit their crimes. Focusing purely on the types of crime committed does not provide optimal explanatory targets. The psychological and social difficulties exhibited by offenders exist on a normal-abnormal continuum of clinical symptoms and therefore are within the purview of psychopathology theory and research.

Third, dynamic risk factors are composite constructs containing putative causal elements, state factors, and contextual features (Ward, 2015; Ward & Beech, 2015). They are not theoretically coherent concepts because referring to them in their unmodified form is likely to result in referential failure (i.e. the inability to pick out specific causes) or simply confusion (i.e. by creating uncertainty concerning what is being referred to). If the focus is on contextual or state factors then in order to formulate an effective intervention plan you need to identify the causal processes that created them. However, if the emphasis is on the causal elements of dynamic risk factors then you need some way of elucidating the different processes involved to make sure that you provide a comprehensive outline of the different causal systems associated with the state and contextual features. Either way, something like the RDoC framework that can help researchers identify different types of causal networks (e.g. biological, psychological, social, environmental) and their interactions is likely to be helpful.

Fourth, dynamic risk factors and their incorporation into the risk, need, and responsivity principles are used to allocate offenders into risk bands, which in turn partly determines what intervention streams they are offered (Andrews & Bonta, 2010). This is conceptually similar to the way DSM-5 diagnostic criteria are based on symptom clusters to arrive at specific diagnoses for treatment purposes. Both classification systems suffer from the difficulty that grouping individuals together based on surface, or state features does not provide sufficient knowledge of the pertinent causal processes. This lack of knowledge makes the resultant intervention plans overly general and vague. A unique strength of a methodological framework such as the RDoC is that it can help researchers sort causal processes into their various types and to distinguish them from symptoms, or state factors such as loneliness and sexual arousal in the case of sex offenders.

Finally, once the causal processes associated with specific dynamic risk factors have been depicted it is easier to appreciate (1) the extent to which they are distributed across the different types of causal processes (e.g. emotional dysregulation may have positive and negative affective components) and (2) how the different processes dynamically interact to cause offence related problems. Attempting to model these relationships without possessing adequate theoretical understanding is a bit like driving blind.

Dynamic risk factor research framework

We would like to present a way of conceptualising dynamic risk factors drawing from the RDoC and transdiagnostic ideas reviewed above. We have made a number of adjustments to the RDoC matrix because of the differences between mental disorders and problems associated with offending. In particular, we have stressed the importance of interpersonal processes in the genesis of crime; especially the way they can directly elevate the risk of reoffending (see Hannah-Moffat, 2016). With some modifications, we endorse the assumptions underpinning the RDoC and transdiagnostic perspectives:

- Problematic affective, cognitive, behavioural, and physiological states associated with crime are proximally caused by psychological and social processes within certain contexts;
- The functioning of these psychological and social processes is best construed in dimensional terms, and therefore the differences between normative, dysfunctional, and prosocial behaviour are ones of degree;
- Offence related psychological states, while proximally mediated by psychological processes, are best explained by reference to the development of the organism and its interaction with its social, physical, and cultural environments.
- Ideally, aetiological factors (e.g. developmental adversity, head injury, learning history), psychological and neurobiological causal mechanisms, and their development and interaction over time within certain contexts will all figure in a comprehensive explanation of crime related states;
- The classification and treatment of offence associated psychological and social states should be based on our best theories of core psychological processes and their causal interactions;
- Therefore, the optimal explanatory strategy for the conceptualisation, and explanation of crime and its associated problems is that of integrative pluralism. This involves constructing theories at different levels, each level containing emergent properties that are not reducible to the others, and which collectively provide a rich account of the onset, development, and maintenance of criminal behaviour and its associated problems.

It should be evident from the above list of assumptions that we recommend dividing dynamic risk factors into their presumed causal processes, contextual features, and psychological and social states. Because they are composite constructs they are really only summaries of items that predict reoffending. From an explanatory viewpoint, in their classical form they do not genuinely refer to causal processes but rather are

Table 1. Dynamic risk research framework.

Dynamic risk factor	Intimacy Deficits (e.g. emotional congruence with children)			
	Levels of analysis			
Causal processes	Biological	Behavioural	Phenomenological	Contextual
Negative affective systems				
Positive affective systems				
Cognitive systems				
Intrapersonal social processes				
Self-regulation				
Interpersonal social systems				

markers for a number of different factors: general causes, states of affairs, psychological states, and social circumstances. We will now briefly outline the *Dynamic Risk Research Framework* (DRRF – see Table 1).

Following the lead of the RDoC matrix there are two types of concepts in the DRRF, causal processes on the vertical axis and levels of analysis on the horizontal axis. The proposed causal processes in the DRRF are *negative affective systems* (e.g. threat detection, avoidance behaviour), *positive affective systems* (e.g. approach motivation, cost benefit analysis, locating rewards), *cognitive systems* (e.g. cognitive control systems, attention processes, declarative memory), *intrapersonal social processes* (e.g. internal; working models, self-conceptions, self-knowledge), *self-regulation systems* (e.g. regulation of arousal, coordination of internal systems, construction of action plans), and *interpersonal social systems* (e.g. affiliation and attachment systems, vicarious learning).

The levels of analysis included in our framework are *biological* (e.g. neurotransmitter disturbances, fMRI data on executive functions), *behavioural* (e.g. how individuals react under stress), *phenomenological*, or the first person perspective (e.g. experiences of fear, emotional loneliness), and *relational* (e.g. social network analysis, collateral reports, interpersonal observations). The purpose of data collection is to provide evidence for the causal processes on the horizontal axis. The idea is to first tease out the causal components of a dynamic risk factor such as intimacy deficits and to develop a provisional causal model of the component processes and their interaction. The various levels of analysis should then direct researchers to collect more data and to further refine the depiction of the network of causal systems, or even the addition of further casual processes.

In order to clarify the way the DRRF can enable researchers to separate out the distinct components of dynamic risk factors and guide subsequent theory development and evaluation, we will use the example of intimacy deficits, or more specifically, emotional congruence with children (Mann et al., 2010; Thornton, 2013). According to Thornton's (2013) recent review the general dynamic risk factor of dysfunctional relational styles contains a number of distinct factors. These include emotional congruence with children, lack of intimate adult relationships, and dysfunctional self-esteem (low or narcissistic). In an empirical study of dynamic risk factors Mann et al. (2010) describe emotional congruence with children in the following way:

> Emotional congruence with children refers to feeling that relationships with children are more emotionally satisfying than relationships with adults. The offender who is emotionally congruent with children may find children easier to relate to than adults, may feel he is still like a child himself, and may believe that children understand him better than adults do. He often feels himself to be "in love" with his child victims, as if the relationship was reciprocal. (p. 201)

It is apparent that the dynamic risk factor of emotional congruence with children is a composite construct and refers to a number of implicit or explicit disparate causal factors, contextual features, and state variables. However, for the purposes of exposition we will ignore state variables such as loving feelings or anxiety and instead concentrate on the hypothesised causes alluded to in the above quote. For simplicity sake we will look more closely at the assertions that offenders who experience emotional congruence with children may find them easier to relate to than adults and believe that they understand them better. It is clear that a number of the systems listed in the DRRF appear to have prima facie explanatory relevance for this factor:

- negative affective systems: views adults as threats and employs avoidance strategies to manage fear and anxiety;
- positive affective systems: views children as sources of reward and more likely to provide him with love, sexual pleasure and care. He is likely to seek out opportunities for engagement with children;
- cognitive systems: displays attentional bias towards signs of affection from children or indicators that it might be possible to become involved with them sexually and emotionally (e.g. cues signifying vulnerability, lack of supervision);
- intrapersonal social processes: has a tendency to view himself as vulnerable and unsafe, living in a dangerous world; he lacks understanding of his motives due to expectancy and interpretational biases;
- self-regulation systems: lacks the capacity to soothe himself and effectively control negative physiological arousal; seeks interaction with children to do this and constructs elaborate grooming strategies to accomplish this based on problematic beliefs and goals;
- interpersonal social systems: has an insecure attachment style and dysfunctional internal working models in which affiliation seeking strategies are entirely directed towards daily interactions with children, including sexual contact. He may also belong to deviant social networks that approve of adults having sex with children.

It is possible to elaborate more deeply and fully on the above theoretical analyses, by drawing from contemporary sex offender theory and research. However, even the somewhat cursory sketch provided is enough to show how the DRRF framework can be used to sift through the various causal elements either explicitly stated or implied in dynamic risk factors and their description. We hope it is obvious how a single dynamic risk factor (or one aspect of a risk factor) contains a number of distinct and possibly conflicting causal claims. But more importantly, that it is possible to analyse emotional congruence with children into different types of causal processes, that interact to generate state factors (situations, feelings of fear or loneliness, etc.) or 'symptoms' evident in individuals who feel emotionally drawn to children. Once deconstructed into its separate causal processes and their interactions, data can be collected at different levels to provide a rich explanatory mosaic; biological, emotional, cognitive, behavioural, and contextual. Researchers can work through all the causal strands evident in any dynamic risk factor and create causal network models to depict the way they impact on each other, and how they develop across time within specific types of contexts (social, physical, cultural). Once this work progresses, we suspect it will then be relatively easy to make theoretical links between the different types of dynamic risk factors, and hence create a conceptual bridge between the domains of risk prediction and explanation. For example, the dynamic risk factor of offence supportive attitudes and beliefs overlaps with emotional congruence with children through the mutual involvement of attentional, cognitive, intrapersonal, interpersonal, and self-regulation causal processes.

From risk factors to causes

The dynamic risk-causation framework described in this paper meshes well with Bradford Hill's (1965) guidelines for forming causal inferences in epidemiology. He formulated nine guidelines that were intended to collectively provide researchers with reasonable grounds for deciding that risk factors such as smoking may be a cause of a disease, for example, of lung cancer (for a discussion of 2015 see Ward, 2015). The first four of Bradford Hill's guidelines are concerned with basic methodological requirements necessary to establish causal relationships, such as a strong association with an specific outcome, consistency, specificity (e.g. to particular groups, body systems and sites, and diseases), and temporality (i. e. an hypothesised cause preceding an outcome). However, the remaining five guidelines are more theoretically oriented and recommend that researchers infer causal processes that are plausible, exhibit coherence with existing knowledge, demonstrate the expected functional relationships, are supported by experimental evidence, and are developed using models from domains that have similar causal relationships. In our view, the DRRF and its accompanying assumptions would be expected to provide the data and knowledge to support the move from risk factor status to that of causal process.

Conclusions

The challenge for researchers and clinicians is to know how best to use the information provided by dynamic risk factors. They are at the very least markers of causal processes in offenders as well as being reasonable predictors of reoffending. However, it is their explanatory role that is most in question, the problem being how to overcome the issues of internal complexity and vagueness arising from their composite nature. In this paper we have drawn from psychopathology research and theory on the conception and classification of mental disorders. In our opinion, the assumptions and methodological tools provided by RDoC and transdiagnostic theorists can be profitably adapted to the forensic and correctional fields to better focus research into the causes of offending. Dynamic risk factors are usefully construed as boundary riders that indicate significant offence related phenomena and possible causes within a specific domain, for example, emotional functioning or interpersonal relationships. A conceptual framework such as the DRRF may be of use in translating this valuable information into deeper, coherent explanations, and ultimately, more streamlined and precise intervention strategies.

References

American Psychiatric Association. (2013). *Diagnostic and statistical manual of mental disorders.* (5th ed.). Arlington, VA: American Psychiatric Association.

Andrews, D. A., & Bonta, J. (2010). *The psychology of criminal conduct*. New Providence, NJ: Anderson.

Barlow, D. H., Farchione, T. J., Fairholme, C. P., Ellard, K. K., Boisseau, C. L., Allen, L. K., & Ehrenreich-May, J. (2011). *Unified protocol for transdiagnostic treatment of emotional disorders*. New York, NY: Oxford University Press.

Beech, A. R., & Ward, T. (2004). The integration of etiology and risk in sexual offenders: A theoretical framework. *Aggression and Violent Behavior, 10*(1), 31–63. doi:10.1016/j.avb.2003.08.002

Borsboom, D. (2008). Psychometric perspectives on diagnostic systems. *Journal of Clinical Psychology, 64*(9), 1089–1108. doi:10.1002/jclp.20503

Borsboom, D., Epskamp, S., Kievit, R. A., Cramer, A. O. J., & Schmittmann, V. D. (2011). Transdiagnostic networks: Commentary on Nolen-Hoeksema and Watkins (2011). *Perspectives on Psychological Science, 6*(6), 610–614. doi:10.1177/1745691611425012

Bradford Hill, A. (1965). The environment of disease: Association or causation? *Proceedings of the Royal Society of Medicine, 58*, 295–300.

Casey, S. (2015). Dynamic risk and sexual offending: The conundrum of assessment. *Psychology, Crime, & Law*, 22(01–02), 104–123.

Cording, J. R., Beggs-Christofferson, S. M., & Grace, R. C. (2015). Challenges for the theory and application of dynamic risk factors. *Psychology, Crime, & Law*, 22(01–02), 84–103.

Cuthbert, B. N., & Kozak, M. J. (2013). Constructing constructs for psychopathology: The NIMH research domain criteria. *Journal of Abnormal Psychology, 122*(3), 928–937. doi:10.1037/a0034028

Durrant, R. (2015). Putting risk factors in their place: An evolutionary-developmental approach to understanding risk. *Psychology, Crime, & Law*, 22 (01-02), 17–32.

Garland, E. L., & Howard, M. O. (2013). A transdiagnostic perspective on cognitive, affective, and neurobiological processes underlying human suffering. *Research in Social Work Practice, 24*(1), 142–151. doi:10.1177/1049731513503909

Hannah-Moffat, K. (2016). A conceptual Kaleidoscope: Contemplating 'dynamic structural risk' and an uncoupling of risk from need. *Psychology, Crime, & Law*, 22(01–02), 33–46.

Kincaid, H., & Sullivan, J. A. (2014). *Classifying psychopathology: Mental kinds and natural kinds*. Cambridge, MA: MIT Press.

Klepfisz, G., Daffern, M., & Day, A. (2015). Understanding dynamic risk factors for violence. *Psychology, Crime, & Law*, 22(01–02), 124–137.

Lilienfeld, S. O. (2014). The Research Domain Criteria (ROC): An analysis of methodological and conceptual challenges. *Behaviour Research and Therapy, 62*, 129–139. doi.org/10.1016/j.brat.2014.07.019

Mann, R. E., Hanson, R. K., & Thornton, D. (2010). Assessing risk for sexual recidivism: Some proposals on the nature of psychologically meaningful risk factors. *Sexual Abuse: A Journal of Research and Treatment, 22*(2), 191–217. doi:10.1177/1079063210366039

Mansell, W., Harvey, A., Watkins, E., & Shafran, R. (2009). Conceptual foundations of the transdiagnostic approach to CBT. *Journal of Cognitive Psychotherapy: An International Quarterly, 23*(1), 6–19. doi:10.1891/0889-8391.23.1.6

Morris, S. E., & Cuthbert, B. N. (2012). Research domain criteria: Cognitive systems, neural circuits, and dimensions of behavior. *Dialogues in Clinical Neuroscience, 14*, 29–37.

Polaschek, D. L. L. (2015). Desistance and dynamic risk factors belong together. *Psychology, Crime, & Law*, 22(01–02), 171–189.

Serin, R. C., & Chadwick, N. (2015). Dynamic risk and protective factors. *Psychology, Crime, & Law*, 22 (01–02), 151–170.

Thornton, D. (2015). Developing a theory of dynamic risk. *Psychology, Crime, & Law*, 22(01–02), 138–150.

Thornton, D. (2013). Implications of our developing understanding of risk and protective factors in the treatment of adult male sexual offenders. *International Journal of Behavioral Consultation and Therapy, 8*, 62–65. doi:10.1037/h0100985

Vernham, V., & Nee, C. (2015). Dysfunctional expertise and its relationship with dynamic risk factors in offenders. *Psychology, Crime, & Law*, 22(01–02), 47–67.

Wakeling, H. C., Beech, A. R., Szumski, F., & Fremantle, N. (2015). Problems in the measurement of risk in sexual offenders. *Psychology, Crime, & Law*, 22(01–02), 68–83.

Ward, T. (2015). Dynamic risk factors: Scientific kinds or predictive constructs? *Psychology, Crime, & Law*, 22(01–02), 2–16.

Ward, T., & Beech, A. R. (2015). Dynamic risk factors: A theoretical dead-end? *Psychology, Crime & Law*, *21*(2), 100–113.

Index

For Product Safety Concerns and Information please contact our EU
representative GPSR@taylorandfrancis.com
Taylor & Francis Verlag GmbH, Kaufingerstraße 24, 80331 München, Germany

www.ingramcontent.com/pod-product-compliance
Ingram Content Group UK Ltd.
Pitfield, Milton Keynes, MK11 3LW, UK
UKHW050054200926
475702UK00019B/2833
* 9 7 8 0 3 6 7 1 0 9 5 6 1 *